The Beginning of the Gospel

Introducing the Gospel According to Mark

Eugene LaVerdiere, S.S.S.

VOLUME 2

Mark 8:22–16:20

A Liturgical Press Book

THE LITURGICAL PRESS
Collegeville, Minnesota

1   2   3   4   5   6   7   8

Library of Congress Cataloging-in-Publication Data

LaVerdiere, Eugene.
    The beginning of the Gospel : introducing the Gospel according to Mark / Eugene LaVerdiere.
        p.   cm.
    Includes bibliographical references.
    ISBN 0-8146-2574-6, vol. 2 (alk. paper)
    1. Bible. N.T. Mark I–VIII, 21—Commentaries. I. Title.
BS2585.3.L38 1999
226.3'077—dc21   98-44957
                                              CIP

Contents

Table VII

An Outline for Part Two
Jesus and the Coming of the Kingdom of God
Mark 8:22–16:8

Table VIII

An Outline for Part Two, Section IV
Following Christ on the Way
Mark 8:22–10:52

Table IX

An Outline for Part Two, Section V
The Coming of the Lord Jesus
Mark 11:1–13:37

Table X

An Outline for Part Two, Section VI
The Passion and Resurrection of the Son of God
Mark 14:1–16:8

Table XI

An Outline for the Alternate Ending of Mark
Mark 16:9-20

VII

❧ Part Two ❧

Jesus and the Coming of the Kingdom of God

Mark 8:22–16:8

Introduction

In the first part of the Gospel, Mark told the story of Jesus and the mystery of the kingdom of God (1:14–8:21). The story began with a summary of Jesus' mission and ministry: "After John had been arrested, Jesus came to Galilee proclaiming the gospel of God. 'This is the time of fulfillment. The kingdom of God is at hand. Repent, and believe in the gospel'" (1:14-15). At the end, Mark left us with a question: "Do you still not understand?" (8:21).

Everything Jesus said and did announced the coming of the kingdom of God, including the breaking of the bread for the five thousand and the breaking of the bread for the four thousand (6:34-44; 8:1-9). The disciples had not understood about the bread (6:52; 8:14-21) and its relationship to the mystery of the kingdom. If they had understood about the bread, they would have known the mystery of the kingdom of God that was granted to them (4:11).[1]

---

[1] No one can fully comprehend the mystery of the kingdom of God. Knowing the kingdom is like knowing God. Both would take more than a lifetime, even more than the entire life of the Church. The mystery of God is inexhaustible. So is the mystery of the kingdom.

In the first section (1:14–3:6), Jesus called disciples to follow him, to be with him, and take up his mission (1:16-20). He taught them what the proclaiming of the kingdom of God would entail. Like Jesus, they should expect strong resistance and opposition, particularly from the Pharisees and their scribes (1:21–3:6).

The first section is extremely fundamental for the nature of Christianity and the Church. It shows how the nature of the Church is based on Jesus' call. The Hebrews, the Israelites, and the Jews were born as such. For them, circumcision was just a sign of their identity. Unlike the Hebrews, the Israelites, and the Jews, Christians are not born as such. We are called to be Christians. Unlike circumcision, baptism is an effective sign for us.

In the second section (3:7–6:6a), Jesus created the Twelve as the basis of a new Israel that would include Gentiles as well as Jews, forming a Church for all peoples (3:13-19). He then showed them how the new Israel challenged his relatives, the scribes who came from Jerusalem, and the people of his native place (3:20–6:6a). It would be the same for them (see 10:28-30).

The second section builds on the first. It shows how, called by Christ, the Church is universal. The new Israel, as the community of the Twelve of Christ, transcends every natural relationship, including those that were based on family, ethnicity, race, and nationality. The Israel of old united twelve tribes into one people. The new Israel would unite all peoples in a people of God. For the early Church, it was a great challenge to be, in fact, a universal church, as it is today.

In the third section (6:6b–8:21), Jesus sent the Twelve on mission, giving them authority over unclean spirits as they preached the gospel of repentance (6:7-30). Jesus showed them the nature of their mission when he broke the bread on the Jewish as well as on the Gentile side of the sea (6:34-44; 8:1-9). For them, crossing from the Jewish to the Gentile shore implied a major cultural and religious shift and challenged valued traditions. The crossing was extremely difficult (6:31–8:21).

In presenting the mission of the Church, the third section builds on the first and the second. Called by Christ, and constituted as the community of the Twelve, the Church is missionary by nature. As Christians, we are called for the kingdom of God. Since the kingdom of God is universal, the Christian community, the Church, is called to be universal. To be universal, the Church has to reach to every nation and people.

In the first part, Jesus also taught the crowd in parables. When the Twelve questioned him about the parables, Jesus said: "The mystery of the kingdom of God has been granted to you. But to those outside everything comes in parables" (4:11). The mystery of the kingdom of God unfolded before their eyes as Jesus proclaimed the gospel of God (1:14-15), healed and exorcised those who came to him (3:7-12), and taught around the villages (6:6b). But the Twelve did not understand.

In the boat with Jesus, the Twelve crossed to the other side, but they had forgotten to bring bread. They had only one loaf with them. Jesus asked them, "Why do you conclude that . . . you have no bread? Do you not yet understand or comprehend? Are your hearts hardened? Do you have eyes and not see, ears and not hear?" (8:16-18a).

At the end, Jesus reminded them of the breaking of the bread. "'And do you not remember, when I broke the five loaves for the five thousand, how many wicker baskets full of fragments you picked up?' They answered him, 'Twelve.' 'When I broke the seven loaves for the four thousand, how many full baskets of fragments did you pick up?' They answered [him], 'Seven.' He said to them, 'Do you still not understand?'" (8:18b-21).

The mystery of the kingdom of God had been given to the Twelve of Christ (4:11), but they did not understand. Otherwise, they would have understood about the twelve wicker baskets and the seven baskets of fragments they had gathered. Did the communities in the time of Mark understand that the baskets were for the universal Church?

In the second part of "the beginning of the gospel," Mark tells the story of Jesus and the coming of the kingdom of God. The story begins when Jesus with the Twelve arrived at Bethsaida and cured a blind man (8:22-26). It ends with the women's flight from the tomb of Jesus, saying "nothing to anyone, for they were afraid" (16:8).

The story of the coming of the kingdom of God unfolded on the way to the passion and resurrection of Jesus Christ. Called by Christ, constituted as the Twelve, and sent on mission, the disciples followed him on the way. At every step of the way, Jesus taught them. The passion and resurrection had implications for every aspect of the life of the Church.

Literary Characteristics

As we introduced the first part of the Gospel (1:14–8:21), we examined the Gospel's literary characteristics. As we have seen, they tell us a lot about the nature and the purpose of the Gospel of Mark. Now as we introduce the second part of the Gospel (8:22–16:8), we shall focus on the literary characteristics of the second part. Some of them are common to the whole Gospel, but others are very distinctive.

As an action story, telling what Jesus did, the first part had relatively little dialogue and just a few discourses. Two of the discourses, however, were quite long, the one on teaching in parables (4:1-34), and the one on the tradition of the elders (7:1-23). As a teaching story, presenting what Jesus taught, the second part has very few action stories and much more dialogue and many discourses, long and short.

The first part included many healing stories. In the first section (1:14–3:6), Jesus cured a demoniac in the synagogue at Capernaum (1:21-28), the mother-in-law of Simon at home (1:29-31), a paralytic also at home (2:1-12), and a man with withered hand (3:1-6) in the synagogue. In the second section (3:7–6:6a), Jesus cured a Gerasene demoniac (5:1-20), raised the daughter of Jairus to life, and cured a woman with a hemorrhage (5:21-43). In the third section (6:6b–8:21), Jesus cured the daughter of a Syrophoenician woman (7:24-30) and a deaf man with a speech impediment (7:31-37). Even the summaries focused on Jesus' healing of the sick and expelling unclean spirits or demons (1:32-34; 3:7-12; 6:53-56).

The first part also included five crossings of the sea (4:35-41; 5:21; 6:45-52; 8:10; 8:14-21), three of them told in detail. There were also two stories of the breaking of the bread, one on the Galilean shore of the sea (6:34-44) and one on the Gentile shore (8:1-9). As a flashback, the first part included the story of the imprisonment of John the Baptist and his execution (6:17-29).

The second part includes only three healing stories, all three in the fourth section (8:22–10:52). Two of the stories show how Jesus healed the blind, one at Bethsaida (8:22-26) and the other on leaving Jericho (10:46-52). The third story shows how Jesus cured a boy possessed with a mute spirit (9:14-29). The fourth section also includes the story of the transfiguration (9:2-8). The fifth section tells the story of Jesus' triumphant entry into Jerusalem (11:1-11), the cursing of the fig tree (11:12-14, 20), and the cleansing of the Temple (11:15-19). The sixth section, the story of the Jesus' passion and his resurrection (14:1–16:8), stands apart.

In the second part, Jesus still preaches and teaches by what he does, but now the emphasis is on his word and the content of his teaching. Significantly, Jesus is often addressed as "teacher" (*didaskale*), ten times in all.[2] By contrast, in the first part Jesus was referred to as a teacher only once (5:35) and he was addressed only once as "teacher" (4:38).

---

[2] Jesus is addressed as "teacher" (*didaskale*) in 9:17, 38; 10:17, 20, 35; 12:14, 19, 32; 13:1; and 14:14.

The second part includes the longest discourse of the Gospel, the eschatological discourse on the Mount of Olives (13:1-37). Besides, we have many short discourses, on what it means to follow Christ, applying it to various aspects of Christian life and to particular categories of people (8:34-38; 9:35-49; 10:5-12, 23-31, 38-45; 12:1-12, 24-27; 14:6-9). Very often, a short dialogue introduces the discourse.

Both parts include several sayings of Jesus. In the first part, the sayings are based on common observation and common sense. For example, in the story of Levi (2:13-17) Jesus says, "Those who are well do not need a physician, but the sick do" (2:17). And in the story of the Syrophoenician (7:24-30), Jesus says, "for it is not right to take the food of the children and throw it to the dogs" (7:27).

In the second part, however, many of them are in the form of a hyperbole, intended to shake up the hearers to what is at stake. For example, concerning scandalizing children in the faith, "If your hand causes you to sin, cut it off" (9:43). Concerning wealth, Jesus says, "It is easier for a camel to pass through [the] eye of [a] needle than for one who is rich to enter the kingdom of God" (10:25).

In the first part, each section was introduced by a summary of Jesus' mission and ministry (1:14-15; 3:7-12; 6:6b). In the second part, each section (8:22–10:52; 11:1–13:37; 14:1–16:8) is introduced by a prophetic, symbolic action, a cure of a blind man (8:22-26), the entry to Jerusalem (11:1-11), and the anointing of Jesus (14:3-9) and the plot against him (14:1-2, 10-11).

Like the action stories, the teaching stories are tightly written and related to one another with the conjunction *kai* (and). In the first part, the adverb *euthys* (immediately, suddenly, just then) appeared thirty times, as we would expect in action stories. In the second part, it appears only ten times.

As in the first part, the adverb *palin* is also used to connect a later event to a previous event (10:1, 10, 24, 32; 11:3, 27; 14:61, 69, 70; 15:4, 12, 13), six of them in the passion account. But the adverb is also used to emphasize a significant repetition (8:25; 12:4; 14:39, 40). In the first part, the effort was to connect the various events into one story. In the second, the emphasis is on the forward movement to the passion and the resurrection.

In the first part, we had three examples of intercalation, called a Markan sandwich (3:20 [22-29] 31-35; 5:21-24a [25b-34] 35-43; 6:7-13 [14-29] 30). In the second part, we have only one, the cursing of the fig tree and the cleansing of the Temple (11:12-24 [15-19] 20-25).[3] But in the passion and resurrection (14:1–16:8), Mark developed the

---

[3] For Markan sandwiches, see James R. Edwards, "Markan Sandwiches, The Significance of Interpolations in Markan Narratives," *Novum*

literary device into an interlocking pattern, in which the main story line is interrupted repetitively by disparate stories that interpret the main story step by step.[4]

Symbols and Images

Telling the story of "the beginning of the gospel," Mark employed many images, as Jesus had done when he proclaimed "the gospel of God." Speaking of the kingdom of God, Mark, like Jesus, needed images. The kingdom of God may be present in our midst, transforming our history into a history of salvation, but it also transcends history. As such, the kingdom of God is a mystery. Symbolic language and images allowed Mark to speak of the mystery without betraying or trivializing it.

There are other reasons why Mark used symbols and images. Like John, Mark presented the life of Jesus and his disciples as the "sacrament" of the life of the risen Lord and the early Church. Distinguishing between the life of Jesus and of risen Lord, Matthew and Luke are much less symbolic, except in their Gospels' infancy and resurrection narratives, where they present the ultimate origin and destiny of Jesus, both of which transcend human history.

Handing on the tradition of Jesus' preaching and teaching, Mark made Jesus' parables an integral part of his Gospel.[5] The images in the parables were based on common observation. From their earliest years, everyone had participated in a wedding feast, where the bridegroom was present with the wedding guests (2:19-20). From experience, everyone knew that sewing a piece of unshrunken cloth on an old cloak would ruin the cloak (2:21). Everyone knew what would happen if new wine was poured in old wineskins (2:22), and how it is in sowing seed (4:2-9, 14-20, 26-29). Everyone understood when

---

Testamentum XXXI, 3 (1989) 193–215. For the cursing of the fig tree and the cleansing of the Temple, see 206–08.

[4] Besides the four in our list of Markan sandwiches, James Edwards includes five more, four of them in the passion and resurrection narrative (14:1-2[3-9] 10-11; 14:17-21[22-26] 27-31; 14:53-54[55-65] 66-72; 15:40-41[42-46] 47-16:8). Besides these, he includes the beginning of the discourse in parables (4:1-9[10-13] 14-20), op. cit. 197–98, 208–09, 211–15.

[5] As Paul J. Achtemeier observed, Mark was faithful to the traditions he received, but "however faithful he may have been to those traditions, he also had in mind the need to say something to his readers by way of those traditions." See Paul J. Achtemeier, "'He Taught Them Many Things': Reflections on Marcan Christology," *The Catholic Biblical Quarterly* 42:4 (October 1980) 465–81, 466.

Jesus compared the kingdom of God to a mustard seed, the smallest of the seeds that would become the largest of plants (4:31-32).

Steeped in the early Jewish culture with its biblical literature, the Gospel of Mark reflects the scriptural tradition. It was normal for him to relate Jesus and the events in his life to biblical personages, such as King David and the Suffering Servant and events, such as the exodus. Most often, Jesus used natural images. Mark turned to well-known biblical images.

Some symbols permeate the entire Gospel, for example, clothing, beginning with John the Baptist, who was "clothed in camel's hair, with a leather belt around his waist" (1:6), and concluding with the young man in the tomb who was "clothed in a white robe" (16:5). Describing the transfigured Jesus, Mark did not allude to his features but to his clothes, which "became dazzling white, such as no fuller on earth could bleach them" (9:3).[6] In the biblical world, as in many cultures today, clothing expressed the identity of the person.

Throughout the Gospel, the home *(ho oikos, he oikia)* is also symbolic, particularly the home of Simon Peter (1:29-31) that became Jesus' home (2:1; 3:20). That is where Jesus spoke in private to the disciples (see 7:17; 9:28, 33; 10:10). Like the boat, Jesus' home represented the Church. There were those who entered the home, and there were those who stayed outside. Only those inside were granted the mystery of the kingdom of God (4:10-12).

In the first part of the Gospel, two images were very prominent, the sea *(he thalassa)* and bread *(artos)*. Both images were at the center of a cluster of images. Also prominent was the desert *(ho eremos* or *eremos topos)* and the mountain *(to oros)*. The first part also included many other images, especially, but not only, in Jesus' parables.

In the second part, two different images are prominent. Instead of the sea, there is the way *(he hodos),* and instead of bread, there is the cup *(to poterion).* Like the sea and bread, the way and the cup are at the center of a cluster of images. The way and the cup are basic for the movement of the whole second part. When they are not mentioned, they are always present in the background. The second

---

[6] Mark also used the symbol of clothing in the parable of sowing unshrunken cloth on an old garment (2:21), in the story of the Gerasene deomoniac (5:15), of the woman with a hemorrhage (5:28-30). He also used it in the instruction for the mission of the Twelve (6:9), in the cure of the blind beggar named Bartimaeus (10:50), in Jesus' triumphal entry to Jerusalem (11:7-8), and in the eschatological discourse (13:16). Garments are also prominent in the account of Jesus' passion and resurrection (14:52; 15:17-20, 24, 46; 16:5).

part also has other important images, such as the cross *(ho stauros)*, the fig tree *(he syke)*, and the stone *(ho lithos)* at the entrance of the tomb, but they are limited to one or two sections.

The Way *(he hodos)*

The first set of images is related to the way *(he hodos)*.[7] The way is a prominent biblical theme, particularly in wisdom literature, where it refers to a way of life (see Prov 2:7-20; Pss 1:1; 32:8; 101:2, 6), but also in prophetic literature, where it refers to the way of the Lord (see Isa 40:3). In prophetic literature, the way is associated with the coming of the Lord. Drawing from both, Mark applied the theme to the way of Jesus, where it refers to the way of life demanded by the kingdom of God. More specifically, it refers to Jesus' way to Jerusalem and to his passion and resurrection.

In a biblical synthesis of Malachi 3:1, Exodus 23:20 and Isaiah 40:3, Mark's prologue introduced the way of the Lord and applied it to the way of Jesus (1:2-3). As a new Elijah, John the Baptist was sent to prepare the way of Jesus.

In the first part of the Gospel, "the way" refers to a path or road in general. It refers to a path that the disciples made while picking heads of grain (2:23). In Jesus' parable of the sower, it refers to a path where seed fell (4:4, 15). It also refers to a journey. In Jesus' instruction to the Twelve, it refers to their mission: "He instructed them to take nothing for the journey [*eis hodon*]" (6:8). In the second story of the breaking of the bread, Jesus says, "If I send them away hungry to their homes, they will collapse on the way [*en te hodo*]" (8:3).

The image of the way in the first part has theological connotations. For example, the instructions for the missionary journey (6:7-9) evoke Israel's exodus from servitude. The missionary journey of the Twelve would be a new exodus. But the image does not refer to the way of Jesus, as it did in the prologue (1:2-3). In the second part, the way is the way of Jesus.

"The way" is the way of Jesus Christ, the Son of man, journeying to Jerusalem, the city of his passion and resurrection. As such, the way is intimately related to the following of Christ (8:27; 9:33, 34; 10:17, 32). The following of Christ means being with him in solidarity and taking up his mission. On the way, going up to Jerusa-

---

[7] For the use of "the way" *(he hodos)* in Mark's Gospel, see Elizabeth Struthers Malbon, *Narrative Space and Mythic Meaning in Mark* (Sheffield: JSOT Press, 1991) 59–60, 68–71.

lem, Jesus preceded them (10:32), as he would do in Galilee after his resurrection (14:28; 16:7).

There were those who are on the way, following Jesus on the way. Others were beside the way (10:46). At the Jesus' entry to Jerusalem, the crowd spreads their cloaks on the way (11:8). Those preceding and following him on the way acclaimed him as the one who comes in the name of the Lord (11:9).

The Cup *(to poterion)*

The second set of images revolves around the symbol of the cup *(to poterion)*.[8] Mark does not speak of the cup as an object in itself. In Mark, as in rest of the New Testament, the cup refers to an action, as today we refer to the time for the cup. Drinking the cup, or participating in the same cup, implies solidarity with Jesus and the community of the followers. As in the case of "the way," the cup image, like baptism, is related to Jesus and his passion and resurrection. The disciples had to drink the cup that Jesus drank to enter the kingdom of God (10:37-39).

The cup is part of Jesus' Last Supper and the Church's Lord's Supper. As such, it is related to Jesus' prayer of thanks to God and blood of the covenant to be shed for many. It is also related to the fruit of the vine that Jesus would drink new in the kingdom of God (14:22-25). It is also part of Jesus' prayer to his Father at Gethsemane. Like Jesus, the disciples should not seek the cup, on the contrary, but they should accept the cup if the Father wills to give it to them (14:36).

Structure and Movement

The first part of the Gospel (1:14–8:21) raised the question of Jesus' identity. It was concerned with the implications of following Jesus, the basis of a disciple's relationship to him, and the mission that flowed from that. All three aspects of their life were determined by who Jesus was. Jesus' identity made all the difference.

The major issue in the first part was the universal scope of Jesus' mission, which transcended the Judaism into which he was born and raised. The same universality applied to Jesus' followers. Being with Christ did not depend on family origin, on being Jewish or Gentile, or being male or female. Every human being could be a follower of Christ. The Church consequently had to be universal in its outreach and universal in its welcome.

---

[8] For the theme of the cup, see Jakob Obersteiner, "Cup," *Encyclopedia of Biblical Theology,* edited by Johannes B. Bauer (New York: Crossroad, 1981).

The second part of the Gospel (8:22–16:8) takes up the question of Jesus' identity where the first left off. Beginning with the confession of Peter that Jesus was the Christ (8:29), the story brings it to the centurion's confession of Jesus as the Son of God (15:39). It is concerned with the cost of discipleship, ethical concerns, both general and particular, and being in solidarity with Christ in his passion, burial, and risen life, all of which are determined by Jesus' identity.

In the first part, Mark focused on the breadth of the mission required by the kingdom of God. In this second part, Mark focuses on the depth of commitment needed to realize the universal mission. Like the first part, the second raises the question of Jesus' identity. The depth of their commitment, no less than its breadth, depends on who Jesus is. What then did it mean for Jesus to be the Christ, and what did it require of him and his followers?

The three sections of the first part of the Gospel (1:14–3:6; 3:7–6:6a; 6:6b–8:21) led to the introduction of the second part, with its story of the blind man of Bethsaida (8:22-26) and Peter's confession of Jesus as the Christ or Messiah (8:27-30). To see and understand (8:14-21), the disciples had to have a new sight. The blind man is symbolic of the disciples' blindness. Like the blind man, they needed new sight to understand who Jesus was as the Christ.

As such, the introduction of the second part (8:22-30) can be seen as transitional. The elements in the two stories look back to previous sections of the Gospel. At the same time, they look forward to the sections still to come. It can be seen as the conclusion of the first part, but also as a summary or compendium of the entire second part. The whole of the second part tells about the opening of the eyes of the disciples and Jesus as the Christ.

Like the first part, the second is divided into three sections, forming the fourth to the sixth sections of the Gospel:

Section IV: Following Christ on the Way (8:22–10:52),
Section V: The Coming of the Lord Jesus (11:1–13:37),
Section VI: The Passion and Resurrection
    of the Son of God (14:1–16:8).

In the first part, the three sections were built up in the same way. In the second part, their structure and movement are quite different.

Section IV: Following Christ on the Way (8:22–10:52)

Throughout the fourth section, the emphasis is on the following of Christ. In the first three sections, Jesus called the disciples, created the Twelve, and sent them on mission. In the fourth section, the christological focus is on Christ as the Son of Man. In the section, Jesus announces his passion and resurrection and spells out their implications for every aspect of Christian life.

1. **Jesus Heals the Blind (8:22-26; 10:46-52).** The framework for the fourth section is provided by two stories in which Jesus opens the eyes of a blind man (8:22-26; 10:46-52). To follow Christ, the disciples, the Twelve, and the Church have to see. The stories of the cure of the blind men form an inclusion. As such, the opening of the eyes is the encompassing theme for this section.

2. **Who Is Jesus? (8:27-31).** Intimately associated with the first story of the opening of the eyes (8:22-26) is the identity of Jesus and Peter's confession that he was the Christ (8:27-30). Together they form the introduction, which follows the pattern observed in the first three sections. Each one had two parts, one focusing on Jesus (1:14-15; 3:7-12; 6:6b) and the other on the disciples (1:16-20; 3:13-19; 6:7-30). Here, the cure of the blind man is about Jesus' mission, and Peter's confession is about the faith of the disciples.

3. **Prophetic Announcements of the Passion and Resurrection of the Son of Man (8:31–10:52).** The body of the section (8:31–10:45) is neatly divided into three parts. Each of them is introduced by Jesus' prophetic announcement of the passion and resurrection of the Son of Man (8:31; 9:30-31; 10:32-34). As the human being, Jesus accepts all the conditions associated with humanity, including mortality.

   After each prophetic announcement, the disciples reject the passion in various ways (8:32; 9:32; 10:35-37), and Jesus addresses them directly on the matter (8:33; 9:33-34; 10:38-40). The exchange between Jesus and the disciples sets out a context for broader considerations regarding the implications of the passion and resurrection for everyone who follows him (8:34–9:29; 9:35–10:31; 10:41-45).

4. **Jesus, the Son of David (10:46-52).** In the conclusion (10:46-52), Jesus cures a beggar named Bartimaeus of his blindness. Cured, Bartimaeus followed Jesus on the way to Jerusalem, the city of the passion and resurrection. The conclusion introduces the title, Son of David, that would be treated in the fifth section (11:1–13:37). Like the title Son of Man, Son of David also must be considered in relation to Jesus' identity and mission as the Christ.

Section V: The Coming of the Lord Jesus (11:1–13:37)

In the fourth section, the Gospel emphasized the following of Christ on his way *(he hodos)* to Jerusalem, the place of his passion and resurrection (8:22–10:52). In the fifth section, the Gospel presents Jesus' royal entry to Jerusalem as symbolic of his return in glory at the parousia (11:1–13:37).

In the fourth section, the christological focus was on the Christ as the Son of Man. In the fifth, it is on Christ as the Son of David. Countering earthly views of Jesus' Davidic kingship, the Gospel shows how in Jesus the kingdom of David is transformed and fulfilled in the kingdom of God.

1. **Jesus' Entry to the Temple at Jerusalem (11:1-11).** In the fourth section, the way *(he hodos)* to Jerusalem formed the literary framework. In the fifth, the geography forms the framework. The section begins on the Mount of Olives (11:1-7), from which Jesus enters Jerusalem and the Temple area (11:8-11). In reverse, the section ends with Jesus leaving the Temple area (13:1-2), from which he returns to the Mount of Olives (13:3-37).

2. **The Cursing of the Fig Tree and the Cleansing of the Temple (11:12-25[26]).** After Jesus' triumphal entry to Jerusalem and its Temple, Jesus returns to Bethany, and on the following day, he returns to the Temple for two symbolic actions, the cursing of the fig tree (11:12-14, 20-25[26]) in which the Gospel sandwiched the cleansing of the Temple (11:15-19). Together, Jesus' entry into Jerusalem and the cursing of the fig tree and the cleansing of the Temple form the introduction of the section. Like the previous sections, the first unit focuses primarily on Jesus (11:1-11) and the second on the disciples (11:12-25[26]).

3. **Jesus in the Temple (11:27–12:44).** The body of the section includes a series of confrontations between Jesus and the various groups that came to him in the Temple at Jerusalem. First came the Sanhedrin, the chief priests, the scribes and the elders, who confronted Jesus on the matter of authority (11:27–12:12). Second came the Pharisees and the Herodians who brought up the question of paying tribute to Caesar (12:13-17). Third came the Sadducees who tried to ridicule Jesus' teaching on the resurrection (12:18-27). Fourth, one of the scribes came on the scene to question Jesus about the Law (12:28-34). Fifth, Jesus addressed everyone in general

concerning teaching of the scribes that the Christ is the Son of David (12:35-37). Sixth and finally, he warned everyone, and the disciples in particular, against adopting the behavior of the scribes, who exalt themselves and take advantage of the helpless poor (12:38-44).

4. **Jesus and the Destruction of the Temple (13:1-37).** Leaving the Temple, Jesus (see 11:12-25) predicted its destruction (13:1-2) and returned to the Mount of Olives (13:3; 11:1-11). On the Mount of Olives, overlooking the Temple area, he addressed a discourse to the disciples on the theme of his return as the Son of Man in glory (13:3-37). The conclusion (13:32-37) introduces the title, Son of God (13:32), that would be treated in the sixth section. Like the titles Son of Man and Son of David, the title, Son of God, must be considered in relation to Jesus' identity and mission as the Christ.

Section VI: The Passion and Resurrection of the Son of God (14:1–16:8)

The story of Jesus' passion and resurrection forms the final section of the Gospel. Everything in the Gospel has been directed toward this great climactic event. In a sense, the whole Gospel, beginning with the prefatory title (1:1) and the prologue (1:2-13), and including the previous five sections, can be seen as an introduction for Jesus' passion and resurrection. In this section, the christological focus is on Christ as the Son of God.

1. **The Conspiracy (14:1-11).** As in the other sections of the Gospel, the passion and resurrection has a special introduction (14:1-11). It tells about the conspiracy to destroy Jesus and the offer made by one of the Twelve to betray him (14:1-2, 10-11) as well as the story of a meal in Bethany, in which a woman anointed Jesus as the Christ in view of his death and burial (14:3-9). The rest of the story of the passion and resurrection can be divided into four parts.

2. **The Betrayal of Jesus and His Arrest (14:12-52).** First, there is the account of Jesus' betrayal and arrest. It begins with the preparation for the Passover and ends at Gethsemane where Jesus had gone to pray after the Last Supper.

3. **Jesus' Trial and Condemnation (14:53–15:15).** Second, there is the story of Jesus' trial and condemnation. It begins at the house of the high priest and ends at the palace of Pilate.

4. **Jesus' Torture and Death (15:16-41).** Third, there is the account of Jesus' torture and death by crucifixion. It begins inside the praetorium and ends at the place called Golgotha.

5. **Jesus' Burial and Resurrection (15:42–16:8).** Finally, there is the story of Jesus' burial and the proclamation of his resurrection. It begins with the request of Joseph of Arimathea for Jesus' body and ends with the group of women fleeing the tomb and saying nothing to anyone, "for they were afraid."

6. **The Silence of the Women (16:8).** The story of the passion and resurrection has no conclusion. Instead, there is the silence the women, leaving us to wonder and to ponder as we did earlier at the end of the first part (8:21). And so, we go back to prefatory title and the prologue and reread "the beginning of the gospel of Jesus Christ [the Son of God])" (1:1). That is the way it is with the Gospel. There is no exhausting its mystery.

In this introduction for the Gospel's second part (8:22–16:8), we have reviewed its major literary characteristics. We have also reviewed the prominent symbols and images in this first part, namely, the way *(he hodos)* and the cup *(to poterion)*. Finally, we proposed a literary structure for the second part, showing how the passion and resurrection dominate its three sections.

Now, we are ready to enter the fourth section, "Following Christ on the Way" (8:22–10:52), beginning with the opening of the eyes of a blind man at Bethsaida (8:22-26) and then Peter's confession that Jesus is the Christ (8:27-30).

VIII

rc~ Section IV ~n

Following Christ on the Way

Mark 8:22–10:52

Jesus and his disciples finally arrived at Bethsaida (8:22). After Jesus had broken the bread for the five thousand (6:34-44), he made his disciples get into a boat. His intention was that the disciples should precede him to the other side *(eis to peran)* to Bethsaida, while he dismissed the crowd (6:45). Bethsaida was at the border of Galilee and the Decapolis.

The crossing proved extremely difficult. Even though Jesus came to the disciples on the sea, as the Lord had come to the Israelites while crossing the sea (see Ps 77:20-21), they did not reach the other side at Bethsaida. Instead, they landed on the same side below Capernaum at Gennesareth (6:53).[1]

At the time, the disciples were not ready to go to the other side. Jesus had begun to form them. But they were still not fully prepared for their mission to the Gentile world. As Jews, they avoided eating with Gentiles. They did not understand that their mission had to be universal. And so, Jesus showed how "the tradition of the elders" was subordinate to the commandment and the word of God (7:1-23). They also saw how Jesus responded to a Gentile woman pleading with him to drive a demon out of her daughter (7:24-30)

---

[1] For Gennesaret, see Douglas R. Edwards, "Gennesaret," *The Anchor Bible Dictionary* (New York: Doubleday, 1992) II:963.

15

and how Jesus opened the ears and loosed the tongue of a Gentile so that he could hear and proclaim the gospel of God (8:31-37).

With that, the disciples were prepared for the breaking of the bread with Gentiles. Jesus then broke the bread in the Decapolis (see 7:31) for four thousand people, including Gentiles as well as Jews (8:1-9), and returned to the Jewish side (8:10). And finally, the disciples got into the boat with Jesus and headed to Bethsaida (8:13; see 8:22).

But even as they crossed the sea to the other side, they still did not understand the full implications of what Jesus did. They had eyes but they did not see! To follow Christ on the way, their eyes had to be opened fully. When they arrived at Bethsaida, Jesus opened the eyes of a blind man (8:22-26). Symbolically, Jesus was opening the eyes of the disciples and the eyes of Mark's readers.

The second part of the Gospel according to Mark (8:22–16:8) opens with a section on following Christ on the way (8:22–10:52). Framed by two stories in which Jesus cures blind men of their blindness (8:22-26; 10:46-52), the whole section is about blindness and the sight Jesus gives.

The section tells how Jesus had to open the eyes of the disciples to follow him on the way to the passion and resurrection. Applying the passion and resurrection of Jesus to the most basic aspects of Christian life, Mark offers a synopsis of Christian ethics. For Mark, Christian ethics or moral theology can not be divorced from the following of Christ as expressed in baptism and the Eucharist (see 10:35-40).

An Overview

The disciples were there when Jesus broke *(kataklao, klao)* the five loaves for the five thousand (6:34-44) and the seven loaves for the four thousand (8:1-9), and they all saw what happened. They even gathered up the fragments *(ta klasmata)* left over. Even so, they did not understand about the loaves (6:52). Later, when Jesus asked them how many baskets they had picked up, they answered, "Twelve," and "Seven." But even then, they still did not understand (8:18b-21). They had eyes but they did not see (8:18a).

The fourth section (Mark 8:22–10:52) tells how Jesus opened the eyes of the disciples. The section begins with Jesus opening the eyes of a blind man at Bethsaida (8:22-26). It ends with Jesus opening the eyes of a blind man as Jesus was leaving Jericho with the disciples on the way to Jerusalem (10:46-52).

To understand about the loaves and what they implied for their mission, the disciples had to see that Jesus was the Christ and, as the Christ, he was the Son of Man who would suffer greatly, be handed over, put to death, and rise again after three days. They also had to see and accept the implications of Jesus' death and resurrection for his followers, beginning with themselves. It was all part of following Jesus "on the way" *(en te hodo)*.

The general outline of the section is quite clear. It opens with a story of a blind man whom Jesus cured in two stages (8:22-26). The first stage represents the partial blindness and distorted vision of the disciples. The second announces the full vision needed to follow Jesus on the way.

After the two-stage cure (8:22-26), the Gospel presents various opinions on Jesus' identity, culminating with Peter's confession that Jesus was the Christ (8:27-30). The story shows how the people, the disciples, and even Peter were partially blind to Jesus' identity.

The section then unfolds in three movements, each introduced by Jesus' announcement of the passion and resurrection of the Son of Man, each focusing on a particular set of concerns for his followers (8:31–9:29; 9:30–10:31; 10:32-45). The story ends with a story of a blind man named Bartimaeus, whom Jesus cured in one stage (10:46-52). Seeing, he could follow Jesus on the way to Jerusalem.

The first movement (8:31–9:29) opens with Jesus' first prophetic announcement of the death and resurrection of the Son of Man (8:31) as Jesus and his disciples were on the way to the villages of Caesarea Philippi (see 8:27). Hearing the announcement, Peter took Jesus aside and rebuked him (8:32). Peter was partly blind to Jesus' identity as the Christ. He did not accept that as the Christ Jesus would be killed and rise after three days.

Peter's rejection of the passion provides the context for Jesus' teaching on the radical demands of discipleship and the conditions for effective Christian ministry. This first movement addresses the most fundamental issues for everyone who follows Christ and takes on his mission.

Like the first movement, the second (9:30–10:31) also opens with a prophetic announcement of the death and resurrection of the Son of Man (9:31), now as Jesus and the disciples were beginning a journey through Galilee (9:30). In their partial blindness, the disciples did not understand the announcement and were afraid to ask (9:32). Instead, they argued among themselves on the way which disciple was the greatest (9:33-34).

The disciples' inability to understand invited Jesus' teaching on true greatness and on a wide range of human relationships, including attitudes toward wealth. This second movement speaks to basic community concerns as Christians were emerging from Judaism and were exposed to the influence of the pagan world.

Like the first and second movements, the third (10:32-45) opens with a prophetic announcement of the death and resurrection of the Son of Man, now as Jesus and the disciples were on the way to Jerusalem (10:32-34). As a climactic announcement, the third spells out in detail the events of Jesus' passion. After the first announcement, Peter rebuked Jesus (8:32). After the second, the disciples as a body avoided the implications for them (9:32-34). After the third, James and John asked Jesus to sit at the right and at the left of Jesus in his glory (10:35-37).

Jesus had stressed the ignominy of the passion, but James and John focused on the glory of the resurrection. Their focus invited Jesus' teaching on their baptismal and Eucharistic commitment in following the Son of Man who came "to serve and to give his life as a ransom for many" (10:45). The third movement addresses basic problems affecting Christian leadership as Jesus' followers emerged into the Gentile world.

Setting and *Dramatis Personae*

We begin our reflections on the following of Christ and its implications for Christian life (8:22–10:52) by examining the geographical and chronological settings and the personages who play a role in the section. Focusing on where and when an event is situated and on who are involved in the event makes it much easier to enter the story and to make it our own.

As in the previous sections, geography in general and the specific temporal indications are symbolic and support the development of Mark's theology. In this section, land journeys replace sea journeys, and the theological expression, "after three days," is complemented by a new expression, "after six days." We also meet a few new personages, but mostly, the section focuses on personages that were already introduced and further develops their historic roles, beginning with Jesus.

Geographical Setting: On the Way

The fourth section begins at Bethsaida (8:22-26), a village (see 8:26) on the other side of the sea at the border of the Decapolis (see 6:45). From Bethsaida, the section focuses on "the way" *(he hodos)* to the villages of Caesarea Philippi (8:27–9:1). The theme of "the way" *(he hodos)* was introduced in the prologue (1:2-13; see 1:2) and in the first part of the Gospel (6:8; 8:3). In this section, "the way" is intimately related to the following of Christ. Jesus announces his passion and resurrection on the way and spells out its implications. The section describes five journeys of Jesus with his disciples. Besides the journey to the villages of Caesarea Philippi (8:27–9:1), there is a journey through Galilee (9:30-32) with a stop at Capernaum (10:33-50). The third journey is from Capernaum into the district of Judea opposite the Jordan (10:1-16). The destination for the fourth is not specified (10:17-31). In the fifth journey, Jesus and his disciples are on the way to Jerusalem[2] (10:32-52), the city of his passion and resurrection (see 10:32-34).

The fifth journey (10:32-52) is the climax of the whole section. The four previous journeys were oriented to the passion and resurrection (8:31; 9:31), but the geographical destination was not specified. The journey to Jerusalem (10:32-52) also introduces the next section (11:1–13:37), which begins with Jesus' entry into Jerusalem. On the way to Jerusalem, the city of Jesus' passion and resurrection, Jesus teaches his followers a whole way of life.

In this fourth section, a high mountain *(oros hypsolon)* is the setting for the transfiguration (9:2-8). Coming down from the mountain, Jesus forbade his disciples to tell what they had witnessed until the Son of Man would have risen from the dead (9:9). He also explained the relationship between Elijah and John the Baptist (9:11-13). As in the stories in which Jesus created the Twelve (3:13-19) and made his disciples get into a boat while he was dismissing the crowd (6:45-52), the mountain is the mountain of God, evoking the Old Testament stories of Sinai and Horeb.

The home *(oikos, oikia)* is again a setting where Jesus taught the disciples by themselves (9:28-29; 9:33-50; 10:10-12; see 7:17). In Mark, when Jesus taught the disciples at home, he applied his teaching to pastoral situations that the Church would encounter, after his passion and resurrection, particularly in the time of Mark.

The section began with a story set in Bethsaida, where Jesus gave sight to a blind man (8:22-26). After restoring his sight, Jesus sent him home *(eis oikon autou),* instructing him not to go into the village (8:26). The section ends with a story set in Jericho and on the way from Jericho, where Jesus gave sight to another blind man

---

[2] For the name of Jerusalem, Mark, like John, uses exclusively the Hellenistic form, *Hierosolyma* (see 3:8, 22; 7:1; 10:32, 33; 11:1, 11, 15, 27; 15:41) instead of the Semitic form, *Hierosalem.* See J. H. Moulton, *Grammar of New Testament Greek,* vol. II (Edinburgh: T. & T. Clark, 1920) 147–48.

(10:46-52). This time, Jesus sent him on his way *(hypage)*. But as a follower of Jesus, his way had become the way of Jesus, the Christ, the Son of Man, to Jerusalem and his passion and resurrection (10:52). At the beginning of the story, the blind beggar was beside the way *(para ten hodon,* 10:46). Now he was following Jesus on the way *(en te hodo,* 10:52).

Temporal Setting: When They Arrived at Bethsaida

In this section, most temporal references are relative to a place, to an event, or to an experience. For example, the introductory story (8:22-26) opens with a temporal clause: "When they arrived [*kai erchontai*] at Bethsaida" (8:22), and the concluding story (10:46-52) also opens with a temporal clause: "They came to Jericho. And as he was leaving [*kai ek poreuomenou autou*] Jericho with his disciples" (10:46).

The section has many other examples: "Along the way" (8:27); "As they were coming down the mountain" (9:9); "when they came to the disciples" (9:14); "Once inside the house" (9:33); "When Jesus saw this" (10:14); "As he was setting out on a journey" (10:17).

Other temporal references are simply sequential, introduced by the adverb *euthys* ("immediately," 10:52) or the conjunction *kai* ("now," "then," or "and"), for example: "Then [*kai*] he sent him home" (8:26), "Now [*kai*] Jesus and his disciples set out for the villages of Caesarea Philippi" (8:27).

The section also refers to the time of Jesus' resurrection with the expression "after three days" *(meta treis hemeras,* 8:31; 9:31; 10:34).[3] The early tradition and the other Gospels situated the resurrection "on the third day" *(te hemera te trite,* 1 Cor 15:4). For pastoral reasons, Mark stressed the duration between Jesus' death and his resurrection. For the Markan communities, the suffering of the passion—including their own passion—seemed to be extremely long, and the resurrection was long in coming.

Also in this section, the Gospel also refers to eschatological events, relating them to Jesus' life, passion, and resurrection. Speaking to the crowd, Jesus solemnly announces, "Amen, I say to you, there are some standing here who will not taste death until they see that the kingdom of God has come in power" (9:1). Immediately, Mark pre-

---

[3] The theme of "three days" was introduced in the third section (6:6b–8:21) in conjunction with the breaking of the bread for the 4,000 people (8:1-9). At the beginning of the story, Jesus said to his disciples: "My heart is moved with pity for the crowd, because they have been with me now for three days *(ede hemerai treis)* and have nothing to eat" (8:2).

sents Jesus transfiguration, situating it "after six days" (*meta hemeras hex,* 9:2). Jesus would rise from the dead "after three days," and the transfiguration occurred "after six days," prefiguring Jesus' glorious manifestation when he would come in power in the fullness of the kingdom of God.

Coming down from the mountain after the transfiguration, Jesus told the disciples not to say what they had seen "except when the Son of Man had risen from the dead" (9:9). Interpreting the resurrection eschatologically, the disciples ask: "Why do the scribes say that Elijah must [*dei*]⁴ come first?" (9:11). Answering them, Jesus says, "Elijah will indeed come first and restore all things" (9:12). And referring to John the Baptist, Jesus continues, "But I tell you that Elijah has come" (9:13).

Dramatis Personae

The cast of personages in the fourth section includes Jesus and the disciples, in particular the Twelve (9:35-37; 10:35-45; see 3:13-19), Peter (8:29; 10:28), Peter, James, and John (9:2-8), James and John (10:35-40), and John (9:38). There is also the anonymous crowd, the scribes (9:14), the Pharisees (10:2-9), a father and his son (9:17-27), a child (9:36-37), some children (10:13-16), a rich man (10:17-22), and two blind men, of whom one remains anonymous (8:22-26), and the other named Bartimaeus (10:46-52).

As in the previous sections, Jesus is principal personage. For the first time since the prefatory title (1:1), Jesus is called the Christ (*ho Christos),* the Anointed One, that is, the Messiah (8:29). In the same section, Jesus also refers to himself as the Christ, while speaking to the Twelve (see 9:35) while responding to John (9:38): "Anyone who gives you a cup of water to drink because you belong to Christ . . ." (9:41). Usually, Jesus refers to himself as the Son of Man (8:31; 9:9, 12, 31; 10:33). At the end of the section, Jesus is also called "Son of David" (10:47-48), a title that is developed in the following section (see 11:9-10; 12:35-37).

In the first section (1:14–3:6), Jesus presented himself as the Son of Man in relation to his authority to forgive sins (2:10) and as the lord of the Sabbath (2:28). In this section, Jesus speaks of himself as the Son of Man in relation to his passion and resurrection (8:31; 9:9, 12, 31; 10:33).

---

⁴ In Mark, the verb *dei* (must, it is necessary) expresses prophetic necessity in relation to the events of salvation history and the eschaton (see 8:31; 9:11; 13:7, 10, 14; 14:31).

As a prophet, Jesus announced his passion and resurrection. As a teacher, he spelled out the implications of the passion and resurrection for the disciples and those who would come later, living in the Gentile world of the Roman Empire.

The section also relates Jesus and his mission to John the Baptist and his preparatory mission for the third and fourth times, each time in connection with Elijah. In the prologue, John the Baptist, wearing the garments of Elijah, prepared the way for the Lord Jesus (1:6-8, 9-11). When Jesus sent the Twelve on mission, Jesus' identity came up in relation to John the Baptist and Elijah (6:14-16, 17-29).

In this section, Jesus himself raises the question of his identity. Some people said that he was John the Baptist, others Elijah (8:27-28). Later, Jesus explains that Elijah had already come in the person of John the Baptist (9:11-13). In the prologue and here, the mission of John the Baptist is presented as both historical and eschatological.

The crowd has played a crucial role from the beginning of the Gospel. In the first section (1:14–3:6), the Gospel showed how the rapid growth of the crowd affected Jesus' life and ministry (1:32-33, 35-39, 45; 2:1-4, 13). In the second (3:7–6:6a), it showed how the ethnic diversity of the crowds, including Gentiles as well as Jews (3:7-9), affected the very nature of the Church. The Church had to be universal. In the third (6:6b–8:21), the great and diverse crowds, now including women as well as men, affected the mission of the Church. The Church was sent to evangelize all peoples.

In the fourth section (8:22–10:52), the crowds are with Jesus and the disciples or in the background. They represent the mission field of the Church. Jesus' teaching on the way is for the disciples, but, ultimately, it was for the crowds.

Jesus Heals a Blind Man (8:22-26)

This is the first time in Mark's Gospel that a section opens with a healing story (8:22-26). The previous three sections all opened with a summary of Jesus' mission and ministry (1:14-15; 3:7-12; 6:6b). The first part of the Gospel (1:14–8:21) included many healing stories, but this the first time Jesus heals someone of blindness. This is also the first time that Jesus heals someone in two stages.

There were ten healing stories in the first part of the Gospel (1:14–8:21), five in the first section (1:14–3:6), three in the second (3:7–6:6a), and two in the third (6:6b–8:21). In the first section, Jesus healed a demoniac (1:21-28), Simon's mother-in-law (1:29-31), a leper (1:40-45), a paralytic (2:1-12), and a man with a withered hand

(3:1-6). In the second, Jesus healed the Gerasene demoniac (5:1-20), the daughter of a synagogue official (5:21-24, 35-43), and a woman with a hemorrhage (5:25-34). In the third, he healed the daughter of a Syrophoenician woman (7:24-30) and a deaf-mute (7:31-37).

There were also four summaries of Jesus' healing activity, one at the gate of Simon's home (1:32-34) and another beside the sea, where people came to Jesus from Gentile lands as well as Jewish (3:7-12). The third summary tells of cures at the synagogue of Jesus' native place (6:5), and finally, in the villages, towns, and the countryside in the vicinity of Genesareth (6:53-56).

In healing people or driving out unclean spirits and demons, Jesus proclaimed the gospel of God (see 1:14-15; 3:7-12; 6:6b), first to Jews (1:14–3:6), then to both Jews and Gentiles (3:7–6:6a; 6:6b–8:21). Now, healing the blind man, Jesus was symbolically healing his disciples of their own blindness. The story directly responds to Jesus' question toward the end of the previous section: "Do you have eyes and not see" (8:18)?[5]

When Jesus and the disciples were at Bethsaida, people brought to Jesus a blind man *(kai pherousin auto typhlon)* and begged him *(kai parakalousin auton)* to touch him *(hina auto hapsetai,* 8:22). Earlier, they had brought to him a deaf man with a speech impediment *(kai pherousin auto kophon kai mogelalon)* and begged him *(kai parakalousin auton)* to lay his hands on him (8:31). Later, people would bring children to him *(kai prosepheron auto paidia)* that he might touch them *(hina auton hapsetai,* 10:13).[6] As in Matthew and Luke, every sense is important in Mark's Gospel, not only the senses of sight and hearing, but also the sense of touch.

Then Jesus "took the blind man by the hand and led him outside the village" (8:23a). In stories intended for the early Church, Jesus took the disciples aside and taught them in private, particularly at home. Here, he took the blind man outside the village. At the end of the story, Jesus sent him home *(eis oikon),* forbidding him to enter

---

[5] The symbolism of the story is narrowly connected with its function in the literary structure of the whole section (8:22–10:52). On its own, outside the section, the story would have been nearly meaningless. Probably, that is why it was omitted in the Gospels of Matthew and Luke. In Matthew's Gospel, Jesus healed two blind men instead of one on leaving Jericho (Matt 20:29-34; see Mark 10:46-52).

[6] As in the stories of the breaking of the bread (6:34-44; 8:1-9) and other stories (see 11:1-11 and 14:12-16), Mark follows a familiar pattern in 7:31-37; 8:22-26; 10:13-16.

the village (8:26). In Mark, the story of the blind man addressed the early Church, in particular, Mark's readers.

Jesus put spittle on the blind man's eyes and laid his hands on him *(epitheis tas cheiras auto,* 8:23b). This is the second time Jesus used spittle in a cure. Healing the deaf man with a speech impediment, Jesus put his finger into his ears, and spitting, touched his tongue (7:33). Now Jesus put spittle on the eyes of the blind man.

This is also the fourth time that Jesus laid his hands on a person (5:23; 6:5; 7:32; 8:23-25; see also 10:16b). In Galilee, one of the synagogue officials named Jairus pleaded with Jesus to lay his hands on his daughter (5:23). Jesus took the child by the hand and commanded her to rise (5:41). Later, in his native place, Jesus cured "a few sick people by laying his hands on them" (6:5). Later yet, in the Decapolis, people brought a deaf man to Jesus and begged him to lay his hand on him (7:32).

Now, the people who brought the blind man begged him to touch *(hapsetai)* him (8:22). Responding, he laid his hands on the blind person, not only once, but twice (8:23-25). In Mark, when Jesus touches someone, he lays his hands on the person (see also 10:13, 16, and 1:41).

After laying his hands on *(epitheis tas cheiras)* the person *(auto),* Jesus asked him, "Do you see anything?" *(Ei ti blepeis).* With that question, the story recalls Jesus' question to the Twelve: "Do you have eyes [*ophthalmous echontes*] and not see [*ou blepete*]?" (8:18). At the time, Jesus did not expect a response from the Twelve. The question was rhetorical. Now, Jesus asked a real question and expected an answer from the blind man. Looking up *(anablepsas),* the man responded, "I see [*blepo*] people looking like trees and walking" (8:24).

Emphasizing the blindness, again *(palin)*[7] Jesus laid his hands on *(epetheken tas cheiras)* on his eyes *(epi tous ophthalmous autou)* and he saw clearly *(kai dieblepsen,* 8:25a). Again we have to recall Jesus' question to the Twelve: "Do you have eyes and not see?" (8:18). The blind man had eyes and he did not see. When Jesus laid his hand on his eyes, his eyes were cured of their blindness. Now he could see *(eneblepsen)* everything clearly (8:25).

---

[7] For the use of the adverb *palin* (again) in Mark, see David Barrett Peabody, *Mark As Composer,* New Gospel Studies 1 (Macon, Ga.: Mercer University Press, 1987) 136–137. To this point, *palin* was employed in the same way in 2:1, 13; 3:1, 20; 4:1; 5:21; 7:14; 7:31; 8:1; 8:13.

Who Is Jesus? (8:27-30)

Leaving Bethsaida (8:22-26), "Jesus and his disciples set out for the villages of Caesarea Philippi" (8:27). On the way *(en te hodo)*, Jesus asked the disciples two questions: "Who do people say that I am?" and "But who do you say that I am?" Together, the story of the blind man (8:22-26) and the interchange between Jesus and the disciples (8:27-30) introduce the whole section.

The opinions concerning Jesus' identity are closely related to the story of the blind man. The disciples' response to the first question shows that people were blind to who Jesus was. Some said that Jesus was John the Baptist, others Elijah, and others one of the prophets (8:28). Peter's response to the second question, "You are the Messiah," and Jesus' warning not to tell anyone, show that the disciples' vision of Jesus might be distorted (8:29-30). The rest of the section deals with their distorted vision.

The identity of Jesus has been an important theme from the beginning of the Gospel. In the prefatory title, Mark described "the beginning of the gospel" as "the gospel of Jesus Christ, [the Son of God]" (1:1). The prologue presented Jesus as God's beloved Son (1:9-11). The first section (1:14–3:6) related the identity of Jesus to the call of the disciples (1:22, 24, 27; 2:7, 10). The second section (3:7–6:6a) related it to the creation of the Twelve and to the universality of the Church (4:38; 5:41; 6:1-6a).

In the double introduction (8:22-26, 27-30) of the fourth section, the question of Jesus' identity (8:27-30) comes up after people begged him to touch the blind man. Responding, Jesus laid hands first on him and later on his eyes (8:22-26). At the end of the second section, Jesus' identity (6:3) was also related to the mighty deeds he wrought by his hands (6:2) when he laid his hands on the sick (6:5).

Everything in the Church depends on who Jesus is, including the mission of the Church. After sending the Twelve on mission, the question of Jesus' identity is brought up. Mark reports that King Herod heard about the mission of the Twelve. Some people thought Jesus was John the Baptist raised from the dead. Others were saying that he was Elijah, or a prophet like the other prophets. King Herod was convinced that Jesus was John the Baptist whom he had beheaded but was raised up (6:14-16).

Introducing the fourth section, Jesus himself raises the question of his identity (8:27-30). First, he asked his disciples, "Who do people say that I am?" Their answer recalls the opinions presented in connection with the mission of the Twelve: "John the Baptist, others Elijah, still others one of the prophets" (8:27-28; see 6:14-16).

Jesus then pointed the question to the disciples: "But who do you say that I am?" Again, everything objectively depends on who Jesus is. And for the disciples, everything, including following him on the way, depends on the disciples' recognition of his identity.

Peter answered, "You are the Messiah," that is, the Christ, the Anointed One. But as we shall see, Peter and the disciples did not accept that Messiah would die and rise after three days. They were like the blind man who saw "people looking like trees and walking." Before telling anyone about him (8:30), Jesus had to cure their blindness with his teaching.

The First Movement: Implications of the Passion and Resurrection for Christian Life (8:31–9:29)

Jesus cured a man of blindness, but at first the cure was only partial and the man's vision was very distorted. He saw people that looked like trees walking. That was in Bethsaida (8:22-26; see 6:45).

Jesus and his disciples then set out for the villages of Caesarea Philippi. On the way *(en te hodo),* Jesus asked his disciples two questions: "Who do people say that I am?" and "Who do you say that I am?" Speaking for the disciples, Peter answered that Jesus was the Christ, but Jesus ordered them to speak to no one about him (8:27-30).

At this point in the story, we do not yet know why Jesus forbade the disciples to reveal his identity. He himself had been going around Galilee proclaiming the gospel and the imminence of the kingdom. He had been crisscrossing the Sea of Galilee, curing the sick, casting out demons, and feeding the hungry. This was not the kind of behavior expected of someone who did not want anyone to know about him.

However, we did receive an indication in the first stage of the blind man's cure. He could see, but his vision was distorted. Could it be that Peter's faith was just as distorted as the blind man's vision? With that, the disciples would distort the gospel of Jesus Christ. The answer comes in the brief exchange that follows as Jesus and his disciples continue on the way *(en te hodo; see 8:3, 27).*

In this first movement (8:31–9:29), Jesus announces that the Son of Man must suffer greatly, be rejected by the Sanhedrin, be killed, and rise after three days (8:31). Immediately, Peter took Jesus aside and began to rebuke him (8:32), but Jesus rebuked him in return (8:33). After this dialogue, Jesus summons the crowd together with his disciples and speaks of the basic implications of the passion for the life and mission of his followers (8:34-38). He then applies the passion to their ministerial life (9:1-29).

Introducing the transfiguration (9:2-8), Mark adds a traditional saying of Jesus concerning the coming of the kingdom of God in power (9:1). In conclusion, he relates the transfiguration to his resurrection and their ministry (9:9-13). After the transfiguration, this first movement concludes with a story of Jesus driving an unclean spirit from a young boy, showing how faith and prayer is critical for their ministry (9:14-29).

Jesus' First Prophetic Announcement (8:31-32a)

Jesus then began to teach his disciples "that the Son of Man must suffer greatly and be rejected by the elders, the chief priests, and the scribes, and be killed, and rise after three days" (8:31). This is the first of several prophetic announcements of the approaching passion of Jesus. Mark added that Jesus spoke the word *(ton logon)* openly *(parresia)*. Jesus made his message, his gospel, very clear.

Two further announcements would be just as clear (9:31; 10:32-34). After the transfiguration, Jesus also refers to the Son of Man's rising from the dead (9:9), a statement that clearly presupposes his passion. Referring to the coming of Elijah, he also asked the disciples about how it is written "regarding the Son of Man must suffer greatly and be treated with contempt?" (9:12). Concluding a mini-discourse, Jesus announces that the Son of Man came "to give his life as a ransom for many" (10:45).

A number of events also had suggested that Jesus' life might end with passion. At least there were those who wanted it so. After a series of conflicts with Jesus and his disciples (2:1–3:6), the Pharisees had already taken counsel with the Herodians against Jesus, seeking to put him to death (3:6). Later, the scribes from Jerusalem had accused Jesus of driving out demons by the prince of demons (3:23). Nor should we forget the conflicts with the Pharisees and the scribes from Jerusalem over the traditions of the elders (7:1-13) and Jesus' refusal to grant the Pharisees a sign from heaven (8:11-13). The Pharisees' plotting to have Jesus put to death looms over all these later conflicts.

Besides, at the very beginning of Jesus' mission, an ominous reference was made to the handing over of John the Baptist (1:14). Since Jesus had been a follower of John (1:7), should we not expect him to be handed over as well? During his ministry, Jesus was closely associated with John, at least in the mind of Herod, who had put John to death (6:14-16). Many others thought of Jesus as a new John the Baptist (8:28). All of these were literary indications that, like John, Jesus might sooner or later suffer a violent death (see 6:17-29).

The first announcement of Jesus' passion (8:31) and those that follow take the story far beyond all previous intimations of Jesus' death by introducing a divine foil to the plotting of the Pharisees. Three days after his passion and death, Jesus would rise from the dead. Jesus may have been John's follower, and as such he would die a violent death, but he was far more than John (1:7-8). As such, Jesus would rise.

The story of Jesus' conflicts with the Pharisees and the scribes and the way Mark presented John the Baptist did indeed point to Jesus' eventual passion. At least they raised the possibility of it, and even the probability. But the prophetic announcement in 8:31 marks the first time Jesus himself spoke clearly of his passion-resurrection, and the Gospel made a point of noting it (8:32a).

Jesus, the Son of Man. The prophetic announcement does not refer to Jesus with the personal pronoun. Jesus did not teach them that *he* must suffer greatly, but that the Son of Man must suffer greatly. The title Son of Man appeared earlier in the first section of the Gospel (1:14–3:6) in two sayings that were attributed to Jesus: "the Son of Man has authority to forgive sins on earth" (2:10), and "the Son of Man is lord even of the sabbath" (2:28). This earlier context emphasizes the authority of the Son of Man. In the fourth section, the context emphasizes the passion and resurrection of the Son of Man.

Both of these contexts refer to Jesus as *the* human being, fulfilling God's plan for humanity as presented in Genesis. While subject to God, the human being was meant to have authority over all things on earth. However, the human being did not enjoy God's immortality. The human being was not God, the creator, but a co-creator. It was the lot of Adam to die, something Adam rejected. Trying to be like God, Adam grasped for God's immortality (see Phil 2:6-11). Because of this, Adam could no longer claim full humanity as God had intended. That was for Jesus, *the* Son of Man, to reestablish, by accepting the most basic human limitations, which is to suffer and die.

Jesus was indeed the Son of Man, and the various references to Jesus' suffering and death in 8:22–10:52 all refer to the Son of Man. In various ways, they also reflect the particular manner of Jesus' death. Jesus did not only accept to die. He gave his life as a ransom for many (10:46).

Rejection by the Sanhedrin. The Son of Man would suffer greatly *(polla pathein)*, and be rejected by the elders, the chief priest, and the scribes. Given the scribes' long-standing opposition to Jesus, who taught with authority and not as one of them (1:22), we would expect that they would have a role in Jesus' death. However, until now, the elders and the chief priests did not have any part in Mark's Gospel. They were not even mentioned.

Given the prominent role of the Pharisees in the first part of the Gospel and their association with the scribes, we would expect the Pharisees would have a role in Jesus' death. Surprisingly, Jesus does not mention them in his announcements of the passion. As we shall see, they have no role in account of the passion (14:1–16:8).

The introduction of the elders and the chief priests in Jesus' first great announcement of the passion presupposes the actual account of the passion. In the passion's opening statement, we learn that the chief priests and the scribes were seeking a way to arrest Jesus and put him to death (14:1). Both groups, that is, the chief priests and scribes, are mentioned in the third prophetic announcement of the passion (10:33).

Later in the passion story, in the description of those who accompanied Judas to Gethsemane, all three, the chief priests, the scribes, and the elders, are mentioned (14:43), and again when Jesus was before the high priest (14:53) and before Pilate (15:1). On that final occasion, Mark explains that the chief priests with the elders and the scribes constitute the Sanhedrin.

The Sanhedrin was an official governing body in Jerusalem, a Jewish council with authority in religious matters over the Jewish community. In Jesus' first announcement (8:31), the Gospel places the responsibility for the killing of Jesus on this official body. In the passion itself, the greatest responsibility for Jesus' death would be attributed to the chief priests, who are singled out from the rest of the Sanhedrin (14:55; 15:3).

The Sanhedrin, that is, the chief priests, the elders, and the scribes, are responsible for the death of Jesus precisely as the Son of Man. With this realization, the full impact of the title, Son of Man, is felt. Judaism's religious governing body did what it could do to destroy the life and work of the one whose mission was to reestablish humanity on the way *(en te hodo)* God had originally intended. However, by having Jesus killed, they unwittingly assured the fulfillment of his mission. It was far from the intention of the chief priests, but as part of the Sanhedrin, they also fulfilled their priestly sacrificial role. The ironies of Jesus' passion are beginning to unfold.

A Message for the Disciples. There are times in Mark's Gospel when Jesus addressed the crowds or even the Pharisees and the scribes, but the prophetic announcement of the passion was addressed to the disciples, those whom Jesus had just forbidden to tell anyone about him (8:30). In the Markan context, the fact that the addressees were disciples is related to the purpose of the announcement.

Jesus' prophetic announcements of the passion and resurrection are often referred to as predictions. For example, Mark 8:31 is titled "The First Prediction of the Passion" in several editions of the New Testament. Unfortunately, the title tends to distort the reader's attention. Instead of hearing it as a proclamation, we await its verification by subsequent events.

Viewing the announcement as a prediction can suggest that it had an apologetic intent, and that is how it has sometimes been used in apologetics. Or again, taking into account that it was addressed to the disciples, it may suggest a pastoral intent, as though Jesus had merely intended to prepare the disciples for the difficulties of the approaching passion.

The purpose of the announcements is indeed pastoral, but not as a forewarning. Rather, it is that there was a serious problem in the attitudes of the disciples. Jesus made these announcements because the disciples, while accepting that Jesus was the Christ, did not accept his passion and resurrection as the Son of Man. They sought a Christ or Messiah of earthly glory, not a suffering and rising Messiah.

The pronouncements were genuinely prophetic, but not as predictions. They penetrated to the core of Jesus messianic mission and tried to open the minds of the disciples, who so far had been unable to see or understand and who even seem to be suffering from hardness of heart. Like the blind man, the disciples need to have their eyes opened that they might see perfectly. They needed to see that Jesus had to die to everything that limited him humanly. Otherwise, there could never be a mission to all human beings.

Peter Rebukes Jesus (8:32b)

Peter, the one who had just confessed that Jesus was the Christ (8:29), responded negatively to Jesus' prophetic announcement of the passion and resurrection. First, he took Jesus aside from the others. Peter did not want the other disciples to hear Jesus speak in this vein. He then began to rebuke Jesus directly (8:32b). He did not want Jesus to continue with his announcement of the passion and resurrection.

Jesus had barely begun to teach the disciples about the passion when Peter began to rebuke him about this teaching. From Mark's presentation, we see that the passion of Jesus, the Son of Man, was a problem for the disciples. But for the moment we remain in the dark as to the precise nature of the problem.

In Matthew's Gospel, Peter's rebuke is presented as an obstacle to Jesus' personal pursuit of his way to the passion. For Matthew, Peter was thus tempting Jesus (16:22-23). Not so in Mark, where Peter is tempting not Jesus but the disciples. Mark had shown this by having Peter take Jesus aside from the disciples.

In Return, Jesus Rebukes Peter (8:33)

Peter had barely begun to rebuke Jesus, when Jesus in turn rebuked Peter. Since Peter had taken Jesus aside from the others. Jesus turned back toward them. With his eyes fixed on the disciples, he spoke to Peter in startling terms. Jesus addressed Peter as Satan (8:33a), a designation he had used earlier in responding to the scribes from Jerusalem: "How can Satan drive out Satan . . . If Satan has risen up against himself and is divided, he cannot stand; that is the end of him" (3:23-26). Peter was speaking as Satan, that is, as the Adversary. Jesus could not possibly accept his rebuke. He would then be acting with the mind of Satan. So doing, he would not stand, and that would be the end of his mission.

Jesus was warning the disciples against being tempted by Peter who was now acting as Satan. Jesus did more than call Peter Satan. He ordered Peter to get behind him. The expression, "Get behind me" *(opiso mou)* is very easily misinterpreted. For instance, the older edition of Mark's Gospel in the New American Bible rendered it, "Get out of my sight," as though it were both a reproach and a banishment. Jesus' rebuke was indeed a reproach, but it was not a banishment, just the opposite.

As we saw in the call of the disciples (1:16-20), to go or come behind someone is a way of referring to the following of someone. It first appeared in the Gospel in relation to Jesus' coming after John the Baptist, who announced that "one mightier than I is coming after me" *(opiso mou,* 1:7). After 8:33, it appears again in 8:34 when Jesus speaks to the crowd along with his disciples: "Whoever wishes to come after me *[opiso mou].* . . ."

In Mark's Gospel, to come behind or after someone has nothing to do with spatial or temporal relationships. It is not a matter of coming later or being situated at the back of someone. It has to do with the personal relationship, that of a disciple in the following of Christ.

At the very beginning of the Gospel, when Jesus saw Simon and brother Andrew casting their nets, he called them: "Come after me [*Deute opiso mou*], and I will make you fishers of men." Leaving their fishing nets, they followed him (1:16-18). Now Peter had abandoned his commitment to follow Christ, and Jesus was calling him back: "Get behind me [*Hypage opiso mou*]." As it was, Peter was not thinking like God, but as human beings think (8:33).

Rebuking Jesus, Peter was not so much rejecting what the passion meant in Jesus' life. He was rejecting what it implied for the life of his followers. Jesus was indeed the Christ, the Messiah, as Peter confessed (8:29). But as the Christ, Jesus was also the Son of Man. As the Son of Man, Jesus was mortal. Not only did Jesus accept his mortality, he even gave his life for others (8:33b). As followers, the disciples were called to do the same.

Following Christ, the Son of Man (8:34-38)

Jesus' announcement of the passion (8:31-32a), Peter's rebuke (8:32b), and Jesus' response to Peter (8:33) introduce further teaching aimed at a wider audience (8:34-38). In 8:31-33, Jesus' concern was with Peter and the other disciples. In 8:34-38, Jesus' teaching is intended for all, including the Markan communities.

While the two units (8:31-33, 34-38) are distinct, they are also closely related, as can be seen from the expression *opiso mou* (behind or after me), which associates the general challenge for every disciple (8:34) with the special challenge given to Peter (8:33). The relationship can also be seen from the title Son of Man, which appears both at the beginning of the first unit and at the end of the second unit, relating the passion and the resurrection of the Son of Man (8:31) with his future coming in glory (8:38).

Jesus' message in 8:34-38 is given in the form of a little discourse laying down the conditions for following Christ, the Son of Man. As in all Jesus' discourses in Mark's Gospel, the mini-discourse on the conditions of discipleship looks beyond the context of the early disciples to Jesus to all those who would come in the future.

The discourse has a little introduction: "He summoned the crowd with his disciples [*syn tois mathetais autou*] and said to them" (8:34a). In the introduction, Mark associates the crowd with Jesus' disciples as potential disciples.

After the introduction, the discourse is composed of six sayings traceable in some form to Jesus' ministry in Galilee. Like most of Jesus' preaching and teaching, the sayings acquired a new significance with Jesus' passion and resurrection, and this is reflected in their wording. Taking up one's cross would not have made any sense prior to Jesus' own crucifixion (8:34).

When Mark as an evangelist shaped the traditional sayings into a discourse, he focused their meaning still further, and this can also be seen in their wording. In the earlier tradition, Jesus spoke to the disciples about losing their life for his sake. In Mark, Jesus speaks to them about losing their life for his sake "and that of the gospel" (8:35). Mark advances the tradition by identifying Jesus with the gospel (see 10:29; 1:1; 14:9).

"Whoever Wishes to Come after Me *(opiso mou)* . . ." **(8:34).** The discourse opens with a general principle: "Whoever wishes to come after me must deny himself, take up his cross, and follow me" (8:34). As when Jesus called the first disciples (1:16-20), Jesus did not force anyone to come after him. As then, his call is an invitation. Nor is Jesus' invitation elitist. It is issued to all. But while all are called, there are conditions for coming after Christ, the Son of Man.

In the first section (1:14–3:6), when Jesus called the first disciples to come after him (1:16-20), the focus was on the purpose of the call. They would be fishing for human beings. In the second (3:7–6:6a) and third (6:6b–8:21) sections, the focus was on the Church and its universal mission. They would be fishing for Gentiles as well as Jews. Now, in the fourth section, the focus is on what it is required to fish for human beings.

The conditions are three. First, one who wants to come after Jesus must deny himself *(aparnesastho heauton)*. To deny oneself is to re-nounce all claims on oneself. It shows a willingness to be claimed by Christ, the Son of Man. Those who deny themselves place them-selves totally at the disposition of Christ.

Second, one who wants to come after Jesus must take up his or her cross *(arato ton stauron autou)*. To take up one's cross is to join Jesus in offering one's life for others. Such is the purpose for deny-ing oneself, and such is the nature of Jesus' claim on his disciples. To be totally at the disposition of Christ means concretely taking one's cross.

Third, one who wants to come after Jesus must follow *(akoloutheito)* him. To follow Jesus is to join him on the way *(en te hodo)* to his pas-sion and resurrection (8:31). It expresses a commitment to be with Jesus on a life journey characterized by self-renunciation and the demands of the cross.

"For Whoever Wishes to Save His Life . . ." (8:35). The three conditions for coming after Jesus, denying oneself, taking up one's cross and following Christ as the Son of Man, are not the stuff of ordinary wisdom or asceticism. They are part of Jesus' new teaching (see 1:27) that cannot be understood apart from his passion and resurrection. There had to be a rationale for those extraordinary demands. It comes in the form of two contrasting sayings:

> For whoever wishes to save his life will lose it, but whoever loses his life for my sake and that of the gospel will save it (8:35).

Both sayings are in the form of generalizations with a protasis and an apodosis. Together, they form an antithetical parallelism, in which the second contrasts with the first.

In the first saying, "For whoever wishes to save his life" *(protasis)* "will lose it" *(apodosis)* Jesus presents a challenge. Apart from the second, "but whoever loses his life for my sake and that of the gospel" *(protasis)* "will save it" *(apodosis),* the first saying would remain a total enigma.

Antithetical parallelism is quite common in wisdom poetry, especially in Hebrew wisdom literature. Where are two examples from the book of Proverbs:

> The greedy man stirs up disputes,
>   but he who trusts in the LORD will prosper (Prov 28:25).

> The fool gives vent to all his anger;
>   but by biding his time, the wise man calms it (Prov 29:11).

In each case, the two statements are parallel, but they also stand in contrast.

Antithetical parallelism also appears in Hellenistic wisdom. Here are two examples from the Wisdom of Solomon:

> But let our strength be our norm of justice;
>   for weakness proves itself useless (Wis 2:11).

> For blest is the wood through which justice comes about;
>   but the handmade idol is accursed, and its maker as well (Wis 14:7-8).

Finally, antithetical parallelism is fairly common among the sayings of Jesus. Here are two examples from Matthew's Gospel:

> Every good tree bears good fruit, and a rotten tree bears bad fruit (Matt 7:17).

> Do not store up for yourselves treasures on earth, where moth and decay destroy, and thieves break in and steal. But store up treasures in

heaven, where neither moth nor decay destroys, nor thieves break in and steal (Matt 6:19-20).

As in Mark 8:35, all but the last of these parallelisms contrasts two positive affirmations. In the last, Matthew 6:19-20, the antithesis consists in a positive-negative contrast. In that case, the second member does little to advance the thought beyond affirming the opposite. If Mark 8:35 were a positive-negative antithesis, it would read like this:

> For whoever wishes to save his life will lose it,
> but whoever does not wish to save his life will save it.

With two positive statements, the second member usually drops or adds something and moves the thought forward. In Mark 8:35, the second part of the antithesis drops the idea of wishing and adds a reference to Jesus and the gospel. With that deletion and the addition, the thought is greatly enriched. Losing one's life does not depend on one's own will but on ones' relationship to Jesus and the gospel.

If the antithesis were perfectly parallel, it would read like this:

> For whoever wishes to save his life will lose it,
> but whoever wishes to lose his life will save it.

This does not correspond to what Jesus said, and it would not be true. In fact, it would be contrary to Jesus' prayer at Gethsemane: "Take this cup away from me, but not what I will but what you will" (14:36).

For Jesus, losing one's life was not a matter of choice or volition, as though it were a value in itself. It was a matter of acceptance and only for the sake of something beyond it, that is the will of his Father. Without wanting to lose one's life, one could accept its loss for the sake of Christ and that of the gospel. Those who lose their life as followers of Christ, that is, as people whose life is patterned on Christ and the gospel, save their life. Such is the Christian paradox.

The wisdom of following Christ and losing one's life makes sense only in the light of Christ's passion and resurrection. By losing his life, Jesus saved both his own life and that of others. Therein lies the wisdom of the cross, of which St. Paul wrote so eloquently to the Corinthians (1 Cor 1:18-25).

The distance between the wisdom of the cross and conventional wisdom can be measured by the mockery of the chief priests and the scribes seeing Jesus on the cross: "You who would destroy the temple and rebuild it in three days, save yourself by coming down from the cross" (15:29-30). "He saved others; he cannot save himself" (15:31). It takes the second saying to grasp the irony in their taunts.

The second saying on "whoever loses his life" is needed to understand the first: "Whoever wishes to save his life." Whoever rejects the implications of the following of Christ, who gave his life for others, certainly will lose it. But whoever refuses to join Christ in the passion will not join him in the resurrection.

"What Profit Is There . . ." (8:36-37). After presenting the rationale (8:35) for denying oneself, taking up one's cross, and following Christ (8:34), the discourse raises two rhetorical questions in support:

> What profit is there for one to gain the whole world and forfeit his life? What could one give in exchange for his life? (8:36-37).

Again we have two contrasting parallel sayings, forming an antithetical parallelism, but now in question form. This kind of antithesis reflects a prophetic inspiration rather than the sapiential. It appears quite frequently in Paul, at times in a series of questions in the style of Stoic diatribes. Here is an example from 1 Corinthians:

> Where is the wise one? Where is the scribe? Where is the debater of this age? Has not God made the wisdom of the world foolish? (1 Cor 1:20).

The three short questions in the first member of the antithesis may have been inspired by Isaiah 19:12 and 33:18. The question in the second member shows the futility of trying to answer them.

Here is an another example from the Letter to the Romans:

> Do you suppose, then, you who judge those who engage in such things and yet do them yourself, that you will escape the judgment of God?

> Or do you hold his priceless kindness, forbearance, and patience in low esteem, unaware that the kindness of God would lead you to repentance? (Rom 2:3-4).

In Mark 8:36-37, the first member of the antithesis is quite direct. The question, "What profit?" invites the answer, "No profit at all!" For one who loses his life, all the goods of this world are of no value whatsoever. But there is another aspect to the question. Life refers to eternal life, and the focus is on the relative value of the goods of this world. What value is it to gain everything else if someone loses the one thing that is more precious than anything else?

The second member of the antithesis returns to the Christian paradox presented in 8:35. While it is true that nothing, not even the whole world, is enough to repurchase the life one has lost, there is something one can exchange for one's life. We can exchange our earthly life for eternal life. That is precisely what we do when we lose our life for the sake of Jesus and the gospel (8:35).

"Whoever Is Ashamed of Me . . ." (8:38). Up to this point, Jesus' discourse has focused on soteriological considerations, that is, on the matter of gaining eternal life by following Christ through his passion to the resurrection. The sixth and final saying in the discourse introduces the perspective of eschatology. It consists in a warning, a conditional threat. Should the arguments not prove persuasive, here was a final reason for denying oneself, taking up one's cross, and following Christ:

> Whoever is ashamed of me and of my words in this faithless and sinful generation, the Son of Man will be ashamed of when he comes in his Father's glory with the holy angels (8:38).

The warning begins by recalling 8:35. The reference to "whoever is ashamed of me and my words" parallels "whoever loses his life for my sake and that of the gospel." For Christians, refusing to lose one's life for Jesus' sake is the same as being ashamed of him. As the motive for not losing one's life, the notion of shame is quite specific. Like the entire discourse (8:34-38), the saying is addressed to the Markan communities and anyone for whom the cross was a stumbling block or foolishness (see 1 Cor 1:23).

Jesus spoke of those who are ashamed of him and his words as belonging to "this faithless and sinful generation." The expression, "in this generation" *(en te genea taute)* has negative connotations, but not only as a temporal reference. There are those who belong to this generation, and there are those who do not belong.

While "this generation" stands in contrast with the final coming of the Son of Man, it does not refer to the present era, but rather to the people living in it. Nor does it refer to everyone in the present era, but only those who are ashamed of Christ and his words.

The expression has already appeared in reference to the Pharisees, whose hearts were hardened (3:5), who rejected Jesus and his message and demanded a sign from heaven to test Jesus (8:11-12). In response, sighing "from the depth of his spirit," Jesus said, "Why does this generation [*he genea aute*] seek a sign? Amen, I say to you, no sign will be given to this generation [*te genea taute*]" (8:12). The Pharisees could not see that, when Jesus broke the bread and nourished four thousand with seven loaves with seven baskets of fragments left over (8:1-9), he had given them a sign from heaven.

The Son of Man, who had authority to forgive sins on earth (2:10), who was lord even of the Sabbath (2:28), and who had to suffer greatly, be rejected, be killed, and rise after three days (8:31) would also return in his Father's glory with the holy angels (8:38). That final great event in the story of the Son of Man is further developed in the great eschatological discourse in chapter 13:

> And then they will see "the Son of Man coming in the clouds" with great power and glory, and then he will send out the angels and gather [his] elect from the four winds, from the end of the earth to the end of the sky (13:26-27).

The vision of the Son of Man coming in the clouds with great power is a reference to Daniel 7:13. It would also be Jesus' answer to the high priest during the interrogation before the Sanhedrin (14:61).

Jesus warns the crowd with his disciples that at the final moment, when history comes to an end, the Son of Man will be ashamed of those who had been ashamed of him and his words. Since they had refused to take up their cross and follow him on the way, giving their life for his sake and that of the gospel, he would refuse to give them life. They may have gained the whole world, but they would not join him in his Father's glory with the holy angels.

Jesus' reference to "this generation" invited some statement concerning those living in this present era but not part of "this faithless and sinful generation." There were also other questions to consider regarding the Son of Man, the kingdom of God, and the coming of Elijah. These matters are treated in the next unit (9:1-13), which includes the story of Jesus' transfiguration (9:2-8).

"He Was Transfigured before Them" (9:1-13)

Jesus' discourse on the conditions of discipleship (8:34-38) ends with a strong warning: "Whoever is ashamed of me and of my words in this faithless and sinful generation (8:38; see 8:12; 9:19; 13:30), the Son of Man will be ashamed of when he comes in his Father's glory with the holy angels."

In the context of Jesus' prophetic ministry, the warning was very clear. The attitude of people toward Jesus would determine the attitude of Jesus when he comes as the Son of Man. At the same time, the warning must have shocked Jesus' listeners with its reference to "this faithless and sinful generation." But that is what a prophetic warning is meant to do.

There is something of the hyperbole about prophetic warnings, and a hyperbole does not make distinctions. Had Jesus distinguished between those who belonged to "this faithless and sinful generation" and others who did not, the warning would have lost its prophetic impact.

In the years after Jesus' death and resurrection, the saying became part of a traditional body of teaching, and the early Christians turned to it along with other sayings in their ministry or evangelization, catechesis, and preaching. In such pastoral settings, the warning's original impact could easily be maintained. Christian evangelization, catechesis, and preaching were not very far from Jesus' prophetic ministry.

But the early Christians also turned to Jesus' teaching for understanding and guidance as they faced new situations and challenges. This second type of setting called for light and wisdom rather than prophetic warnings. Accordingly, what had been an effective hyperbole, sure to stir Jesus' listeners, became a source of confusion for Christians seeking clarity and direction. Hyperbole jolts people out of their lethargy and sets them thinking and acting. It does not show them what to do. Removed from its original prophetic context, the saying lost both its meaning and its impact.

For Christians trying to understand the world in which they lived and seeking guidance regarding their role in it, Jesus' reference to "this faithless and sinful generation" raised a lot of questions. What of those who followed Jesus faithfully? How could they be considered part of "this faithless and sinful generation?" Surely the Son of Man would not be ashamed of everyone!

Jesus' warning also referred to the Son of Man's coming in glory. That too raised important questions. What could the Son of Man's coming be like? Did it presuppose the coming of Elijah? If so, was not Elijah to restore all things? Why then did Jesus say that the Son of Man would suffer greatly?

These questions needed answers. If they were left unanswered, how could anyone take seriously Jesus' call to deny oneself, take up one's cross, and follow him? Why not do what Peter did and rebuke Jesus for his announcement of the passion and resurrection?

The purpose of Mark 9:1-13 is to respond to these questions and objections. The unit includes a distinct saying of Jesus (9:1), the story of the transfiguration (9:2-8), and a discussion about the coming of Elijah (9:9-13).

"There Are Some Standing Here . . ." (9:1). The unit begins with a solemn pronouncement: "Amen, I say to you, there are some

standing here who will not taste death until they see that the kingdom of God has come in power" (9:1). This additional pronouncement provides the distinction called for by the general statement in
8:38. There may have been those of whom the Son of Man would be
ashamed (8:38), but there were also those who would see the kingdom of God in power (9:1).

Originally, this saying about some "who will not taste death" was
not associated with the sayings in 8:34-38. This can be see from the
opening phrase, "He also said to them." Mark uses this phrase to
join previously unrelated statements of Jesus.[8] It can also be seen
from the statement itself, whose reference to those "who will not
taste death" is out of step with the previous statements about taking up one's cross (8:34) and losing (8:35) or forfeiting one's life
(8:36). Finally, there is the pronouncement's solemn tone, not found
in the previous sayings.

The introductory expression, "Amen, I say to you," focuses attention on the words that follow. It emphasizes the message and gives
great solemnity to its presentation, whether oral or written.

The expression is very frequent in the Gospels, where it appears
exclusively in the sayings of Jesus. This is the third time it appears
in Mark's Gospel (see 3:28; 8:12). Its form is even more solemn in
John's Gospel where the "Amen" is repeated: "Amen, amen, I say to
you" (John 1:51; 5:19, 24, 25; 6:26, *passim*).

The expression has two components, "Amen" and "I say to you."
The second refers to the narrator's introduction, "He also said to
them," and places nearly the same words on the lips of Jesus. The
result is a striking shift in point of view. What was first presented
from the narrator's standpoint is now presented from that of Jesus.
Rhetorically, this too contributes to the solemnity of the statement.

The first component, the word "Amen," has a liturgical origin well
attested in the New Testament letters and the book of Revelation
as well as in the Old Testament. Typical is its use in Romans 9:5:
"God who is over all be blessed forever. Amen." In the Old Testament,
a double "Amen" provides the whole first book of Psalms (Psalms
1–41) with a solemn and formal conclusion. It serves the same function for books two and three at the end of Psalms 72 and 89.

The most basic use of "Amen" is as a response of the liturgical assembly for a prayer recited by a leader or choir. There is an explicit
reference to this usage in the book of Psalms at the conclusion of

---

[8] In the first part of the Gospel, the expression, "He also said to them
(kai elegen autois)," was used six times, always in discourse material (2:27;
4:13, 21, 24; 6:10; 7:9).

book four: "Let all the people say, amen! Hallelujah!" (Ps 106:48; see also Jer 11:4).

"Amen" was also used in private prayer where it indicated a person's serious commitment to the prayer, much as we do today when we add "Amen" to the Lord's Prayer and other prayers. This second usage, in which "Amen" acts as a simple conclusion, evokes the liturgical context as an experiential backdrop for someone's private prayer. Its primary purpose, however, is to state emphatically that we really mean what has been expressed in prayer.

It is a simple step from this use of "Amen" to its use as an introduction for an important statement. Jesus' expression, "Amen, I say to you," says, "I really mean what I am about to say," and it says this with the solemnity associated with liturgical prayer.

Jesus' practice was not unprecedented. In 1 Kings 1:36, Behaiah responds to King David, "So be it! May the LORD, the God of my lord the king, so decree!" The introductory "Amen" emphasizes the prayer and conveys great earnestness.

Jesus' pronouncement was fully worthy of so solemn an introduction. He told those standing about him that some of them would not die before seeing that the kingdom of God had come in power. While resolving the problems raised by 8:38, with its reference to "this faithless and sinful generation," the second saying raised a lot of new problems. At the time when the Gospel was written, many of the Christians had already died, including some of Jesus' closest disciples and apostles. Would anyone be left to see the kingdom of God come in power?

There were those in Mark's community who expected the end and the full manifestation of the kingdom to come at any moment, and Jesus' pronouncement appeared to support their belief. Mark, however, did not accept this view. The gospel had to be preached to all nations (13:10). Only then would Jesus' return in kingly glory (13:5-9, 24-26).

Jesus' pronouncement had to be reinterpreted, and the expectations to which it gave rise redirected. Such is the purpose for the story of the transfiguration (9:2-8) in the context of Mark's Gospel.

"After Six Days . . ." (9:2-8). In itself, the story of Jesus' transfiguration was open to several interpretations.[9] It could be read as

---

[9] For the biblical background of the story of the transfiguration in the Mark's Gospel, see Joel Marcus, *The Way of the Lord, Christological Exegesis of the Old Testament in the Gospel of Mark* (Louisville: Westminster/ John Knox Press, 1992) 80–93.

an anticipation of Jesus' appearance to the disciples as risen Lord or even of his ultimate manifestation in glory at the *parousia*. Many have suggested that the story was originally a resurrection story that was later read back into the earthly life of Jesus, where it counterbalanced the Gospel's emphasis on Jesus' suffering and death.

There is some truth to all of these interpretations, and all provide insight into the story's origins and early history. But to know how Mark interpreted it, we need to pay close attention to the literary context provided for it in Mark's Gospel. Like sayings, stories can mean many things. We need the context to know what an author intends to convey.[10]

Whatever may have been the story's origins, Mark told it at this point in the Gospel to demonstrate the truth of Jesus' pronouncement that some standing with him would not taste death until the kingdom of God had come in power. For Mark, the pronouncement had already been fulfilled. The kingdom of God was manifested in power when Jesus was transfigured before Peter, James, and John, three of those whom Jesus had referred to as "standing here" (9:1). Therefore, even all who had surrounded Jesus should die before the *parousia,* his pronouncement remained true.

There is no answering whether Mark viewed the event as belonging to the post-resurrection life of the early church or as belonging to Jesus' ministry in Galilee. Mark's Gospel prescinds from such historical considerations. His purpose was to tell Jesus' story and present his message meaningfully and effectively. For this, he frequently drew on the Church's post-Easter life and experience.

We saw a good example of this in the second story of the breaking of the bread, the one that took place among the Gentiles (8:1-9). Historically, this happened only after Jesus' resurrection when the Church broadened the scope of its mission beyond Judaism. Mark told it to bring out the implications of "the beginning of the gospel of Jesus Christ [the Son of God]" (1:1) for both Jews and Gentiles.

Only three of the disciples witnessed Jesus' transfiguration, Peter, James, and John, the same who would witness Jesus' agony at Gethsemane (14:32-42; see also 5:37). Jesus led the three up a high mountain, a special place in Mark's Gospel for prayer and contemplation (see 6:46), apostolic commissioning (3:13-19), and as here

---

[10] For allusions to the Old Testament, especially the Mosaic typology, see Joel Marcus, *The Way of the Lord, Christological Exegesis of the Old Testament in the Gospel of Mark*, op. cit., 81–93.

extraordinary revelation (9:2-8).[11] On the mountain, the three would be alone *(monous;* see 4:10, *kata monas)* with Jesus in private *(kat' idian,* see 4:34; 13:3).

The transfiguration was a private event, and it would remain so until after the resurrection, in keeping with Jesus' injunction (9:9). Hence the reason why so many, even in Mark's time, did not realize that some already had seen the kingdom of God come in power (see 9:1).

The transfiguration itself is very striking for its emphasis on Jesus' garments. After stating that Jesus was transfigured in the presence of Peter, James, and John, Mark describes Jesus' clothing, which became dazzling white. We may wonder why Mark did not focus on Jesus' features. We need to recall that clothing in the ancient world, as in so many cultures today, expresses a person's identity. It was consequently quite natural to describe Jesus' transfiguration in terms of his clothing.

The statement that no fuller on earth could have bleached Jesus' garments so white indicates his transcendent identity. The description thus prepares for the message of the voice from the cloud declaring: "This is my beloved Son. Listen to him."

The voice from the cloud evokes the voice from the heavens at Jesus' baptism declaring: "You are my beloved Son, with you I am well pleased" (1:11). But there is a great difference between the two moments. At the baptism, the voice addressed Jesus in the second person: "You are my beloved Son." At the transfiguration, it addresses the three disciples: "This is my beloved Son." Jesus' transfiguration is to be understood in relation to his baptism, which is a dying and rising event (see 10:37-38).

The heavenly voice also affirms the authority of Jesus' teaching and asks Peter, James, and John to listen to him. In this context, Jesus' teaching refers to his passion and resurrection, to taking up one's cross and losing one's life. It also includes harsh words for those who are ashamed of him in this faithless and sinful generation and hopeful words about some seeing the kingdom of God come in power. Jesus' teaching contained no contradictions. All of it was true, and the disciples were asked to accept it as coming from God's beloved Son.

Together with the transfigured Jesus there appeared Elijah along with Moses, two towering figures from the Old Testament, symbols

---

[11] For the symbol of the mountain in Mark's Gospel, see Elizabeth Struthers Malbon, *Narrative Space and Mythic Meaning in Mark* (Sheffield: JSOT Press, 1991) 84–89; for its role in the story of the transfiguration, see 85–86.

respectively of the Prophets and the Law. With Moses and Elijah, the entire Old Testament joined in conversation with Jesus glorified. Of the two, the story emphasizes Elijah: "Elijah appeared to them along with Moses" (9:4). This is in keeping with the discussion in 9:11-13 regarding the coming of Elijah.

The Greek verb *ophthe,* indicating the appearance of Elijah along with Moses, is in a form that is well known from the Septuagint, where it is used exclusively to say that the Lord, God, the angel of the Lord, or the glory of the Lord appeared. In the New Testament, it expresses how Christ appeared after his resurrection (see 1 Cor 15:6-8; Luke 24:34). The transfiguration story associates the appearance of Elijah and Moses with these special contexts of extraordinary divine manifestations.

Overwhelmed by the vision of Jesus' transfigured and of Elijah and Moses, Peter exclaimed, "Rabbi, it is good that we are here! Let us make three tents: one for you, one for Moses, and one for Elijah" (9:5). Peter has still a long way to go in his understanding of Jesus. Even with Jesus transfigured, the best form of address he could manage was Rabbi, which means teacher. Even so, the experience moved him to want to preserve the moment forever, as though the *parousia* itself had come. But that is the way it is with the coming of the kingdom in power.

The story tries to account for Peter's reaction: "He hardly knew what to say, they were so terrified" (9:6). In this way, Mark prepares the reaction of the women at the tomb on hearing the extraordinary news of the resurrection of Jesus of Nazareth, the one who was crucified (16:6). The women said nothing to anyone, they were so afraid (16:8).

The account of the transfiguration is rich in literary allusions to the story of Moses and the exodus, beginning with the six days and the mountain. Jesus' transfigured appearance, the overshadowing cloud, and the voice from the cloud evoke when Moses stayed on the Mount Sinai for six days before God called out to him from the midst of the cloud and the glory of the Lord appeared to the people like consuming fire (Exod 24:16-17). It also evokes Elijah's encounter with God on Mount Horeb (1 Kgs 19).

The event ended as suddenly as it began. When the voice from the cloud became still, the three disciples looked around and saw no one but Jesus alone with them (9:8). Jesus had taken the disciples up the mountain alone (9:2). He would come down from the mountain the same way, alone with the three disciples (9:9-13). Earlier they had been with the other disciples and the crowd (8:34–9:1). Now they would return to them (9:14).

Peter, James, and John had been among the other disciples and the crowd (8:34–9:1). But Jesus had selected them to accompany him up a high mountain where they could be apart by themselves *(kat' idian)*. It is there that Jesus was transfigured before them (9:2-8). After the transfiguration, they came down from the mountain (9:9-13), and they rejoined the disciples and the crowd (9:14-29).

"Coming Down from the Mountain" (9:9-13). As Peter, James, and John came down from the mountain, Jesus ordered them not to tell anyone about what they had seen until the Son of Man had risen from the dead (9:9). Apart from the death and resurrection of Jesus, the transfiguration would not have made any sense to those that had not experienced it. They were not prepared to hear about the appearance of Elijah and Moses, the cloud that overshadowed them and the voice from the cloud.

Following Jesus' command, the disciples kept the matter to themselves (9:10a). Mark's Gospel presupposes that the story of the transfiguration was not disclosed until Jesus had risen from the dead.

The resurrection of the Son of Man would enable the disciples to understand the transfiguration. But Jesus' reference to it at this point in the Gospel also raises some further questions. What did Jesus mean when he spoke of rising from the dead (9:10b)? If Jesus had to rise, he must first have to die! And if that was the case, why did the scribes say that Elijah had to come first (9:11)? In Jewish tradition and in the disciples' understanding, Elijah's return was supposed to prepare the way for the Lord's glorious coming, not for his death. As in 7:1-23, Jesus had to situate and interpret the tradition.

This was not the first time Jesus spoke of the Son of Man's rising from the dead. In a solemn announcement of the passion, he had made it quite clear that the Son of Man would "rise after three days" (8:31). On that occasion, Peter rejected Jesus' announcement (8:32). It was not so much the resurrection he objected to as the passion and death it presupposed.

The same was not true as Jesus spoke to Peter, James, and John of the resurrection as they were coming down from the mountain. This time, however, the disciples' reaction was somewhat different. Instead of rejecting the resurrection, they questioned what it meant.

The disciples' question was not theoretical. They were not inquiring into the meaning of the term "resurrection" and the reality to which it referred. In the context of the first-century synagogue, these were plain enough. Nor was it just that Jesus' personal resurrection, or any individual resurrection, ran contrary to the teaching of the Pharisees, who expected that the resurrection would be a general event at the consummation of history.

In the course of Jesus' ministry in Galilee, this would have been a factor, but not for the Markan communities, who accepted Jesus' personal resurrection in faith. Rather, the disciples were asking about Jesus' resurrection because it presupposed his death. The communities needed to recall Jesus' passion as they went through a passion of their own.

Like Peter after Jesus' first announcement of the passion, the three could not understand why Jesus had to die. Persecution, suffering, and death were a big problem for Jesus' disciples, as later on they were for the Markan communities, and in Mark Jesus addressed the problem directly (8:34–9:1). That was before the transfiguration (9:2-8). Now, after the transfiguration, the disciples had yet another difficulty. Jesus' teaching about the Son of Man's death and resurrection did not fit the scribal teaching about Elijah's coming.

The problem was quite simple. The disciples expected Elijah to come and prepare the Lord's manifestation in glory, not his suffering and death. Besides, had not Elijah just appeared along with Moses in the glorious manifestation of the transfiguration (9:4)? And did not the transfiguration announce and prefigure the Lord's final coming?

Jesus took up the objection and carefully spelled out what seemed to be two contradictory beliefs. It was indeed true that Elijah would come first to restore all things. It is also true that this raised an important question about the Scriptures that the Son of Man must suffer greatly and be treated with contempt (9:12). But the two statements were not irreconcilable. Nor were the Scriptures on which they were based, Malachi 3:1-24 for the coming and the mission of Elijah, and the songs of the suffering servant, especially Isaiah 52:13–53:12, for the passion of the Son of Man.

"Elijah has come, and they did to him whatever they pleased, as it is written of him" (9:13). Jesus' reference to the Scriptures may be to 1 Kings 19:2-10, which tells of how Elijah was persecuted by Jezebel. The disciples thought of Elijah's coming as something that would take place in the future. At the beginning of Jesus' ministry, that had been the case, but no longer. Elijah already had come in the person of John the Baptist, the one clothed in Elijah's garment of camel's hair with a leather belt around his waist (1:6; see 2 Kgs 1:8). John the Baptist prepared the way of the Lord (1:2-3) by proclaiming a baptism of repentance (1:4). In John, Elijah had also prepared the way of the Lord by his personal suffering and death (6:14-29).

Jesus reinterpreted the role of Elijah by broadening the disciples' understanding of the Scriptures. He was thus able to show how

Elijah's coming was related to Jesus' passion as well as his glorious manifestation. With that, the disciples had everything needed to understand what Jesus meant by referring to the Son of Man's rising from the dead (9:10).

Most of the basic issues regarding Jesus' passion and resurrection have now been dealt with. Following Christ meant taking up one's cross. But it also meant joining him in his mission, and for that something else was needed.

Encountering Evil Spirits (9:14-29)

There should be no mistake. Jesus' messianic mission (8:27-30) meant nothing less than a decisive victory over evil (9:14-29). This became clear for the first time when Jesus entered the synagogue at Capernaum and cured someone who had an unclean spirit (1:21-28; see also 1:32-34). And again when he went in the Gentile territory of the Gerasenes where he banished a Legion of unclean spirits from a man living among the dead (5:1-20; see also 3:11-12). Jesus' victory was fulfilled through his death and resurrection (8:31-33).

The Twelve were given a share in Jesus' mission to drive out demons (3:15). Sending them out on a mission, Jesus had given them authority over unclean spirits (6:7). The mission of the disciples, like that of Jesus, was consequently to drive out demons. Jesus had given them authority to do this. In its exercise they needed to follow him on the ways of the passion and resurrection (8:34-38). But to be effective, they also needed something else.

The story of Jesus' expulsion of a mute and violent spirit (9:14-29) is about that something else. Effectiveness in the mission required faith and prayer. On the surface, the story seems to be about a boy possessed by a mute spirit as well as Jesus' power to drive it out. But these are but the vehicle for a story about faith and prayer.

The story tells how the disciples had not been able to expel a mute spirit from a young boy. The boy thus remained within the power of the destructive spirit that actually tried to kill him. The boy was now brought before Jesus, and Jesus ordered the mute and deaf spirit to come out of him. When the spirit came out, the boy became like a corpse. Seeing him, many thought that he was dead. But Jesus took the boy by the hand and raised him up. The story is about dying and rising. It deals with baptism and how the disciples needed faith and prayer to be effective in this most basic ministry.

With the Disciples and the Crowd (9:14-16). After coming down the mountain, Jesus came with Peter, James, and John to the disciples. When they approached the disciples, "they saw a large crowd around them and scribes arguing [*syzetountas*] with them" (9:14). As soon as *(euthys)* the crowd saw Jesus, they were overwhelmed with awe (*exethambethesan,* 9:15a). Immediately they ran up to him and greeted him (9:15b).

The crowd knew Jesus. They knew his ministry and his teaching. They recognized that Jesus taught "as one having authority and not as the scribes" (1:22). Hence their reaction on seeing him. In the synagogue at Capernaum, they were also overwhelmed with awe *(ethambethesan)* and argued *(syzetein)* among themselves: "What is this? A new teaching with authority. He commands even the unclean spirits and they obey him" (1:27).

With the crowd's reaction, the scribes disappear altogether from the story. Their role, which was antagonistic as in previous occasions,[12] is replaced by the role of the crowd, which was trying to understand what was happening. At the same time, attention moves away from the disciples as well. The story now focuses almost entirely on the crowd, which expected to benefit from the disciples' ministry but in this case the crowd was disappointed. The disciples are referred to in the story but they have no role in it until the very end when Jesus joins them at home (9:28-29).[13]

The disciples may not play an active role in most of the story, but their argument with the scribes provides the setting for the rest of the story, and their presence in the background is felt all the way through. Upon being greeted by the crowd, Jesus asked the crowd, including the scribes, "What are you arguing about with them?" that is, "What are you arguing about with the disciples?" (9:16). At this point, the action focuses even more sharply on one single member of the crowd, the father of the boy that was possessed by the mute spirit.

Jesus and the Father of the Boy (9:17-18). Jesus' question to the scribes, "What are you arguing about with them," was answered by someone in the crowd, who indirectly identified himself as the parent of a boy possessed by the mute spirit (9:17). The parent, who was in fact the boy's father (see 9:21), addressed Jesus: "Teacher"

---

[12] For the attitude of the scribes, see 2:6-7, 16; 3:22; 7:1-5.

[13] This literary device is familiar to us from previous sections of the Gospel where Jesus addresses the crowd and later speaks to the disciples or some of the disciples in private (see 4:1-9; 7:14-15) and later speaks to the disciples in private (4:10-25; 7:17-23). See also Jesus' teaching to the crowds (8:34–9:1) and the story of the transfiguration on the mountain and Jesus' teaching to the disciples coming down from the mountain (9:2-13).

(Didaskale), a Greek title that became prevalent as the early Christians moved away from their Jewish roots into the Gentile world.

In Mark's Gospel, the Hebrew equivalent for the Greek title *Didaskale,* that is, *Rabbi,* was not completely set aside (see 9:5; 11:21; 14:45), but Teacher *(Didaskale)* was the most common way of addressing Jesus (see 4:38; 5:35; 9:38; 10:17, 20, 35; 12:14, 19, 32; 13:1; 14:14).

The boy's father said how he brought his son to Jesus and described the symptoms of the boy's possession in some detail. When the mute spirit seizes the boy, "it throws him down; he foams at the mouth, grinds his teeth, and becomes rigid" (9:18a). We are reminded of the Gerasene demoniac, who could not be restrained, even with a chain, and spent "night and day among the tombs and on the hillsides . . . crying out and bruising himself with stones" (5:3-5). In both cases, the unclean and mute spirits were extremely destructive and the person had no control over his behavior.

But the differences between the two were also considerable. While the mute spirit rendered the boy helpless, the unclean spirit endowed the Gerasene with great strength. The Gospel places us before two kinds of violence, one that subdues and one that unleashes. We note also that the Gerasene "was always crying out" (5:5), while the boy uttered not a sound, a fact quite remarkable, giving the history of unclean spirits in Mark's Gospel (see 1:23-26, 34; 5:6-9). The fact is reflected in the spirit's primary description as "a mute spirit" (9:17).

The boy's father then told Jesus that he had asked Jesus' disciples to drive the mute spirit out of his son but they had been unable to do so (9:18b). We now know what the argument had been about. The scribes and the disciples had been arguing about why they were unable to expel the mute spirit. Recall that Jesus had sent the Twelve on mission with authority over unclean spirits (6:7). Summarizing their mission, the Gospel said that the Twelve drove out many demons (6:13).

As presented by Mark, the dispute seems to reflect a problematic situation within the Christian community rather than a controversy between the disciples and the scribes in the course of Jesus' ministry. The scribes, who were outsiders, are more likely to have scoffed and walked away than to have argued about the disciples' failure.

"O Faithless Generation" (9:19). Jesus' opening question, "What are you arguing about with them?" was addressed to the whole crowd, including the scribes. And even though a single person answered the question, Jesus continued to address the whole crowd. He began with an apostrophe, spoken to all in general but with the disciples in mind: "O faithless generation, how long will I be with you? How long will I endure you?" (9:19a).

The expression, "faithless generation," recalls a similar expression in 8:12 and especially in 8:38, where Jesus spoke of "this faithless and sinful generation." As negative as it is, the expression introduces the theme of faith into the story by calling attention to its absence. The question, "How long will I be with you?" deals not so much with time as with solidarity. In the Christian mission, Jesus is with those who have faith, not with the faithless of this generation.

After the apostrophe to this "faithless generation," Jesus asked the crowd to bring the boy to him (9:19b), and the crowd did so (9:20a). At this point, attention focuses directly on the boy, and we observe him through Jesus' eyes.

Jesus and the Boy (9:20). Responding to Jesus' request, the crowd brought the boy to him. Upon seeing Jesus, the spirit threw the boy into convulsions. At this point, the story moves into the second description of the boy's condition, which confirms the earlier statement made by the boy's father (9:18). "As he fell to the ground, he began to roll around and foam at the mouth" (9:20).

There is a point to such repetition. Besides emphasizing the boy's terrible state, the description is presented from different points of view. First, we witness the boy's behavior from the point of view of the father when he describes it to Jesus. Then, we witness it from the point of view of Jesus observing it.

Help My Unbelief (9:21-24). Jesus then questioned the boy's father about how long this had been happening to the boy. "Since childhood," he replied (9:21). The boy's condition had never been different. Being possessed by a "mute spirit" *(pneuma alalon)* was his life story.

The father went on, explaining how the spirit had often thrown the boy into fire and into water trying to kill him (9:22a). This is the third description of the boy's condition. Like the first (9:18), it describes the boy from the point of view of his father. It also shows that the boy could not have been worse off. Very often, the "mute spirit" tried to destroy the boy.

The father appeals to Jesus: "But if you can do anything, have compassion on us and help us" (9:22b). For the boy, it was a matter of life and death. The previous time when the father described what the mute spirit did to his son, he said, "I asked your disciples to drive it out, but they were unable to do so" (9:18). Now, he prefaces his plea with a conditional clause, "But if you can do anything."

Jesus picked up on a single element in the father's plea, "If you can!" and responded very forcefully: "Everything is possible to one who has faith [*to pisteuonti*]," that is, to one who believes (9:23). There is no question about Jesus' power, but its effectiveness depends on faith.

In this respect, we recall the episode in the synagogue at Nazareth where Jesus was unable to perform any mighty deed "apart from curing a few sick people by laying his hands on them" (6:5). That was on account of their lack of faith (*apistia*, 6:6a). By contrast, we also remember the woman he cured of a long-standing hemorrhage. Her faith *(pistis)* had saved her (5:34). Through the faith of a child's father and mother, Jesus would even be able to raise a young girl to life (5:35-43).

The boy's father took up Jesus' challenge and cried out, "I do believe [*pisteuo*], help my unbelief [*apistia*]" (9:24). Faith is not a matter of all or nothing. There may be pockets of unbelief in one who believes. The father's confession of faith and prayer for faith may reflect a setting in the early Christian communities as well as in the ministry of Jesus. In both cases, faith was associated with repentance *(metanoia)*. Both were essential elements in Jesus' proclamation of the gospel of God (1:14-15).

Dying and Rising (9:25-28). As the crowd gathered, Jesus focused entirely on the boy. He rebuked the unclean spirit, much as he had rebuked the wind when a storm threatened the disciples in the little boat while they were crossing the sea for the first time (4:39).

"Mute and deaf spirit," Jesus commanded, "come out of him and never enter him again!" (9:25). We have already been told that the boy had been possessed since childhood. He would be possessed no more. Jesus called him from one state, that of enslavement by an evil spirit, to a new state where he would be truly himself.

Shouting and throwing the boy into a final convulsion, the spirit left him. This is the fourth description of the boy's condition. As with the second, we observe it as an event observed by Jesus. Earlier the father had said that the spirit often tried to kill his son. Now the boy became still, like a corpse, and many thought him dead (9:26), "but Jesus took him by the hand, [and] raised him up" (9:27). As earlier in the Gospel,[14] the expression for "raising him" *(egeiron auton)* evokes the resurrection of Jesus.

[14] Jesus raised the boy *(egeiron auton)* as he raised Simon's mother-in-law (1:29-31) and the daughter of Jairus (5:21-24, 35-43).

Jesus did not merely help the boy get up. He raised him up, that is, he gave him a share in his risen life. Confirmation for this interpretation comes from the fact that the story goes on to say that the boy stood up. This addition would have been superfluous if Jesus' action of raising him were not a reference to the resurrection. In this context, after Jesus raised him up, he had to get up.

The story of the exorcism is rich in baptismal imagery and teaching. It is a story of dying and rising, in which Jesus is victorious over the destructive forces of evil and their grasp over a person. Even Jesus' command to the mute and deaf spirit had a liturgical ring to it: "Mute and deaf spirit, I command you: come out of him and never enter him again!" (9:25).

Jesus and the Disciples (9:28-29). We are told nothing of the reactions of the crowd, of the boy's father, or of the boy. Nothing is said about their amazement.[15] Instead, the scene shifts immediately to the house, as though Jesus and the disciples were already in Capernaum (see 9:33). The house or home is no longer closely associated with a geographical location. The home is wherever Jesus and his disciples gather and where Jesus speaks to them in private (*kat' idian,* see 9:21).

The disciples have a question, "Why could we not drive it out?" (9:28). Their question echoes an earlier statement made by the possessed boy's father: "I asked your disciples to drive it out, but they were unable to do so" (9:18). Their inability had been the cause of an argument between the scribes and the disciples at the beginning of the story (9:14-16).

Jesus' answer to them was very simple and straightforward: "This kind can only come out through prayer" (9:29). This is the first time prayer is mentioned in the story. But the story had actually included a prayer. After the boy's father professed his faith, he immediately added a prayer, "Help my unbelief" (9:24).

Taken as a whole, the story is an instruction on faith and prayer for early Christians, in particular those in Mark's communities, who were engaged in baptismal ministry. Many must have been struggling with their ministry and wondering about its lack of success: "Why could we not drive it out?" The matter must have been a source of argument in their communities.

[15] In stories with baptismal connotations, Mark does not describe the reaction of the person who is healed or given life (1:29-31; 5:21-24, 35-43; 5:25-34; 10:46-52). Sometimes, he gives their response. Simon's mother-in-law ministered to them, and Bartimaeus followed Jesus on the way.

Mark told a traditional story of an exorcism in Jesus' ministry that had developed in the community's baptismal catechesis. He used the story for presenting and emphasizing the most basic requirement in this ministry, that is, faith and prayer.

The Second Movement: Implications of the Passion and Resurrection for a Christian Community (9:30–10:31)

With the story of Jesus and the boy afflicted by a mute spirit, the first movement (8:31–9:29) of the section comes to a close. In 8:31–9:29, the Gospel showed the implications of the passion for Christian life and ministry. It dealt with the radical commitment to follow Christ and with the basic issues of faith and prayer.

In the second movement (9:30–10:31), the focus is on the implications of the passion for relationships among Christians and attitudes towards possessions. The second movement deals with six basic issues regarding life within the Christian community:

- the nature of true Christian greatness (9:33-37);
- the Christian attitude toward outsiders who act in Jesus' name (9:38-41);
- scandal, leading others to sin (9:42-50);
- marriage and divorce (10:1-12);
- accepting the kingdom of God as a child (10:13-16);
- the Christian attitude toward possessions and wealth (10:17-31).

The second movement (9:30–10:31) is loosely patterned on the first. It begins with Jesus' prophetic announcement of the passion and resurrection of the Son of Man and with the reaction of the disciples (9:30-32; see 8:31-33). It continues with a discourse on the conditions of discipleship (9:33-50; see 8:34-38). The movement then continues with a second journey (10:1-9; see 9:2-13), some special teaching for the disciples at the home (10:10-16; see 9:28-29), and concludes with a third journey (10:17-31).

Jesus' Second Prophetic Announcement (9:30-32)

"They left from there and began a journey through Galilee" (9:30a). Jesus and the disciples left the mount of the transfiguration and the place where they came after coming down from the mountain of God. Since Mark did not identify the mountain, the geography is quite vague, but adequate from a literary point of view. Mark's concern was to separate the teaching and the events of the second movement (9:30–10:31) from the first (8:31–9:29). He did this by noting the departure of Jesus and the disciples from where they had been and by indicating the beginning of a new journey through Galilee.

This Galilean journey would be different from the others. Jesus "did not wish anyone to know about it" (9:30b). It was to be a secret journey. Until now, Jesus often taught the disciples and the crowd together (see 8:34; 9:14) even if he did provide special instruction for the disciples afterwards (see 9:2-8, 28-29). In this journey, Jesus would teach the disciples by themselves from the beginning. The earlier teaching was intended for all. The new teaching addressed situations and issues that were internal to the community.

Jesus' public teaching in Galilee was over, but only for a time. He would take it up again after the passion and the resurrection when, as risen Lord, he would again go before his followers in Galilee. There they would see him. They would listen to him anew. But this time, they would understand his teaching (see 14:28; 16:7).

On their journey through Galilee, "he was teaching his disciples" (9:31a). As in 8:31–9:29, Mark opens Jesus' new teaching with a summary announcement of the passion and resurrection of the Son of Man: "The Son of Man is to be handed over to men and they will kill him, and three days after his death he will rise" (9:31b).

This second announcement of the passion and the resurrection takes up the first (8:31) like a solemn rhetorical refrain, but it is shorter and quite different. Gone is the emphasis on the necessity *(dei)* of the passion and the resurrection. Gone too are the references to the suffering of the Son of Man and his rejection by the elders, the chief priests, and the scribes.

The second announcement is rich in other ways. It brings additional elements that comment on the first announcement and advance it theologically. Instead of repeating that the Son of Man would "suffer greatly," the announcement declares that the Son of Man would "be handed over." Like the expression, "suffer greatly," "to be handed over" was an allusion to the suffering servant in Isaiah 52:13–53:12, showing that the passion of the Son of Man was according to a divine plan and purpose.

The verb "to be handed over" *(paradidonai)* first entered Mark's Gospel with reference to John the Baptist at the beginning of Jesus' Galilean ministry: "After John had been arrested" (1:14), that is, handed over. In Mark's time, the Christian usage of *paradidonai* was very old. Paul included it in the liturgical tradition that he brought from Antioch on his first mission to Corinth: "the Lord Jesus, on the night he was handed over" (1 Cor 11:23).

Then, instead of focusing on the Son of Man's rejection by the elders, the chief priests, and the scribes, the second announcement looks beyond the Sanhedrin and makes a universal statement. The Son of Man would be handed over into the hands of human beings. It also contrasts the part of God with the part of human beings in the passion and death of Jesus. The Son of Man would be handed over by divine counsel, but he would be killed by human agency.

"But they did not understand [*egnooun*] the saying [*to hrema*]" (9:32a). The verb *agnoeo* indicates ignorance, and the context suggests willful ignorance. The disciples did not know what Jesus was saying, but then they knew enough to be afraid: "and they were afraid to question him" (9:32b), afraid to ask about what he was saying. They were afraid because they did not want to hear the answer.

True Christian Greatness (9:33-37)

On their journey through Galilee (see 9:30), "they came to Capernaum" (9:33a; see 1:21; 2:1), and went to the house of Simon and Andrew, which the Gospel repeatedly refers to as the home of Jesus and the disciples (see 1:29; 2:1; 3:2; 7:17; 9:28). "Once inside the house, Jesus began to ask them, 'What were you arguing about on the way [*en te hodo*]?'" (9:33).

The disciples were afraid to ask Jesus about the passion and the resurrection of the Son of Man, but that did not keep them from arguing among themselves. When Jesus asked them about their argument, "they remained silent," for "they had been discussing among themselves on the way [*en te hodo*] who was the greatest" (9:34).

Jesus announced his passion and death, and the disciples argued over who was greatest among them. The contrast between Jesus and the disciples was glaring. Like Peter earlier (8:32), the disciples were unable to face the passion. Nor could Mark's community. The disciples' concern with being greater than the others raises the first of the six issues that the Christian community needed to address in light of Jesus' passion and resurrection.

The disciples never told Jesus what they had been discussing on the way, but Jesus did not have to be told. He knew. Their argument over who was the greatest provided the setting (9:33-34) for Jesus' discourse to the Twelve (9:35-50). In the discourse, Jesus treats the three issues, beginning with being the first and the last.

This would be one of the longer discourses in Mark, recalling the one on "the tradition of the elders," when addressed the Pharisees and some scribes together with the disciples (7:1-23). It recalls too the discourse on parables, when Jesus spoke to a large crowd along with his disciples (4:1-34). On both those occasions, there had also been special teaching for the disciples at home (7:17-23) or somewhere in private (4:10-25).

This time, the entire discourse was given at home and addressed not to the disciples in general but to the Twelve (9:35a; see 3:14; 4:10; 6:7). To present it, Jesus took the formal seated position of the teacher (9:35a; see 4:1; 13:3; Matt 5:1; 13:1; 24:3; Luke 4:20). Capernaum, the home, the Twelve, Jesus sitting down, everything pointed to the importance of this discourse for the disciples and the early Christian community.

The discourse opens with a solemn generalization stating the conditions for being first: "If anyone wishes to be first [*protos*], he shall be the last [*eschatos*] of all and the servant [*diakonos*] of all" (9:35b). The theme of being first and last dominates the whole movement and returns in its last verse: "But many that are first will be last, and [the] last will be first" (10:31).

Among the Twelve, the first will be both last and the servant of all. The term for servant, *diakonos,* appeared earlier as a verb in the story of Simon's mother-in-law, whom Jesus raised from a fever and who then served *(diekonei)* the community at its very beginnings in the home of Simon and Andrew (1:31; see also 1:13).

The form of the opening statement, "If anyone wishes [*ei tis thelei*] to be first . . . ," recalls the introduction of Jesus' discourse in the previous movement: "Whoever wishes [*ei tis thelei*] to come after me . . ." (8:34). After stating a general condition for one who wishes to be first, Jesus provided a dramatic illustration. Placing a child in the midst of the Twelve, he put his arms around it and said to them: "Whoever receives one child such as this in my name, receives me; and whoever receives me, receives not me but the One who sent me" (9:36-37).

Jesus invited the Twelve to measure their greatness against that of a child. A child is not concerned about being the greatest or the first. Nor was Jesus, though in fact he was by far the greatest. In the arms of Jesus, the child showed how the least could indeed be the greatest and the last could be first.

Jesus also invited the Twelve to look beyond themselves to a simple child. Rather than be preoccupied about who was the greatest, they should welcome a child such as this in Jesus' name. In doing so, they would be welcoming Jesus himself. More than that, they would be welcoming the one who sent him.

With regard to this issue, Jesus' first concern was to describe the one who is truly the greatest (9:35). He then confronted the Twelve with the emptiness of their self-preoccupation and directed their attention to those who seem, but only seem, to be least (9:36-37). The disciples were taken up with their own importance. Jesus made them reflect on the importance of a little child.

An Outsider Who Acts in Jesus' Name (9:38-41)

The second issue was raised by John, one of the four who were first called (1:16-20) and one of the three who witnessed the transfiguration (9:2-8): "Teacher, we saw someone driving out demons in your name, and we tried to prevent him because he does not follow us" (9:38). Preoccupied with being the greatest, the disciples could not tolerate anyone who challenged their supposed superiority.

John spoke for the Twelve in recognizing and addressing Jesus as teacher *(didaskale)*. Earlier, the disciples had not been able to cast out a demon from a young boy (9:17-18). Now they saw someone casting out demons and they tried to put a stop to it because the person did not follow them. But the outsider drove out demons in Jesus' name.

Seated, in the position of the teacher, Jesus proceeded to teach them. First, he dealt with the particular case: "Do not prevent him" (9:39a). Then, providing the reason, he broadened the issue. Jesus' response applied to a wide range of situations and cases: "There is no one who performs a mighty deed in my name who can at the same time speak ill of me" (9:39b).

The name represents the person. That is why whoever receives a child in Jesus' name receives Jesus himself (9:37). The name also communicates the identity of the person. John did not appreciate the implications of Jesus' name because like the other disciples he had a distorted vision of Jesus' identity (see 9:32-34). If John understood who Jesus really was, he would have known that anyone who performs a mighty deed in Jesus' name could not speak ill of him (9:39b).

We recall that a mighty deed depended not only on the power of the person who performed it, but also on the faith of the one who would benefit from it (see 6:2, 5; see also 5:34; 9:23-24). The disciples' concern was limited to those who performed the deed, and Jesus began by addressing that concern. Someone who performs a mighty or powerful deed *(dynamis)* does not have the power *(dynesetai)* to speak ill of Jesus. That would be a contradiction.

Jesus then presses the question even further. It is not merely a matter of a person not being against us: "Whoever is not against us is for us" (9:40). Anyone who acts in Jesus' name must be recognized as contributing to our efforts, even when they are not among those who follow the Twelve.

Jesus ends his response to John with a simple but very striking example about "anyone who gives a cup of water to drink because you belong to Christ" (9:41a). The expression "you belong to Christ" (*Christou este,* literally, "you are of Christ") stands out. It presupposes considerable experience and reflection in the Christian community. For the context of Jesus' historical ministry in Galilee, we would expect an expression like, "because you are my disciples." In the context of the Church, we see that the disciples thought of themselves in relation to Christ.[16] It was a short step from calling themselves "of Christ" to calling themselves Christians (Acts 11:26).

The person who gives you a cup of water because you are of Christ will not go without a reward. This was a very serious matter for the early Christians, and Jesus highlighted the point with a solemn rhetorical expression we recognize from other moments in the Gospel that were equally serious: "Amen, I say to you" (9:41b; see 9:1).

With regard to the second issue, Jesus' concern was to help the disciples see that those who were not followers were not necessarily against them. On the contrary, when the disciples were taken up with being the greatest, Jesus pointed to a little child. When they objected that others were performing mighty deeds in Jesus' name, Jesus called their attention to someone who offers them a simple cup of water. The disciples were taken up with being personally great and doing great things. Responding, Jesus spoke to them of little people and simple gestures. All was not as it appeared.

Scandal, Leading Others to Sin (9:42-50)

The first and most basic issue was surfaced by the disciples' discussion on the way about who was the greatest (9:33-34). The second issue, raised by John, was about outsiders driving out demons in Jesus' name (9:38). The third issue was not raised by anyone, at least, not explicitly. When Jesus responded to the second issue, he took it up immediately. It had to do with scandal, causing others to sin: "Whoever causes one of these little ones who believe [in me] to sin, it would be better for him if a great millstone were put around his neck and he were thrown into the sea" (9:42).

---

[16] Referring to baptism in Galatians 3:26-29, Paul addressed the Galatians as "children *(huioi)* of God in Christ Jesus." Baptized into Christ they had clothed themselves with Christ. Clothed with Christ, they had a new identity. Paul refers to that identity as belonging to Christ: "And if you belong to Christ," literally, "if you are of Christ *(Christou)*" (Gal 3:29).

The third issue flows immediately from the previous one. A disciple who was taken up with being the greatest *(meizon)* was not apt to be very concerned about one of the little ones who believed *(hena ton mikron touton ton pisteuonton)*. Besides, disciples who tried to prevent others from doing great things in Jesus' name did not necessarily stop there. They could go further and cause them to sin, especially if they considered those people to be insignificant little people.

Jesus' mention of reward (9:41) invited consideration of the alternative, that is, punishment. Jesus had just announced that those who offered a cup of water to drink because someone was of Christ (9:41). He now added that those who caused others to sin would surely be thrown into the fire of Gehenna (9:42-48).

The One Who Causes Others to Sin (9:42). The disciples' concern with being the greatest (9:34) easily leads to preventing others from doing good (9:38). It could also escalate to causing others to sin, that is, to giving scandal (9:42). Very likely, as with previous issues, the problem of scandal had arisen in the early Church. The passage is not about scandal given by just anyone, but by the disciples, by those who followed Jesus on the way.

Jesus addressed the issue of scandal with a set of four sayings. The first is a generalization in the third person singular similar to several others in this section of the Gospel: "Whoever causes . . . to sin" *(kai hos an skandalise,* literally, whoever scandalizes). The form of the generalization recalls, "Whoever wishes to come after me . . ." (8:34); "Whoever wishes to save his life . . ." (8:35); "Whoever receives one child such as this . . ." (9:37; see also 9:35, 40, 41). Its concern with serious infidelity calls to mind an earlier saying, "For whoever is ashamed of me and my words . . ." (8:38).

A number of expressions in the saying need careful examination. First, who are "these little ones who believe [in me]"? Second, what about having "a great millstone . . . around the neck," and being "thrown into the sea?"

Those "who believe" *(ton pisteuonton)* are those who are not part of "this faithless *[apistos]* and sinful generation" (8:38; 9:19). Those who believe are those for whom all things are possible *(panta dynata to pisteuonti,* 9:23). They are those who pray for help with their unbelief even as they profess their belief *(pisteuo, boethei mou te apistia,* 9:24).

Among those who believe, there are "these little ones" *(ton mikron touton),* those who are not concerned with being the greatest *(meizon,* 9:34). They are like a little child, the children in the faith *(ton toiouton paidion,* 9:37). "These little ones" could refer to all of Jesus' disciples. In 10:24, Jesus addresses his disciples as "children" *(tekna).* They might even refer to all those who act in Jesus' name but do not become associated with the followers (9:39).

One of these little ones is a matter of great concern to Jesus. The same should be true of his disciples. The expression "one of these little ones who believe [in me]" highlights the importance of even the least of Jesus' followers and draws attention to the perfidy of causing one of them to sin.

The seriousness of causing the least believer to sin is further emphasized by the images of what should be done to the perpetrator. It would be better for that person to have a great millstone placed around his neck and be thrown into the sea.

Millstones were of various shapes and sizes. There were simple domestic millstones that could be turned by hand for grinding wheat and other grain products. The mill consisted of two round stones, one of which was fitted over the other. The lower stone, which was convex, was stable. The upper stone, which was concave and had an opening at the top for pouring in the grain, was rotated over the other. Such mills, many of which were in the general shape of an hourglass, are common in the ruins of ancient Roman cities. This is the kind spoken of in Matthew 24:41 and Luke 17:35 in Jesus' reference to "two women . . . grinding at the mill together." Even a relatively small domestic mill required a heavy millstone. Even operating a small mill was very hard work.

There were also much larger mills, those found in professional milling establishments. The mill itself usually consisted of two large thick stone wheels, one of which was moved around the other, which lay on the ground. The upper wheel was ordinarily turned by a donkey, and it was called a "donkey millstone" *(mylos onikos).* This is the kind of stone that was rolled across the entrance to the tomb of Jesus (15:46). It is also the "very large millstone" that ought to be put around the neck of one who scandalizes even the least of those who believe.

With such a stone around the neck, anyone would be quickly dragged down to the depths where the jaws of death lurk, even to the gates of the netherworld (see Jonah 2:1-11). Being cast into the sea was a terrible fate. It is what happened to the legion of unclean spirits when they were permitted to enter the swine upon leaving the Gerasene demoniac (5:11-13).

The One Who Sins (9:43-48). The first saying is in the third person singular, beginning with "Whoever causes" (9:42). The following three sayings are in the second person singular, beginning with a similar expression "If your hand (foot, eye) causes." The three, which form a set (9:43-48), can certainly be considered among the most striking hyperbolic expressions in the entire New Testament.

The first saying deals with the one who gives scandal, the one who causes a believer to sin (9:42). The following three sayings address those who might be scandalized, warning them not to be scandalized (9:43-48).

The first saying, with its image of a great millstone around someone's neck and being thrown into the sea, was an extremely strong hyperbole, not likely to be forgotten. The following three are even stronger. Together, they leave no doubt that scandal was a grave concern for Jesus, for the early church, and for Mark the evangelist.

Each hyperbole calls attention to a part of the human body: "If your hand causes you to sin, cut it off . . . And if your foot causes you to sin, cut it off . . . And if your eye causes you to sin, pluck it out." In each of these cases, what we have is a startling prophetic statement intended to jolt the audience into realizing what is at stake in this matter of giving or receiving scandal. Such is the nature of a hyperbole. A moral hyperbole is not a moral prescription. Its purpose is to change attitudes and behavior.

Each of the three sayings recalls the expression from the first, "it would be better for him" (9:42). However, in keeping with the form of 9:43-48, it is cast in the second person:

"It is better for you to enter into life maimed than with two hands to go into Gehenna" (9:43);

"It is better for you to enter into life crippled than with two feet to be thrown into Gehenna" (9:45);

"Better for you to enter the kingdom of God with one eye than with two eyes to be thrown into Gehenna" (9:47).

Each saying presents an alternative, "to enter into life," that is, "to enter the kingdom of God," or "to be thrown into Gehenna." The kingdom of God was the object of Jesus' preaching. It is what gave meaning to Jesus' life and mission. If a disciple did not enter into life, into the kingdom of God, the disciple's life would have been futile.

While the kingdom of God is a major theme in Mark's Gospel, the same is not true of Gehenna, and the image requires some explanation. The term Gehenna renders the Greek *geenna,* which in turn renders the Aramaic *ge-hinnam* and the Hebrew *ge-hinnom.* This last is an abbreviated form of *ge-ben-hinnon,* meaning Valley of the

Son of Hinnom. The name refers to a real place, a valley southwest of Jerusalem.

In Old Testament times, a cultic shrine, a high place called Topheth, dedicated to Baal, was built there, and the Valley of the Son of Hinnom became associated with human sacrifice. Jeremiah spoke loudly to condemn the practice and the place: "In the Valley of Ben-hinnom they have built the high place of Topheth to immolate in fire their sons and their daughters" (Jer 7:31). It would therefore become a place of death and would be called "the Valley of Slaughter" (7:32; see also Jer 19:1-9, 32-35; and 2 Kgs 23:10).

In an allusion to Jeremiah, Isaiah referred to the same place: "They shall go out and see the corpses / of the men who rebelled against me; / Their worm shall not die, / nor their fire be extinguished; / and they shall be abhorrent to all mankind" (Isa 66:24). This is the very last verse in Isaiah, and it is the one quoted in Mark: "their worm does not die, and the fire is not quenched" (9:48).

The enduring punishment by fire became a major theme in the intertestamental literature, and the theme was taken up in the New Testament. It was left to the New Testament to associate eternal punishment by fire with the name Gehenna. Very probably, this development was inspired by prophetic literature, notably, Isaiah 66:24 and Jeremiah 7:31.

Salted with Fire (9:49-50). Jesus' discourse to the Twelve in the home at Capernaum (9:35-50) dealt with three major issues: wanting to be the greatest, dealing with others who were driving out demons in Jesus' name, and scandalizing others or being scandalized by them. The first dealt with relationships within the community, the second considered relationships with outsiders, and the third seems to have included both. The discourse now comes to a conclusion.

The conclusion includes prophetic announcement: "Everyone will be salted with fire" (9:49), as well as a short exhortation: "Salt is good, but if salt becomes insipid, with what will you restore its flavor? Keep salt in yourselves and you will have peace with one another" (9:50). So ends Jesus' private discourse to the Twelve in the home at Capernaum.

The conclusion's major image is salt, and we are told many things about salt. Salt is good, but it can become insipid. When that happens, there is nothing to restore its flavor. Some of this we know from elsewhere in the New Testament. We read in the Sermon on the Mount: "You are the salt of the earth. But if salt loses its taste, with what can it be seasoned? It is no longer good for anything but to be thrown out and trampled underfoot" (Matt 5:13).[17]

In his *Natural History,* Pliny the Elder is usually quite straightforward and matter-of-fact. But on the matter of salt, he waxes eloquent. In the midst of a description of the values and uses of salt, he exclaims: "Heaven knows, a civilized life is impossible without salt, and so necessary is this basic substance that its name is applied metaphorically even to intense mental pleasures. We call them *sales* (wit); all the humour of life, its supreme joyousness, and relaxation after toil, are expressed by this word more than by any other" (Book XXXI, 88).

In the Old Testament, salt was used for purification. In one of the stories of Elisha, we read that when the water in a place was bad and the land unfruitful, he requested that a new bowl with salt be brought to him. He then took the bowl to the spring and threw the salt into the water, thereby purifying it permanently (see 2 Kgs 2:20).

Salt was also used in the cleansing of a child at birth. Its absence was noteworthy: "As for your birth, the day you were born your navel cord was not cut; you were neither washed with water nor anointed, nor were you rubbed with salt, nor swathed in swaddling clothes" (Ezek 16:4).

It may be this association with purification inspired the expression "salted with fire." While the basic metaphor in the conclusion of the discourse is salt, the Gospel uses the term salt metaphorically. The salt referred to is fire. Two distinct metaphors for purification are brought together into one image, salt and fire. Suggested by the references to unquenchable fire in 9:43 and 48, fire comes with a new association, that of purification.

The very last words of the discourse ask that the disciples keep salt in themselves, that they would have peace with one another. In the Old Testament, salt was related to their covenant relationship with the Lord and with one another. The covenant was referred to as "[a covenant of salt] before the Lord" (Num 18:19) and as the "salt of the covenant of your God" (Lev 2:13).

Even in the New Testament, partaking of salt together was an expression of covenant. In Acts 1:4, we read that "while meeting with them, he enjoined them not to depart from Jerusalem, but to wait for 'the promise of the Father.'" The verb, translated as "meeting with" is *synalizo,* literally means "while having salt with." The

---

[17] For the theme of salt in antiquity, including the Old and New Testaments, see E. LaVerdiere, *The Breaking of the Bread* (Chicago: Liturgy Training Publications, 1998) 37–65.

simple verb *alizo* means to salt or give flavor. Jesus was restoring the flavor of the apostolic community, "salting" them, that they might have flavor in themselves.

With that background, we can offer a good interpretation for the complex of metaphors in Mark 9:49-50. Even if the disciples had failed as followers of Christ—by trying to be the greatest, by preventing others to drive out demons in Jesus' name, by scandalizing others or being scandalized—their life and mission would be restored. They would not be destroyed with fire, but purified, salted with fire. The salt of their covenant may have become insipid, but if they attended to Jesus' exhortation, they would again enjoy covenant peace with one another.

Marriage and Divorce (10:1-12)

The fourth issue in the second movement is about marriage and divorce.[18] First, Mark lays out the setting and shows how the passage is related to the previous passages and to the general flow of the Gospel. Jesus set out from the home in Capernaum, and went into Judea (10:1a). Again the crowds gathered, and again he taught them (10:1b).

While Jesus was teaching, Pharisees approached to test him in the matter of marriage, divorce, and remarriage.[19] In their interchange, Jesus turned the tables on them (10:2-9). The encounter with the Pharisees deals with divorce in relation to the Old Testament and early Jewish life.

Then, at home with the disciples, Jesus adds further teaching about marriage and divorce. With the Pharisees, he spoke of divorce that was initiated by men. Now with the disciples, he broadens the teaching to include women (10:10-12). In this, Jesus deals with divorce in relation to the Gentile world.

Into the District of Judea (10:1). Jesus had been traveling through Galilee teaching the disciples (9:30-32). The journey had brought them to Capernaum, and once inside the house, he questioned the disciples about their conversation on the way (9:33-34). He then sat down *(kathisas)* and addressed the Twelve with a special discourse (9:35-50).

[18] For an analysis of Mark 10:1-12 and a pastoral application, see E. LaVerdiere, "Marriage and Divorce in the Gospel according to Mark (chapter 10:1-12)," *The Way* (January 1994) 53–64.

[19] In the ancient world, whether Israelite, Jewish, Greek, Roman, or Christian, the question of divorce always implied remarriage.

Now, rising *(anastas),* he then "set out from there." The discourse was over. So was the journey through Galilee. Leaving Capernaum and Galilee, Jesus went into the districts of Judea *(ta horia tes Ioudaias)* over by the Jordan *(peran tou Iordanou,* 10:1a).

As usual, Mark opens the story with the setting. Every word is important. "Rising" *(anastas)* is not just a stock expression to introduce Jesus' journey. It responds to his "sitting down" *(kathisas)* earlier in 9:35 and effectively indicates the end of Jesus' formal teaching and the beginning of a new journey.

But there is a difficulty concerning the geography of the journey. The preposition *(peran)* used with the genitive usually means "across" or "beyond," as in Mark 3:8: "A large number of people . . . from Idumea, from beyond *(peran)* the Jordan." Were *peran* translated in the same way in 10:1a, it would mean that Jesus "went into the district *(ta horia,* literally, the districts) of Judea beyond the Jordan." But there are no districts of Judea beyond Jordan, that is, on the eastern side of the Jordan. The difficulty was perceived very early on, and many manuscripts inserted the word "and" *(kai)* between "the district[s] of Judea" and "beyond the Jordan," thereby eliminating the difficulty.

This is the only time Mark ever refers to "the district[s] of Judea." Elsewhere he refers to "Judea," purely and simply (3:7; 13:14), or to "the Judean countryside" *(chora,* 1:5). In 10:1a, the term *horion,* usually employed in the plural, *horia* (see 5:17; 7:24, 31), refers to the districts of the territory of Judea.

The word *peran* can indeed mean "across" or "beyond" (see 3:8), hence its use as a substantive with the article to mean "the other side" (see 4:35; 5:1, 21; 6:45; 8:13). But it can also mean "over against" or "opposite," as it frequently does in Pausanias' *Description of Greece* (second century A.D.). Pausanias wrote, for example, of something located "opposite the grave" *(peran de tou taphou,* 2.22.2), and of a town hall built "beside the exit" *(para ten exodon)* "opposite the gymnasium" *(tou gymnasiou peran,* 5.15.8). The emphasis in these examples, as in Mark 10:1a, is on the location, not on a destination.

It may be that Mark associated the districts of Jordan with Judea, recalling that people came to Jesus from Judea and from across the Jordan (3:7-8). Doing that, he may have extended the districts of Judea across the Jordan, as he would extend Jesus' teaching for the Jews (10:2-9) to the Gentiles (10:10-12). This is the first time that Jesus goes into Judea and near the Jordan River after his baptism (see 1:9-11).

It may be also that Mark wanted to say that Jesus went into "the districts of Judea opposite the Jordan," that is, "over by the Jordan," or "next to the Jordan." From the districts of Judea over by the Jordan, Jesus would thus be well positioned for his journey to Jerusalem (10:32), which would take him through Jericho (see 10:46). Jericho was situated between the lower Jordan and the old Roman road leading up to Jerusalem.

"Again [*palin*] crowds gathered around him and, as was his custom, he again [*palin*] taught them" (10:1b). Jesus' Galilean ministry had ended with the special teaching for the Twelve (9:35-50). He was now in the districts of Judea over by or across the Jordan. Mark connected Jesus' encounter with the Pharisees (10:2-9) with previous episodes with a simple term "again" *(palin)*.[20] Again *(palin)* crowds gathered, and again *(palin)* Jesus taught them.

Crowds had gathered around Jesus many times before. The previous time was in 9:14-15 when he came upon the disciples arguing with scribes surrounded by a large crowd. Earlier, Jesus taught the crowds when he summoned them with his disciples to teach them what it meant to be his follower (8:34). In the background, we also recall the great crowds that Jesus taught in the desert (6:34) and for whom he broke the bread (6:35-44; 8:1-9). After the breaking of the bread, Jesus had dismissed the crowd, only to summon them later (7:14).

Jesus often had special teaching for the disciples (see 7:17-23; 9:28-29), for the Twelve (see 9:35-50), and even for an inner circle made up of Peter, James, and John (see 9:2-13), but much of his teaching was intended for the disciples with the crowds. It is in this public setting that the Pharisees approached Jesus with a question about the lawfulness of divorce (10:2).

Jesus Tested by the Pharisees (10:2-9). When Jesus was teaching the crowds (10:1), the Pharisees approached him with a question: "Is it lawful [*existin*] for a husband [*andri*] to divorce [*apolusai*, dismiss] his wife [*yynaika*]?" We are immediately told that "they were testing him" *(peirazontes auton,* 10:2).

The conflict between the Pharisees and Jesus goes back to the beginning of the Gospel. At first, the Pharisees questioned Jesus and his disciples why they did not observe the law and follow the tradition of the elders:

"Why does he [Jesus] eat with tax collectors and sinners?" (2:16);

"Look, why are they [the disciples] doing what is unlawful *(ouk existin)* on the sabbath?" (2:24);

[20] For Mark's use of *palin,* see David Barrett Peabody, *Mark As Composer,* op. cit., 137–39.

"Why do your disciples not follow the tradition of the elders but instead eat a meal with unclean hands?" (7:5).

Later, already bent on having him put to death, they "began to argue with him, seeking from him a sign from heaven to test him" (*peirazontes auton,* 8:11). Now they were testing him (*peirazontes auton*) concerning divorce (10:2). Their question presupposes Jesus had a public position on divorce that was accepted in general in Mark's communities. It also presupposes that some were calling Jesus' teaching into question. Note how Mark could not take it for granted that the Pharisees were only testing Jesus. Stating that explicitly, he felt some might have understood it as an honest request for Jesus' view on divorce. And if that is the case, it also means that divorce was being discussed in the communities.

Jesus answered the Pharisees with a question of his own: "What did Moses command you?" (10:3). The Pharisees had asked whether divorce was lawful, and Jesus asked them to spell out the law. In the context, "Moses" refers to the lawgiver as well as to the five great scrolls of the Law. The Pharisees replied that "Moses permitted [*epetrepsen*] him [the husband] to write a bill of divorce [*biblion apostasiou*] and dismiss [*apolysai*] her" (10:4).

Divorce in the Old Testament.[21] To situate the response of the Pharisees and Jesus' teaching, we need to examine the Old Testament's teaching on divorce as well as how it was interpreted in early rabbinical tradition. In Mark 10:4, the Pharisees referred to the Deuteronomy 24:1-4, the major Old Testament passage on divorce:

> When a man, after marrying a woman [*labe gynaika,* literally, takes a woman] and having relations with her [*synoikese aute,* cohabiting with her] is later displeased [*me heure charin*] with her because he finds in her something indecent [*aschemon pragma,* an unseemly or shameful matter], and therefore he writes out a bill of divorce [*biblion apostasiou*] and hands it to her, thus dismissing her [*kai exapostelei auten*] from his house [*ek tes oikias autou*]:
>
> if on leaving his house she goes and becomes the wife of another man [*andri*], and the second husband [*aner*], too, comes to dislike her and

[21] For brief treatment of divorce in the Old Testament, see Roland de Vaux, *Ancient Israel, Its Life and Institutions* (New York: McGraw-Hill, 1961) 34–36. See also D. Freeman, "Divorce," *The International Standard Bible Encyclopedia* (Grand Rapids, Mich.: William B. Eerdmans, 1979) I:974–76; and Robert W. Wall, "Divorce," *The Anchor Bible Dictionary,* 2:217–18.

dismisses her [*kai exapostele auten ek tes oikias autou*] by handing her [*kai eis tas cheiras autes*] a written bill of divorce [*biblion apostasiou*];

or if this second man [*aner*] who has married her, dies;

then her former husband [*aner*], who dismissed her [*exaposteilen auten*], may not take her as his wife [*gynaika*] after she has become defiled.

That would be an abomination [*bdelygma*, see Mark 13:14] before the LORD, and you shall not bring such guilt upon the land which the LORD, your God, is giving you as a heritage.

I have included many terms from the Septuagint (third century B.C.) because it constitutes an early interpretation of the Hebrew text. Some key expressions in Deuteronomy 24:1-4 are present in Mark 10:2-4. One of the expressions is *biblion apostasiou* (a written notice of divorce). In both, the ordinary words for husband and wife are *aner* (man) and *gyne* (woman).

Even the differences in terminology are helpful. In Deuteronomy, the expression for divorce is *apostello auten* (send her away) *ek tes oikias autou* (from his home). It corresponds to the expression for marriage, *lambano gynaika* (to take a wife) and *synoikese aute* (to cohabit or share a home with her). In Mark 10:2-4, the expression used by the Pharisees for divorce is *apolyo* (to release or set free).

The Septuagint's expression, "to send away," seems harsher, but it is closer to the reality of divorce. The woman was in fact sent away. The Pharisees' expression is more euphemistic. It also implies that the woman was free to remarry.

Contrary to what the Pharisees said, Deuteronomy does not state that Moses permitted divorce. Presupposing that divorce was practiced, it regulates the practice by giving a procedure to follow. Once the woman was remarried, the prior divorce was permanent. The first husband could never claim her back. It thus definitely freed the woman and protected her from the man who had been her first husband.[22]

The actual procedure for divorce was simple. The husband wrote a bill of divorce, placed it in the woman's hand, and sent her away from his house. From Deuteronomy, one could infer that Moses permitted divorce. But in context, the regulations could be understood quite differently, as is seen in Jesus' position (10:5-9).

---

[22] In Egypt, when Abram (Abraham) presented his wife Sarai (Sarah) as his sister to the pharaoh, and when the pharaoh found out that Sarah was not Abraham's sister, but his wife, he summoned Abraham and said to him: "How could you do this to me! Why didn't you tell me she was your wife?" Abraham could take back Sarah as his wife, because he did not divorce her (see Gen 12:10-20; see also 20:1-18).

Before moving to Jesus' teaching, we need to complete the picture regarding divorce in the Old Testament. Deuteronomy also addressed two cases in which divorce was absolutely prohibited. The first case is about a husband who accused his wife falsely of not being a virgin at the time of their marriage (Deut 22:13-17). Such a man shall be flogged (see Deut 25:1-3) and fined one hundred silver shekels to be given to the girl's father. "She shall remain his wife [*kai autou estai gyne*], and he may not divorce her [*exaposteilai auten*] as long as he lives" (Deut 22:18-19).

The second case is about a man who had relations with a virgin who was not already betrothed (Deut 22:28). He had to pay the girl's father fifty silver shekels and take the woman as his wife. "He may not divorce her [*exaposteilai auten*] as long as he lives" (Deut 22:29).

There are also two instances in the historical literature of the post-exilic period where divorce was absolutely required. The first is described in Ezra 9–10. When the deportees returned from Babylon, they found many that remained in Jerusalem had married foreign women (Ezra 9:1-15). It was decreed that all the Israelites with foreign women had to send them away (Ezra 10:1-44). Described in Nehemiah 13:23-29, the second also involves Israelites who married foreign women. Although it does not refer explicitly to divorce, it is clearly implied: "Thus I cleansed them of all foreign contaminations" (Neh 13:30).

The two instances in Ezra and Nehemiah presuppose the law of Deuteronomy 7:1-4, which strictly prohibited marriage with foreigners: "You shall not intermarry with them, neither giving your daughters to their sons nor taking their daughters for your sons" (Deut 7:3). The reason for the prohibition was that "they [daughters of the foreigners] would turn your sons from following me to serving other gods" (Deut 7:4).[23]

Divorce in Early Judaism.[24] To understand the position of the Pharisees and Jesus' teaching about divorce, we also need to know how Deuteronomy 24:1-4 was interpreted in rabbinical Judaism.

---

[23] In the mid-fifth century, the prophet Malachi raised his voice against Judah, which was breaking the law and violating the covenant by marrying idolatrous women (Mal 2:10-11). By marrying a woman whose family was committed to other gods, Judah, Israel, and even Jerusalem had violated the covenant which God had given them. Marriage was not a specifically religious institution, but like every other aspect of life, it had religious implications (Mal 2:12).

[24] For a brief treatment of divorce in early Judaism, see Joachim Jeremias, *Jerusalem in the Time of Jesus* (Philadelphia: Fortress Press, 1969) 370–71.

For this, we turn to the Mishnah and to its tractate entitled *Gittin* ("Bills of Divorce"). It appears in the Mishnah's third division, *Nashim* ("Women"). The passage that refers to Deuteronomy 24:1-4 gives three positions regarding the grounds for divorce (9:10).[25]

In the Mishnah, as in early Judaism, the legality of divorce was generally taken for granted and the procedure from Deuteronomy 24:1-4 was practiced. The questions being discussed by the scribes and rabbis had to do with the grounds of divorce. This can be seen from Matthew's Gospel, which reflects a Jewish-Christian context. In Mark, the question asked by the Pharisees was "Is it lawful for a husband to divorce his wife" (Mark 10:2). In Matthew, the question was "Is it lawful for a husband to divorce his wife for any cause whatever?" (Matt 19:3).

The fact that in Matthew's prologue, Joseph had considered divorcing Mary indicates that divorce was considered lawful. Otherwise, Joseph would not even have considered the matter. A divorce would have allowed Joseph to marry another woman, and if the grounds for the divorce had been made public, they would have made Mary subject to death by stoning in front of her father's house (see Deut 22:22-27).

The Mishnah gives three opinions on the grounds for divorce. The first is that of the House of Shammai:

> The House of Shammai says,
>
> > "A man should divorce his wife only because he has found grounds for it in unchastity, since it is said, 'Because he has found in her indecency in anything'" (Deut 24:1).

The House of Shammai drew its inspiration from its founder, Shammai Ha-Zaken ("the Elder"), who lived from around 50 B.C. to A.D. 30. His attitude and that of the school (*beth,* house) was more stringent than others. Shammai was a contemporary of Jesus.

The position of the House of Shammai hinged on the interpretation of the term "indecency," a vague term in Hebrew, *'erwat dabar,* which the House of Shammai understood as "unchastity," and which appears in Matthew's Gospel as *porneia* (sexual immorality, 5:32; 19:9). A literal rendering of the Hebrew would be "an indecent thing" (see Deut 23:15).

---

[25] See Jacob Neusner, *The Mishnah, A New Translation* (New Haven: Yale University Press, 1988) 487. The purpose of this new translation was "to present the Mishnah in as close to a literal rendition of the Hebrew as is possible in American English" (ix). It thus allows us to appreciate the flavor of the original Hebrew.

The second opinion is that of the House of Hillel:

> And the House of Hillel says,
>
> "Even if she spoiled his dish, since it is said, 'Because he has found in her indecency in anything'" (Deut 24:1).

The House of Hillel drew its inspiration from its founder Hillel Ha-Zaken ("the Elder"), who lived in the latter part of the first century A.D. and the beginning of the second. His attitude and that of the school was generally lenient. The later works of the New Testament were written during his lifetime.

The example given, "even if she spoiled his dish," implied that just about anything the woman might do might be grounds for divorce. The opinion hinged on an extremely broad interpretation of *'erwat dabar* ("an indecent thing"). A similar interpretation is reflected in the Pharisees question as it appears in Matthew: "Is it lawful for a man to divorce his wife for any cause whatever *(kata pasan aitian)?*" (Matt 19:3).

The third opinion is that of Rabbi Aqiba (Akiva), who lived from around A.D. 50 to 135:

> R. Aqiba says,
>
> "Even if he found someone else prettier than she, since it is said, 'and it shall be if she find no favor in his eyes'" (Deut 24:1).

Rabbi Aqiba's position was the broadest of all. The woman herself need not have given cause for divorce. It was enough that the man's attention was drawn to someone else. This interpretation hinged on the phrase, "if she found no favor in his eyes" (Deut 24:1). Somehow, the woman was blameworthy for losing favor in her husband's eyes.

It should be noted that in all three interpretations of Deuteronomy 24:1-4, it was always a matter of a man divorcing his wife, never of a woman divorcing her husband. In this respect, Mark 10:2-12, which addresses the possibility of a woman divorcing her husband, stands almost unique in biblical literature. Mark did have a precedent in Paul who considered marriage and divorce involving a believer, man or woman, and an unbeliever, man or woman (see 1 Cor 7:12-16).

The Teaching of Jesus (10:5-9).[26] When the Pharisees asked Jesus, "Is it lawful for a husband to divorce his wife?" he asked them,

---

[26] For a short treatment of divorce in the teaching of Jesus and the New Testament, see A. D. Verhey, "Divorce," *The International Standard Bible Encyclopedia,* I:976–78.

"What did Moses command you?" (10:3). They replied, "Moses permitted him to write a bill of divorce and dismiss her" (10:4). Responding, Jesus did not question their interpretation of Deuteronomy. Instead, Jesus declared that Moses wrote this commandment "because of the hardness of your hearts" (10:5). Apart from their hardness of heart *(sklerokardia),* Moses would never have written that commandment, and the "law of creation" would have applied.

Referring to the story of creation, Jesus said to them, "But from the beginning of creation [*apo de arches ktiseos*], 'God made them male [*arsen*] and female [*thely,* see LXX, Gen 1:27]. For this reason a man [*anthropos*] shall leave his father and mother [and be joined to his wife], and the two shall become one flesh [see LXX, Gen 2:24].'" Commenting, Jesus said, "So they are no longer two but one flesh." Jesus concluded: "Therefore what God has joined together, no human being [*anthropos*] must separate" (10:6-9).

Genesis does not speak of divorce. It speaks of marriage and the way it joins two human beings, one male and one female, into one flesh, into one single person. The marriage union is not a secondary historical development but part of creation itself. Since the union comes from a divine act, no man can sever it.

Jesus' teaching is very far away from the teaching of the House of Shammai, of the House of Hillel, and of Rabbi Aqiba. Bypassing the discussions on the grounds for divorce, Jesus took a stand against divorce itself. There may have been various interpretations of Deuteronomy 24:1-4, but all concurred in assuming that divorce was lawful. We understand, then, what prompted the Pharisees' question.

Cardiosclerosis. The word "cardiosclerosis" does not appear in any dictionary, but its meaning is obvious, "hardening of the heart" *(sklerokardia).* The term appears for the first time in Mark 10:5 (see also Matt 19:8 and Mark 16:14). In three other references, Mark uses other expressions. Referring to the synagogue and the Pharisees, the expression is *porosis tes kardias,* that is, hardness of heart (3:5). Referring to the disciples, we have the noun *kardia* (heart) with a participle of the verb *poroo* (6:52; 8:17).

In the Septuagint, the ordinary way to refer to hardness of heart is through the active voice of the verb *sklerynein* (to harden) and the noun *kardia* (heart). It appears most frequently in the story of the plagues in Egypt, where the subject is God. It is God who hardens the heart of pharaoh (see Exod 4:21, 22; 8:19; 9:12 *passim*). Jesus could not have been alluding to any of these passages. In Jesus' statement, hardness of heart is something reprehensible. It is not God's doing, but that of the Pharisees and disciples.

A passage from Psalm 94:8-9 (LXX) very likely underlies Jesus' statement:

> Do not harden your hearts [*me skerynete tas kardias*] as in the rebellion, at the day of testing [*peirasmou*] in the desert, when your fathers tested [*epeirasan*], examined and saw my works.

The corresponding Hebrew text (Ps 95:8-9) is more familiar:

> Do not harden your hearts as at Meribah,
>   as on the day of Massah in the desert.
> There your ancestors tested me;
>   they tried me though they had seen my works.

In the Psalm 94, God did not harden their hearts, but the people themselves hardened their hearts. In this, the Psalm corresponds to the situation in Mark 10:5, where the people themselves were responsible for their hardness of heart.

We note also how the Psalm refers to the day of testing in the desert and the way the ancestors had tried God. In Mark 10:2-4, the Pharisees tested Jesus. By referring to the hardness of heart and to Psalm 94:8-9, Jesus associated the way they were testing him with the way their ancestors long ago tested the Lord in the desert.

A Prophetic Response. Jesus was not the first in the Bible to raise his voice against divorce. After the prophet Malachi spoke out against intermarriage with foreigners (Mal 2:10-12), he denounced divorce among Israelites (Mal 2:13-17). Foreign influence had led to the proliferation of divorce. The prophet saw this especially reprehensible when an Israelite divorced an Israelite wife in order to marry a foreigner.

Like Jesus, Malachi appealed to the story of creation.

> This also you do: the altar of the LORD you cover
>   with tears, weeping and groaning,
> Because he no longer regards your sacrifice
>   nor accepts it favorably from your hand;
> And you say, "Why is it?"—
>   Because the LORD is witness
>   between you and the wife of your youth,
> With whom you have broken faith
>   though she is your companion, your betrothed wife.
> Did he not make one being, with flesh and spirit:
>   and what does that one require but godly offspring?
> You must then safeguard life that is your own,
>   and not break faith with the wife of your youth.

> For I hate divorce,
>> says the LORD, the God of Israel,
> And covering one's garment with injustice,
>> says the LORD of hosts;
> You must then safeguard life that is your own,
>> and not break faith.
> You have wearied the LORD with your words,
>> yet you say, "How have we wearied him?"
> By your saying, "Every evildoer
>> is good in the sight of the LORD,
> And he is pleased with him";
>> or else, "Where is the just God?" (Mal 2:13-17).

The expression, "the wife of your youth," helps us to grasp the situation. A man may have been quite pleased with his wife when she was young, but later he divorced her to take a younger woman. Rabbi Aqiba must not have read this text! In the post-exilic context, the man might even have divorced his wife to marry an attractive foreign woman. Proverbs 2:16-17 describes a similar case, warning men who forsake the companion of their youth and forget the covenant of their God.

In the face of such practices, Malachi appealed to the creation story: "Did he [the LORD] not make one being, with flesh and spirit. . .?" The couple is one being. The husband must consequently safeguard what is in effect his own life. For Malachi, divorce is equivalent to self-destruction: "You must then safeguard life that is your own."

The prophet's strongest statement against divorce comes from God, "I hate divorce." It amounts to covering one's garment with injustice. In the Bible, garments express a person's identity. By covering one's garment with injustice, injustice becomes a person's identity. That is what divorce does.

Malachi's prophecy stands in the background of Jesus' statement on divorce and helps us to appreciate its character. Like Malachi, Jesus was not providing legislation. His intention was prophetic. Jesus wanted people to see what was at stake and respond accordingly. Divorce was not a light matter. The fact that it became very widespread called for stern words. What was at stake was the disintegration of the marriage institution itself.

It is important to recall the greater context for Jesus' teaching on divorce. The main theme in this section (8:22–10:52) is the cost of discipleship. Following Christ, the Son of Man, on the way and taking up the cross did not invite distinctions. The whole section is filled with hyperbolic sayings. Every little unit is designed to open the eyes of people who could not see (see 8:22-26; 10:46-52).

Sometimes Jesus told stories. Sometimes he developed the ways of wisdom. Other times he spoke out prophetically, as in the case of divorce. He spoke as the conscience of the early Christians to stem the tide of divorce and hold back the rising flood of infidelity. Some members in Mark's communities appear to have forgotten or challenged Jesus' teaching. Being countercultural was not easy. Mark's Gospel reminded them of Jesus' prophetic message and preserved it for future generations.

At Home with the Disciples (10:10-12). In Mark 10:5-9, Jesus spoke of divorce with an eye to the Jewish context of early Christianity. In that context, divorce was possible only for the husband, and that accounts for the one-sided question of the Pharisees: "Is it lawful for a husband to divorce his wife?" (10:2). For the Pharisees, it did occur to ask the question in reverse: "Is it lawful for a wife to divorce her husband?"

There seem to have been some exceptions, but these were too few to influence the moral climate. Consequently, Jesus' radical stance prohibiting a man to divorce a woman could be seen as defending the position of the wife, who could be dismissed for little or no reason at all. Defending the position of women would be consistent with Jesus' concern for women in general (see 1:29-31; 5:25-34; 7:24-30; 14:3-9). But the broader intention was to strengthen marriages among the disciples. In view of that, Jesus aligned the marriage institution with God's design in creating man and woman.

In Judea, crowds, including Pharisees, gathered around Jesus, and Jesus taught them (10:1-9). With Mark 10:10, the setting changes. Jesus was now away from the crowds and the Pharisees "at home again" *(eis ten oikian palin)* with the disciples. The word "again" *(palin)* is related with being at home, not with the disciples' questioning. It connects 10:10-12, Jesus' further teaching on divorce, to 9:33-50, the previous time Jesus was at home giving special teaching to the disciples.

Instructing the disciples at home away from the crowds is already an established pattern in the Gospel (see 7:17-23; 9:28-29; see also 4:10-25). In all these cases, Jesus prepared the disciples for situations that would arise once the community had moved out of the Jewish environment into the Gentile. Each case applies Jesus' teaching, which was originally for the Jewish environment, to challenges from the Greco-Roman world.

In Mark's Gospel, the home of Jesus and the disciples was at Capernaum in Galilee (see 1:29; 2:1; 3:20; 7:17; 9:33). In 10:1, we read that Jesus left Galilee for Judea over by the Jordan. How then could he suddenly be at home with the disciples (10:10)? For Mark, the home was defined far more by a set of relationships than by a particular place. It corresponded to the Church (see 3:20, 31-35), the community of the Twelve (3:13-19). Mark was free to evoke the home wherever Jesus and the disciples happened to be. Like the mountain, the sea, the boat, the desert, and the way, the home had acquired profound symbolic significance within the special world of the Gospel.

The disciples questioned Jesus about what he said about divorce (10:10; see 10:2-9). As on other occasions, Jesus did more than explain what he said. He developed his teaching still further. He applied the teaching on divorce to the Greco-Roman world, where divorce had become extremely frequent and could come from the wife as well as from the husband.

As his message for the Jewish environment, Jesus' message for the Gentile world was uncompromisingly prophetic:

> Whoever divorces [*apolyse*] his wife and marries [*gamese*] another commits adultery [*moichatai*] against her; and if she divorces [*apolysasa*] her husband and marries [*gamese*] another, she commits adultery [*moichatai*] (10:11-12).

In the Gentile world, the Christians had to deal with cases where wives divorced their husbands as well as with cases where husbands divorced their wives. Jesus consequently extended his earlier prohibition to include the wife. He also added that remarriage was adulterous. In this, his message was nothing if it was not countercultural. We recall that John the Baptist was imprisoned and beheaded for his prophetic stance on Herod's marriage with his brother's wife (6:17-29).

The addition of the phrase, "and marries another," was not needed in the Jewish and Greco-Roman contexts, where a succession of marriages was commonplace. Jesus' teaching presupposes a Christian context such as in 1 Corinthians 7:10b-11:

> A wife should not separate [*me choristhenai*] from her husband—and if she does separate [*choristhe*] she must either remain single [*meneto agamos*] or become reconciled to her husband—and a husband should not divorce [*me aphienai*] his wife.

Paul received that teaching from the Lord (1 Cor 7:10a), forbidding divorce by a husband or by a wife. But if the wife divorces her husband, it forbids the woman to remarry.

In Mark 10:11-12, Jesus addresses situations where a man divorces his wife and remarries, and where a wife divorces her husband and remarries. In such cases, they commit adultery against the person they divorced. The divorced wife had rights over her husband. By remarrying, the husband violated her rights. He also did violence to his own person, since in marriage he and his wife had become one flesh. The same reflections apply to the husband who had been divorced by his wife.

Roman Law and Practice.[27] To appreciate Jesus' teaching on divorce, remarriage, and adultery, we need to view it against the background of Roman law[28] and practice. In the early years of the Roman Republic, every marriage[29] was viewed as *cum manu,* that is, with the wife's passage into the power of her husband. Everything the wife acquired subsequently became automatically the property of her husband.

When a husband repudiated his wife, she had no appeal. However, the husband did need grounds for divorcing his wife. These grounds were presented to his family, that is, to his father and his brothers. Acting as a domestic tribunal, they accepted or rejected the grounds. In the third century B.C., if the wife could not bear a child constituted grounds for divorce.

By the second century B.C., marriage *sine manu,* that is, without the wife's passage into the power of her husband, was rapidly becoming the rule. In such cases, the woman was either in the power of her father or *sui juris,* or a juridical independent. In this context, just about any pretext could suffice for divorce.

By the first century B.C., marriage *sine manu* had completely replaced the old form of marriage *cum manu,* and the woman could divorce her husband as easily as he could divorce her. Her family, that is her male relatives, could come forward and take her back to

---

[27] For a general presentation on marriage and divorce in Roman life, see Jerome Carcopino, *Daily Life in Ancient Rome* (New Haven: Yale University Press, 1940) 95–100; see also Hugh Last, "The Social Policy of Augustus," in *The Cambridge Ancient History,* edited by S. A. Cook, F. E. Adcock, M. P. Charlesworth (Cambridge: Cambridge University Press, 1934) 10:441–56.

[28] See Barry Nicholas, *An Introduction to Roman Law* (Oxford: Clarendon Press, 1962) 80–90; Max Kaser, *Roman Private Law*, translated by Rolf Dannenburg, 2nd ed. (London: Buttersworths, 1968) 238–49.

[29] In the Western world today, marriage is either a religious and legal act or a purely legal act, whereas in the Roman world it was neither of these, but a social fact regulated by Roman private law. See Kaser, op. cit., 238.

her family home, and if she had no male relatives, she could personally declare herself free.

At the beginning of the first century A.D., in the age of Augustus, divorce became extremely common, at least among the upper classes. An eloquent witness to the situation was left by Quintus Lucretius Bespillo, a consul in 19 B.C., in a stone epitaph to his wife Turia, who died between 8 and 2 B.C.:

> Seldom do marriages last until death undivorced;
> but ours continued happily for forty-one years.[30]

Our knowledge for the general population is limited, because Roman literature dealt mainly with the aristocracy and the wealthy class. We can assume, however, that divorce had become just as common among the lower classes. Otherwise there would have been no point to developing Jesus' teaching in Mark 10:10-12, which was intended for ordinary people.

Divorce became so widespread among Roman citizens that Augustus enacted a law[31] requiring divorced people to remarry. His intention was to stem the fall in the birth rate among Roman citizens, especially in the upper classes, but all the law did was encourage further divorce. With multiple marriage came multiple divorce.

The breakdown of the Roman family and the high rate of divorce were noticed by Roman writers. And indeed, the subject came up quite frequently. Most often, writers refer to the women who divorced their husbands and rarely to the husbands who divorced their wives. The fact that the writers were men contributed to this one-sidedness. But the main factor was that there was nothing unusual about a man divorcing a woman, while a wife divorcing her husband was something new, dealing a serious blow to the Roman family and household, once a proud institution and the foundation of the Roman society.

We expect the satirists, Martial and Juvenal, to comment on the matter. Juvenal let loose against Sartorius, for whom three wrinkles on his wife's face or even a runny nose were grounds enough to send Bibula packing (*Satire* VI, 142–48). Later in the same *Satire*, Juve-

---

[30] See Ludwig Friedlander, *Roman Life and Manners under the Early Empire* (London: Routledge & Sons Limited, 1928) I:243.

[31] According to the *Lex Julia de maritandis ordinibus* (18 B.C.) and the *Lex Poppaea* (A.D. 9), men aged 25–60 and women 20–50 who were unmarried, widowed, or divorced were obliged to marry unless they already had at least three children. Note that a celibate was not in compliance with this law. See Kaser, op. cit., 243.

nal rails against a woman who lords over her husband but soon relinquishes her kingdom. That woman moves from home to home and from husband to husband—eight in five autumns—wearing out her bridal veil until she comes full circle to the imprint of her own body in the bed she first abandoned (219–30).

Martial sneered at Telesilla, who was marrying her tenth husband. This was no longer marriage, but legal adultery. An honest prostitute was less offensive (*Epigrams,* Book VI, 7). Writers of satires and epigrams are not historians, but they do provide a window onto attitudes and mores. Each barb contains a grain of truth. Otherwise, it would have no impact.

Seneca, the moral philosopher, can usually be taken more seriously, but even he got carried away with disgust:

> Is there any woman who still blushes at divorce now that certain illustrious and noble women no longer count the years by the number of consuls but by the number of husbands, and now that women leave home to marry, but marry only to divorce? (*On Benefits* III, 16, 2).

These few passages from Roman writers provide a good idea of the situation regarding marriage and divorce in the Roman world in New Testament times. They make it clear that to be effective Jesus' response to the Pharisees was not enough. It had to be supplemented with further teaching that took the Roman Empire into consideration.

Speaking out of the Jewish context, the Pharisees had asked about the lawfulness of divorce. Knowing that Moses himself provided for situations where divorce occurred, they meant to test Jesus in relation to Moses. Jesus responded that Moses permitted divorce only because of their hardness of heart. However, with the kingdom of God at hand and in the following of Christ, the Son of Man, there could be no divorce. For this, Jesus appealed to God's purpose in creating male and female. The Pharisees had asked a legal question. In response, Jesus gave them a prophetic answer (10:3-9).

The Gentile Christians, however, were influenced not so much by Jewish customs and traditions but by life and mores in the Greco-Roman world. Looking beyond the Jewish context, Mark had Jesus address the situation in his readers' world. At the risk of becoming irrelevant, Jesus' message had to be adapted and applied. In Mark, Jesus thus took into consideration situations where women divorced their husbands. He also drew out the implications for adultery when a husband or a wife divorced his or her partner and remarried (10:10-12). This last teaching was given to the disciples at home. It is Jesus' special message to the young Church once it moved into the Gentile world.

Children and the Kingdom of God (10:13-16)

A society can be measured by the way it deals with its children.[32] For Jesus, children were a living, personal symbol for those who enter the kingdom of God. The fifth issue in this second movement (9:30–10:31) is about children and the kingdom of God. "Let the children [*ta paidia*] come to me; do not prevent them, for the kingdom of God belongs to such as these" (10:14).

The kingdom of God is the central theme of Jesus' message and ministry (see 1:14-15). In this passage, Jesus says that the kingdom of God belongs to children and to those who are like them. And "whoever does not accept the kingdom of God like a child will not enter it" (10:15).

The Gospel's passage on children (10:13-16) brings together two important themes in the teaching and ministry of Jesus, children and the kingdom of God, showing how the two themes are related to Jesus' person. Jesus' admonition to the disciples, "Let the children come to me; do not prevent them, for the kingdom of God belongs to such as these" (10:14), implies that the kingdom of God is realized in his very person.

Context and Development. The image of children was introduced earlier (9:35-37) in this movement (9:30–10:31). On a journey through Galilee, Jesus had announced his passion and resurrection, but the disciples did not understand (9:30-32; see 8:31). Once at home in Capernaum, Jesus inquired about what they were discussing "on the way" *(en te hodo),* but they remained silent. "On the way" to his passion and resurrection, the disciples had been arguing about who was the greatest (9:33-34).

To show how a disciple was truly great, Jesus took a child *(paidion),* placed it in the midst of the Twelve, and put his arms around the child. Whoever received such a child in his name received Jesus as well as the one sent him (9:35-37). Those who want to be first had to be like a child *(paidion),* to be the last and a servant *(diakonos)* of all. They would thus enter into the mystery of Jesus, the living sacrament of God's presence with them (see 6:50-51).

---

[32] For the background concerning children in ancient Rome and in the New Testament world, see *The Family in Ancient Rome,* edited by Beryl Rawson (Ithaca, N.Y.: Cornell University Press, 1986); Carolyn Osiek and David L. Balch, *Families in the New Testament World* (Louisville: Westminster/John Knox Press, 1997) 156–73.

The image of children is taken up again and further developed in 10:13-16, in which Jesus blesses the children. To enter into the kingdom of God, the disciples had to accept the kingdom like a child: "Amen, I say to you, whoever does not accept the kingdom of God like a child will not enter it" (10:15). From a literary standpoint, the blessing of the children (10:13-16) is an integral part of Jesus' teaching in Judea over by the Jordan (10:1-31). There Jesus taught the crowds, met the Pharisees' challenge regarding marriage and divorce (10:1-9), and applied his teaching to the Greco-Roman context in which the disciples would later be immersed (10:10-12). Jesus' teaching on marriage and divorce flows directly into the blessing of the children. It is likely that the two came from different traditions, but from the literary point of view they now form one event.

Just as the image of the child challenged the disciples concerning true greatness (9:36-37), now it challenged the disciples and the crowds concerning marriage and divorce (10:13-16). To accept Jesus' teaching on marriage and divorce they had to accept the kingdom of God like a child. Those who did not accept the kingdom like a child would not accept Jesus' teaching and would not enter the kingdom of God.

The story is quite short and very simple. The introduction shows people bringing children to Jesus in order that he would touch them, but the disciples rebuked them (10:13). The body of the story tells how Jesus reacted to the rebuke and presents his teaching on children and the kingdom of God (10:14-15). The conclusion shows Jesus embracing the children, blessing them, and placing his hands on them (10:16).

People Were Bringing Children to Jesus (10:13a). They were bringing children *(paidia)* to Jesus that he might touch them, but the disciples rebuked them (10:13). Although a change of setting is not indicated, the passage presupposes that Jesus and the disciples were no longer at home (10:10-12) but in an open place with the crowds (10:1-9). We saw a similar shift in the parable discourse (4:1-34), in which Jesus addressed a large crowd by the sea (4:3-9; see 4:1-2) and taught the Twelve alone with those with them (4:10-25). The concluding parables presuppose that Jesus was again teaching the crowd by the sea (4:26-32; see 4:33-34).

The Gospel says nothing about those who brought the children. We may suppose the parents brought them. The story's focus is on the disciples and on the children, not on those who brought the children. If Mark wanted to suggest the presence of the parents, he would have used another Greek word for the children, namely *tekna*,[33] which refers to a child in relation to his parents (see 7:27; 10:29, 30; 12:19; 13:12). Like the words "son" and "daughter," *teknon* (child) evokes the correlative term "parent."

Throughout 10:13-16, the Greek term for child is not *teknon* but *paidion*, referring to the child's age, not to its relationship to his parents. The focus is entirely on the child's age and status in relation to others in the community. The word refers to a young boy or girl past infancy,[34] but still too young to assume adult responsibilities, which come after the age of twelve (see 5:39-41; 7:28-30; 9:24 and 9:36-37).

That Jesus Might Touch the Children (10:13b). The reason people brought children was that Jesus might touch *(hapsetai)* them. There was something extraordinary about being touched by Jesus and touching Jesus. This is the seventh and last time that touch is mentioned in the Gospel, where it appears always with reference to Jesus.

The first time was when Jesus touched a leper and made him clean (1:41-42). The Law forbade people to touch one who was unclean, particularly a leper (Lev 5:3; Num 5:2-4), but the prohibition did not apply to Jesus, since his touch made an unclean person clean. Later, a woman with a long-standing hemorrhage was cured upon touching Jesus' cloak. Touching Jesus in faith brought her salvation, peace, and healing (5:25-34). Touch was a vital component of Jesus' ministry. It was even mentioned in two important summaries of his ministry (3:7-12; 6:56).

On three occasions, Jesus' touch is associated with the imposition of hands. When people brought a deaf man who was unable to speak and asked Jesus to lay his hand on him, Jesus put his fingers into the man's ears and touched his tongue. As Jesus' commanded, "Be opened!" the man was cured (7:31-37). When people brought a blind man to be touched by Jesus, Jesus laid hands on him the first time, and the man saw, but in a distorted way. When he laid his hands on him again, he saw perfectly (8:22-26). When people brought children that Jesus might touch them (10:13b), Jesus embraced and blessed the children and imposed hands on them (10:16).

These references to touching and the imposition of hands were sometimes associated with other physical actions, such as spitting

---

[33] The plural, *tekna*, refers to children. The singular, *teknon*, refers to a child of either sex.

[34] The term for infant or baby is *brephos* (see Luke 18:15).

(7:33; 8:23) and with a person's faith, suggesting an early liturgical context for these stories. The casting out of a demon, the opening of the ears, the releasing of the tongue, and the opening of the eyes also suggest a context close to baptism. The importance given them may indicate Mark intended to evoke a liturgical, baptismal context for his readers (see also 10:38-39).

The Disciples' Rebuke (10:13c). The Greek word for "rebuke" *(epitimao)* is a strong term often associated with Jesus in the Synoptic Gospels. In Mark, it is used for Jesus' forceful command in expelling an unclean spirit (1:25; 9:25) or stilling the wind, bringing calm to a stormy sea (4:39).

The word also describes Jesus' strong warning to unclean spirits not to make him known (3:12) and a similar command to Peter and the disciples not to tell anyone that he was the Christ (8:30). The reason became plain when Jesus announced his passion and resurrection and was rebuked by Peter for teaching this openly (8:32). Peter's rebuke was countered by a severe rebuke by Jesus, "Get behind me, Satan" (8:33).

Peter's rebuke was the first of three instances where the verb is attributed to someone other than Jesus. The second is in 10:13, where the disciples rebuked those who were bringing children to Jesus. The third is when many *(polloi)* rebuked Bartimaeus and tried to silence him as he called out to Jesus (10:48). All three were ineffectual in trying to stifle Jesus' ministry.

Why did the disciples try to prevent people from bringing children to Jesus? For the same reason they tried to prevent an outsider from driving out demons in Jesus' name (9:38). For the same reason someone might have caused of these little one who believed in Jesus to sin (9:42). For the same reason the disciples would be salted with purifying fire (9:49).

The disciples were "on the way," but their preoccupation with being the greatest was inconsistent with following Christ to the passion and resurrection. It distorted their vision. They were like the blind man who could see people but they looked like trees walking. They could not see that the kingdom was for everyone. Not even a child was too insignificant for the kingdom of God.

Jesus' Indignation (10:14a). On seeing what the disciples did, Jesus became indignant and very angry *(eganaktesen)*. In its proper sense, the verb *aganakteo* refers to a violent physical irritation. Here in its metaphorical sense, it indicates a strong emotional reaction against what someone has done (10:41; 14:4).

Angry reactions are usually accompanied by angry words. Here, Jesus' gentle words seem oddly out of step with his anger. Jesus' anger and indignation were altogether directed against what the disciples had done. His message was entirely taken up with what could and ought to happen, that is, the children coming to him.

"Let the Children Come to Me" (10:14b). Jesus' response is addressed to the disciples, but its focus is on the children. The opening command, "Let the children come to me" *(erchesthai pros me),* recalls several other passages in the Gospel where people were brought to Jesus (2:3) or came on their own to be cured (1:40, 45; 3:8) or taught (2:13) by him. Later, there would also be Bartimaeus, the blind beggar, who called to Jesus and came to him because he wanted to see (10:50). As with the children, those who were already on the way rebuked Bartimaeus, but Jesus intervened.

For the sake of emphasis, the opening positive command is followed immediately by a negative command, "Do not prevent them" *(me kolyete auta),* that is, "Do not prevent the children from coming to me." The second command recalls when Jesus' disciples tried to prevent someone who was not following them from driving out demons in Jesus' name. Jesus had the same answer: "Do not prevent him" *(me kolyete auton,* 9:38-39).

"For the Kingdom of God Belongs to Such as These" (10:14c). The kingdom of God *(he basileia tou theou)* is one of the dominant images in Mark's Gospel (1:14-15). It played a major role in the discourse on parables (4:10-12, 26-29, 30-32) and was introduced by the story of the transfiguration (9:1-8). It is also a key element for various relationships among Jesus' followers (9:47; 10:14-15, 23-25).

The kingdom of God later figures again three times, first in Jesus' encounter with a scribe who was "not far from the kingdom of God" (12:28-34). It also was part Jesus' announcement at the Last Supper: "Amen, I say to you, I shall not drink again the fruit of the vine until the day when I drink it new in the kingdom of God" (14:25). The last mention is in the description of Joseph of Arimathea as one "who was himself awaiting the kingdom of God" (15:43).

The reason the children should be allowed to come to Jesus is that "the kingdom of God belongs to such as these" *(ton gar toiouton estin he basileia tou theou),* more literally, "the kingdom of God is of such as these." The Greek expression is akin to the traditional beatitudes, "for theirs is the kingdom of heaven" (cf. Matt 5:3, 10), meaning more than that the kingdom of God belongs to them. The kingdom of God is also realized in them, as in those who are poor in spirit, awaiting all things from God. That is why to receive one child in Jesus' name is to receive him and the one who sent him (9:37).

The kingdom of God, a transcendent reality in which the entire universe will be one under God, belongs to the children. The kingdom of God counters to every ambition to be "the greatest." It belongs to the very least, the ones who are last, the children (9:34-37), to the "little ones who believe" (9:42) and to those who are like them (10:14).

The image of the child is at the very heart of the gospel reversals, expressed in the beatitudes (Matt 5:3-10; Luke 6:20-22) and in Mary's hymn of praise, the *Magnificat* (Luke 1:46-55). They are also proclaimed in Jesus' passion and resurrection and are implied in the call to follow Christ, in which those who lose their life for the sake of Christ will save it (8:35).

"Amen, I Say to You" (10:15a). When the disciples tried to prevent children from coming to Jesus (10:13), Jesus responded directly: "let the children come to me; do not prevent them, for the kingdom of God belongs to such as these" (10:14). But that was only the first part of his response. As on many other occasions, the reason Jesus gave invited a far broader application. The kingdom of God does not belong to the children alone, but to all "such as these."

The second part of Jesus' response went beyond the immediate setting and challenged everyone concerned with entering the kingdom of God: "Amen, I say to you, whoever does not accept the kingdom of God like a child will not enter it" (10:15). This solemn pronouncement is similar to others in this section of Mark, including the conditions of discipleship (8:34-37; 8:38; 9:35, 37, 40, 42; 10:11-12, 29-30, 43, 44).

The opening words, "Amen, I say to you," separate the general principle (10:15) from the circumstances (10:13-14) and give the pronouncement the great solemnity that is associated with liturgical prayer. It appears here for the fifth time in Mark's Gospel (see 3:28; 8:12; 9:1, 41), where it always introduces a decisive pronouncement that had become critical for Mark's communities. "Amen, I say to you" invokes Jesus' authority in a matter that was disputed and brings the discussion to a close.

"Whoever Does Not Accept the Kingdom of God Like a Child" (10:15b). The kingdom of God transcends every earthly kingdom and embraces all of creation. Like creation, it is a free work of God, a work of grace, which human beings can accept but cannot initiate or bring about. Accepting the kingdom of God means openness to the transcendent and a readiness to live under divine rule. To illustrate the required openness and readiness, Jesus challenged the disciples and the crowd with the image of a child.

The disciples were somewhat prepared for the image (9:36-37), but the crowd must have been puzzled. Jesus had already given them parables of the kingdom of God, its tiny beginnings and mysterious growth (4:26-29, 30-32), but here was a new kind of parable with the image of a child. To get at the gospel image of the child, we need to strip away a number of cultural attitudes that are foreign to the biblical world and which obscure the image and distort Jesus' message.

Being like a child has nothing to do with a child's innocence, a personal state for which adults may wistfully long but can never regain. The Gospel is not romantic in its view of children. Nor is it escapist. When it speaks of being like a child it offers a serious and realistic challenge.

Very little in the ancient portrayal of the child could be termed romantic, an attitude springing from the humanism and the individualism characteristic of the Western world from the time of the Renaissance. In the biblical and early Jewish world, the child was seen not as an individual, but as a member of the family who gave it birth. The child belonged first to the community, and when the parents had a boy circumcised they fulfilled their duty to the community. Like others, the child was a sinner from birth and shared in the sins of the community. We have an eloquent witness from the psalmist: "True, I was born guilty, / a sinner, even as my mother conceived me" (Ps 51:7).

That is why a young boy participated in the great feasts and was associated with the people's prayers and expiatory offerings as soon as he no longer needed to be with his mother (*Sukkah* 2.8). A young boy was obliged to keep the feasts when he could take his father's hand (Hillel) or ride on his shoulders (Shammai) to the Temple.[35]

Unlike the adult, who was a big sinner, the child growing up was just a little sinner, taking part as a child in the way people oppressed one another. For the child that often meant being "bold toward the elder" and "base toward the honorable" (Isa 3:5). Besides, children could be quite senseless, unruly, and easily deceived (see Wis 12:24-26; 15:14). They were not to be pampered and indulged but disciplined:

> A colt untamed turns out stubborn;
>   a son left to himself grows up unruly.
> Pamper your child and he will be a terror for you,
>   indulge him and he will bring you grief (Sir 30:8-9; see 30:1-13).

[35] See H. L. Strack and Paul Billerbeck, *Kommetar zum Neuen Testament aus Talmud und Midrash* (Munich: Beck, 1922–1961) 2:146.

Why then does the kingdom of God belong to the children if not for their innocence? An answer comes from the people who were brought to Jesus, or came to be touched by him, or reached out to touch him. All were in need and knew they were in need. There were the sick, who needed healing and life, and the lame, the blind, the deaf, and the mute, who needed to walk, to see, to hear, and to speak. In every case, those who came to Jesus were quite helpless and totally dependent on the gift of God.

Like them, children are also helpless and dependent regarding the most basic necessities for living. Because they are little, and by reason of their stage of life and level of development, as well as their place in the community and position in the family, children are in fact dependent on others for just about everything. They are also ready to receive from others what they themselves cannot provide, even when they are not aware of that.

This attitude of radical dependence, openness to others, and readiness to receive is quite natural for children. But for adults, it must be acquired. For this, adults must repent, undergo a *metanoia,* a radical change in their attitudes and behavior, and open their minds and hearts in faith to the truth and reality of the kingdom of God (1:14-15). The adult challenge by the image of children was a matter of accepting to be the least, as a child truly is, rather than the greatest, as adults yearn to be (9:34-37). Before God, adults are in fact children, and being like a child means accepting that fact. And that is the way adults accept the kingdom of God like a child.

"Will Not Enter It" (10:15c). But "whoever does not accept [*hos an me dexetai*] the kingdom of God like a child will not enter [*ou me eiselthe*] it." To accept the kingdom of God is to subject oneself to the rule of God and all that implies regarding life and relationships. To enter into the kingdom is to receive all the blessings that flow from living under God's rule.

In this second context, where the focus is on entering the kingdom, "the kingdom of God" is seen as a place which can be approached and entered (10:15c; see 9:45; 10:23-25). In other contexts, the kingdom refers to a definitive manifestation of divine sovereignty (1:15; 15:43) or to a graced relationship in which God's sovereignty is recognized (10:14, 15a; 12:34). As a place, the kingdom is associated with retribution. The alternative was to enter Gehenna: "Better for you to enter [*eiselthein*] into the kingdom of God with one eye than with two eyes to be thrown into Gehennna, where 'their worm does not die, and the fire is not quenched'" (9:47-48).

Matthew developed this aspect of the image of the kingdom in the conclusion of Jesus' eschatological discourse (Matt 25:31-46). The kingdom is where the righteous enjoy eternal life (Matt 25:46). It has been prepared for them "from the foundation of the world." Blessed by the Father of Jesus, they will inherit it at the decisive judgment.

Unlike Mark, Matthew refers to the kingdom as the kingdom of heaven rather than the kingdom of God, giving rise to the popular view of "heaven" as the place of eternal reward. Following Mark, we would describe "heaven" as entering into the living presence of God. In the present context (10:15), the notion of "entering the kingdom of God" introduces the next passage, whose central concern is inheriting eternal life and entering into the kingdom of God (10:17-31).

Then Jesus Embraced the Children (10:16a). Jesus' action more than fulfills the hopes of those who brought the children. They wanted Jesus to touch them. For Jesus, touching them meant embracing them, blessing them, and imposing hands on them. Jesus had just spoken of entering the kingdom of God. The coming of the children to Jesus as symbolic of entering the kingdom of God, and Jesus' embrace and blessing, along with the imposition of hands, were symbolic of eternal life in the kingdom of God.

In embracing *(enagkalisamenos)* the children, Jesus embraced those to whom the kingdom of God belongs. The verb *enagkalizomai* means to take into one's arms or put one's arms around. In the New Testament, it appears only here and in 9:36, where Jesus also puts his arms around a child. In both cases, Jesus does this for the benefit of the children, but also for the benefit of all who were invited to be "such as these."

Jesus' embrace does not merely come from a deeply loving human being. It comes from the Christ (8:29), proclaiming the advent of the kingdom of God (1:14-15), and of the Son of Man, who would be handed over to men, put to death but would rise after three days (9:31). Jesus' embrace had awesome implications. Embraced by Jesus, the children and those like them joined in Jesus' proclamation of the kingdom and were taken into the mystery of his dying and rising.

And Jesus Blessed the Children (10:16b). The verb for Jesus' blessing *(kateulogeo)* appears nowhere else in the New Testament. As a compound form of the simple verb *eulogeo* (to bless) it emphasizes the effectiveness of Jesus' blessing. Blessing the children, Jesus invokes on them all the good things that flow from their participation in Jesus' passion and resurrection.

In Mark's Gospel, as elsewhere in the New Testament, blessing is associated with prayer. Later in the Gospel, Jesus' triumphant entry into Jerusalem would be accompanied by a blessing prayer, identifying the coming of Jesus with "the kingdom of our father David":

> Hosanna!
>> Blessed [*eulogemenos*] is he who comes in the name of the Lord!
>> Blessed [*eulogemene*] is the kingdom of our father
>>> David that is to come!
> Hosanna in the highest!" (Mark 11:9-10).

The first blessing comes from a prayer of petition, praise, and thanksgiving in Psalm 118:25-26: "LORD, grant salvation! (Hosanna) . . . Blessed is he who comes in the name of the Lord." Referring to the kingdom of David, the second blessing does not announce the restoration of David's kingdom but eschatological kingdom that is to come. Elsewhere Jesus' blessing is a liturgical act addressed to God, who is blessed in gratitude for the gift of Christ's body and blood in the Eucharist (6:41; 8:7; 14:22).

Jesus' blessing of the children bestows on them the kingdom which is to come but already present in the signs of the breaking of the bread. The children belong to the liturgical assembly of the Church. The blessing came as Jesus' response to those who tried to prevent the children from coming to Jesus.

Jesus Imposed His Hands on the Children (10:16c). The story ends with Jesus placing his hands on the children *(titheis tas cheiras ep' auta)*. Jesus embraced the children, drawing them to himself as the Christ and enveloping them in the passion and resurrection of the Son of Man. He blessed them, dismissing the objections of those who tried to keep them away from him and effectively invoking on them the blessings of the kingdom of God.

By placing his hands on them, Jesus then took possession of them, fulfilling the sure hope contained in his blessing. With Jesus' hands on them, they were full of life (see 5:23), cured of all illness (see 6:5), able to hear and speak (see 7:32), and see clearly (see 8:23, 25). The children, in their openness to the kingdom of God, are in the hands of Jesus. "The kingdom of God belongs to such as these!"

Wealth and the Kingdom of God (10:17-31)

How should a Christian view wealth and possessions? After Jesus' teaching on marriage and divorce (10:1-12) and on children in the kingdom of God (10:13-16), Mark presents Jesus' teaching regarding wealth and possessions (10:17-31). Wealth in the kingdom of God is the sixth and last issue treated in this movement (9:30–10:31).

"What must I do to inherit eternal life?" The question came from one who "had many possessions [*ktemata polla*]" (10:22). Jesus' response was simple and demanding. Besides observing the commandments, people had to sell their possessions, give the proceeds to the poor and follow Jesus. That is what someone must do to inherit eternal life and "enter the kingdom of God" (10:23).

The story of Jesus' encounter with the wealthy man (10:17-31)[36] associates eternal life with the kingdom of God and shows how the two are related to the following of Christ. The goal of Jesus' journey is the kingdom of God. To follow him, disciples must part with all earthly possessions and attachments.

Context and Developments. The theme of voluntary poverty was first introduced in the Gospel when Jesus sent the Twelve on their missionary journey (6:7-13) with instructions to take nothing for the journey: "no food, no sack, no money in their belts" (6:8). The disciples found these instructions extremely difficult to follow when they were faced with the demands of the ministry (see 6:35-38; 8:4-5).

Voluntary poverty was also implied in Jesus' teaching that those who wished to come after him on the way had to deny themselves, take up his cross and follow him (8:34). In this section (9:30–10:31), the general call for self-denial and mortification in following Christ is applied to a wide range of attitudes and relationships.

Jesus' teaching on property, possessions, and even family, concludes Jesus' teaching in the districts of Judea over by or opposite the Jordan (10:1-31). A first challenge came from the Pharisees regarding the law of Moses on divorce (10:1-12). A second came from the disciples who tried to prevent people from bringing children to Jesus (10:13-16). Now a third challenge came as a simple question concerning what someone has to do to inherit eternal life (10:17).

The story unfolds in two parts. In the first part, someone who was not a disciple approached Jesus (10:17-22). A brief exchange on the conditions for inheriting eternal life ends with his going away sadly. He was one of those who do "not accept the kingdom of God like a child" and "will not enter it."

---

[36] In Matthew, the wealthy man becomes a rich young man (Matt 19:16-30; see 19:20, 22). In Luke, he becomes a rich official (Luke 18:18-30).

In the second, Jesus addresses the disciples on the subject of wealth and entering the kingdom of God (10:23-31). The passage deals with the humanly impossible and divinely possible. It also deals with the reward both "in this present age" and "in the age to come" for accepting Jesus' challenge (10:30).

Jesus' concluding statement, "But many that are first will be last, and [the] last will be first" (10:31), recalls Jesus' challenge at the beginning of the section, "If anyone wishes to be first, he shall be the last of all and the servant of all" (9:35). We are reminded that the fundamental problem "on the way" is trying to be "the greatest" (9:34), instead of accepting to be the least.

As He Was Setting Out on a Journey (10:17a). Jesus was setting out *(ekporeuomenou autou)* on a journey *(eis hodon)*. Until now, Mark introduced journeys without the noun *hodos*. Early in the section, Jesus left *(exelthen)* with his disciples for the villages of Caesarea Philippi (8:27a). Leaving there *(dexelthontes)* they then journeyed *(paraporeuonto)* through Galilee (9:30) and came *(elthon)* to Capernaum (9:33; see also 10:1).

In each instance, the journey is indicated first by a verb, but only later by the noun *hodos* (8:27b; 9:33, 34), referring to a "journey," "way," or even "road," depending on the context. The various journeys were loosely related, if at all, in tradition and history. The symbolic term *hodos* unites these journeys in one great Christian journey.

While in the district of Judea over by the Jordan (10:1), Jesus was setting out on a journey (10:17a), but the first time, there is indication of a destination. What is important is that Jesus was setting out. The present journey will soon continue with the ascent to Jerusalem. But for now it is interrupted by the arrival of someone with a question.

At the start, we know nothing about the man. The story refers to him simply as "one" *(heis,* 10:17b). From his question, we know that he was not a disciple. From the brief dialogue, we learn that he faithfully observed the commandments from his youth (10:20). Only at the end of the story we learn that he had many possessions (10:22).

The man's precipitous entry is very striking. Running up *(prosdramon)* to Jesus, he knelt down *(gonypetesas)*. Most people simply come to Jesus, gather near or around him, or follow him. Those who are sick or in some other way helpless, like the children, are usually brought to Jesus.

But in the Gospel the man's entry has a precedent. There was the crowd running up to *(prostrechontes)* Jesus when he came down from the mount of transfiguration (9:15). And there was the Gerasene with the unclean spirit, who ran up *(edramen)* and prostrated himself *(proskynesen)* before Jesus (5:6). But now the man does not prostrate himself before Jesus. In Mark, prostration is a gesture of homage. The gesture could be done out of fear, or done in mockery, as the soldiers did during the passion (15:19). For the Gerasene, whose unclean spirit addressed Jesus as "the Son of the Most High God," the gesture was a travesty, done in mock-worship.

The man did not prostrate himself but simply knelt down *(gonypeteo)*. His gesture recalls that of the woman with the hemorrhage, who fell before Jesus *(prosepesen auto)* and of the Syrophoenician woman, who fell at Jesus' feet *(prosepesen pros tous podas autou,* 7:25). But it recalls most especially that of the leper, who, according to many important manuscripts, knelt down *(gonypeton)* before him (1:40).

Running up to Jesus demonstrates the man's eagerness. Kneeling before reveals a humble suppliant. But as the story shows, the man was too eager, and his slow, sad departure contrasts with his hurried, expectant arrival (10:22).

The Request (10:17b). The man addresses Jesus as "teacher" (10:17, 20), a title used by the disciples (4:38; 9:38; 10:35; 13:1) as well as outsiders (5:35; 9:17; 12:14, 19, 32) in Mark's Gospel. Even Jesus refers to himself as "the teacher" (14:14). Jesus was not an ordinary teacher. People were astonished at his teaching, "for he taught them as one having authority and not as the scribes" (1:22; see 1:27). Still, no one up to this point had called him, "Good teacher." Goodness is a divine quality revealed in the Lord's enduring mercy:

> Give thanks to the LORD, who is good,
> whose love endures forever (Ps 118:1).[37]

The man kneeling before Jesus attributes the divine quality to him.

The man then asks Jesus, what he must do "to inherit eternal life" *(zoe aionion)*. Eternal life is not the same as natural immortality which flows from having an immortal soul. Eternal life is a gift of God, graciously granted to those who have died in their rising from the dead. Its first mention in the Bible is in the book of Daniel:

> Many of those who sleep
>   in the dust of the earth shall awake;
> Some shall live forever,
>   others shall be an everlasting horror and disgrace (12:2).

---

[37] See also 1 Chron 16:34 and 2 Chron 5:13.

The alternative to eternal life is "everlasting horror and disgrace." It is consequently something qualitative and not merely a matter of endless duration.[38] While eternal life is a free gift of God, there are conditions for its granting. Hence the man's request about what he must do to inherit it.

Jesus' Response and the Man's Answer (10:18-20). Before answering the man's question, Jesus questions the way he addressed him. "Why do you call me good? No one is good but God alone" (10:18). Jesus' response recalls Deuteronomy's introduction to the great commandment: "Hear, O Israel! The LORD is our God, the LORD alone!" (Deut 6:4; see Mark 12:29).

Any goodness that is in Jesus is from God and must be recognized as such. The man who ran up to Jesus saw the goodness in Jesus as independent of divine goodness. He therefore did not realize that God's gift of eternal life would come to him through Jesus. Having disassociated the goodness of Jesus from the goodness of God, he did not associate the following of Christ with the observance of the commandments.

Jesus then turns to the man's question, "What must I do to inherit eternal life?" and responds to it in two stages. First, he recalls what the man already knows, the commandments, and he recites six of them, including five prohibitions and one positive command (10:19). Second, he asks him to sell his possessions, give the proceeds to the poor, and follow him (10:22).

Four of the prohibitions come from Exodus 20:13-16 and Deuteronomy 5:17-21:

> You shall not kill.
> You shall not commit adultery.
> You shall not steal.
> You shall not bear false witness.

The general prohibition not to commit adultery recalls the special Markan teaching on divorce and adultery for Christians in a Greco-Roman setting (10:11-12).

The fifth prohibition is not found with the other commandments: "You shall not defraud." It is drawn from a Deuteronomic list of statutes and decrees concerning justice, equity, and charity (Deut 24:6–25:4):

---

[38] See also 2 Macc 7:9.

> You shall not defraud a poor and needy hired servant, whether he be one of your own countrymen or one of the aliens who lives in your communities (Deut 24:14-15; see Sir 4:1).

In the New Testament, a similar concern surfaced in 1 Corinthians:

> Now indeed [then] it is, in any case, a failure on your part that you have lawsuits against one another. Why not rather put up with injustice? Why not let yourselves be cheated [defrauded]? Instead, you inflict injustice and cheat [defraud], and this to brothers (1 Cor 6:7-8).

Jesus' recitation of the commandments does not follow the order given in Exodus and Deuteronomy. In the Old Testament, the positive command, "honor your father and your mother," is given before the others. In Jesus' response, it comes last, in the climactic position. Recall that in the Old Testament, fulfilling this commandment held the promise of a long life:

> Honor your father and your mother, that you may have a long life in the land which the Lord, your God, is giving you (Exod 20:12; see Deut 5:16).

However, the man kneeling before Jesus was asking what he had to do not to have a long life on earth but to inherit eternal life. For this, fulfilling the commandments was necessary but not adequate.

Jesus' reproach, "Why do you call me good?" (10:18), was well taken but not understood. The man addressed Jesus anew as "teacher," not as "good teacher," but failed to see what God's gift of eternal life comes through a person's relationship with Jesus Christ. He kept the commandments from his youth, from the age when he was first taught them (see Ps 71:17) and through all the years he could have transgressed them (10:20). The expression "from my youth" is equivalent to "all my life" or "from the beginning of my life." But keeping the commandments from his youth was not enough to inherit eternal life. He was still lacking in one thing (10:21).[39]

Jesus Loved Him (10:21a). The story of Jesus and the children focused on Jesus' touch and how he embraced the children, blessed them, and placed his hands on them (10:13-16). Earlier Jesus had placed a child in the midst of the Twelve and put his arms around the child (9:36-37). Jesus welcomes the children and makes them his. The children belong to Jesus, as do all who are like them, and that is why the kingdom of God belongs to them.

[39] See Gen 8:21; 1 Sam 12:2; Ps 71:17; Acts 26:4.

The story of Jesus and the wealthy man focuses on Jesus' gaze, a loving and potentially transforming gaze, calling the man to come and follow him, as many others had been called before. The telling of all this is extremely simple: having set his gaze *(emblepsas)*[40] on him, Jesus loved *(egapesen)* him (10:21a). Jesus looked the man in the face. The same verb is used later in the story when Jesus looks directly at his disciples with the message that things impossible for human beings are possible for God (10:27).

The verb employed makes a big difference. Simple verbs of seeing, such as *blepo* (to look on or at) and *horao* (to see) are often used in the sense of knowing and understanding. The difference between *blepo* and *eidon* stands out when Jesus quotes Isaiah 6:9 about those who look *(blepo)* but do not see *(horao)*.

Emblepo adds a nuance of concentration. By fixing his gaze on the wealthy man, Jesus focuses our attention on him and stirs in us a sense of expectation. When Jesus looks into someone's eyes, he has a purpose. The purpose is immediately revealed. Having fixed his gaze on the wealthy man, Jesus loved *(egapesen)* him.

The verb for love *(agapao)* does not refer to an ordinary human sentiment. For this, another verb *(phileo)* would have been used. In Mark, the verb *phileo* is used only once, in the passion story referring to Judas' hypocritical expression of love (14:44). The love Jesus has for the man before him is used in the first commandment: "You shall love [*agapeseis*] the Lord with all your heart, with all your soul, with all your mind, and with all your strength" (12:30). The same love is again found in the second commandment: "You shall love [*agapeseis*] your neighbor as yourself" (12:31).

To view this love as a mere feeling or affection would trivialize it. As in John's reference to the disciple Jesus loved (*agapao,* John 13:23), the love of Jesus for the man kneeling before him speaks Jesus' attitude toward him, his commitment to him, and invites the man to respond in kind. Jesus' love remains even in the face of rejection.

"You Are Lacking in One Thing" (10:21b). The man's question, "What must I do to inherit eternal life?" (10:17) had already been answered in part. He was not to address Jesus as "good," for God alone is good. Then there was the matter of observing the commandments, and Jesus had recalled several of these, beginning with the fifth, "You shall not kill," and ending with the fourth,

---

[40] The verb *emblepo* is a compound of *blepo* (to look) and *en* (in).

"Honor your father and mother" (10:18-19). But these were only part of the answer, and so Jesus continues, "You are lacking in one thing" (*hen se hysterei,* 10:21b).

Jesus' emphasis is on the "one thing" *(hen),* not on its lack. Having fulfilled every other requirement (10:20), eternal life was within his grasp. Jesus' response recalls Psalm 23 (LXX 22:1) that nothing is lacking to me *(ouden me hysterei)* because the Lord is my shepherd. We remember too that Jesus' heart was deeply moved for the crowd "for they were like sheep without a shepherd" (6:34a). The crowd also was lacking, and Jesus filled their lack by becoming a shepherd to them: "He began to teach them many things" (6:34b). With the man now before him, Jesus is again ready to fill the one thing lacking. Jesus loved him, but was the wealthy man ready to follow Jesus the shepherd?

Jesus' response was unexpected. An ordinary teacher might have answered that to inherit eternal life one has to present offerings for sacrifices at the Temple and contribute to its treasury, observe the Sabbath study the Torah. The house of God had vast expenses and required enormous revenues. For a mobile population, rarely able to get to the Temple, the Sabbath and the Torah were extremely important.

Jesus began with a solemn command, "Go" *(hypage),* as earlier when Jesus addressed a leper (1:44), a paralytic (2:11; see 2:19), the Gerasene demoniac (5:19), and the woman cured of a hemorrhage (5:34). He gave the same command to the disciples at the breaking of the bread (6:38), the Syrophoenician woman (7:29), and Peter in need of being recalled to the following of Christ (8:33).

The command, "Go" *(hypage),* is later balanced by a second command, "Come" *(deuro).* The man first had to go and fulfill a preliminary but essential prerequisite for inheriting eternal life. He had to sell everything he had and give to the poor. He then had to come and fulfill the main requirement, that is, to follow Christ.

The one thing lacking, with its two closely related components, evokes the call of the first disciples, when Jesus commanded Simon and Andrew to come *(deute,* plural of *deuro)* after him. On that occasion Jesus did not ask the disciples to sell their possessions and give to the poor, but they did have to leave their nets (1:16-18). Afterwards, when he called James and John they had to leave "their father Zebedee in the boat along with the hired man" (1:19-20). It also evokes Jesus' instruction to the Twelve going on mission, to take with them "no food, no sack, no money in their belts" (6:8).

As fishermen, the first disciples had to leave everything associated with fishing for fish. They would then come after Jesus to cast the net of the gospel of God. So did the Twelve and the Church on mission. The man asking for eternal life had many possessions. To follow Jesus, he had to leave everything associated with earthly wealth. Coming after Jesus, he would find treasure in heaven.

Jesus' response relates the following of Christ to wealth and possessions and develops two new aspects, giving to the poor and the destiny of those who follow Christ to the passion and resurrection (see 8:31; 9:30-31). First, the man had to sell what he had. Those who deny themselves, who renounce all claims on their person that Christ may claim them (8:34), have also renounced all claims on their wealth and possessions that Christ may claim them. Concretely, this means giving to the poor *(ptochoi)*.

This is the first of three references to "the poor." The second describes a woman so poor *(ptoche)* that her contribution of two coins *(lepta)* to the Temple treasury was all she had (12:41-44). Unlike the scribes that took advantage of her under the pretext of reciting lengthy prayers (12:38-40), a follower of Jesus must not take from the poor but must give to the poor.

The third reference to the poor comes at the beginning of the passion when a woman anointed Jesus with costly spikenard. Some at table protested the waste of perfumed oil, which could have been sold and the money given to the poor *(ptochois)*. Jesus defended her and dismissed the protest as hypocrisy (14:3-9). The purpose for selling one's possessions and giving to the poor was to follow Christ. Those who were protesting had no intention to follow Christ.

On their mission, the apostles would be welcomed into the homes of those to whom they ministered. Having left everything behind (see 6:8-9) and as itinerant apostles (6:10), they would be blessed with hospitality. But there would be times when they would not be so welcomed (6:11). Even so, there was never any question about their ultimate reward. Those who sold whatever they had and gave to the poor would have treasure in heaven *(thesauron en ourano,* 10:21c).

This is the first and only time the term "treasure" is found in Mark's Gospel. Having sold his earthly treasure and inheriting treasure in heaven, the man with many possessions would receive eternal life (10:17). But the term "heaven" is used quite frequently. From the heavens—the plural reflects Semitic influence—the Spirit descends (1:10) and God's voice is heard (1:11). Heaven is God's dwelling, and so Jesus looked up to heaven to bless God at the breaking of the bread (6:41) and at the cure of a deaf person (7:34). As God's dwelling, heaven is associated with the kingdom of God in which one enjoys the fullness of life. Its alternative is Gehenna (see 9:43).

Having sold his possessions, the man would be like a child, entirely dependent on God and ready to accept the kingdom of God (10:15).

Having inherited eternal life, he would then follow Christ into the kingdom of God where the treasure of eternal life awaits him.

The Man Went Away Sad (10:22). It had seemed so simple. Only one thing was lacking. He had to sell his possessions and give to the poor. Jesus loved him, but the love was not for him alone. To follow Christ, he had to extend Jesus' love to the poor. The man's parting reaction contrasts with his enthusiastic arrival. Hearing Jesus' invitation and the conditions for following him, "his face fell" *(stygnasas)*. The verb *stygnazo* evokes a darkened sky and refers to the clouding of the man's features.

Instead of following Christ, the man went away sad *(lypoumenos),* for he had many possessions. Mark withheld that the man was wealthy until the very end of the story. He was not sad because he had many possessions but because he could not bring himself to fulfill the one that was lacking to inherit eternal life.

Jesus' Special Teaching for the Disciples (10:23-31)

Like the story of Jesus and the children (10:13-16), the story of Jesus and the man with many possessions (10:17-22) could easily stand on its own, and in the early tradition it may well have done so. But in Mark's Gospel, it serves as a springboard for further teaching on the subject of wealth, the following of the Christ, and the kingdom of God (10:23-31). This latest teaching, addressed specifically to the disciples, completes Jesus' prophetic message on relationships in the community of the followers (9:30–10:31).

The transition from the story (10:17-22) to the teaching (10:23-31) is effected through Jesus' eye movements. Jesus had fixed his eyes *(emblepsas)* on the man kneeling before him. Once the man left, Jesus looked around *(periblessamenos)* and spoke to his disciples (10:23a). The device reappears in 10:27, when Jesus again fixes his eyes *(emblepsas)* on the disciples, alerting the reader that something very important is about to be imparted.

"How Hard It Is . . ." (10:23b-25). The man was unable to part with his many possessions. With this image still fresh before the disciples, Jesus exclaimed: "How hard it is for those who have wealth to enter the kingdom of God!" (10:23b). The disciples were amazed *(ethambounto),* shocked at Jesus' words (10:24a; see 10:32), and with good reason. In Jewish teaching, wealth and possessions were not a problem or hindrance but a blessing (see Sir 11:21-22). There was no question of having to give up one's possessions to be a good person.

Job, for example, "a blameless and upright man . . . who feared God and avoided evil" (Job 1:1) was blessed by God with enormous wealth (1:10). When the Lord tested Job, taking away his livestock, house, family, and health, Job remained the Lord's faithful servant and his prayer was acceptable to the Lord. And so "the LORD restored the prosperity of Job," doubling what he had before (Job 42:10). Job continued to fear God and avoid evil until he "died, old and full of years" (Job 42:17).

Wealth, of course, could be an obstacle for a miser (Sir 14:3-10), for someone who was inordinately attracted by gold and driven by the pursuit of it (Sir 31:5-7). But it was not an obstacle for those who used it freely and generously, mindful that, like all human beings, they were destined to die (Sir 14:11-19). Gold was a test, but a test one could pass. A rich person who was blameless "has been tested by gold and come off safe, and this remains his glory" (Sir 31:8-10).

But Jesus went far beyond conventional religious wisdom. By ordinary standards, the man who went away sad was a good person, one who observed the commandments. Job was also a good person, blessed with many possessions, and he lived to be "old and full of years." But the man who went away sad had not asked how he could live to be "old and full of years," but how to inherit "eternal life." It was one thing for someone with wealth to be upright and live a long life. It was another for someone with wealth to inherit eternal life and enter the kingdom of God.

Jesus did not say it is hard for those who have wealth to fear God and avoid evil. What he did say was that it is hard for those who have wealth to enter the kingdom of God. Noting the disciples' reaction, Jesus addressed them again, this time more directly: "Children, how hard it is to enter the kingdom of God!" (10:24b). The repetition leaves no doubt that the matter was very important. The kingdom of God makes special demands on those who have wealth and possessions.

Jesus addressed the disciples as "children" *(tekna),*[41] a title which can be understood as an expression of endearment, as a sign of warmth and intimacy. As we have seen (see 10:13-16), ordinarily it refers to the child's relationship to its parents. In this sense, a man in the sixties remains the child *(teknon)* of his parents. The disciples, taught by Jesus, would receive eternal life by following him into the kingdom of God. In relation to eternal life, they were indeed his children.

---

[41] See also 2:5; 7:27; 10:29, 30; 12:19; 13:12.

Parting with one's wealth was not the only condition for entering the kingdom of God. One had also to respond to the needs of the poor. In this, Jesus took up a challenge embedded in Israelite wisdom and brought it a step further.

The prophetic tradition was strong in denouncing those who oppress, afflict, or defraud the poor and in defending the needy against violence, injustice, and degradation (see Amos 2:6-7; 4:1-3; 8:4-14; Hos 12:8; Isa 10:1-2; 11:1-4). But it said little about giving to the poor and alleviating their plight (see Amos 5:11-12). The legal tradition prohibited acts of injustice against the poor (Exod 20:15-17; 22:21-23; 23:6; Deut 15:7-8) and asked generosity in making loans to the poor (Exod 22:24-26; Deut 24:10-15), but it said little about giving to them (see Deut 15:10-11; 26:12).

For giving to the poor, we turn to two texts in the wisdom tradition (Sir 3:29–4:6; Tob 4:7-11, 16). For Sirach, the purpose of giving alms to the poor was to atone for one's sins (see Sir 3:29; 4:3-4). For Tobit, giving alms insured against a possible day of adversity (see Tob 4:7-9). For Tobit, the measure of giving depended on the amount of wealth people had. Those who had great wealth were expected to give more, but everyone had to give, including those who had little (Tob 4:10-11).

Both Sirach and Tobit can be seen in the background of Jesus' teaching, but Tobit stands closest when he speaks of avoiding death by giving alms (Tob 4:10). Jesus took such teaching much further. Giving to the poor was a condition not only for avoiding death. It was a condition for inheriting eternal life in the kingdom of God.

Jesus repeated *(palin)* his exclamation, "How hard it is to enter the kingdom of God!" (10:24b). And he buttressed it with a very striking saying: "It is easier for a camel to pass through [the] eye of [a] needle than for one who is rich to enter the kingdom of God" (10:25).

The saying is extraordinary both as a hyperbole and as a comparison. As a hyperbole, it can be classed with the other hyperbole in this movement (9:30–10:31): "If your hand causes you to sin, cut if off" (9:43); "If your foot causes you to sin, cut it off" (9:45); "And if your eye causes you to sin, pluck it out" (9:47). All of these hyperbole express Jesus' prophetic intention to have the disciples recognize and accept Christian values.

What makes the hyperbole so effective is its graphic image. For those who do not understand a hyperbole, the tendency is to explain it away. Recognizing that wealthy, excellent Christians cannot be excluded from the kingdom, some have suggested that the needle refers to a narrow gate of the city, through which a camel could actually pass, so long as it was not carrying a large burden. Similarly, a wealthy person that was not attached to possessions could enter the kingdom of God. Unfortunately, there is no basis for a gate called "the needle." Such explanations destroy the hyperbole's effectiveness. They also make the subsequent exchange between the disciples and Jesus meaningless.

"Then Who Can Be Saved?" (10:26). If the disciples "were amazed" *(ethambounto)* at Jesus first comment, they "were exceedingly astonished" *(perissos exeplessonto)* on hearing him repeat it with this very graphic and uncompromising saying. Their question, "Then who can be saved?" (10:26) can be paraphrased as follows: "If that is the case, then how can anyone possibly be saved?" The story of Jesus' encounter with the man who went away sad and Jesus' subsequent teaching was intended to bring them precisely to that question.

There had been several references to "saving" and "being saved" in the Gospel. In the first part of the Gospel (1:14–8:21), the verb "save" *(sozo)* appears in Jesus' response to those who objected to his healing on the Sabbath: "Is it lawful to do good on the sabbath rather than do evil, to save life rather than to destroy it?" (3:4). It next appears in Jairus' plea that Jesus come lay hands on his daughter "that she may get well [*sothe,* to be saved] and live" (5:23). "Being saved" is the silent hope of a woman who had been hemorrhaging for seven years (5:28). She touched Jesus' garment (5:29) and Jesus declared, "Daughter, your faith has saved you" (5:34). Finally, it is mentioned in a summary of Jesus' healing activity (6:56).

In all these cases, people were saved from some infirmity or illness, from a debilitating condition that diminished or threatened their life. Ultimately, salvation is from death (see 3:4; 5:35), and it consists in being restored to life. Each of the cases deals with salvation from physical ailments, infirmities, and death and grants physical well-being and life, but they also suggest a broader range of meaning.

For the woman with the hemorrhage, being saved was associated with faith and the gift of peace (5:34). Jairus' daughter is described as "not dead but asleep" (5:39), an expression indicating faith in the resurrection (see 5:41-42; 1 Thess 4:13-16).

In the Gospel's second part (8:22–16:8), the theme of salvation first enters in one of Jesus' sayings on the following of Christ: "For whoever wishes to save [*sosai*] his life will lose it, but whoever loses his life for my sake and that of the gospel will save [*sosei*] it" (8:35). Up to this point, salvation consisted in giving health and life. As in the Old Testament, it dealt with anything that threatened life. Now in 8:35, it is associated with the cross (8:34), losing one's life for the sake of Christ and the gospel. Salvation is no longer seen as a deliverance from physical death or restoration to earthly life.

Death and salvation are now viewed as compatible with one another. Indeed, dying for Christ and the gospel has become a source of salvation. In this sense, salvation looks beyond earthly life and suggests a new kind of life associated with Christ's dying and rising (see 8:31). In the second part of the Gospel, it is no longer a matter of salvation from death but of salvation through death.

What was only suggested in 8:35 becomes explicit in the disciples' question, "Then who can be saved?" (10:26). For the first time in Mark's Gospel, salvation is viewed in terms of eternal life (10:17) and entering the kingdom of God. Salvation is not just from infirmity, illness, and death but from earthly life itself, even for one in good health who fulfills the commandments (10:19-21).

The disciples raised the question at this point because the conditions for eternal life and salvation seemed impossible to meet. Jesus had led them to this point, and he agreed with their astonishing conclusion. For human beings, achieving salvation and eternal life, transcending earthly and temporal existence, are indeed impossible. Those who have wealth cannot fulfill the conditions for entering the kingdom of God, no more than a camel can pass through the eye of a needle (10:25). Nor can any other human being. But what is impossible for human beings is not impossible for God (10:27a).

"All Things Are Possible for God" (10:27). Jesus concludes with a general statement, "All things are possible for God" (10:27b), all things including salvation (10:26) for eternal life (10:17) in the kingdom of God (10:24). In 9:23, Jesus said, "everything is possible to one who has faith." In 10:27b, he states that God ultimately makes things possible for those who have faith.

Salvation, eternal life, and the kingdom of God are the work not of human beings but of God. For many Christians, who view immortality as a natural attribute of beings with a spiritual soul, such a statement may be puzzling. But for the early Christians, who rarely distinguished body and soul and viewed eternal life in terms of resurrection, there was nothing unusual about it. Even in 2 Corinthians 5:1-10, where Paul presupposed the distinction of body and soul, immortality is a pure gift of God "who has given us the Spirit as a first installment" (2 Cor 5:5).

"We Have Given Up Everything and Followed You" (10:28-30). The response came from Peter, the one who had confessed that

Jesus was the Christ (8:29), but did not accept his passion and resurrection (8:32). He had to be recalled to the following of Christ
(8:33). The disciples had accepted Jesus' challenge (10:21; see 8:34).
Unlike the man who had many possessions (10:17-22), but like children (10:13-16), they gave up everything and followed Jesus (1:16-
20; 6:7-13).

With a solemn "Amen" (see 3:28; 8:12; 9:1, 41; 10:15), Jesus then
spells out what they have given up and what all must give up: house,
brothers, sisters, mother, father, children, and lands (10:29). The list
includes everything that comprises wealth (house and lands) and
every family relationship (brothers, sisters, mother, father, and children). The list includes those who provide for people in their infancy
and childhood (mother, father), in their grown-up years (brothers,
sisters), and in their old age (children). The term for children is
tekna (see 10:24), not *paidia* (see 9:36; 10:13-16). It was not required
to give up one's wife because a wife did not provide for her husband.
On the contrary, a disciple had to provide for his wife.

Giving up everything and everyone is not done for its own sake
but for that of Christ and the gospel. The expression "for my sake
and that of the gospel" appeared earlier in 8:35, where losing one's
life to save it was first introduced. In Mark, the identification of the
gospel with Jesus Christ parallels John's identification of the Word
of God with Jesus Christ.

At this point, we expect Jesus to say that those who give up
everything will inherit eternal life, but he adds they will also benefit greatly in this life. We are reminded of Job, but in the case of the
disciples the restoration will be not in kind. In this present age *(en
to kairo touto),* in the decisive time of opportunity, they will receive
a hundred times more: houses (homes) and brothers and sisters and
mothers and children and lands.

The list recalls 3:20-21, 31-35, defining the home, the relatives,
and the mother and brothers and sisters of Jesus as "whoever does
the will of God" (3:35). That extended meaning of brother, sister,
and mother is now applied to the disciples, whose brothers, sisters, mothers, and children are all those who join in the family of
Jesus' followers. Their house or home is wherever the disciples
gather.

Along with houses and relatives, those who give up everything
will also receive persecution *(diogmos)* in this present age *(en to
kairo touto).* Like Jesus, who was persecuted unto death, they will
then receive eternal life in the age to come *(en to aioni to erchomeno).*
The theme of persecution (see 4:17) announces the disciples' future
share in the passion of Jesus (see 10:39) as well as the persecution

that the community would undergo at the hands of family members (13:9-13) who rejected the new Christian household (3:20, 34; 4:11-12).

"But Many That Are First . . ." (10:31). A concluding saying echoes 9:35 and brings this movement (9:30–10:31) to a close. The movement developed what constitutes true greatness in the following of Christ. In the process, it dealt with a broad range of relationships for which the image of a child *(paidion)* provided the needed perspective (see 9:37).

Becoming like a child, the disciples would recognize their own worth and that of others, including those who acted in Christ's name but did not follow with them (9:38-41) and the least of believers, who could so easily be led astray (9:42). Purified, they would have peace with one another (9:49-50). The disciples would also be faithful in marriage, as befits children of the kingdom (10:1-12), in spite of efforts made to prevent them from coming to Jesus (10:13-16), and they would give up their possessions, give to the poor, and follow Christ into the kingdom of God (10:17-30).

But all this would not be for everyone. Many who are first *(protoi)* in this age *(en to kairo touto)* may not seize the opportunity offered them and they would be last *(eschatoi)* in the age to come *(en to aioni to erchomeno)*. Conversely, those who are last *(eschatoi)* in this age will be first *(protoi)* in the age to come (10:31).

This was the second movement (9:30–10:31) in Jesus' healing the blindness of the disciples (see 8:22-26). The story of healing began in 8:27–9:29, where the Gospel anchored discipleship in Jesus Christ and in the passion and resurrection of the Son of Man (8:27-38). It also situated discipleship in history and eschatology (9:1-13) and dealt with the disciples' basic need for faith and prayer (9:14-29).

After the second movement, which dealt with various relationships, we now move to the third movement (10:31-45), which deals with issues affecting leadership in the community, namely, ambition and the exercise of authority. The third movement, in which Jesus completes his teaching concerning the blindness of the disciples, introduces the opening of the eyes of the blind beggar at Jericho. Receiving his sight, he follows Jesus on the way to the passion and resurrection.

The Third Movement:
Implications of the Passion and Resurrection
for Christian Leadership (10:32-45)

First, people brought a blind man to Jesus (8:22). Then, Jesus asked his disciples: "Who do people say that I am?" (8:27). Jesus cured the blind man of his blindness in two stages. In the first stage, his vision remained quite distorted (8:23-24). So was the people's view of Jesus (8:28).

Now the man could see quite clearly, but he was not to speak to anyone in the village (8:25-26). Was there still something lacking to his sight? Did he have the kind of vision needed to follow Jesus "on the way" *(en te hodo)?* Peter announced that Jesus was the Christ, the Messiah, but Jesus forbade him to tell anyone (8:29). Was his view of the Christ deficient in some way?

Peter's hopes for Jesus as the Christ were quite different from those of Jesus, and so were those of the other disciples. Twice, Jesus announced that, as the Son of Man, the Christ would suffer, be put to death, and rise after three days (8:31; 9:31). The first time, Peter rebuked Jesus for speaking in this vein (8:32). The second time, the disciples simply did not grasp what Jesus said. Afraid to ask, they turned instead to discuss who of them was the greatest (9:32-34). Peter's rebuke and the disciples' avoidance of the matter brought a response from Jesus (8:33; 9:35-37) and invited more extensive teaching on the implications of the passion and resurrection for those who followed Christ as the Son of Man "on the way" (8:34–9:29; 9:38–10:31).

With that we have come to the beginning of a new movement (10:32-45). Again Jesus announces that the Son of Man would suffer, die, and rise again, but in much greater detail (10:32-34). Again the disciples react negatively. This time, James and John request positions of honor when Jesus comes into his glory (10:35-37). And again Jesus responds to them (10:38-40), as he did earlier to Peter and the disciples, and goes on to address the other ten on the meaning and exercise of authority for those who followed him "on the way" to Jerusalem (10:41-45).

The entire section (8:22–10:52) concludes with the cure of a blind beggar, as Jesus and the disciples are leaving Jericho for Jerusalem. This time, unlike the introductory cure (8:22-26), Jesus does not forbid him to go into the village. The man, who was once blind and sat "beside the way" *(para ten hodon),* now had the sight needed to follow Jesus "on the way" *(en te hodo)* to Jerusalem (10:46-52).

Jesus' Third Prophetic Announcement (10:32-34)

"They were on the way" (*esan de en te hodo,* 10:32). Earlier, Jesus and his disciples had set out for the villages of Caesarea Philippi (8:27). Then they had gone through Galilee (9:30) and came to Capernaum (9:33). They had even gone into the districts of Judea over by the Jordan (10:1). For the first time, Jesus came to Judea. They were now "going up to Jerusalem" (*anabainontes eis Hierosolyma*) for the first time.[42]

On previous occasions, many came to Jesus from Jerusalem. Some came while he was teaching by the sea and followed him in the hope of being cured (3:7-8, 10). Others came to him at home, charging that he was possessed by Beelzebul and driving out demons by the prince of demons (3:22). Pharisees also came, together with scribes from Jerusalem (7:1), to confront Jesus' disciples on not following "the tradition of the elders" and eating with unclean hands (7:5). Now it was time for Jesus to go up to Jerusalem, together with his disciples, other followers, and the Twelve. They were going for a definitive confrontation with those who had long sought to destroy him (3:6).

As earlier, being "on the way" is an image for following Christ to his passion and resurrection (8:27; 9:33-34). But for the first time, the journey's destination is given. Until now, "the way" has remained quite vague. Now it is very clear. They were going up to Jerusalem, to the city of David and the place of God's dwelling, rich with memory, some joyous and some sorrowful. Jerusalem was about to become the city of Jesus' passion and resurrection.

Jesus Was Going Before Them (10:32). "On the way," Jesus was going before them (*en proagon autous*). He was going before his disciples (10:23), those he had just addressed as children (*tekna,* 10:24) and who gave up everything to follow him (10:28).

"Going before" (*proago*) can refer to "going earlier" (6:45) or "going in front of" (11:9), indicating someone's relative position to others on a journey. But in this case, given the symbol of "the way," it refers to Jesus' personal relationship to his disciples. As his followers, Jesus' disciples came after him (see 1:16-20; 8:34). As their leader, Jesus went before them, showing the way and modeling the life to which he called them (see also 14:28; 16:7).

The disciples were amazed (*kai ethambounto*), awestruck, as they were when Jesus told them "how hard it is for those who have wealth to enter the kingdom of God" (10:23). On that occasion, they

---

[42] Since Jerusalem was built on a set of hills high in the mountains of Judea, one always went up (*anabaino*), never down (*katabaino*) to Jerusalem.

were taken aback by his words (10:24). The verb *thambeomai* appears one other time in the New Testament, also in Mark, when all in the synagogue were amazed *(ethambethesan)* at Jesus' new teaching with authority (1:23-27). On the way going up to Jerusalem, the disciples were now in a state of amazement, the cumulative effect of Jesus' teaching concerning the way to his passion and resurrection and their implications for the life of the followers (8:27–10:31).

They had learned from Jesus of the passion and resurrection (8:31; 9:31), and they were quite disturbed. After the first announcement, Peter rebuked Jesus (8:32), and after the second, the disciples who did not understand were too afraid *(ephobounto)* to ask about it (9:32). Even so, Jesus had gone to great lengths to map "the way" and make clear what it meant to follow him (8:33–9:29; 9:33–10:31). Now Jesus was leading them to Jerusalem. Many had come from Jerusalem to be healed by him (3:8), but many others had come to denounce him as possessed and demonic (3:22). There was reason for the disciples' amazement.

The disciples were amazed, while "those who followed were afraid" *(hoi de akolouthountos ophobounto)*. The distinction Mark draws between the disciples and those who followed may appear somewhat strange, since the first disciples were also the first followers (1:16-20). Ordinarily, Mark does not distinguish between the disciples of Jesus and those following him, but early on, in the story of Levi (2:13-17), he did provide the grounds for the distinction.

The story of the call of Levi (2:13-14) follows the pattern set in the call of Simon and Andrew (1:16-18, 19-20). Invited to follow Jesus, Levi was associated with the first disciples, even though he would not be included among the Twelve (3:13-19). After Levi's call, there is a dinner at which many *(polloi)* tax collectors and sinners joined Jesus and the disciples (2:15-17). Mark emphasizes that many tax collectors and sinners *(esan gar polloi)* were following Jesus *(kai ekolouthoun auto)*. At this point in the Gospel, only a few had been called. Referring to the followers, Mark anticipates a later time when there would be great crowds following Jesus from Galilee, Judea, Jerusalem, as well as from Idumea, Transjordan, the region of Tyre, and Sidon (3:7-8). Mark distinguished the crowds of followers from the disciples who were asked to prepare a boat because of the large crowds of followers (3:9).

The disciples were followers (see 6:1; 10:23, 28), but there were other followers who were not called disciples (8:34; 10:21). The disciples represented a special group of followers with roots in the days of Jesus' first Galilean ministry. The other followers, that is, those who were afraid, included those who joined the disciples in Jesus' second Galilean ministry (see 14:28; 16:7). Among these were the members of the communities addressed by Mark's Gospel.

In 10:32, Mark thus distinguishes the early follower-disciples from the large crowd of followers who come later. The follower-disciples were amazed as they accompanied Jesus on the ascent to Jerusalem. But the large crowd of followers were afraid as they too followed Christ to the passion and resurrection.

The same distinction between the follower-disciples and the later followers reappears at the arrest of Jesus when the disciples (14:32) all abandoned him and fled (*kai aphentes auton ephygon pantes,* 14:50), but a certain young man was following him (*kai neaniskos synekolouthei auto,* 14:51). The compound verb *synekolouthei* (following with) may indicate that the young man was with Jesus' following, but it may also suggest that he was following with those others for whom the original journey had become a paradigm for Christian living.

The Passion and Resurrection of the Son of Man (10:33-34). The first prophetic announcement of the passion (8:31) was given to the disciples (8:17, 33), including Peter (8:29) who rejected the announcement and rebuked Jesus for making it (8:32). Its direct implications regarding the following of Christ were then addressed to the crowd whom Jesus summoned with his disciples (8:34–9:1). The second announcement (9:31) was again given to the disciples, who could not understand and were too frightened to ask about it (9:32). Its first implications were spelled out at home as special teaching for the Twelve (9:35-50).

Unlike the two earlier announcements, the third was not addressed to the disciples in general but to the Twelve *(tous dodeka),* whom Jesus took aside again *(palin),* as he had done for Peter, James, and John at the transfiguration (9:2). The previous time Jesus took aside the Twelve he spoke to them concerning relationships in the community, on true greatness, on attitudes toward those who invoked his name but were not following with them, and on the seriousness of scandalizing the little ones who believed (9:35-50). The time before that he sent the Twelve on mission (6:7-13). And the time before that he established them as the Twelve "that they might be with him and he might send them forth to preach and to have authority to drive out demons" (3:14-15; see 3:13-19).

This time, he called them aside to begin telling them "what was about to happen to him" *(ta mellonta auto symbainein).* What Jesus now had to say referred to the things that were about *(ta mellonta)* to happen. They already knew something of what it would mean to "be with him" (*hina osin met' autou*, 3:14). But on the way, going up to Jerusalem, Jesus would reveal a lot more.

But even this was only the beginning. The introductory expression, "he began to tell them" *(erxato autois legein)*, which Mark frequently uses, especially in summaries, implies a continuation. That continuation would come shortly, in Jerusalem, but even later in the life of the Church, when they would meet persecution (see 10:30; 13:9-13), and Jesus would continue to address them through the Gospel (1:1).

Going Up to Jerusalem. As in 8:31 and 9:31, the Greek particle *hoti,* an ancient equivalent for today's quotation marks, presents Jesus' announcement as a direct quotation: "Behold, we are going up to Jerusalem" (10:33).[43] We have just heard the same statement, but it was while standing with the narrator contemplating Jesus and the others from a distance. We now hear it again from Jesus as he announces it to the Twelve. Jesus' introductory "behold" *(idou)* invites us to stand with the Twelve, to view the assent to Jerusalem through their eyes and listen to the announcement with their ears.

"We are going up [*anabainomen*] to Jerusalem." The first person plural includes the Twelve in a journey that is consciously decided upon and deliberately undertaken. This is not merely the journey of Jesus. It is the journey of Jesus and the Twelve, those whom have been established to be with him even as he goes to his passion and resurrection.

Having focused the attention of the Twelve on their journey to Jerusalem, Jesus proceeds with a solemn announcement: "The Son of Man will be handed over" *(paradothesetai).* The announcement is very explicit on what is about to happen. As in 8:31 and 9:31, Jesus refers to himself as the Son of Man, the human being who "has authority to forgive sins on earth" (2:10) and "is lord even of the sabbath" (2:28), but is also subject to suffering and death. Like the suffering servant of the Lord (see Isa 52:12–53:13) and John the Baptist before him, the Son of Man will be handed over by God to humiliation, suffering, and even death, the most radical human limitation.

In the first announcement Jesus said that the Son of Man had to suffer, be rejected by the elders, the chief priests, and the scribes, and be killed (8:31). In the second, he said that the Son of Man is to

[43] For the theological significance of Jerusalem, see Alois Stoger, "Jerusalem," in *Encyclopedia of Biblical Theology, The Complete Sacramentum Verbi,* edited by Johannes B. Bauer (New York: Crossroad, 1981) 409–19; Philip J. King, "Jerusalem," *The Anchor Bible Dictionary,* op. cit., 3:764–65.

be handed over to men who will kill him (9:31). The third presents the passion in two phases. First, it describes the role of the chief priest and the scribes, "who will condemn him to death and hand him over to the Gentiles." Second, it describes the role of the Gentiles, "who will mock him, spit upon him, scourge him, and put him to death." The chief priests and the scribes would condemn him to death, and the Gentiles would actually put him to death.

Until now, Jesus' enemies consisted mainly of the Pharisees (3:6; 7:1; 8:11, 15), whose sphere of influence centered on the synagogue, and the scribes associated with them (3:22; 7:1). In Jerusalem, the role of the Pharisees would be taken over by the chief priests, whose sphere of influence revolved around the Temple, the scribes and the elders associated with them.

The role of the chief priests and the scribes begins to evoke the succession of events in the passion story. First, they would condemn Jesus to death *(katakrinousin),* and then they would hand him over *(paradosousin)* to the Gentiles. The account of Jesus' condemnation is told in 14:53-65, and the account of Jesus' being handed over to the Gentiles is told in 15:1-15a.[44]

After Jesus was handed over to the Gentiles, they would "mock him, spit upon him, scourge him, and put him to death" (10:34). As with the two actions of the chief priests and the scribes, the four actions of the Gentiles refer to the passion account (see 15:15b-20). Writing the announcement, Mark presented his readers with an interpretive summary of the events told in the passion story.

Jesus' announcement began on a positive note. Being handed over (10:33a) was a saving event, notwithstanding the human betrayal, mockery, and torture through which it came about (10:33b-34a). It also ended on a positive note: "but after three days he will rise" (10:34b; see 8:31; 9:31). The expression "after three days" was a departure from tradition.[45] There is ample precedent for situating Jesus' resurrection "on the third day,"[46] but there is no such precedent for Jesus' resurrection "after three days."

---

[44] Used in the active voice, the verb *paradidomi* is a historical term, describing human agency in Jesus' betrayal and death. Used in the passive, as earlier in 10:32, *paradidomi* is a theological term, evoking divine agency in Jesus' death.

[45] Early tradition referred to Jesus' resurrection as "on the third day" (see 1 Cor 15:4), not "after three days." Later, Matthew and Luke would abandon Mark's wording in favor of the traditional expression (Matt 16:21; 17:22; 20:19; Luke 9:22; 18:33).

[46] See the *Midrash Rabbah* on the deliverance of Isaac (see Gen 22:3). Commenting on Isaac's deliverance, *Midrash Rabbah* refers to the theo-

The reason for the departure from tradition may lie in the very wording of the expressions. "On the third day" *(he trite hemera)* highlights that particular day, associates it with salvation, and gives it symbolic significance. "After three days" *(meta treis hemeras)* underlines the length of time elapsed between the first and the third day.

The expression, "after three days," may have been inspired by the reference to Jesus rebuilding the Temple "in three days" *(dia trion hemeron,* 14:58). In relation to the rebuilding of the Temple, three days was a very short time. For people experiencing the passion, three days was a very long time. With the expression, "after three days," Mark may have intended to encourage the communities. Jesus did not rise immediately, but only after three days. Likewise, their persecution would not end immediately. It surely would end, but while it lasted, they needed to persevere.

Like the temporal expression, "after three days," the verb for the resurrection of Jesus *(anistemi)* is not the one used in the early tradition *(egeiro,* see 1 Cor 15:4).[47] As with the expression, "after three days," Mark's intention (see also 8:31; 9:31) may have been pastoral. There are places where Mark uses the verb *egeiro* to indicate when Jesus raises someone from death (12:26) or illness (1:31; 2:9, 11, 12; 9:27; 10:49) or when someone is raised up (6:14, 16; 12:26; 14:28; 16:6). In Jesus' announcements, using *anistemi* (to rise) may have been influenced by the early Christian vocabulary presenting death in terms of sleep. *Anistemi* is the ordinary verb to describe rising from sleep.

In 1 Thessalonians 4:14, we read: "For if we believe that Jesus died and rose [*aneste*], so too will God, through Jesus, bring with him those who have fallen asleep [*tous koimethentes*]. In the following verses, we read that those who have fallen asleep, that is, those who are dead in Christ, will rise *(anestesontai)* first (1 Thess 4:15-16). The same terms appear in an early Christian hymn: "Awake, O sleeper [*ho katheudon*], / and arise [*anasta*] from the dead" (Eph 5:14).

Mark is very well aware of this early Christian usage. In the story of the raising of Jairus' daughter, Jesus declares that "the child is not dead [*ouk apethanen*] but asleep" *(alla katheudei,* 5:39). Jesus commands her to rise *(egeire,* 5:41), and she "arose [*aneste*] immediately and walked around" (5:42).

phany in Exodus 19:1, to Hosea's prophetic announcement that God would raise up his people "on the third day" (Matt 6:2; LXX 6:3), and several other events in which the Lord saved his people. See Pierre Grelot, *The Resurrection and Modern Biblical Thought,* ed. Paul DeSurgy, tr. Charles Underhill Quinn (New York: Corpus Books, 1996) 18–19, 24–25.

[47] Save for Luke 18:33, Matthew and Luke abandoned Mark's wording in favor of the traditional verb (see Matt 16:21; 17:22; 20:19; Luke 9:22).

To refer to Jesus' resurrection after three days, Mark chose terms associated with the rising of those who have fallen asleep and were dead in Christ. Early baptismal catechesis would constitute a likely context for those terms. Drawing on their baptismal catechesis surely would have strengthened those who risked death during a time of persecution.

The Request of James and John (10:35-37)

When Jesus spoke of the passion and resurrection of the Son of Man, he emphasized the passion (10:33-34), as he did on previous occasions (8:31; 9:31), but never with such solemnity or in such detail. The disciples heard Jesus' message on the resurrection, but seem to have heard nothing else. Ignoring everything Jesus said about the passion, James and John asked to join him in glory: "Grant that in your glory we may sit one at your right and the other at your left" (10:37).

After the first prophetic announcement (8:31), Peter rebuked Jesus (8:32). After the second (9:31), the disciples did not understand and were too afraid to ask. Instead, they argued about which of them was the greatest (9:32-34). After Jesus' third announcement, James and John seized on Jesus' reference to the resurrection and on the glory that it could mean for them. No one, not Peter, not the disciples, and not James and John, was able to face and accept the passion.

James and John were among the first disciples (1:19-20). Like Peter, they had been fishermen and were following Jesus as "fishers of human beings" (cf. 1:16-18). They had accompanied Jesus to the home of Simon and Andrew where Jesus raised Simon's mother-in-law from a fever to a life of ministry (1:29-31). They were also included among the Twelve and named right after Simon Peter, even before Simon's brother Andrew (3:13-19).

With Peter, James and John had experienced the transfiguration (9:2-8). When Jesus told them not to speak of it until "the Son of Man had risen from the dead," they questioned "what rising from the dead meant" (9:9-10). Even now, as they asked Jesus for a special place with him in glory, they had no idea what resurrection meant. Sometime after the transfiguration, John sought Jesus' approval after trying to prevent someone who was not following them from driving out demons in Jesus' name (9:38).

Besides Peter, James and John were the two most significant disciples following Jesus and among the community of the Twelve. The Gospel treats them accordingly. Together with Peter, they raised the most basic issues regarding the following of Christ and were the vehicle for Jesus' most challenging teaching.

James and John came to Jesus with a very bold request: "Teacher, we want you to do for us whatever we ask of you" (10:35). No one had ever approached Jesus with a similar request. Jairus came to Jesus pleading that he would cure his daughter (5:23). A woman with a hemorrhage, hoping to touch Jesus' clothing, did not even dare to utter her request (5:28). A Syrophoenician woman begged Jesus to drive a demon from her daughter (7:26). Others begged Jesus to lay his hand on a deaf man (7:32). The disciples, including James and John, came to Jesus seeking information or an explanation (9:11, 29; 10:17).

In every other case, people approached Jesus modestly as one did a respected teacher. No one had ever demanded anything of Jesus, let alone without indicating what was being demanded. Testing the limits of what Jesus was willing to do for them, James and John demanded Jesus give them whatever they would ask.

Jesus answered with a question: "What do you wish me to do for you?" (10:36). He would address the same question to Bartimaeus, the blind beggar of Jericho (10:51). Unlike James and John, however, Bartimaeus approached Jesus very humbly, appealing to his generosity: "Jesus, Son of David, have pity on me" (10:47-48). Bartimaeus asked Jesus to be merciful to him. James and John tried to get from Jesus what they wanted.

Jesus' Response (10:38-40)

In the first part of the Gospel (1:14–8:21), one of the major symbols was the bread *(artos).* In this second part (8:22–16:8), the bread is not mentioned except in the liturgical formula cited at the Last Supper (14:22). The corresponding symbol is the cup *(poterion).* The first reference to the cup is here in Jesus' response to James and John: "Can you drink the cup that I drink?" (10:38b).

The symbol of the cup has a rich background in the Old Testament. The cup that overflows expresses rejoicing and communion with God (see Ps 23:5). The cup is also a symbol for someone's lot, as in Psalm 11:6, where it refers to God's wrath and divine judgment on the wicked: "[He] rains upon the wicked / fiery coals and brimstone, / a scorching wind their allotted cup." Closely related is the cup one drinks to the dregs (see Ps 75:9). A person's lot may also consist in salvation. In this case, we have the cup of salvation: "I will raise the cup of salvation / and call on the name of the LORD" (Ps 116:13).

Jesus asked James and John if they could drink the cup that he drinks? Could they drink the cup of his suffering and death (see 10:33-34), giving "his life as a ransom for many" (10:45). In other words, could they drink the cup of Jesus' passion? In Mark's context, the symbol of the cup is drawn from the liturgical text for the Lord's Supper (14:23-25), but Jesus was referring not so much to the liturgical celebration as to the celebration's relationship to the passion.

The cup of Jesus' passion is in fact the cup of salvation. Jesus was asking the two disciples if they were able to join him in the work of salvation, not their own salvation but that of others. Jesus was applying to them a saying that he had given to the crowd with the disciples: "For whoever wishes to save his life will lose it, but whoever lose his life for my sake and that of the gospel will save it" (8:35). Asking them if they could drink the cup was asking them if they were able to lose their lives for Jesus' sake and that of the Gospel.

The image of the cup is immediately related to that of baptism (*baptisma,* 10:38c), which also refers to the passion. Being baptized with the baptism with which Jesus is baptized means suffering the passion that Jesus suffers. To appreciate the image, we need to think of baptism not so much as cleansing or purification, but as dying with Christ and being buried with him to live with one and one day rise with one (see Rom 6:3-4). Such is the theology of baptism that underlies the baptismal creed in 1 Corinthians 15:3b-5:

> that Christ died for our sins in accordance with the scriptures; that he was buried; that he was raised on the third day in accordance with the scriptures; that he appeared to Cephas, then to the Twelve.

Like the cup, the baptism refers not so much to the liturgical event as to its relationship with the passion. Until now, the term baptism *(baptisma)* was used only in relation to the mission and ministry of John the Baptist (1:4). The same is true for the verb baptize *(baptizo,* 1:4, 5, 8, 9; see also 6:14, 24), except for two references. The verb, to baptize, is applied to the rites of water purification practiced by the Pharisees and other Jews (7:4). John the Baptist also contrasted Jesus' baptism with his own: "I have baptized you with water; he will baptize you with the holy Spirit" (1:8).

Except for John's reference to Jesus baptizing with the holy Spirit, the Gospel emphasizes Jesus' baptism by John and by God. Jesus was baptized by John, but as he came up from the water, the Spirit came down upon him and a heavenly voice declared that he was God's beloved Son (1:10-11). Such is also the case when Jesus asked James and John, "Can you . . . be baptized with the baptism with which I am baptized?" The question refers to the event in which Jesus was baptized. It does not refer to Jesus' baptizing mission. For Mark, John was the Baptist, and Jesus was the Baptized.

What it meant for Jesus to be baptized was fully revealed in the passion. Jesus asked James and John if they could go with him to the passion. They were already on the way, but they tried to avoid what Jesus had outlined in detail (10:33-34).

Astonishingly, James and John responded that they could drink the cup Jesus drank and be baptized in the baptism with which he was baptized. When Jesus asked if they could, he also said that they did not know what they were asking (10:38a). Now, in saying that they could, they did not know what they were promising (10:39a).

Still, the cup Jesus drank they would drink, and the baptism with which Jesus was baptized they would indeed be baptized. Such was Jesus' response to them (10:39bc) as he drew their attention away from the quest for glory and redirected it to the passion. There would be no glory without the passion.

Concluding, Jesus returned to their original request and told them that sitting at his right or his left is not for him to give "but is for those for whom it has been prepared" (10:40). Jesus was speaking as the Son of Man. As such he was always open to the will of God. This was wonderfully expressed in Jesus' prayer at Gethsemane: "Abba, Father, all things are possible to you. Take this cup away from me, but not what I will but what you will" (14:36). Jesus was asking James and John to have the openness regarding the Father's will. It is the Father who would raise Jesus from the dead (14:28; 16:6). It is also the Father who would grant places in glory.

Jesus' Message to the Ten (10:41-45)

When James and John, two of the Twelve, asked Jesus for special places in glory, the ten others heard them and became indignant because James and John wanted to be above the rest in glory. As readers, we are tempted to join them in their indignation. It is as though James and John did not hear Jesus' message to the Twelve about wanting to be the greatest (9:33-37). In order to be the first of all, they had to become the last of all and the servant *(diakonos)* of all (9:35).

Like other emotions, indignation can be blind, masking ambitions not unlike those of James and John. After speaking to James and John, Jesus responded to the Ten with a mini-discourse (10:41-45). They needed to learn what it meant to be the servant of all (9:35). The discourse sums up Jesus' entire teaching on following him on the way to the passion and resurrection. Jesus' followers must not only be the servants *(diakonoi)* of all but the slaves *(douloi)* of Christ. Like Jesus, the Son of Man, they must be ready to give their lives "as a ransom for many."

Noting the indignation of the Ten, Jesus called them over. As leaders and men with authority, they had to avoid behaving like the Gentiles. They should be looking to Jesus, the Son of Man, as their exemplar. The Ten knew how those who are regarded as rulers among the Gentiles *(hoi dokountes archein)* lord it over *(katekyrieuousin)* and how their great ones *(hoi megaloi)* bear down on the others and make their authority felt *(katechousiazousin,* 10:42). It must not be like that with the Twelve (10:43a).

The reference to "those regarded as rulers" is ironic, recalling Paul's reference to James, Kephas, and John as "those of repute" *(tois dokousin),* "those reputed to be important" *(ton kikounton einai ti),* and "those reputed to be the pillars" *(hoi dikountes styloi,* Gal 2:10). But Paul's irony had to do with those who appealed to the importance of James, Kephas, and John to undermine Paul's authority. It did not have to do with the actual importance of the three apostles.

In Mark, the irony lay in the fact that those regarded as the rulers among the Gentiles were actually not very important. Being a genuine leader or ruler does not depend on those who regard them as such. As truly great, they do not need to bear down on others and make their authority felt. Their authority is recognized as the people in the synagogue at Capernaum recognized Jesus' authority (1:21-28).

At the beginning of the discourse, Jesus distinguishes "the Ten" from "those who are recognized as ruler over the Gentiles." The distinction bears directly on the expected attitudes and behavior of the Twelve, but it also seems to imply that the Church was not a Gentile community. The distinction appears inconsistent with the many passages pointing to a Gentile community and setting. The inconsistency is only apparent.

In Jesus' life, membership in the community was exclusively Jewish. A few years after Jesus' death and resurrection, the community spread to Gentile centers such as Caesarea Maritima and Antioch on the Orontes and many Gentiles were converted. As a minority, the Gentile members adopted many Jewish traditions and practices. In some communities, Gentiles eventually became the majority. By the time of Mark, the communities that were predominantly Gentile had moved far away from their Jewish origins, and even the ordinary Jewish customs had to be explained (see 7:3-4).

The contrast between "the Ten" and "those who were recognized as rulers over the Gentiles" shows that the followers of Gentile ori-

gin did not think of themselves as Gentiles. We see a similar phenomenon in John's Gospel, where Jesus' disciples are distinguished
from "the Jews." In this we sense the emergence of a new reality, a
tertium quid, comprising those who are of Christ (*Christou,* 9:41).
In Pauline terms, those who are of Christ are neither Jews nor Gentile (see Gal 3:26-28; Col 3:11). From their baptism, they have a distinct identity.

Among the Ten and in the community of the Twelve, anyone who
wished to be great *(megas)* had to be the servant *(diakonos)* of all
(10:43b), and anyone who wished to be first *(protos)* had to be the
slave *(doulos)* of all (10:44). The contrast with the Gentile world
could hardly be greater.

Jesus had already spoken to the Twelve of being first and what it
meant (9:35). In doing so, he compared himself to a child, to one who
clearly was the last (9:36-37). Becoming first by being a servant represented a striking reversal of values. Jesus made that reversal
even more dramatic. He challenged the Ten to become the slaves
(douloi) of all.

Servant and Slave.[48] There is a big difference between a servant
and a slave. A servant *(diakonos)* is someone hired for a set of tasks
and compensated according to the terms agreed upon. A slave *(doulos)* is not hired but owned by someone who may or may not com-
pensate the slave. In the Greco-Roman world, it was not uncommon
for a slave to be compensated for the service rendered, but this had
nothing to do with an agreement. It was entirely up to the owner's
discretion.

The basic difference between a servant and a slave is a matter of
freedom. A servant is a free person who has chosen to work as a servant and could opt for another form of work. Servants are also free
to choose the household in which they will work, and they can
transfer to another household should conditions be unsatisfactory.
By the same token, servants whose work is deemed unsatisfactory
can be dismissed.

---

[48] For the institution of slavery in the Ancient Near East and in the Old
and New Testaments, see Muhammad A. Dandamayev, "Slavery," *The An-
chor Bible Dictionary,* 6:58-65, and S. Scott Bartchy, ibid., 65–73; in Jewish
life, see Joachim Jeremias, *Jerusalem in the Time of Jesus* (Philadelphia:
Fortress Press, 1969) 110–11, 312–16, 334–37, 345–51; Dale B. Martin,
Slavery as Salvation, The Metaphor of Slavery in Pauline Christianity
(New Haven: Yale University Press, 1990); and Carolyn Osiek and David L.
Balch, *Families in the New Testament World* (Louisville: Westminster John
Knox Press, 1997) 174–92.

A slave, on the contrary, is not a free person and has no choice about being a slave or about his or her owner. Before the age of Augustus and the *Pax Romana,* one became a slave by being captured in war. With Augustus and in the years following, one became a slave by being born of a female slave, being kidnapped, and by incurring an overwhelming debt (see Matt 18:24-25). An abandoned child could have been given slave status in a home. For a foundling, the condition of slave could make the difference between life and death. Unlike a servant, a slave could not transfer to another household, and instead of being dismissed, a slave could be sold.

A slave's work may have been identical to that of a servant and of greater dignity than the work of many a slave owners. A slave might even be better treated than a servant. Still, it is hard to imagine a servant choosing to be a slave for the sake of more important work or better living conditions. There was something inherently onerous about being a slave.

Mark's readers knew about servants and slaves firsthand. In the Roman Empire of the first century, it was not unusual for people to have servants. Even those of fairly modest means could ordinarily afford to hire a servant. Some of Mark's readers may even have been slave owners, and others may have been slaves. It is estimated that one out of five people in the Roman Empire was a slave. In large, prosperous cities, the ratio was even higher. The population of Rome itself included approximately one slave for every three people.

Jesus' discourse began the mini-discourse with two parallel statements about how among the Gentiles those who are regarded as rulers lord it over them, and their great ones make their authority felt (10:42). Jesus told the Ten that it could not be so among them (10:43a). Jesus continued with two other parallel statements on how it must be among them: "Whoever wishes to be great [*megas*] among you will be your servant; whoever wishes to be first among you will be the slave of all" (10:43b-44).

The parallelism points to a similarity between a servant and a slave. It also calls attention to the difference between them. The saying concerning the servant recalls an earlier saying: "If anyone wishes to be first, he shall be the last of all and the servant of all" (9:35). In that saying, "all" refers to the Twelve, not to the whole human race. The same is true in 10:43b, where Jesus refers to the Ten with the pronoun "you" and "your."

Being "your servant" refers to the internal relationships and attitudes within the community of the Twelve. Unlike those who rule among the Gentiles, whoever wishes to be great among the Twelve will be the servant of all. Being servant in the Christian sense is not the same as being an ordinary servant. It has nothing to do with choosing an employer, being hired, quitting, or being fired. Christians, particularly Christians in authority, are asked to think of themselves as the servants of the others in their service *(diakonia)* of the Gospel. Being a slave in the Christian sense is far more radical than being a Christian servant. It speaks of someone's life condition. The fact that such a condition was freely chosen also distinguished a Christian slave from an ordinary slave. The Christian is asked to adopt the condition of a slave not just in relation to other Christians but vis-à-vis the entire human community. It means denying oneself (see 8:34), giving up all personal claim on oneself, and allowing oneself to be claimed by Christ and all those who were called to be of Christ *(Christou,* 9:41). It meant being claimed by the mission of Christ in view of the Gospel and the kingdom of God.

The Mission of the Son of Man (10:45). As servant and slave, the Christian is a follower of Jesus Christ, the Son of Man, who was both a servant and a slave: "For the Son of Man did not come to be served but to serve and to give his life as a ransom for the many" (10:45).

Being a servant *(diakonos)* and serving *(diakoneo)* describes Jesus' relationship to the Twelve and the community of followers. It corresponds to the pastoral nature and function of the Church. Being a slave *(doulos)* describes Jesus' relationship to God, to the kingdom of God. The kingdom of God has to be as universal as creation. Being a slave thus corresponds to the apostolic or missionary nature of the Church.

In the passion, Jesus fulfills his mission as a slave. To express this, Mark evokes a passage from one of the great Isaian songs of the suffering servant:

> Because of his affliction
>   he shall see the light in fullness of days;
> Through his suffering, my servant shall justify many
>   [*douleuonta pollois*],
>   and their guilt he shall bear.
> Therefore I will give him his portion among the great,
>   and he shall divide the spoils with the mighty,
> Because he surrendered himself to death
>   and was counted among the wicked;
> And he shall take away the sins of many,
>   and win pardon for their offenses (Isa 53:11-12).

In the expression "a ransom for many," "many" is a correlative for the one servant and slave. The sufferings of the one slave are redemptive for the sins of the many, that is, for the sins of all. Jesus' passion fulfills his mission and provides a basis for the universal mission of the Church. As followers of Christ, the *doulos,* the Church offers its life "as a ransom for many."

Jesus Heals a Blind Beggar (10:46-52)

The fourth section of the Gospel now concludes with a story in which Jesus heals a blind beggar at Jericho (10:46-52), framing the whole section (8:22–10:52). The section was introduced by a story in which Jesus healed a blind man at Bethsaida (8:22-26).

The section provides a christological basis for Christian ethics, grounded in the passion and resurrection, sacramentally expressed in baptism and the Eucharist, and informed by Christ's prophetic teaching. Divided in three movements (8:31–9:29; 9:30–10:31; 10:32-45), it shows how every aspect of Christian life flows from solidarity with Christ.[49]

Introducing the section, the first healing story (8:22-26) was followed by a story on the identity of Jesus (8:27-30). The concluding story (10:46-52) includes the theme of Jesus' identity, introducing the next section. The sight Jesus gives is the sight of faith, seeing Jesus as he really is, knowing him as the Christ, and accepting the implications of following him on the way to the passion and resurrection. The body of the section (8:31–10:45) shows how Peter, the disciples in general, and James and John were blind, and how Jesus healed their blindness little by little as he taught them.

The concluding story (Mark 10:46-52) is about a blind man named Bartimaeus sitting beside the road, begging as Jesus was leaving Jericho with his disciples and a sizable crowd (10:46). Jesus and his disciples were on the way to Jerusalem (see 10:32). Hearing that it was Jesus of Nazareth, he cried out to him, "Jesus, Son of David [*Huie David Iesou*], have mercy on me" (10:47).

The story tells how Bartimaeus reached out to Jesus in spite of those who were surrounding him. Coming up to Jesus, he threw off his cloak, and with his sight restored followed him on the way to Jerusalem (10:48-52). It is the story of a blind beggar who put off his former self. It is a very baptismal story.

---

[49] In his theology, Paul related every aspect of Christian life to Christ as "belong(ing) to Christ" (*Christou,* literally "of Christ," Gal 3:29), being "with Christ" (*syn Christo,* Rom 6:8), and being "in Christ" (*en Christo,* Rom 6:11). All three are related to Christian baptism.

The stories in which Jesus heals the blind should be read in light of each other. The story of the blind man of Bethsaida (8:22-26) is rich in liturgical drama. Jesus led a blind man by the hand outside the village, separating him from his former life and relationships. He then put spittle on the blind man's eyes, imposed hands on him, and in two stages restored his sight. After the first stage, Jesus asked, "Do you see anything?" After the second, he ordered, "Do not even go into the village." With his eyes opened, there was no returning to his former life. Instead, Jesus sent him home.

The story of the blind beggar of Jericho (10:46-52) is rich in liturgical drama. Like the story of Bethsaida (8:22-26), that of Jericho is primarily an action story. It was not a word story, unlike most of the stories in 8:27–10:45. In a word story, Jesus' teaching carries the story. In an action story, the story carries Jesus' teaching.

The story of Bartimaeus has a brief introduction, presenting the setting and the personages (10:46). The body is told in two parts, like a drama in two acts. The first part tells how Jesus called Bartimaeus. It emphasizes Bartimaeus' distance from Jesus and shows how he overcame it (10:47-49). The second part tells how Bartimaeus responded. It shows the transformation that took place in Bartimaeus and how it changed the course of his life (10:50-52).

They Came to Jericho (10:46)

On their way to Jerusalem (see 10:32-34), Jesus and the disciples came to Jericho (10:46a). This is the first and only time that Jericho is mentioned in the Gospel, but it needed no introduction.[50] In Jesus' day, Jericho was a splendid oasis city built in Roman style with fine palaces, gardens, pools, baths, a theater-hippodrome complex, and other public buildings that were part of a Roman city. The city had been rebuilt over a number of years by Herod the Great and further embellished by his son Archelaus, both of whom appreciated things Roman.

Herodian Jericho stood on a plain just south of the great earth mound covering the ruins of biblical and pre-biblical Jericho. In Mark's time, Vespasian made Jericho a staging point for the Roman campaign against Judea, as Joshua had done with biblical Jericho many centuries earlier.

When Mark says that Jesus and his disciples came to Jericho, he means the Herodian city, today often referred to as New Testament

---

[50] For the history and the archeology of the pre-biblical Jericho, Old Testament Jericho, and Herodian Jericho, see T. A. Holland and Ehud Netzer, "Jericho," *The Anchor Bible Dictionary,* 3:723–40.

122 The Beginning of the Gospel

Jericho. But in the first-century Christian imagination there was no separating New Testament Jericho from the Old Testament city associated with Joshua and the liturgical seige that collapsed its mighty wall.

As Jesus was leaving Jericho with his disciples and a large crowd, the son of Timaeus, named Bartimaeus, was sitting by the roadside. It was the right place for a beggar to be. Jericho was an agricultural center and a winter resort for Jerusalem's aristocracy. It was also a crossroad for people traveling east-west and north-south. There was always lots of movement in and out of Jericho, especially on the Jerusalem-Jericho road.

Bartimaeus was not "on the way" *(en te hodo)* with Jesus and the disciples, but "by the roadside" *(para ten hodon)* where he sat begging. Mark uses the Greek expression *en te hodo* throughout 8:22–10:52 as an image for Christ's journey to his passion-resurrection and for the following of Christ.

Bartimaeus was blind. Perhaps he was like so many other blind people who gathered in busy places to beg. Perhaps he was like those who had eyes to see, but could not see. Perhaps he was both, but whether Bartimaeus was blind physically or spiritually was not Mark's concern. From a literary point of view, Bartimaeus' blindness is symbolic of the blindness of all who have not had their eyes opened in faith by Christ.

Mark introduced Bartimaeus as "the son of Timaeus" rather than by his personal name, adding the name afterwards and indicating he was blind. The usual way to introduce someone is to give the name first, as when Mark introduced James, the son of Zebedee (1:19). It may be that Timaeus was better known or more prominent than his son, but Mark tells us nothing else about him.

It may also be that the designation, "son of Timaeus," was meant to parallel the messianic title, "Son of David," which Bartimaeus uses when crying out to Jesus (10:47-48). In this case, "the son of Timaeus" would highlight Bartimaeus unimportance, in contrast with the great importance of Jesus. Bartimaeus was the son of an unknown father with a Greek name. Jesus was the son of King David!

Jesus Calls Bartimaeus (10:47-49)

In the body of the story, the first part tells how Bartimaeus cried out to Jesus (10:47-48) and how Jesus summoned him (10:49). We are not told how Bartimaeus learned Jesus was passing by. But the story implies that Bartimaeus knew that Jesus, the Messiah *(ho Christos),* the Son of David, was now on the way to Jerusalem.

Bartimaeus' Cry (10:47-48). Some translations[51] render Bartimaeus' cry as "Jesus, Son of David." Following the Greek text, Bartimaeus' addresses Jesus as "Son of David," adding the name, "Jesus," only afterwards. The story emphasizes the title, "Son of David," not the name Jesus. When repeating the cry, Bartimaeus uses only the title, "Son of David," without mentioning the name.

In Mark's time, the title "Son of David" was emerging as a theological interpretation of Jesus' historic life and mission (see Mark 11:10; 12:35-37). Early tradition related Jesus to David. A creed Paul quoted in Romans 1:3-4 referred to Jesus as descended from David according to the flesh. But before Mark the title itself did not appear in New Testament writings. By the time of Matthew and Luke-Acts, the title would acquire a secure place among the major titles of Jesus. Between Paul and the later Synoptics, Mark represents an intermediary stage in which the meaning of the title had yet to be clarified.

In 8:22–10:52, Mark clarified the title, "Christ," and associated it firmly with the dying and rising of the Son of Man. In 11:1–13:37, Mark associated the messianic title, "Son of David," with Christ's glorious return as the Son of Man. Just as the title, "Christ," had to be purified of all political and military expectations, the title, "Son of David," had to be purified of hopes for a restoration of David's earthly kingdom.

Have Pity on Me. Bartimaeus cried out, pleading with Jesus to have pity on him. "Have pity on me" *(eleeson me),* he cried. We recognize his plea from the liturgy's *Kyrie, eleison,* "Lord, have mercy." We also recall Jesus' command to the Gerasene demoniac: "Go home to your family and announce to them all that the Lord in his pity has done for you" *(pepoieken kai eleesen se, 5:19).*

"Have pity on me, O Lord," is an ancient prayer formula, appearing sixteen times in the Greek version of the Psalms (LXX, the Septuagint). In Psalm 6:3, for example, the prayer is for healing: "Have pity on me, LORD, for I am weak; / heal me, LORD, for my bones are trembling." In Psalm 26:11 (LXX 25), the prayer is for redemption: "But I walk without blame; redeem me, be gracious to me" *(elesson me).* In Psalm 27:7 (LXX 26), the prayer is for salvation: "Hear my voice, LORD, when I call; / have mercy on me and answer me. . . . / do not forsake me, God, my savior." In Psalm 51:1 (LXX 50), the Psalmist

[51] For example, the New Revised Standard Version (NRSV), Revised New American Bible (RNAB), and New International Version (NIV). In this instance, the New Jerusalem Bible (NJB) is more literal.

pleads for forgiveness: "Have mercy [pity] on me, o God, in your goodness; / in your abundant compassion blot out my offense."

In the Psalms, the prayer is addressed to God, the Lord, the *Kyrios.* In Mark 10:46-47, Bartimaeus addresses the prayer to the Son of David. In this, the Gospel suggests that there is more to Jesus than Son of David, as we see later in an exchange concerning David's relationship to the Son of David: "David himself calls him 'lord'; so how is he his son?" (12:36-37). Bartimaeus was a beggar in more ways than one. Bartimaeus was begging for more than alms, and his pleading, "have pity on me," was actually a prayer.

Many rebuked Bartimaeus, trying to silence him. We remember how Jesus used the verb "rebuke" *(epitomao)* to silence unclean spirits (1:25; 3:12; 9:25), to quiet the wind (4:39), and to warn Peter not to tell anyone about his being the Christ (8:30). We remember also how Peter rebuked Jesus when he spoke of his passion and resurrection (8:32) and how Jesus rebuked him in return (8:33). But especially we remember how the disciples rebuked those who brought children to Jesus (10:13). Many were now doing the same to Bartimaeus, but Bartimaeus persisted all the more in his prayer.

Jesus' Command (10:49). Two things are very striking about Jesus' response. First, instead of calling for Bartimaeus directly, Jesus asked the disciples, those who were with him on the way, to call him. This mediation by the disciples may reflect the ecclesial context in which the story was handed down. Then, Jesus did not allude to the title "Son of David" as he did when Peter declared him to be the Christ (8:27-30). But Peter had rebuked Jesus for teaching about the passion-resurrection, whereas the blind man of Jericho was ready to follow him on the way.

Following Jesus' command, the disciples summoned Bartimaeus. As the story puts it, "They called the blind man, saying to him, 'Take courage; get up, he is calling you.'" The disciples transmitted the call to the blind beggar, enabling Jesus to act in and through them. Such mediation was not needed in the historical setting, where distance was not a factor. But it makes sense in the Markan community setting, where temporal distance from the days of Jesus was very much a factor. Through his followers, Jesus continued to call the blind beside the road to join him on the way to the passion and resurrection.

The mediation may point to an adaptation of the story to a later ecclesial setting, more specifically, to a baptismal setting. Mark did something very similar for a Eucharistic setting of the breaking of bread for the five thousand (6:34-44), in which the disciples mediated between Jesus, the one who broke the bread, and the communities of fifty and a hundred. In the story of Bartimaeus, we hear the early baptismal call to a candidate, one who until now has been beside the road. In this, the community saw itself acting in the name of Christ, and it saw Christ acting through them.

Reading the story in its early ecclesial and baptismal setting, we understand why after being introduced as "the son of Timaeus," Bartimaeus is never again referred to by name. He is simply "the blind one," an apt symbol for all the blind people beside the road crying out to Jesus. The words of Jesus' followers to the blind beggar may approximate a baptismal call formula used in the early Church. If so, every word, including "Take courage" *(tharsei)* and "get up" *(egeire)* is important.

At first, their command, "take courage," makes us smile. Before Jesus caught the blind beggar's attention, they were trying to prevent him from coming to Jesus. But the command fits the baptismal setting. It took great courage to accept the baptism in which Jesus was baptized. The verb *tharseo* ("take courage") occurs only one other time in Mark, when Jesus admonished the disciples in a difficult crossing of the sea: "Take courage, it is I, do not be afraid!" (6:50). It took great courage to cross the sea to the Gentile side. It took courage to follow Jesus on the way to the passion and resurrection.

The command to "get up" *(egeire)* was very appropriate for a blind beggar seated by the road, but in keeping with the story's other baptismal evocations, we might better translate it "arise." In the Gospel, the same command is associated with a number of healings, such as that of Simon's mother-in-law (1:31), the paralytic (2:9-12), the man with the withered hand (3:3), and the boy with the demon (9:27). It is also associated with resurrection from the dead, as in the case of Jairus' little daughter (5:41). The same verb is used with reference to John the Baptist whom some thought was risen from the dead (6:14, 16) and the resurrection of Jesus (14:28; 16:6; see also 12:26).

We are not surprised then to hear Jesus' disciples using the same command to a blind beggar who was still beside the road. The beggar wanted to join Jesus, the Son of David, on the way. For Bartimaeus, it was time to arise.

The first part of the story told how Bartimaeus was called. The second tells how he responded. Like the first part, the second evokes baptism and may even reflect the influence of an early baptismal liturgy. The second part shows how Bartimaeus threw off his cloak, sprang up, and came to Jesus (10:50). It also presents a brief dialogue between Jesus and Bartimaeus (10:51-52a) and tells how Bartimaeus followed Jesus on the way (10:52b).

He Threw Aside His Cloak (10:50)

For a blind beggar, Bartimaeus showed amazing energy and alacrity. He was sitting by the roadside. When Jesus called him, he threw off his cloak, jumped to his feet, and came to Jesus with no sign of hesitation. He also had an amazing sense of purpose. It is as though he was waiting for the signal to come to Jesus. This is not what we expected from a blind beggar.

We understand why a beggar would have removed his cloak while begging. But why would a beggar throw off his cloak upon being summoned? Unlike Bartimaeus, beggars are apt to cling to their belongings. If their cloak is tattered, they do not abandon it until they get a new one. Besides, if beggars have managed to secure a space in a busy place, they do not readily abandon it. Nor do they put all their hopes on one passerby. Beggars stay on their little turf, protectively alert, with a hand continuously held out in hope of obtaining alms.

Bartimaeus did not behave like an ordinary beggar nor like an ordinary blind man. He was begging Jesus, the Messiah, or Christ, the Son of David, to be able to see. The way Bartimaeus threw off his cloak, jumped up, and came to Jesus suggests that he was ready to be with Jesus. He had a sure hope that Jesus would provide everything he really needed. With Jesus, Bartimaeus would no longer be a beggar, and so he threw off his beggar's cloak.

The Greek term for cloak is *himation,* the same that was used in the story of the woman with a hemorrhage (5:27, 28, 30), in a summary of Jesus' healing activity at Gennesaret (6:56) and in the story of the transfiguration, where Jesus' *himatia* (plural) became "dazzling white, such as no fuller on earth could bleach them" (9:3).

The *himation* is a long flowing robe, a mantle, which men wore as an outer garment over a tunic, in Greek a *chiton,* which was worn next to the body as an undergarment. The *chiton* is the garment Jesus mentioned when telling the Twelve not to bring a second garment as they went on mission (6:9). The plural *himatia* could, of course, refer to several cloaks, but it was also commonly used to designate a person's clothing in general.

Clothing and Identity. Several times in the course of this commentary, I focused on the meaning of clothing in Mark's Gospel, beginning with the description of John the Baptist, who "was clothed in camel's hair, with a leather belt around his waist" (1:6).[52] This

---

[52] For the symbol of clothing in the Gospel, see E. LaVerdiere, "Robed in Radiant White," *Emmanuel* 90 (April 1984) 138–42, and "A Garment of Camel's Hair," *Emmanuel* 92 (December 1986) 545–51.

theme is not peculiar to the Synoptic Gospels. It is present throughout the New Testament, albeit in various degrees, as it is in the Old Testament.

In the biblical cultures, as in many cultures today, clothing expressed a person's identity. Intimately associated with the person, it was a personal symbol and played an important role in someone's self-communication. Awareness of the symbolic meaning of clothing enables us to understand Bartimaeus' gesture in 10:50.

Bartimaeus, the son of Timaeus, wanted to join Jesus, the son of David, along with his disciples and the Twelve on the way. To do this, he had to throw off his cloak, the symbol of his former self and way of life, and to put on a new garment, symbolic of his new self and a new life, as he follows Christ on the way to the passion-resurrection. As Jesus had indicated earlier, "No one sews a piece of unshrunken cloth on an old cloak" (2:21). Becoming a disciple of Jesus meant more than patching up one's old identity. It called for throwing off that identity altogether and putting on a new one.

Clothing as a Baptismal Symbol. This is the first time in Mark's Gospel that the clothing theme functions as a baptismal symbol. From very early times, clothing played a key role in Christian baptism, which involved a radical change in the baptized. This change took place on three levels. At the ontological or anthropological level, the change was expressed in terms of dying and rising or of birth and rebirth. At the psychological level, it was presented in terms of night and day, darkness and light, blindness and sight. At the moral level it was described as a *metanoia,* a basic transformation in one's way of thinking, relating, and acting.

At all three levels, baptism meant passing from one to the other. In the story of Bartimaeus, he passes from blindness to sight. The symbolism of clothing expressed all three levels. In baptism, Christians put off the garments of their former self, attitudes, and moral behavior and put on the new.

For this, we have four principal passages from the Pauline letters: Galatians 3:26-29, Romans 13:12-14, Colossians 3:9-11 and Ephesians 4:20-24. Chronologically, the passages span some thirty to forty years of early Christian history, from Galatians and Romans in the 50s to Colossians in the 60s and Ephesians in the 70s or 80s of the first century. All four reflect a level of traditional development and liturgical reflection that antedates the time of the writing.

The oldest text is in Galatians: "For all of you who were baptized into Christ [*eis Christon ebaptisthete*] have clothed yourselves with Christ" (*Christon enedusasthe,* Gal 3:27). All those who put on

Christ in baptism became children of God through faith in Christ (Gal 3:26). By putting on Christ, they acquired a new identity, that of God's children.

Paul does not explicitly refer to putting off the old identity, but it is implied in the following verse, where Paul announces that among them "there is neither Jew nor Greek, there is neither slave nor free person, there is not male and female" (Gal 3:28a). Those who have put on Christ have put off every source of division and everything that prevented them from becoming "all one in Christ Jesus," one in baptism, and one at the table of the Lord (see Gal 2:11-14). Paul also refers to the baptized as those who are "of Christ" *(Christou),* an early designation which appears in Mark 9:41.

The second text is in the Letter to the Romans: "Let us then throw off [*apothometha*] the works of darkness [and] put on [*endusometha*] the armor of light" (Rom 13:12). The works of darkness include orgies and drunkenness, promiscuity and licentiousness, rivalry and jealousy (Rom 13:13). Putting on the armor of light means putting on the Lord Jesus Christ (Rom 13:14).

In 1 Thessalonians, Paul described this special armor in terms of faith, charity, and hope. "Putting on the breastplate of faith and love and the helmet that is hope for salvation" (1 Thess 5:8) is an adaptation of Isaiah's description of the Lord who "put on justice as his breastplate, salvation, as the helmet on his head" (LXX, Isa 59:17).

The third text is from Colossians: ". . . you have taken off the old self [*apekdusamenoi ton palaion anthropon*] with its practices [see Col 3:5-9a] and have put on the new self [*endusamenoi ton neon*], which is being renewed, for knowledge, in the image of its creator" (Col 3:9b-10). In terms reminiscent of Galatians 3:28, Paul continues with the social implications of putting off the old self and putting on the new: "Here there is not Greek and Jew, circumcision and uncircumcision, barbarian, Scythian, slave, free; but Christ is all and in all" (Col 3:11). Then in Colossians 3:12-14, he spells out the practices that flow from the new self, placing special emphasis on love: "And over all these put on love, that is, the bond of perfection" (Col 3:14).

The fourth and final text is in Ephesians: ". . . you should put away [*apothesthai*] the old self [*ton palaion anthropon*] of your former way of life, corrupted through deceitful desires, and be renewed in the spirit of your minds, and put on [*endusasthai*] the new self [*ton kainon anthropon*] created in God's way of righteousness and holiness of truth" (Eph 4:22-24). Paul summed up this dual process of putting off the old self and putting on the new as "learn(ing) Christ" *(emathete ton Christon,* Eph 4:20), which is precisely what every disciple *(mathetes)* was expected to do.

All of these Pauline texts are related to one another, evoking the symbolic value of clothing through the verbs "putting off" and "putting on," and applying it to baptism and its threefold transformation. In baptism, Christians put off their former self along with the attitudes and practices of darkness and put on the new self, namely Christ, along with the attitudes and practices of light.

When Mark wrote his Gospel, the Pauline texts were already part of the faith culture of early Christianity. Recalling them as we read that Bartimaeus "threw off his cloak" as he jumped to his feet and came to Jesus, we can appreciate how apt the gesture was.

It may not have been the gesture expected of an ordinary blind beggar, but it was very much expected from one who sought baptism. By throwing off his cloak, Bartimaeus threw off the garment of his old self together with the way of life he had been living beside the Christian way. He was now ready to put on the new Christian self as he joined Christ on the way of the passion-resurrection.

A Baptismal Dialogue (10:51-52a)

Coming to Jesus, Bartimaeus threw off his cloak. Seen as a historical action, the gesture would have been most unusual. But seen as a symbolic action, a liturgical, baptismal action, it appears absolutely normal. The same is true for the dialogue between Jesus and Bartimaeus (10:51-52a).

Introduction

The Blind:	"Jesus, Son of David [*Huie David Iesou*], have pity on me." "Son of David, have pity on me."
Jesus:	"Call him."
Disciples:	"Take courage; get up, he is calling you."

The Dialogue

Jesus:	"What do you want me to do for you?"
The Blind:	"Master, I want to see."
Jesus:	"Go your way; your faith has saved you."

From the Bartimaeus' opening prayer, "Jesus, Son of David [*Huie David Iesou*], have pity on me," to Jesus' closing dismissal, "Go your way; your faith has saved you," we sense that the story is not an ordinary begging story. We saw how the introduction suggests a baptismal context. The baptismal atmosphere is even more pronounced in the actual dialogue.

The dialogue opens with an introductory question: "Jesus said to him in reply, 'What do you want me to do for you?'" Jesus' question seems strange. As a beggar, Bartimaeus would accept whatever

Jesus gave. But in a baptismal liturgy, the question makes a lot of sense, responding to Bartimaeus' cry, "Son of David, have pity on me," and his throwing off his cloak.

Jesus did not ask, "What do you want me to give you?" but "What do you want me to do for you?" In the story, Jesus knew that Bartimaeus was not asking for money. He was asking for something that an ordinary human being could not give. He was asking for a response to his prayer, "Son of David, have pity on me." Throwing off his cloak, he was ready for what only Jesus could do.

When people told Bartimaeus that Jesus was calling for him (10:49), he is referred not by name but as "the blind man" *(ho typhlos)*. After first identifying "the blind man" as the son of Timaeus, Bartimaeus (10:46), the story never again refers to him by name, but simply as "the blind man."

In relation to the larger story, it made sense to identify "the blind man" as Bartimaeus and to situate him beside the road leading out of Jericho (10:46). But in relation to the baptismal context that shaped the story of Bartimaeus, the blind man's historical identity and the geographical locale are not significant. The constituent elements of a baptismal liturgy are symbols, gestures, and dialogue. In the story of Bartimaeus, "the blind one" is a symbol for all who "have eyes and not see" (8:18) and for all who can be baptized with the baptism with which Jesus is baptized (see 10:38-39).

***Rabbouni,* That I Might See!** Responding to Jesus, the blind man made his prayer for mercy more specific. *"Rabbouni,"* he pleads. *Rabbouni,* a more solemn address than *Rabbi,* is an Aramaic equivalent for *Kyrios* or Lord. And this is the way Matthew and Luke rendered it in their versions of the story (Matt 20:33; Luke 18:41). The only other time *Rabbouni* is used in the New Testament is in John's Gospel, when Mary Magdalene recognizes Jesus as her risen Lord (John 20:16). Referring to that moment, she would tell the disciples, "I have seen the Lord" (John 20:18).

Mark retained a number of Aramaic and Hebrew terms from early tradition, reflecting liturgical expressions, which are strongly resistant to change. This is what explains the persistence of Greek in the familiar *Kyrie eleison* centuries after the liturgy was translated from Greek into Latin.

Most of the other Aramaic terms in Mark are attributed to Jesus: *Talitha koum* ("Little girl . . . arise!" 5:41), *Ephphatha!* ("Be opened!" 7:34), *Eloi, Eloi, lema sabachthani?* ("My God, my God, why have you forsaken me?" 15:34). The retaining of these expressions in Aramaic, all of which had to be translated for Mark's Greek-speaking readers, may stem from liturgical usage. The same may be true of Bartimaeus' Aramaic address, *Rabbouni.*

The blind beggar did not beg the Son of David for money. He begged for sight, and more specifically, to see again, that is to recover his sight *(anablepo)*. It is not, therefore, that he had always been blind, but that at one point he had become blind. Now he wanted to see again.

Bartimaeus, the blind one, was like those to whom everything came in parables that "they may look and see but not perceive" *(blepontes bleposin kai me idosin,* 4:12). Like those who were not with the Twelve *(syn tois dodeka,* 4:10) but outside *(exo,* 4:11; see 3:31), they were not granted the mysteries of the kingdom of God (4:11) and so they could not see. Earlier they had been able to see and understand, but that was before Jesus established the Twelve as the foundation of a new people, a people which would be as universal as the kingdom of God. So long as they were not with the Twelve and part of that people, they were condemned not to see.

Until now, Bartimaeus had not been on the road with Jesus, the disciples, and the Twelve (10:32). He was beside the road, outside the new community of the Twelve. Before Jesus established the Twelve and the people of the Kingdom of God, he was able to see. But now, outside, beside the road, he could no longer understand. He was blind.

So it is that he prayed to be able to see again. To regain his sight, the blind one would have to join Jesus and the Twelve and the community of disciples on the way of the passion and resurrection. There was no other way to the Kingdom of God. Having thrown off his cloak, he came to Jesus. Addressing Jesus as *Rabbouni,* he pleaded that he might see. He was ready to see.

"Go Your Way; Your Faith Has Saved You." Jesus' response seems to ignore the blind one's request. Instead of referring to blindness and new sight, his response is a dismissal, not unlike a liturgical dismissal: "Go your way, your faith has saved you" (10:52).

"Go" *(hypage)* is the command used in 8:33 where Jesus told Peter, "Go [*hypage*] behind me" *(opiso mou),* that is, "Go back into my following." In Mark's Gospel, the verb *hypago* is almost always found in the imperative as a solemn command of Jesus. It is used after a healing or exorcism (1:44; 2:11; 5:19; 5:34; 7:29), in relation to the following of Christ (8:3; 10:21) and in liturgical or liturgically-inspired settings (6:38; 11:2; 14:13). Jesus' command to Bartimaeus corresponds to all these contexts, suggesting that Bartimaeus was being healed in baptism in view of following Christ on the way of the passion and resurrection.

The one use of the imperative *hypage* not ascribed to Jesus is in the resurrection story. It comes from the young man clothed in a white robe solemnly giving the women their Easter commission (16:7). Apart from these instances and 10:52, the verb *hypago* is used three times, all related to a liturgical context, twice in the breaking of bread for the 5,000 (6:31, 33) and once at the Last Supper as an interpretation of the passion: "For the Son of Man indeed goes [*hypagei*], as it is written of him" (14:21).

The dismissal of the blind one is no ordinary dismissal. After the command, Jesus gives the grounds for it: "Your faith has saved you" *(he pistis sou sesoken se)*. Jesus' declaration does not allude to sight but to faith and salvation. From the very beginning, blindness was a liturgical symbol for lack of faith. What the blind man sought all along was to see with eyes of faith, and such was Jesus' gift of liturgical healing. With this theme of saving faith, Mark joins Paul, who saw it as "the will of God through the foolishness of the proclamation to save those who have faith" (1 Cor 1:21). In this regard, witness Paul's message to the Ephesians: "For by grace you have been saved through faith, and this is not from you; it is the gift of God" (Eph 2:8).

Jesus used the same expression, "Your faith has saved you," when addressing the woman suffering from a long-standing hemorrhage (5:34a). On that occasion, Jesus then referred to her affliction: "Go in peace and be cured of your affliction." Both stories are about faith and salvation.

"Immediately He Received His Sight and Followed Him on the Way" (10:52b)

As the story of Bartimaeus ends, he receives new sight and follows Jesus on the way (*en te hodo*, 10:52b; see 10:32-34). Like James and John, he is able to drink the cup that Jesus would drink and be baptized in the same baptism with which he would be baptized (10:39). On the way, he joins Jesus, the Christ, the Son of David, and the Son of Man as a servant and slave. With Jesus he would give "his life as a ransom for many" (10:45).

Throwing off his cloak to follow Christ, he showed that he gave up everything (10:17-31) that he might be saved (10:26-28) and receive a hundredfold in the present age and eternal life in the age to come (10:29-30). Bartimaeus would enter the kingdom of God because, in giving up everything (10:17, 21, 23-25), he accepted the kingdom like a child (10:15). Everything had become possible (10:27) for him because he had faith (9:23) and he turned to Christ, the Son of David, in prayer (9:29).

Bartimaeus was able to come after Jesus because he denied himself, allowed himself to be claimed by Christ, took up his cross and followed him (8:34) on the way of the passion-resurrection. He had heard Jesus' message that, as the Son of Man, he would "suffer greatly and be rejected by the elders, the chief priests, and the scribes, and be killed, and rise after three days" (8:31; see also 9:31; 10:32-34). Bartimaeus saw perfectly, like the blind man of Bethsaida (8:22-26), when he was fully cured (8:25).

Bartimaeus' story, like every Christian's story, is about blindness and sight. To be able to see, he had to deny himself and embrace the cross. With his sight restored, he could join the disciples and follow Christ to the passion and resurrection.

IX

~ Section V ~

The Coming of the Lord Jesus

Mark 11:1–13:37

The fourth section of the Gospel (8:22–10:52) told how Jesus' journey to Jerusalem was a journey to his passion and resurrection. At the beginning of the journey, Peter announced that Jesus was the Christ, that is, the Messiah (8:30). At the end, Bartimaeus cried out to him, "Jesus Son of David," (10:47-48). But throughout the section, Jesus always referred to himself as the Son of Man (8:31, 38; 9:31; 10:31).

As Son of Man, Jesus was the quintessential human being, the very embodiment of what it meant to be human. As Son of Man, Jesus would suffer and die, and rise after three days. He would also give his life as a ransom. As the Son of Man, Jesus challenged every messianic historical expectation, giving new meaning to the titles "Christ" and "Son of David." There is no separating the Christ and the Son of David from the Son of Man.

As the Son of Man, Jesus is the Christ. While on the way *(en te hodo)* to Jerusalem, Jesus taught the disciples what this implied for him and for his followers. He opened their eyes to see that the way of Christ is the way of the Son of Man, a way to redemptive suffering, death, and resurrection (8:22–10:52).

The fifth section shows how Jesus, as the Son of Man, is the Son of David. In Jerusalem, Jesus would teach the disciples the meaning of this second title and its implications for them. He showed them that the reign of the Son of David is also the reign of the Son of Man, whose transcendent reign had nothing to do with earthly glory (11:1–13:37).

The story of Bartimaeus, a blind beggar (10:46-52), concluded the fourth major section (8:22–10:52) of "the beginning of the gospel of Jesus Christ [the Son of God]" (1:1). That section opened with Jesus curing a blind man at Bethsaida (8:22-26). At first, the blind man was cured only partially. At the end, he could see clearly. The second stage of his cure pointed ahead to the perfect sight of Bartimaeus. With his eyes open, Bartimaeus joined Jesus on the way to Jerusalem, ready to be baptized with the baptism with which Jesus is baptized.

While concluding the previous section, the story of Bartimaeus announced the theme of the following section. Jesus is the Son of David. Just as the previous section dealt with what it meant for Jesus to be the Christ, the present section deals with what it means for Jesus to be the Son of David.

In the previous section, popular messianic expectations were refocused on Jesus' passion and resurrection. In the fifth section, popular expectations of a Davidic restoration are refocused on Jesus' coming in glory at the consummation of creation and history.

Jesus was not an ordinary Messiah or Christ. Nor was he an ordinary Son of David. The section shows how Jesus was extremely different from those who had messianic and Davidic pretensions. Indeed, Jesus, the Son of David, was greater than King David (see 12:35-37).[1]

An Overview

Like the previous four sections, the fifth opens with a double introduction, Jesus' triumphal entry into Jerusalem (11:1-11) and the cursing of the fig tree and the cleansing of the Temple (12-26; see 1:14-15, 16-20; 3:7-12, 13-19; 6:6b, 7-30). But unlike the previous sections, it also closes with a double conclusion, the announcement of the destruction of the Temple (13:1-2) and Jesus' eschatological discourse (13:3-37; see 3:1-6; 6:1-6a; 8:14-21; 10:46-52).

The overall structure of the fifth section is similar to the previous section (8:22–10:52), in which the story of the blind man at Bethsaida (8:22-26) and of the blind beggar at Jericho (10:46-52) framed the section. The fifth section is framed by the geographical setting of the Mount of Olives and of the Temple area.

As the section opens, Jesus and the disciples are at Bethany on the Mount of Olives. The first unit presents Jesus' messianic entry into Jerusalem from the Mount of Olives. After looking over the Temple area, Jesus returns to Bethany with the Twelve (11:1-11).

[1] Similarly, in the prologue (1:2-13) we saw that Jesus, the follower of John the Baptist, was greater than John the Baptist.

The next day, Jesus again leaves Bethany for Jerusalem and the Temple area. This second story (11:12-26) tells how Jesus cursed a fig tree (11:12-14, 20-26) and cleansed the Temple area (11:15-19). The story of the Temple interrupts the story of the fig tree. In that, we recognize the sandwich pattern typical of Mark.

The focus in the first story is on the Mount of Olives (11:1-11). In the second, the focus is on the Temple area (11:12-26). Jesus' messianic entry into Jerusalem introduces and provides the grounds for the second story, the cursing of the fig tree and the cleansing of the Temple.

The same pattern reappears at the end of the section, but in reverse order. In the first story, the attention is on the Temple and its great buildings (13:1-2). Imposing as these were, they would all be destroyed. In the second story, Jesus returns to the Mount of Olives opposite the Temple area for the great eschatological discourse (13:3-37). Again, the first story, announcing the Temple's destruction, introduces and points to the second, announcing the fulfillment of creation and history.

The section thus has a double frame, the outer frame with its focus on the Mount of Olives (11:1-11; 13:3-37), and the inner frame with its focus on the Temple area (11:12-26; 13:1-2), giving the following chiastic *(A B B' A')* structure:

A (11:1-11)   Mount of Olives and messianic entry;
B (11:12-26)   Cleansing of the Temple and cursing of the fig tree;
B' (13:1-2)   Leaving the Temple and the announcement of its destruction;
A' (13:3-37)   On the Mount of Olives and the announcement of entry of the Son of Man in glory.

Recognizing the framework is important for interpreting the whole section. It shows that Jesus' messianic entry into Jerusalem (11:1-11) is to be understood in relation to his glorious coming at the consummation of time (13:3-37). In the same way, Jesus' cursing the fig tree and cleansing of the Temple (11:12-26) is to be understood in relation to the Temple's destruction (13:1-2).

Between the opening units (11:1-11, 12-26) and the closing units (13:1-2, 3-37), the section includes Jesus' teaching in the Temple and his confrontations, or conflicts, with various groups and personages (11:27–12:44). Jesus' teaching and confrontations constitute the body of the section. All of the conflicts take place on the same day. In relation to the section (11:1–13:37), it is the third day, beginning with the discovery that the fig tree Jesus cursed was completely withered (11:20-26).

The first confrontation was with the chief priests, the scribes, and the elders, that is, the Sanhedrin, the religious governing and legal body in Jerusalem. It had to do with the basis of Jesus' authority (11:27–12:12). The second was with the Pharisees and the Herodians, an unlikely relationship we first encountered in 3:6. It had to do with the lawfulness of paying taxes to Caesar (12:12-17). The third was with the Sadducees over the question of the resurrection (12:18-27). The fourth was with a scribe over which of the commandments was the first (12:28-34).

In these four confrontations, the initiative came from those who approached Jesus. In the fifth confrontation, the initiative came from Jesus. Teaching a great crowd, Jesus asked how the scribes could claim that the Messiah is the son of David, when David himself called him "lord" (12:35-37). Jesus then warned against behaving like the scribes (12:38-40). Concluding the series of confrontations, Jesus called the attention of the disciples to a plight of a poor widow who was reduced to penury by the religious greed of the scribes (12:41-44).

Setting and *Dramatis Personae*

As we did for the previous sections, we begin our reflections on the coming of the Lord (11:1–13:37) by examining the geographical and temporal settings and the personages who play a role in the story. In the fifth section, the geography and the chronology are very focused. The geographical setting includes the Mount of Olives, Jerusalem, and the Temple area. The temporal setting includes three consecutive days. The personages include various sectors of Jewish life, like the chief priests, the scribes and elders, the Pharisees, and the Herodians and the Sadducees.

Focusing on the Mount of Olives, Jerusalem, and the Temple area, the geography is very symbolic with deep roots in the Old Testament. Focusing on three days, the chronology is also symbolic. The *dramatis personae* represent every important institution at the center of Judaism in the time of Jesus.

Geographical Setting: In Jerusalem

In the prologue (1:2-13), the setting of the mission of John the Baptist and the baptism of Jesus was the desert by the Jordan River. In the first part of the Gospel (1:14–8:21), the principal setting was Galilee. In Galilee, Jesus called the first disciples, constituted the Twelve, and sent the Twelve on mission. He also made them to extend their mission to the Gentiles. For that, they had to cross to the other side of the sea.

In the second part, the principal setting is Jerusalem. From the very beginning of the previous section (8:22–10:52), Jesus and his followers were on the way *(en te hodo)* to Jerusalem, the city of Jesus' passion and resurrection. Now Jesus enters Jerusalem and teaches in the Temple area and on the Mount of Olives (11:1–13:37).

As the fifth section opens, Jesus with his followers and the Twelve (see 10:32) were drawing near to Jerusalem, to the villages of Bethphage and Bethany on the Mount of Olives (11:1). Among the followers was Bartimaeus (see 10:52). The section ends with Jesus sitting on the Mount of Olives overlooking the Temple area. With him were Peter, James, John, and Andrew (13:3).

There is considerable movement, especially at the beginning, but it is confined to a very limited space, taking Jesus from Bethany on the Mount of Olives into Jerusalem and Temple area (11:1-11a) and back to the Mount of Olives and Bethany (11:11b). There is nothing especially significant about Bethphage, save that it marked the approach to Bethany. Bethany has deep traditional roots in the story of Jesus in the Gospels of Mark and John.

In Mark, Bethany is the point of departure for Jesus' entry into Jerusalem and into the Temple area (11:1-11a, 12, 20) and the place of his return at day's end when he saw it was late (11:11b, 19). Bethany is also the place that Jesus would come for a meal at the home of Simon the leper, where a woman would anoint him for his burial (14:3-9) while the chief priests and the scribes were plotting his death (14:1-2).

Both the Mount of Olives and Jerusalem have strong connections with the story of Jesus and the end of his life, but in addition the two brought with them a rich set of associations from the prophetic and narrative history of Israel. In Ezekiel, the Mount of Olives, "the mountain which is to the east of the city" (Ezek 10:23), where the glory of God paused, overlooking the devastation of Jerusalem, upon abandoning the Temple (see Ezek 10:1-22; 11:22-25). King David had followed the same route to the Mount of Olives while fleeing Absalom (2 Sam 15:30-31). In Zechariah, the Mount of Olives figures prominently in the Lord's messianic and definitive battle for Jerusalem (14).

At this point in the Gospel, after several announcements of Jesus' approaching passion (8:31; 9:30-31; 10:32-34), the mere mention of the Mount of Olives and Jerusalem sounds a note that is both ominous and hopeful. The note is ominous because of their connection with suffering and death. It is hopeful because of their association with the return of David and of the glory of the Lord.

The Temple is God's earthly dwelling in the city of David. In some way, it figures throughout the section as the center of Jesus' activity in Jerusalem. The Temple area is seen as the destination of Jesus' journey to Jerusalem (11:1-11). Cleansing it of those selling and buying there, as well as of the paraphernalia of religious and cultic trade, Jesus restores the Temple to its purpose as a house of prayer (11:15-19).

The Temple area is also the site of Jesus' teaching on key issues and a series of confrontations exposing what people and various groups needed in order to take part in the prayer of the renewed Temple (11:27–12:44). It is while leaving the area that Jesus speaks of its destruction (13:1-2). From the heights opposite the Temple he gives a discourse on the signs of the end and the glorious return of the Son of Man (13:3-37).

Temporal Setting: Three Messianic Days

The temporal setting is extremely simple. All the events take place in a period of three days, evoking the days of the passion and resurrection. In Mark, Jesus announced that he would rise "after three days" (8:31; 9:31; 10:34). It also evokes the accusation for which he will be condemned: "We heard him say, 'I will destroy this temple made with hands and within three days I will build another not made with hands'" (14:58).

The first day includes the preparation and Jesus' entry into Jerusalem (11:1-11). The second includes Jesus' cursing of the fig tree and the cleansing of the Temple (11:12-19). The third day includes the rest of the section (11:20–13:37), from the discovery that the cursed fig tree was withered to its roots (11:20-26), to the teaching and confrontations in the Temple area (11:27–12:44). It also includes the announcement of the Temple's destruction (13:1-2), and the final eschatological discourse on the Mount of Olives (13:3-37). Through the discovery of the withered fig tree (11:20-26), the Gospel relates Jesus' teaching to the cleansing of the Temple (11:15-19), the cursing of the fig tree (11:12-14), and Jesus' messianic entry into Jerusalem (11:1-11).

Other temporal indications relate the various events to one another. For example, the indication, "In the course of his teaching he said" (12:38), relates Jesus' denunciation of the scribes (12:38-40) to Jesus' response to their claim that the Messiah is the son of David (12:35-37). The temporal indication, "As he was making his way out of the temple area" (13:1), relates Jesus' announcement of the destruction of the Temple (13:1-2) and his eschatological discourse

(13:3-37) to Jesus' coming into the Temple (11:1-11), his cleansing of the Temple (11:12-26), and his teaching in the Temple (11:27–12:44).

These temporal indications may appear meager but they do contribute to the pace of the story. They also contribute to the coherence and the unity of the story. With the geographical setting, they also enable us to discern the section's literary structure.

Dramatis Personae

The cast of personages includes Jesus, the disciples and the Twelve, and the crowd. Jesus refers to himself as "Master" (*kyrios,* Lord) and refers to his titles, Son of David (12:35-37) and Son of Man (13:26), but he is addressed by the title "Rabbi" (11:21) and "Teacher" (*didaskale,* 12:14, 19, 32; 13:1). Among the Twelve, Peter (11:21) and Peter, James, John, and Andrew are singled out (13:3).

Outside Jesus' triumphal entry into Jerusalem (11:1-11), the crowd has a new role. After the cleansing of the Temple, the chief priests and scribes "were seeking a way to put him to death, yet they feared him because the whole crowd was astonished at his teaching" (11:18). Later, the chief priests, the scribes, and the elders "were seeking to arrest him, but they feared the crowd" (12:12). The fear of the crowd would have an important role in the passion (14:1-2; 15:15).

The cast also includes the chief priests, the scribes, and the elders, that is, the Sanhedrin (11:27–12:12), the Pharisees and the Herodians (12:13-17), the Sadducees (12:18-27), a scribe (12:28-34), the crowd (12:35-40), and the disciples (12:41-44). In the body of the section (11:27–12:44), each group addresses Jesus or is addressed by him in order, one after the other with a key issue.

The disciples play decisive roles in the section's double introduction (11:1-11, 12-26) and conclusion (13:1-2, 3-37), framing the whole section. The disciples are not mentioned in the body of the section, save at the very end in the story of the widow's mite (12:41-44). But within the double frame, every group and issue are relevant to the disciples, if not in Jesus' time, surely in Mark's time. They reflect contemporary controversies and tendencies and in their recent history.

In Jesus' messianic entry into Jerusalem, the disciples accompany Jesus, as do the Twelve (11:1-11). The presence of the Twelve as a renewed Israel open to all peoples is a critical element in Jesus' cleansing of the Temple (see 11:11-12), making it "a house of prayer for all peoples" (11:17).

The disciples are again central to the concluding units. It is they who note the magnificence of the Temple structures (13:1-2). And four of them accompanied Jesus to the Mount of Olives, Peter,

James, John, and Andrew (see 1:16-20; 3:13-19), where Jesus addressed them with his eschatological discourse on the consummation of history and the return of the Son of Man in glory (13:3-37).

Jesus' Entry into Jerusalem (11:1-11)

From Bethsaida (8:22-26), Jesus and his disciples had set out for the villages of Caesarea Philippi (8:27). They then went on a journey through Galilee (8:30), stopping at Capernaum (8:33) and in the Judean district over by the Jordan (10:1). Now they were on the way to Jerusalem (10:32). All the while, Jesus taught his disciples what it meant to follow him "on the way," gradually opening their eyes that they might see perfectly (8:22–10:52).

They had just come up from Jericho (10:46) and were approaching Jerusalem, via Bethphage and Bethany on the Mount of Olives. Jesus sent two of his disciples after a colt. The time had come for Jesus' entry into Jerusalem and into the Temple area, first for a quick overview (11:1-11), then for a radical cleansing, to make God's house a house of prayer for all peoples (11:12-26).

The story of Jesus' entry into Jerusalem shows how Jesus and his disciples left from Bethany on the Mount of Olives (11:1) and returned to Bethany with the Twelve (11:11). In Matthew (21:1-17) and Luke (19:28-48), Jesus' entry into Jerusalem introduces the cleansing of the Temple, which follows immediately, and the two are part of the same event. In Mark, Jesus' entry into Jerusalem is an event by itself, distinct from the cleansing of the Temple, which would take place on the following day.

Much of the story is taken up with the preparations for Jesus' entry (11:1-7) and the popular jubilation welcoming him as he approached from the Mount of Olives (11:8-10). The entry itself is told very simply (11:11a). Since it was already late, Jesus did nothing that day in the Temple area except look around at everything (11:11b).

The story evokes passages from the Psalms, especially Psalm 118, a liturgical celebration in which the king, accompanied by the people, enters Jerusalem and processes into the Temple. We are also reminded of Simon, one of the Maccabees, who earlier entered the city with hymns and songs of praise and cleansed it and the citadel of everything that was impure (1 Macc 13:47-50). "On the twenty-third day of the second month, in the year one hundred and seventy-one, the Jews entered the citadel with shouts of jubilation, waving of palm branches, the music of harps and cymbals and lyres, and the singing of hymns and canticles, because a great enemy of Israel had been destroyed" (1 Macc 13:51). Simon then issued a decree that "this day should be celebrated every year with jubilation" (1 Macc 13:52).

While evoking passages such as these, with their festive and liturgical atmosphere, Jesus' entry into Jerusalem is at the same time strikingly different. Jesus' entry evokes a prophetic passage from the book of Zechariah on the coming of a king-messiah whose entry would be modest, humble, and above all peaceful. The coming of the Lord's Messiah would not be accompanied by the splendor associated with ordinary kings and other rulers (9:9).

Jesus' modest, albeit royal, processional entry into Jerusalem and the Temple is not what people expected of the Son of David. Nor was any of what followed, not the cursing of the fig tree, not the cleansing of the Temple, not the encounters with the Sanhedrin, the Pharisees and Herodians, and others, and most especially not the announcement of the Temple's destruction and the discourse on the Mount of Olives. None of these corresponded to current hopes and expectations regarding the coming of David's Son. Jesus' triumph was not the triumph of earthly kingdoms. It was the triumph of the kingdom of God.

Preparations for the Solemn Entry (11:1-7a)

The preparations for Jesus' entry into Jerusalem (11:1b-7a) are told in two parts: Jesus sent two of his disciples with instructions (11:1b-3), and the disciples then filled Jesus' instructions (11:4-7a). This twofold pattern would reappear early in the next section in the preparations for Jesus' definitive Passover (14:13-16).

Of the two preparations, those for Jesus' entry, for which Jesus takes the initiative, are the more solemn, telling both the instructions and their fulfillment in detail. In the preparations for Jesus' processional entry, the instructions serve as an introduction to their fulfillment by the disciples. For the Last Supper, the initiative comes from the disciples, and emphasis is on Jesus' instructions (14:13-15), not on how the disciples fulfilled them, which is barely mentioned (14:16). For Jesus' entry into Jerusalem, the emphasis is on the fulfillment.

Mark leaves the two disciples nameless both here and in the preparations for the Last Supper. It suffices to know that the two are disciples. The same is true in Matthew (Matt 21:1; 26:17) and in Luke, but only for the entry into Jerusalem (Luke 19:29). The Passover is prepared by Peter and John (Luke 22:8).

Jesus' Instructions (11:2-3). Jesus' told the two disciples: "Go into the village opposite you, and immediately on entering it, you will find a colt tethered on which no one has ever sat. Untie it and bring it here" (11:2). From the beginning we sense something unusual about these instructions. Why did Jesus refer to "the village opposite *you*"? Since Jesus and the disciples were together, would it not have been more normal to refer to "the village opposite *us*."

That would certainly be the case for a realistic telling of a historical event, not, however, for evoking a liturgical procession commemorating Jesus' entry into Jerusalem. In such a procession, Jesus' voice is a voice from the past, from the day, years before, when Jesus entered Jerusalem just before his passion and resurrection. Those sent to make the preparations are the early Christian community reenacting the event liturgically.

We have no independent evidence for such a liturgical procession at this early date, but that does not mean Mark and the Markan community did not think of Jesus' entry into Jerusalem in liturgical terms inspired by Psalm 118 and other processional psalms, and by the story of Simon Maccabee. As such, the immediate background for Mark's story of Jesus' processional entry would not be the historical event itself but its interpretive retelling and liturgical commemoration. Such a liturgical reading of the story in Mark 11:1-11, as we shall see, resolves a few additional anomalies, all of which come from a reading presupposing that the historical event is directly in the background.

In his instructions, Jesus speaks clearly, simply, and with authority. He knows exactly what the disciples will find on entering the village, as though everything had been arranged and prepared in advance, as would be the case for a liturgical enactment. The tethered colt on which no one has ever sat evokes Zechariah 9:9, inviting Jerusalem to rejoice and shout for joy. Her king would come to her as a just savior, riding on an ass, a young donkey, a colt, the foal of an ass.

In the Hebrew text of Zechariah, emphasis is on the messiah-king's entry on an ass or donkey, unlike recent other Davidic kings, who entered through the city gate high in their chariots or on their horses, accompanied by the princes, the leading men of Judah, and the citizens of Jerusalem (Zech 17:25; 22:4). By contrast, Zechariah evokes Jacob's blessing for Judah, who would "tether his donkey to the vine, / his purebred ass to the choicest stem" (Gen 49:11) and the canticle of Deborah singing of Israel's leaders and nobles in the days of the judges "who ride on white asses, / seated on saddlecloths as they go their way" (Judg 5:9-10; see 10:4). With the messianic king entering Jerusalem astride an ass, the colt of an ass, Zechariah summons images of leaders and saviors from Israel's golden age before the days of kings.

Mark retains this rich background from Zechariah but adds something of his own. The Septuagint's translation of Zechariah 9:9 specified that the ass was not just a colt but a new colt, that is, one not yet associated with temporal or political functions. We are reminded of the criteria for selecting the red heifer for sacrifice. Not only was it to be without blemish or defect, but also one on which "no yoke has ever been laid" (Num 19:2) and "that has never been put to work as a draft animal under a yoke" (Deut 21:3). Only such a red heifer was considered fitting for use in a sacred function. In the same way, the messianic-king's entry mounted on a new colt highlights the sacredness of the event.

The savior-king would come as one who was just and meek but also as a sacred figure with a divine mission. Mark emphasizes the sacredness of Jesus' entry even more by spelling out the Septuagint's reference to "the new colt" as one "on which no one has ever sat." This creative Markan detail is not found in John 12:12-15. It would be retained in Luke 19:30 but not in Matthew 21:2.

Foreseeing a possible objection when the disciples came to take the colt, Jesus told them how to reply should someone ask why they were doing this. They should answer: "The Master [*ho kyrios*] has need of it and will send it back here at once" (11:3). It was not ordinary for someone to enter a town and take a donkey that belonged to someone else without so much as requesting it, even if the intention was only to borrow it for a while.

To resolve this apparent anomaly, some have suggested that the reference to the *kyrios* (lord), which the Revised New American Bible has translated as "Master," refers to the owner of the donkey. Jesus, it is argued, would have been recognizing the owner's need and promising to return the colt immediately. But then why would the owner have such urgent need of a mere colt that has not been broken in and has not yet served as a beast of burden? Besides, would it not have been more normal to request the colt from its owner? As it stands, Jesus asks for it as one who has a right to take the donkey and as one whose right was recognized.

The title "Lord" *(kyrios),* as others have argued, more properly refers to Jesus himself, a view that is reinforced in Jesus' teaching concerning David, who referred to the messianic Son of David as "Lord" (12:35-37). It is true that later in Mark 11:1-11, the title "Lord" refers to God when those accompanying Jesus sing, "Blessed is he / who comes in the name of the Lord" (Ps 118:26), but then in 12:35-37 the same title, "Lord," refers both to God and to the Messiah: "The Lord [God] said to my lord [messiah]." Such also seems to be the case in 11:1-11. When Jesus says, "The Master has need of it," the title refers to Jesus as Messiah. In the people's acclamation, "Blessed is he who comes in the name of the Lord," it refers to the Lord God.

By referring to Jesus as Lord, the story further highlights the extraordinary and sacred character of the event. Jesus' entry into Jerusalem as Messiah and king in itself is a definitive event in the history of Israel and the people of God, even apart from the cursing of the fig tree and the cleansing of the Temple. In Mark's reading of Malachi 3:1, John the Baptist was God's messenger sent to prepare the way before the Lord Jesus. Continuing with the same verse from Malachi, we now see Jesus coming to the Temple as the Lord long sought, coming to purify the sons of Levi "that they may offer due sacrifice to the LORD" (Mal 3:3).

Once Jesus had entered there would be no further need of the colt he was the first to ride. It would consequently be returned immediately. Then, if Mark's story does indeed reflect a liturgical telling or enacting of Jesus' entry, the colt in the story would be symbolic of the one Jesus had ridden but then returned in view of the event's commemorative reenactment.

The Disciples Fulfill Jesus' Instructions (11:4-7a). The two disciples went off to fulfill Jesus' instructions (11:4-7a), finding everything just as Jesus said. Jesus had told them that on entering the village they would find a colt tethered. And so they did. They found a colt tethered "at a gate outside on the street." Jesus had told them to untie it, "and they untied it." Point for point, we are told how the disciples found things as Jesus said and how they followed his every instruction.

Jesus had even foreseen that someone might ask them why they were taking the colt, and sure enough, "some of the bystanders said to them, 'What are you doing, untying the colt?'" They answered as Jesus told them, and the bystanders permitted them to proceed. Then, as Jesus requested, they brought the colt to him.

The events are told twice, first in Jesus' voice commanding and announcing, and then in the actual fulfillment, which is told in slightly greater detail. We hear them as the word of Jesus speaking to the disciples and as the disciples listening to him. We then see them as events in the life of the disciples fulfilling Jesus' command.

From a historical point of view, the bystanders' response is fairly puzzling. After all, they were not the owners of the colt but mere bystanders. We can understand why they would object. In a small village, everyone knows everyone else and everyone is concerned with everyone else's business. They might certainly object, but would they then have permitted Jesus' disciples, people unknown to them, to take the colt away?

In a commemorative retelling of the event, however, the dialogue makes sense. As in sung, liturgical dialogue, the presuppositions are not those of a singular event which has taken an unexpected turn. Rather, the presuppositions are in the faith of those telling and hearing the story and at least imaginatively reenacting the event. The bystanders already know the answer to their question, and the disciples know the bystanders will accept their answer:

> Bystanders: "What are you doing, untying the colt?"
> Disciples: "The Master has need of it and will send it back here
> at once."

The early Christians knew the Lord needed this colt and why the colt had to be a new one, one on which no one had ever sat. The logic of such a story is not that of history but of faith celebrating history. It never occurred that the disciples should ask whether in fact anyone had ever sat on the colt. In gospel retelling and imaginative or liturgical enacting, the logic of history is suspended and its role taken over by the logic of faith.

Entry into Jerusalem and into the Temple (11:7b-11)

The disciples brought the colt to Jesus and put their cloaks on it. They provided a saddle of their own cloaks for Jesus' entry into Jerusalem. The Son of David would enter Jerusalem on saddle cloths of disciples' cloaks spread over the colt of an ass on which no one had ever sat.

Cloaks *(ta himatia),* like garments and clothing in general, are very significant throughout Mark's Gospel. As we have seen over and over, their meaning comes from the one who wears them. They express someone's identity and are a symbol of the person. In the Bible, as in so many cultures still today, clothing is a proper symbol, just as someone's name is a proper word. To know what the name means, one must know the person. The same is true of clothing. To know what the clothing represents, one must know the person.

By offering their cloaks as saddle cloths, the disciples symbolically offered themselves to be with the Lord entering Jerusalem. For an ordinary king, disciples' cloaks would not have been much of a saddle, but for the Lord Jesus and the kingdom of God, they were absolutely appropriate. And Jesus sat on them. He accepted the saddle cloths of his disciples' commitment, the saddle cloths of those who had left everything to be with him in Jerusalem for the passion-resurrection.

All was now ready, and the procession could begin. The actual procession, however, is left for us to imagine. Strikingly, there is no mention or notice of Jesus' getting underway and proceeding toward Jerusalem. Indeed, in what follows there is no mention of Jesus' movement at all. It is as though Jesus had become invisible. Everything refers to those who accompanied him, his disciples, of course, but also everyone who would later join Jesus in his solemn entry into Jerusalem for the baptism of his passion-resurrection.

Many people spread their cloaks *(ta himatia)* on the road *(eis ten hodon)*. Not only did Jesus ride seated on the saddle cloths of his disciples, but proceeded into Jerusalem over the cloaks spread out by many "on the road." The clothing symbol is thus linked to the symbol of the road or way, which Mark developed to such great effect in the Gospel's previous section (8:22–10:52). Those with Jesus offer their own persons to carpet the way for his entry into Jerusalem. The image highlights the role of Jesus' followers, and the Church, in the definitive coming of the Son of Man in glory.

Greeks, for whom the theatre was an enormously popular attraction, would have readily recalled *The Agamemnon,* Aeschylus' tragic drama, and the welcome that awaited King Agamemnon at his return to Argos from victory at Troy. His wife, Queen Clytemnestra, has rich purple garments and broideries spread on the way, and invites him not to lower his foot on common ground but to make his way over the carpet of purple into the palace. For Agamemnon, the practice was associated with eastern kings, in particular those of Persia who welcomed and delighted in such lavish displays. Besides, the purple suggested divinity, prompting Agamemnon's reply bidding Clytemnestra to revere him not as a god but as a man. Such excess was not for Greek kings. Still, Agamemnon succumbed to Clytemnestra's pleading, and after removing his strapped sandals, walked over the rich garments and broideries into his palace where the purple of divinity soon became the purple of blood and death.

Aeschylus helps us situate the practice in the Palestine of Jesus and Mark, which had been profoundly influenced by Persia and Persian ways during over two centuries of Persian rule. It also helps us appreciate the simplicity and modesty of Jesus' entry into Jerusalem. The people with Jesus paved his way with the simple cloaks of ordinary pilgrims, not rich purple garments and broideries. Different too would be Jesus' death. Agamemnon's death was brought on by hubris and human pretensions of divinity. Jesus' death came from submission to God's will and divine acceptance of humanity.

Besides their cloaks, people also carpeted Jesus' way with fronds and live vegetation cut from the fields nearby. Again, emphasis is on the sheer simplicity, almost a child's simplicity, of Jesus' royal and messianic entry into Jerusalem as Lord and Son of David.

We are then made to imagine Jesus surrounded by a crowd, some preceding him and some following, all crying hosannas evocative of Psalm 118, especially verses 25 and 26: "LORD, grant salvation. . . . Blessed is he / who comes in the name of the LORD." Jesus remains invisible throughout the procession. Nothing is said of his thoughts or how he reacted to the acclaim and what he saw around him.

The word, "Hosannah," is from the Aramaic rendering of the Hebrew word meaning "grant salvation." When the original Semitic expression is viewed as significant, Mark not only quotes it in a transliteration but immediately gives its Greek translation. In this case, there is no translation, and we must assume that "Hosannah" is used as a joyous acclamation with no specific connotation of prayer for salvation.

The crowd may be crying words from Psalm 118:25-26, but their acclamations bring the whole psalm to mind, as a few verses from the psalm beautifully illustrate:

> In danger I called on the LORD;
>   the LORD answered me and set me free.
> The LORD is with me; I am not afraid;
>   what can mortals do against me? (Ps 118:5-6)
>
> Open the gates of victory;
>   I will enter and thank the LORD.
> This is the LORD's own gate
>   where the victors enter.
> I thank you for you answered me;
>   you have been my savior.
> The stone the builders rejected
>   has become the cornerstone.
> By the LORD has this been done;
>   it is wonderful in our eyes.
> This is the day the LORD has made;
>   let us rejoice in it and be glad (Ps 118:19-24).

It is at this point that the cries of hosannah break in and the acclamation, "Blessed is he who comes in the name of the LORD."

Moving beyond Psalm 118, the crowd continues: "Blessed is the kingdom of our father David that is to come! / Hosanna in the highest!" The kingdom of David is not now. Jesus' entry is but a prophetic announcement and foreshadowing of its coming in the future when it will coincide perfectly with the kingdom of God. With this Mark orients Jesus' entry into Jerusalem along with its liturgical retelling to the ultimate coming of the Son of Man in glory and power, as presented by Jesus in Mark 13.

Attention now returns to Jesus, but only briefly. Jesus entered Jerusalem and went into the Temple area, where he looked around at everything, but since it was already late, he went to Bethany with the Twelve (11:11). By focusing the story on Jesus' entry into Jerusalem and separating it from the cleansing of the Temple, Mark highlights the importance of Jesus' coming as an event significant in itself, something we well appreciate when we see it pointing to the Lord's coming in glory at the consummation of history.

Cursing of the Fig Tree and the Cleansing of the Temple (11:12-25)

Entering Jerusalem for the first time, Jesus went directly to the Temple area and looked around at everything. Since it was already late *(opsias ede ouses tes horas),* he went out to Bethany with the Twelve (11:11).

The expression, "it was already late," gives the reason Jesus did not remain in the Temple and returned to Bethany. On the obvious narrative level, "late" refers to the time of day. On the less obvious symbolic level, it tells what Jesus saw looking around the Temple. For the Temple, it was already late!

In Greek, the expression, "it was already late," is a genitive absolute, a grammatically independent participial clause, introducing a distinct idea, that is related in some way to the rest of a sentence. In English, a genitive absolute can be indicated by parentheses or dashes. The precise meaning of a genitive absolute must be determined from the context.

In this case, the genitive absolute, "it was already late" *(opsias ede ouses tes horas,* literally, "the hour being already late") is related to the clause that precedes it as well as to the one that follows it. It describes what Jesus saw when he looked around the Temple, namely, he saw it was already late for the Temple. And this is the reason Jesus went back to Bethany, not alone, but with the Twelve, the foundations of a people who would include all the nations. He would then return with the Twelve on the following day.

So interpreted, what seemed to be a simple conclusion of Jesus' Messianic entry into Jerusalem is also an introduction for the next day's events, when Jesus, the Davidic Messiah, would curse the fig tree and cleanse the Temple (11:12-25).

The story of the cleansing of the Temple (11:15-19) is told within the story of the cursing of the fig tree (11:12-14, 20-25), presenting the two related events as one story. In this we recognize the sandwich pattern typical of Mark's Gospel. Of the two events, the cursing of the fig tree provides the cleansing of the Temple with a broader context, inviting us to see the Temple event, not as an isolated incident, but as part of a larger development affecting all of Israel. The cleansing of the Temple, for its part, focuses the cursing of the fig tree on Israel's place of worship, inviting us to see the fig tree event as epitomized in the prophetic cleansing and eventual destruction of the Temple.

The second part of the fig tree event, when Peter sees the tree completely withered and remembers what Jesus did (11:20-25), is situated on the day following (11:20). While related to the previous day, Jesus cursed the tree (11:12-14) and cleansed the Temple (11:15-19), it also introduces the next day's confrontations between Jesus and various parties and looks to the whole section's climax in Jesus' final departure from the Temple (13:1-2) and the eschatological discourse on the Mount of Olives (13:3-37).

The Cursing of the Fig Tree (11:12-14)

The previous day, Jesus went into Jerusalem and entered the Temple (11:11a) as the Davidic Messiah. He had come as the Son of David (see 10:46-52) in triumph (11:9-10) but with none of the trappings of wordly power (11:7). Looking around at everything, seeing that it was already late, Jesus returned to Bethany with the Twelve (11:11b). The following day, returning from Bethany with the Twelve, he was hungry (11:12).

Jesus Was Hungry (11:12). Jesus, the Son of David, the Davidic Messiah, was hungry *(epeinasen)*. This is the only time the Gospel speaks of Jesus being hungry. There was another reference of hunger in the Gospel, when Jesus asked the Pharisees, "Have you never read what David did when he was in need and he and his companions were hungry?" (2:25). On that occasion, David went "into the house of God when Abiathar was high priest and ate the bread of offering that only the priests could lawfully eat, and shared it with his companions" (2:26).

When David was hungry *(epeinasen)* he turned to the house of God and took the bread of offering to satisfy his hunger and also that of his companions. Jesus, the Son of David, was now hungry and he was going to the house of God with his companions, the Twelve. But unlike David, Jesus' hunger was not the kind that would be satisfied by physical nourishment. Jesus' hunger was Messianic. He hungered for the kingdom of God, the fulfillment of the kingdom of David, in which all nations would find a home.

A Fig Tree in Leaf (11:13). Seeing from a distance a fig tree in leaf, Jesus went to see if he might not find something on it, but coming to it he found nothing but leaves. For it was not time for figs. Fig trees lose their leaves at the end of the Palestinian dry season and sprout new ones during the rainy winter season. By Passover (see 14:1) fig trees are in full leaf (13:28), but their figs ripen only in June.

By itself, the image of the fig tree does not explain Jesus' reaction when he came to it and found nothing on it. But then, if Jesus' hunger was not an ordinary hunger, the fig tree must not have been an ordinary fig tree. An ordinary fig tree could not satisfy the hunger for the kingdom of God.

In New Testament times, the fig tree had long been a symbol for Israel, especially among the prophets. Mark's story of Jesus and the fig tree evokes several passages in particular. Consider, for example, Micah 7:1-2, which uses the image of the fig tree to refer to Israel and even refers to the Lord's hunger:

> Alas! I [the Lord] am as when the fruit is gathered,
>   as when the vines have been gleaned;
> There is no cluster to eat,
>   no early fig that I crave.
> The faithful are gone from the earth,
>   among men the upright are no more!

The faithful are like early figs for which the Lord craves, but there are none remaining on Israel's fig tree.

Consider, too, Hosea 9:10, 16, which also uses the images of the fig tree for Israel and of the figs for the Israelites:

> Like grapes in the desert,
>   I found Israel;
> Like the first fruits of the fig tree in its prime,
>   I considered your fathers. . . .
> Ephraim is stricken,
>   their root is dried up;
>   they shall bear no fruit.

Because of its wickedness, Israel's fig tree is completely withered and will no longer bear fruit (see also Joel 1:7, 12; Jer 8:13; 24).

Jesus Curses the Fig Tree (11:14). Mark interjects that it was not time for figs, that is for ordinary figs. Well enough, but the kingdom of God was at hand, and ordinary figs were not what Jesus sought. It was time for figs befitting the kingdom of God, figs to satisfy those who hunger for the kingdom. Like the Lord in Micah 7:1-2,

Jesus hungered for faithful Israelites, ready to welcome him "in the name of the Lord" (11:9) as Davidic Messiah.

When Jesus, hungry for the kingdom, approached the fig tree in leaf and found it without fruit, he responded with a terrible judgment: "May no one ever eat of your fruit again!" (11:14). The fig tree of Israel welcomed Jesus with its leaves, but without figs, it was not able to satisfy the Messiah's hunger.

That Jesus spoke to the fig tree should cause no astonishment. Was Jesus not the Lord of history and creation? Had he not rebuked the wind and spoken to the sea, "Quiet! Be still!"? Had not the wind and the sea heard and obeyed him (4:39), as the unclean spirit had done when Jesus cured the demoniac in the synagogue (1:25-26)? The wind and the sea, symbols of chaos and the forces of evil, had threatened the small boat of the church. The fig tree was in leaf but without fruit it was a symbol of Israel's barrenness. It was unprepared for the Davidic Messiah when he came hungry for the kingdom of God.

Jesus did not directly condemn the fig tree to death, but if no one would ever again eat of its fruit, why should it bear fruit? Fruit were to be eaten! And if the fig tree did not bear fruit, why should it live? The purpose of its existence was gone (11:21).

Jesus' cursing of the fig tree may seem a harsh judgment, especially when the passage is seen exclusively as Jesus' judgment against Israel. Similar judgments in the Old Testament were meant to shake Israel out of its complacence (see Mic 7:1-2; Hos 9:10, 16; Joel 1:7, 12; Jer 8:13; 24). But Mark's story of the fig tree was not directed at Israel. It was told to Christians, who needed to hear its message.

The first part of the story of the fig tree ends with the simple statement: "And his disciples heard it," that is, Jesus' curse (11:14b). Jesus' reply to the fig tree of Israel, "May no one ever eat of your fruit again!" (11:14a), was meant as a warning for Mark's community, heir to the disciples who heard it. Should they be unprepared to welcome the coming of the Lord and the kingdom of God, they too would hear Jesus' withering judgment.

The Cleansing of the Temple (11:15-19)

The disciples heard Jesus' reply to the fig tree. With that, the story of Jesus and the fig tree is interrupted, and that of Jesus and the cleansing of the Temple begins (11:15-19). The story of Jesus and the cleansing of the Temple shows just how late it was for the Temple (see 11:11), revealing at the same time why Jesus was so harsh with the fig tree (11:12-14). The Temple, the very center of

Jerusalem, Israel, and Jewish life everywhere, had been made into a den of thieves (11:17).

The story told in 11:12-14 was about Jesus and the Twelve (see 11:11), here seen as disciples who needed to learn what Jesus did and said (11:14b). The story in 11:15-19 shows Jesus continuing to teach them in deed and word.

"They Came to Jerusalem" (11:15a). After the opening statement, "They," that is Jesus and the disciples, "came to Jerusalem" (11:15a), the disciples practically disappear to return at the very end of the episode in a closing statement saying "they went out of the city" (11:19b). The story is about what Jesus did in the Temple (11:15b-17) and how the chief priests and the scribes reacted to it (11:18), but like the cursing of the fig tree, it was intended as a warning for the Twelve disciples, lest they invite a similar cleansing when the Son of Man came with power and glory (13:26). They ought to learn a lesson from the fig tree (13:28).

When Jesus entered the Temple, everything proceeded as though it was previously planned. Nothing is said about what Jesus now saw or what impression it made on him. There is no mention of anger, for example, and this needs to be noted, since so many refer to the episode as an example of righteous anger. But then, there was no need to mention Jesus' reaction. He had already taken stock of the situation the previous evening. Looking around at everything, Jesus had seen that it was already late (11:11). Now on the following day, entering the Temple area, Jesus acted on what he saw the evening before.

Historically, we need to think of the event as unfolding in the court of the Gentiles, the outer court whether Gentiles could enter along with Jews. The scene presents this part of the Temple, the only one open to Gentiles, as overrun with people selling and buying, making it impossible for Gentiles to pray. The Gospel, however, does not mention the court of the Gentiles, but refers simply to the Temple area *(to hieron),* without further specification. For Jesus, as presented in Mark, the whole Temple had been made a den of thieves.

The cleansing of the Temple first tells what Jesus did and taught (1:15b-17) and then how the chief priests and the scribes reacted (11:18). First Jesus set about throwing out those selling and buying in the Temple (11:15b). Then he overturned the tables of the money changers and the seats of those selling doves (11:15c). Finally, he did not allow anyone to carry anything through the Temple (11:16). After this, he taught them, citing the Septuagint version of Isaiah 56:7, "My house shall be called a house of prayer for all peoples," and referring to Jeremiah 7:11, telling that they had made it "a den of thieves."

Those Selling and Buying (11:15b). Immediately on entering the Temple area, Jesus began to throw out those selling and buying in the Temple (11:15a). Jerusalem was a fairly large commercial city, with large market areas for buying and selling, serving not only the local population but also the large number of visitors and Jewish pilgrims who came to Jerusalem from throughout the Roman Empire and even from the Parthian Empire.

These markets were under the legal jurisdiction of the Jewish Sanhedrin, which constituted the principal local authority in Jerusalem, but the taxes paid for purchases went to tax collectors who represented the Roman authority. Because of the many currencies involved, ranging quite widely in value, money changers, conveniently located at the city gate, provided an undeniable service.

An important part of Jerusalem's commerce was directly connected with the Temple, whose ceremonial involved not only sacrificial animals but also fine wood, oil, wine, grain, and incense, not to mention vestments made of costly imported materials and adorned with precious stones. The Temple was under the special jurisdiction of the high priest, and Temple moneys went into the Temple treasury, which was then used for the public sacrifices.

We can understand the temptation to draw commerce connected with the Temple into the Temple itself beyond the reach of Rome's tax collectors. We do not know to what extent this was actually done, but it is the specter held up by Mark in the introductory general statement describing Jesus as throwing out those selling and buying in the Temple (11:15b). The Temple had been turned into a marketplace, and Jesus set about restoring it to its true purpose.

Money Changers and Those Selling Doves (11:15c). After the introductory statement about those selling and buying, which may be more rhetorical than objective—Mark has a tendency to hyperbole—the story specifies that Jesus overturned the tables of the money changers and the seats of those selling doves (11:15c). Whatever may be said regarding other tax moneys, a special Temple tax was to be paid by every adult Jewish male twenty years or older. This tax, which consisted of a half shekel, had to be paid in silver Tyrian coin. The laws and regulations for this tax are in the fourth tractate, *Shekalim* ("shekel dues"), of the Mishnah's second division, *Moed* ("set feasts").

Collection of this tax, destined for the Temple treasury, began on the fifteenth of Adar, the twelfth month of the Jewish calendar, corresponding approximately to our month of March. For this tax "the tables [of money changers] were set up in the provinces; and on the twenty-fifth thereof they were set up in the temple" (*Shekalim,* 1.3). The twenty-fifth of Adar was twenty days before the feast of Passover, which was celebrated the following month on the fourteenth of Nisan.

Normally, we would expect the money changers to be seated at the Temple gates but Mark, along with Matthew 21:12 and John 2:15, imply they may have taken positions in the Temple itself. Since all transactions in the Temple area, including the purchase of doves and other offerings for sacrifice, were conducted in Tyrian currency, Temple money changers must have done a very brisk business.

Sacrificial animals included bulls, calves, sheep, rams, and lambs, as well as doves. Leviticus indicates doves as the proper sacrificial offering for women (Lev 12:6-8; see Luke 2:22-24), lepers (Lev 14:22), and some others (Lev 15:14, 29). In general, doves were the sacrificial offering of the poor. Even they were not to be tolerated in the Temple.

No Temple Short Cut (11:16). After overturning "the tables of the money changers and the seats of those who were selling doves," Jesus "did not permit anyone to carry anything through the temple area" (11:16). Overturning tables and chairs was a specific action. Not permitting people to carry anything through implies that Jesus took control of the Temple area. Like Jesus' authority as the Son of Man to forgive sins on earth (2:10) and his being lord of the sabbath, again as Son of Man (2:28), it speaks of Jesus' authority as Davidic Messiah over the Temple.

In exercising his authority, Jesus was enforcing regulations given in the first tractate, *Berakoth* ("blessings") of the Mishnah's first division, *Zeraim* ("seeds"): "He [a man] may not enter into the Temple Mount with his staff or his sandal or his wallet, or with the dust upon his feet, nor may he make of it a short by-path; still less may he spit there" (*Berakoth,* 9.5). The purpose of these regulations, which reveal deep respect for the holy place, was to safeguard the sanctity of the Temple.

The Temple covered a very large area. Going around it to enter and leave the city, especially while carrying something, took a fair amount of time and energy. We can understand the temptation to take a short cut, gradually transforming the Temple area into a thoroughfare.

"Then He Taught Them" (11:17). After cleansing the Temple, Jesus "taught them." He taught those who had been selling and buying, the money changers and those selling doves, those carrying things through the Temple, and his disciples, the Twelve. He asked them a question: "Is it not written: 'My house shall be called a house of prayer for all peoples'?" (11:17a). Jesus' cleansing of the Temple was to make it once again a house of prayer.

Only Mark includes "for all peoples." Matthew 21:13 and Luke 20:46 omit these words. The expression reflects Mark's general concern for the Christian community's openness to Gentiles as well as Jews. For those familiar with the structure of the Temple, it is clear that the court of the Gentiles, the only part of the Temple where Gentiles could enter and pray, had been made into a marketplace and a thoroughfare, making it impossible for Gentiles to pray. Jesus made the court of the Gentiles once again a suitable place for Gentiles, "all nations," to pray.

Mark, however, does not presuppose such familiarity. In his view the Temple as such, the Lord's house, was to be a house of prayer. It was to be a house of prayer not only for Jews but for Gentiles as well. And that was Jesus' intent in cleansing it. Besides, the Temple had been made into a den of thieves. Dishonesty at changing money and in the sale of doves for sacrificial offerings was an easy temptation. Jeremiah's expression, "a den of thieves," provided a strong prophetic alternative to "a house of prayer," hyperbolic perhaps, but quite effective for awakening people to what was involved.

The Chief Priests and the Scribes (11:18). "The chief priests and the scribes came to hear of it and were seeking a way to put him to death" (11:18a). With that the story moves well beyond the cleansing of the Temple. What Jesus did should normally have provoked an immediate reaction, at least from the money changers and those selling doves, but no such reaction is indicated. As Mark tells it, everyone seems to have remained quite calm, allowing Jesus to teach, interpreting what he did with reference to the Scriptures. The reaction of the chief priests and the scribes presupposes an indeterminate passage of time. In its present form, the story seems to reflect early Christian catechesis concerning Jesus' mission far more than an actual historical event.

The statement that "the chief priests and the scribes came to hear of it," that is, of what Jesus did and taught, recalls the reaction of the Pharisees at the end of the Gospel's first section. Jesus had just challenged the synagogue whether it was "lawful to do good on the sabbath rather than to do evil, to save life rather than to destroy it" (3:4). When they remained silent, Jesus looked around at them angrily and grieved at their hardness of heart. When he proceeded to

cure the withered hand of one of those in the synagogue, "the Pharisees went out and immediately took counsel with the Herodians
against him to put him to death" (3:6).

All this while, the Pharisees and the Herodians have been looking for a way to put Jesus to death. The chief priests and the scribes
now joined in that effort. From the beginning the Gospel insisted on
Jesus' growing fame "throughout the whole region of Galilee" (1:28;
see 1:45; 2:12). People came to him from Judea as well (3:7), and
even from Jerusalem (3:8).

Now with the cleansing of the Temple, in Jerusalem itself "the
whole crowd was astonished at his teaching." Jesus had established
his authority not only in the synagogue (3:1-6) but even in the
Temple, blocking the efforts of the chief priests and the scribes to
put him to death. They feared him, because of the crowd, as they
would continue to fear him (see 12:12) until the beginning of the
passion (14:1-2) and "Judas Iscariot, one of the Twelve, went off to
the chief priests to hand him over to them" (14:10).

"When evening came, they went out of the city," as they did the
previous evening. They would return early the following morning,
to discover just how late it had been for the fig tree, a symbol of
judgment on Israel and a warning for the disciples.

The Lesson of the Withered Fig Tree (11:20-25[26])

The first time Jesus entered Jerusalem, he went into the Temple
area, saw how late it was, and returned to Bethany (11:1-11). It was
indeed very late for the Temple!

The next day, Jesus returned to the Temple area and immediately
set about cleansing it of the sellers and buyers, along with their
chairs and tables, and everything that prevented the Temple from
being "a house of prayer for all peoples" (11:15-19).

On the way, he had come upon a fig tree that was in leaf but without fruit. It may not have been time *(kairos)* for ordinary figs. It was
time *(kairos)* for the kind that could satisfy Jesus' hunger for the
kingdom of God. And Jesus cursed the fig tree, that no one ever
again would be able to eat of its fruit (11:12-14).

The following day, early in the morning, Jesus and the disciples
once again set out for Jerusalem and the Temple area (11:20-25; see
v. 27). The passage includes a short introduction, giving the setting
(11:20), Peter's exclamation at seeing the withered fig tree (11:21),
Jesus' response to Peter (11:22), and three sayings (11:23, 24, 25),
together constituting two-thirds of the passage. Jesus' response and
the sayings constitute a mini-discourse (11:22-25).

The episode is not just an appendix to the cursing of the fig tree and the cleansing of the Temple, allowing Mark to introduce three important sayings of Jesus. The sayings could stand on their own, and may well have done so in early Christian tradition, but Mark has woven them into the story as part of a tightly knit and rhetorically very logical mini-discourse by Jesus.

To see the logic in the discourse, one must view the cursing of the fig tree (11:12-14) and the cleansing of the Temple (11:15-19), not so much as a prophetic judgment on Israel and its Temple worship, but as a prophetic warning to the disciples and the Church in Mark's time.

A brief preliminary paraphrase should help make the order and logic of the passage more obvious. The day after the cleansing of the Temple, Jesus and the disciples set out for Jerusalem and the Temple area (11:20, see v. 26). As they were walking along, they passed by the fig tree and found it withered to its roots (11:20). Peter, remembering how Jesus had cursed the fig tree, exclaimed at what happened (11:21), and Jesus responded: the disciples had to learn the lesson of the fig tree (11:22-25). They needed the "faith in God," literally, the "faith of God" (*pistin theou,* 11:22), a strong faith, indeed, a divine faith that could move mountains (11:23).

With such faith, their prayer regarding the future would surely be answered (11:24) and their past transgressions forgiven, so long as they forgave those against whom they themselves had a grievance (11:25). Their own Temple, one not made with human hands (see 14:58), would thus be a house of prayer for all the nations. Only in this way would they would bear fruit for the kingdom of God and avoid the fate of the fig tree.

The last of the sayings has an affinity to the petition for the forgiveness of sins in the Lord's prayer, all but inviting the readers and copyists to introduce Matthew 6:15 into the text of Mark: "But if you do not forgive others, neither will your Father forgive your transgressions." In some manuscripts this Matthean verse became Mark 11:26. But it is omitted in the best manuscripts as well as in modern translations. However, like many other textual emendations, it does provide important early commentary on Mark 11:25.

The Withered Fig Tree (11:20-21). It was early in the morning, the beginning of a day that would include a whole series of tests and confrontations (11:27–12:34) and further teaching from Jesus in the Temple (12:35-44). The day would end with Jesus and the disciples leaving the Temple and sitting on the Mount of Olives opposite the Temple area for a long discourse (13:1-37).

Jesus and the disciples were walking by, when they saw the fig tree withered to its roots. When Jesus cursed the fig tree, he said, "May no one ever eat of your fruit again!" The curse could have made the fig tree barren. It could also have made its figs tasteless or repulsive. There was nothing to suggest the fig tree was about to wither to its roots.

The disciples had heard Jesus curse the fig tree (11:14), and on seeing the fig tree withered, Peter remembered and exclaimed, "Rabbi, look! The fig tree that you cursed has withered." For the early Christians, remembering was more than recollecting. It enabled someone to see how the past had an impact on the present, giving it meaning, and orienting it into the future. Remembering was a very act of understanding. In this case, remembering disposed Peter to hear Jesus' response.

Later, while Peter was in the courtyard of the house of the high priest, he would again remember a word of Jesus, "Before the cock crows twice you will deny me three times" (14:72; 14:30). In this case, Peter broke down in tears. Remembering disposed Peter for repentance.

Peter addressed Jesus as Rabbi, "My Teacher," as he had done at the transfiguration, "Rabbi, it is good that we are here! Let us make three tents: one for you, one for Moses, and one for Elijah" (9:5). Jesus was teaching Peter and the disciples, and Peter, ever the spokesman (see 8:29; 10:28), recognized Jesus as their teacher.

The story is very visual. Peter invites Jesus to look, "Rabbi, look." Through Peter, Mark also invites his readers to look and see the withered fig tree through the eyes of Jesus.

Jesus' Mini-discourse (11:22-25). Jesus' response to Peter and the others is most unusual: "Have [the] faith of God." In most versions, it is rendered, "Have faith in God," which may be right, but I think there is a far better alternative.

The Faith of God (11:22). The Greek expression, which appears nowhere else in the New Testament, is *echete pistin theou,* literally, "Have (the) faith of God." The translation depends on whether the expression "of God," whose case is genitive, is understood as objective or as subjective.

If the Greek term for "of God" is an objective genitive, the translation, "Have faith in God," would be fine. But elsewhere in Mark's Gospel, where the term "faith" is accompanied by a pronoun (*auton,* "of them," 2:5; *sou,* "your," 5:34; 10:52), the genitive case of the pronoun is not objective but clearly subjective. "Their faith," or "the faith of them," does not mean "faith in themselves," but the faith they themselves have.

I suggest the same may be true in this case, and that the genitive is subjective. Jesus would thus be telling Peter and the others that their faith must equal the faith that God himself has.

Faith has several dimensions. One of those is the interpersonal dimension. From this point of view, faith is based on a personal relationship and consists in a form of trusting knowledge. Since such faith usually implies some kind of dependency, it is hard to imagine that God, the creator of the universe and the lord of history, would have faith in anyone. And so we assume "the faith *of* God" must actually refer to "faith *in* God."

A second dimension of faith is based on someone's personal authority and consists in a form of confident power. It is easy to imagine God having this kind of faith. "The faith of God" would then refer to the divine confidence of God when God commands light and creation into being (see Gen 1:1–2:4a).

Jesus would thus be telling Peter and the others that their faith must equal the faith of God. This divine faith would enable them to do things that are impossible for human beings but possible for God, for whom all things are possible (10:27). But, of course, this faith is itself impossible for Jesus' disciples, since they are not God, but mere human beings. It does become possible, however, if they allow the faith of God, that is, God's effective power, to operate in and through them.

Faith That Moves Mountains (11:23). The first saying refers to one of those things that are impossible for human beings but possible for God: "Amen, I say to you, whoever says to this mountain, 'Be lifted up and thrown into the sea,' and does not doubt in his heart but believes that what he says will happen, it shall be done for him" (11:23).

The saying opens with a favorite expression Jesus used to capture attention and highlight somethings importance: "Amen, I say to you." This is the seventh time Jesus uses the expression in Mark's Gospel (3:28; 8:12; 9:1, 41; 10:15, 29; 11:23). As elsewhere, including later in the Gospel (12:43; 13:30; 14:9, 18, 25, 30), its "Amen" evokes contexts of liturgical prayer.

Mountains do not move by the power of a human will. Nor do they move merely because of a personal relationship someone might enjoy with God. God, however, as the creator of the mountains, can make them move. Having faith in God and with the faith of God at work in them, Jesus' disciples also can make them move.

The saying is a hyperbole. God is not capricious. God respects created nature. The disciples could not expect mountains to obey an order to move, even if they had the very faith of God. The hyperbole was to shake them out of their complacency and make them realize just how great a faith they needed, that it was entirely beyond human reach. Earlier in the Gospel, Jesus did the same with another hyperbole, one that astonished the disciples and occasioned his response about humanly impossible things that were divinely possible: "It is easier for a camel to pass through [the] eye of [a] needle than for one who is rich to enter the kingdom of God." No camel can ever get through the eye of a needle.

Both hyperboles were meant to make the disciples aware of something extremely important. In the "camel" saying, it was to tell them how great an obstacle wealth could be for entering the kingdom of God. In this instance, the disciples needed to know it would not be easy to avoid the fate of the fig tree. To do so, they needed the kind of faith that could come to them only as a gratuitous gift from God. What they could do, however, was pray for that gift.

Faith and Prayer (11:24). Jesus continued the mini-discourse with a second saying, this one having to do with prayer: "Therefore I tell you, all that you ask for in prayer, believe that you will receive it and it shall be yours" (11:24). The disciples not only could but needed to pray for the faith required to avoid the fate of the fig tree.

Like the first saying, the second also refers to faith, but with the verb, "to believe" or "to have faith" *(pisteuo),* from which the Greek noun for "faith" *(pistis)* was derived. But this time, what is intended is the first dimension of faith, the one based on someone's personal relationship with God and consisting in trusting knowledge. The only power the disciples have is that of prayer. Jesus assures them that if they ask it in prayer, "the faith *of* God" will be given them provided they have faith *in* God.

This is the second time in the Gospel Jesus associates prayer with faith. On one occasion, when the disciples were unable to cast out the demon "epilepsy" from a young boy, Jesus personally cast the demon out, saying, "Everything is possible to one who has faith" (9:23). Later when they were alone, the disciples asked why they had been unable to cast out the demon. Jesus told them that this kind of demon could only come out through prayer (9:28-29).

Prayer and Forgiveness (11:25). In order to avoid the fate of the fig tree, the disciples needed to have "the faith *of* God," a faith so great it equaled God's creative power to move mountains. In order to have such faith, the disciples needed to have faith *in* God and pray that he grant it to them. But there was a condition for their prayer to be effective. That condition is spelled out in Jesus' third and last saying in the mini-discourse: "When you stand to pray, forgive anyone against whom you have a grievance, so that your heavenly Father may in turn forgive you your transgressions" (11:25).

To avoid the fate of the fig tree, the disciples had to be concerned about the future, hence their primary need for prayer looks to the future. But they also needed to be concerned about their past transgressions. These stood in the way of their interpersonal relationship with God and needed to be forgiven by God. God was prepared to forgive their transgressions, but on condition they themselves personally forgave anyone who had a grievance against them.

The saying has strong echoes of teaching preserved in Jesus' sermon on the mount in Matthew 6:5-15, especially in the Lord's Prayer, with its reference to the heavenly Father (Matt 6:9) and the petition for forgiveness (Matt 6:12), but also in an independent saying: "If you forgive others their transgressions, your heavenly Father will forgive you" (Matt 6:14).

It is not the one who has offended who forgives, but the one who was offended. That is why Jesus does not ask the disciples to beg forgiveness of those they have offended. What he does ask is that the disciples forgive anyone against whom they have a grievance, whether intended or unintended.

If the disciples forgive others, they will be forgiven. When the disciples are forgiven, they will enjoy the faith relationship to God needed for their prayer to be answered. Having "the faith of God" and avoiding the fate of the fig tree depended entirely on that prayer and God's response to it.

Such was the lesson of the fig tree.

Jesus' Teaching in the Temple (11:27–12:44)

"They returned once more to Jerusalem" (11:27a). This was the third time in as many days Jesus entered Jerusalem, each time going to the Temple area.

The first time, Jesus entered as the Messiah and was greeted with cries of "Hosanna!" Looking around at everything, Jesus saw how late it was for the Temple and all it had come to represent, so he went out to Bethany with the Twelve (11:1-11).

The next day, leaving Bethany for Jerusalem, Jesus was hungry. Finding no fruit on a fig tree, a symbol for Israel, he cursed it. True, the time for figs was past, but Jesus was hungry for the kingdom of God and the fig tree was barren (11:12-14). When they came to Jerusalem, Jesus revealed his authority as the Messiah, cleansing the Temple of sellers and buyers and taking command of it as "a house of prayer for all peoples." When evening came, they again went out of the city (11:15-19).

The next morning, walking back to Jerusalem, Peter marveled how the fig tree was withered to its roots, and Jesus taught them a personal lesson from what happened to the fig tree (11:20-25 [26]).

Returning to Jerusalem for the third time, Jesus taught as the Messiah. We have already seen how it was late for the Temple (11:11) and no longer time for figs (11:13). We now see how the symbol of the fig tree applied to the Jewish leaders and provided a warning for the others, especially for the disciples (11:27–12:44).

While Jesus was walking in the Temple area, various groups and parties came up to him and challenged him, first the chief priests, the scribes and the elders (11:27–12:12), then the Pharisees and the Herodians (12:13-17), then some Sadducees (12:18-27), and finally one of the scribes (12:28-34). Each time Jesus challenged them in return until "no one dared to ask him any more questions" (12:34).

Jesus then proceeded to teach about the scribes and their claims concerning the Messiah (12:35-37). After warning everyone against their behavior (12:38-40), he sat opposite the treasury where a poor widow's contribution inspired an important lesson for his disciples (12:41-44).

Jesus and the Chief Priests, the Scribes, and the Elders: The Authority of Jesus (11:27–12:12)

"They returned once more to Jerusalem" (11:27a), or more literally, "and they came again *(palin)* to Jerusalem." The statement provides the setting for Jesus' teaching "as he was walking in the Temple area" (11:27b) and while sitting "opposite the treasury" (12:41). Jesus would remain in Jerusalem and the Temple area until he went up on the Mount of Olives and gave a great discourse there (13:1-37).

The use of the adverb "again" *(palin)* is typical of Mark.[2] Here in the opening statement, it recalls the previous time Jesus came to

---

[2] Mark often uses the adverb "again" *(palin)* to connect a new event with a previous one. That is how, for example, he connected Jesus' breaking the bread for four thousand people (8:1-9) with his breaking the bread for five thousand men (6:34-44), inviting us to note the development from 6:34-44 to 8:1-9. Earlier in the Gospel, the same adverb *(palin)* associated Jesus' return to Capernaum (2:1) and the controversies in 2:1–3:6 with the first

Jerusalem and the time before that, relating the whole series of controversies (11:27–12:44) to Jesus' Messianic entry into Jerusalem, the cursing of the fig tree, and the cleansing of the Temple.

The encounters in the Temple at Jerusalem recall the controversies that took place at the beginning of Jesus' Galilean ministry (2:1–3:6). At the conclusion of those controversies, the Pharisees took counsel with the Herodians to have Jesus put to death. This time, it is the chief priests, the scribes, and the elders who want to have Jesus arrested (12:12). The Pharisees and the Herodians do reappear, however, trying to ensnare Jesus in his speech (12:13).

As Jesus was walking in the Temple area, the first group to approach him was the chief priests, the scribes, and the elders, the same who were mentioned in the Gospel's first announcement of the passion: "the Son of Man must suffer greatly and be rejected by the elders, the chief priests, and the scribes, and be killed, and rise after three days" (8:31). We recall that when the chief priests and the scribes came to hear of Jesus' cleansing of the Temple, they sought a way to have him put to death but were afraid because of the crowd, which was spellbound at his teaching (11:18).

In the passion, the chief priests, the scribes, and the elders would play a major role in the condemnation of Jesus. At first, their efforts were stymied by fear the people might riot (14:1-2). Eventually, thanks to Judas (14:10-11), they succeeded, arresting Jesus (14:43), bringing him to judgment before the high priest (14:53), and handing him over to Pilate (15:1).

At this last mention (15:1), Mark identifies the chief priests, the scribes, and the elders as the Sanhedrin, the Jewish governing body in Jerusalem.[3] It is not that the entire Sanhedrin approached Jesus while he was walking in the Temple. The setting suggests a small body representing each of its three groups. Later, in the passion story, the whole Sanhedrin would gather first at the palace of the high priest (14:53) and once again before handing Jesus over to Pilate (15:1).

---

time he came to Capernaum (1:21). Jesus' manifestation of authority *(exousia)* in 2:1-12 must consequently be seen in light of the earlier manifestation in 1:21-28.

[3] In *Jerusalem in the Time of Jesus* (Philadelphia: Fortress Press, 1969), Joachim Jeremias described the Sanhedrin as "the highest administrative and judicial authority of Jewry" (151); its members included the chief priests, that is the priestly nobility (196–98), the elders, who represented the lay aristocracy (222–25), and the scribes, a learned class, skilled in scriptural, especially legal, interpretation (236–37).

The Sanhedrin's authority was primarily over Jewish religious matters. But in a religious state, where politics, social life, and the culture were completely pervaded by religion, authority in religious matters extended to just about everything. Any limitations on their authority came from Judaea's status as a prefecture, subject in various ways to the governor of Syria and ultimately to the emperor in Rome.[4]

The Sanhedrin Questions Jesus' Authority (11:28). As the highest authority in Judaism, the Sanhedrin was very concerned about Jesus' authority, directly challenging their own. And so, the high priests, the scribes, and the elders approached Jesus with questions about his authority and who gave it to him: "By what authority *(exousia)* are you doing these things? Or who gave you this authority *(exousia)* to do them?"

They were asking concerning Jesus' authority for cleansing the Temple, taking command of it, forbidding anyone to use it as a shortcut for transporting things, and declaring it "a house of prayer for all peoples." In the context of Mark 11:1–12:12, they also were asking about Jesus' cursing of the fig tree and his messianic entry into Jerusalem.

The chief priests, the scribes, and the elders had no interest in Jesus' messianic mission. Their interest was in drawing out of Jesus some claim of divine authority. They would then be able to accuse him of blasphemy, as they did later in the palace of the high priest (14:61-63). It never occurred to them that Jesus' authority *(exousia)* might actually have been divine.

The chief priests, the scribes, and the elders were challenging Jesus' authority. By what authority was he doing these things? If not his own, who gave him the authority? It certainly did not come from the high priest, who presided over the Sanhedrin, or any of them. Nor did it come from the Romans, who dealt very gently with anything to do with the Temple. The main function of the Roman guard was to ensure order. Who then did Jesus' authority come from?

The matter of Jesus' authority *(exousia)* had already come up very early in the Gospel. Indeed, it was the first major question to sur-

---

[4] "The Sanhedrin's greatest influence was in Judaea, for after Judaea became a Roman province in A.D. 6, the Sanhedrin was its chief political agency. A committee of the Sanhedrin was in charge of finance in the eleven Jewish toparchies into which the Romans had divided the land. Furthermore, the Sanhedrin was at that time the first communal court of justice in the province, and finally it was the highest Jewish court of law in all Judaea" (Jeremias, op. cit., 74).

face. When Jesus came to Capernaum and taught in the synagogue on the sabbath, the people were astounded by his teaching, "for he taught them as one having authority [*exousia*] and not as the scribes" (1:22). Here was "a new teaching with authority" *(exousia),* whom even unclean spirits obeyed (1:27).

Jesus' authority came up again when Jesus returned to Capernaum (2:1) and demonstrated his authority to forgive sins by healing a paralytic. When Jesus said to the paralytic, "Child, your sins are forgiven," the scribes considered the statement as blasphemy (2:5-7). After questioning them about this, Jesus continued: "But that you may know that the Son of Man has authority [*exousia*] to forgive sins on earth"—he said to the paralytic, "I say to you, rise, pick up your mat, and go home" (2:10-11). Later, Jesus would give the Twelve authority over demons (3:15) and unclean spirits (6:7).

Already in the prologue, at the very beginning of the Gospel, John the Baptist proclaimed: "One mightier than I is coming after me" *(opiso mou),* that is, "One of my followers is greater and stronger than I am" (1:7). Implicitly, John was referring to Jesus' authority and to its source. Baptized by John, and so his follower, Jesus was also baptized by the Spirit, revealing him as God's beloved Son (1:9-11). While John was baptizing with water, Jesus would baptize with the Holy Spirit (1:8).

Jesus Responds with a Question (11:29-30). Jesus did not answer the Sanhedrin's questions. Instead, he redirected the dialogue, putting the chief priests, the scribes, and the elders on the spot. They had asked him two questions. He responded with one of his own: "Was John's baptism of heavenly or of human origin?" (11:30). If they answered this question, he would respond to theirs (11:29).

The way the question is introduced is significant. Literally the Gospel says: "Jesus said to them, 'I will ask you one word [*logos*], and you answer me. . . .'" The "word" of Jesus is very important in Mark. Jesus "preached the word" (2:2), "the gospel of God" (1:14), sometimes "in parables" (4:2).

The term *logos* could also refer to a particular word, announcing his passion-resurrection (8:32; see 8:31), inviting someone to follow him (10:22), or praying to his Father (14:39). In the plural, Jesus' words *(logoi)* could refer to his various teachings (8:38; 10:24; 13:31). In his response to the chief priests, the scribes, and the elders, it took the form of a question, incisive as the two-edged sword of the gospel of God.

Jesus' question transferred the matter of authority to another plain altogether. Jesus did not tell them that his authority came from God and that it was invested in him as Son of Man. Nor would he do so unless they declared themselves on the origins of John's authority. Was his baptism of divine origin or human origin? From Jesus' point of view, it was clearly divine. So also for Mark's Gospel.

At the beginning of the prologue, a quotation from Isaiah 40:3 with elements from Malachi 3:1 and Exodus 23:20 had presented John's mission as from God:

> "Behold, I am sending my messenger ahead of you;
>   he will prepare your way.
> A voice of one crying in the desert:
>   'Prepare the way of the Lord,
>   make straight his paths'" (1:2-3).

John's mission was comparable to that of Elijah (Mal 3:23), as could be seen from his garments (2 Kgs 1:7-8). And the mission of Elijah the prophet was surely from God (2 Kgs 1:3).

Discussion and Response (11:31-33). The chief priests, the scribes, and the elders had tried to trick Jesus by admitting that he acted on his own authority or by blasphemy. Deftly blocking their effort, Jesus tricked them in return. There was no way they could answer.

If they admitted that John's baptism was of heavenly origin, they would have to answer for not believing him. That surely would be Jesus' next question (11:31). John's mission was to prepare the way for Jesus, one of his followers who was mightier than John (1:7). He did that "proclaiming a baptism of repentance [*metanoia*] for the forgiveness of sins" (1:4). Had the chief priests, the scribes, and the elders believed John, they would have repented and would now be followers of Jesus, the one whose way John prepared.

On the other hand, if they said John's baptism was of human origin, they had the crowd to fear, "for they all thought John really was a prophet" (11:32). Even Herod was in awe of John, "knowing him to be a righteous and holy man" (6:20). After John was put to death, people thought he had been raised from the dead and the source of mighty powers at work in Jesus (6:14). Again, Jesus was associated with John. People thought John was a prophet, with a divine mission, now being fulfilled in Jesus' mission.

The chief priests, the scribes, and the elders were trapped. There was no way they could answer without admitting their unbelief or risking the judgment, perhaps even a riot, in the crowd. The only way out was to say they did not know. But then Jesus would not have to tell them by what authority he entered Jerusalem as the

Messiah, cursed the fig tree, cleansed the Temple, took command of it, and made it "a house of prayer for all peoples," as it was intended to be. And that is how the dialogue ended.

Jesus Began to Speak in Parables (12:1a). With Jesus' refusal to say by what authority he did "all these things," the encounter with the chief priests, the scribes, and the elders seems to have come to end. But not so. Taking the initiative, Jesus challenged the Sanhedrin as they had challenged him. In the dialogue, Jesus had blocked their offensive. Now he "began to speak to them in parables" and put them on the defensive. They had tried to bring judgment on Jesus. He now brought judgment on them. In a sense the dialogue (11:27-33) had been but an introduction.

Jesus began to speak in parables. We recall the expression "in parables" *(en parabolais)* from the discourse in and on parables (4:1-34; see 4:2, 11). On that occasion, Jesus told those around him who were with the Twelve: "The mystery of the kingdom of God has been granted to you. But to those outside, that is, to those who were not with the Twelve, everything comes in parables, so that

'they may look and see but not perceive,
  and hear and listen but not understand,
  in order that they may not be converted
  and be forgiven'" (4:11-12).

The time of John the Baptist and his "baptism of repentance for the forgiveness of sins" (1:4) was over. John had already been arrested (1:14). It was now time to be "with the Twelve." The mystery of the kingdom of God was given only to those inside "with the Twelve." Those outside *(exo),* apart from the Twelve, would never understand.

Really understanding the parables, that is, responding to them and fulfilling their purpose, requires following Christ with the Twelve. Apart from that, the parables remain opaque, like reflecting on experiences that are totally foreign. After listening to Jesus, the chief priests, the scribes, and the elders knew that Jesus addressed the parable to them, and they were seeking to arrest him. They simply did not have the eyes to see or the ears to hear, and they remained outsiders (12:12).

When Jesus spoke in parables before, his discourse included four parables: the parable of the sower (4:3-8), and those of the lamp (4:21-22), the seed (4:26-29), and the mustard seed (4:30-32). This time the discourse includes only one, the parable of the tenants (12:1-11). Speaking "in parables" describes a way of speaking, not a collection of parables.

Parable of the Tenants (12:1b-11).[5] The parable of the tenants is unique among all the parables attributed to Jesus. Other parables in Mark alluded to Scripture, but not like the parable of the tenants. The conclusion of the parable of the seed that grows of itself, for example, "he wields the sickle at once, for the harvest has come" (4:29), recalls Joel 4:13, "Apply the sickle / for the harvest is ripe." The conclusion of the parable of the mustard seed, "so that the birds of the sky can dwell in its shade" (4:32), recalls Ezekiel 17:23, "Birds of every kind shall dwell beneath it," that is, beneath the cedar of Israel (see also Ezek 31:6).

The parable of the tenants drew on Scripture for its basic framework. The opening description, "A man [*anthropos*] planted a vineyard, put a hedge around it, dug a wine press, and built a tower," comes directly from Isaiah's Song of the Vineyard (5:1-2, LXX), except for one word, "man" *(anthropos)*. In Isaiah, it is the Lord of hosts who planted the vineyard (Isa 5:7).

Part of the parable's story conclusion, "What [then] will the owner of the vineyard do?" (12:9a) recalls Isaiah 5:5, "Now I will let you know what I mean to do." As in the case of Isaiah 5:1-2, however, the allusion is to the Septuagint, which transformed the Hebrew declaration into a question: "Now what shall I [the Lord] tell you I will do . . . ?" Concluding the parable, Jesus adds a formal quotation (12:10-11) from Psalm 118:22-23, again from the Septuagint.

The parable's quotations from and allusive references to Isaiah's Song of the Vineyard (Isa 5:1-6), as well as the formal quotation from Psalm 118, transform the parable into a rich allegory, of which the owner's servants and beloved son are a part. Other parables of Jesus may have a few allegorical elements. Nowhere, however, do these take over the parable so completely (Mark 12:1-11; Matt 21:33-42).

The parable's form in Mark (and Matthew) is quite different from the way Jesus might have told it, where allusions and quotations from Scripture would have come from the Hebrew Bible instead of the Septuagint. The same must be said of the earliest tradition. As we find it in Mark, the parable comes from a later Greek-speaking church, in which the Scriptures were read and quoted from the Septuagint.

Most likely, the parable originated with Jesus, but in another form. Although that form is now impossible to reconstruct, it must have corresponded quite closely to C. H. Dodd's classic definition:

---

[5] Other names for the parable include "The Parable of the Wicked Husbandmen," "The Parable of the Stewards," "The Parable of the Wicked Tenants," and "The Parable of the Defiant Tenants."

At its simplest the parable is a metaphor or simile drawn from nature or common life, arresting the hearer by its vividness or strangeness, and leaving the mind in sufficient doubt about its precise application to tease it into active thought.[6]

As told by Jesus, the parable most likely dealt with an absentee landlord and tenant farmers who took advantage of his absence and stirred up trouble, hoping to appropriate the vineyard. Such situations were not uncommon in the revolutionary climate of first-century Galilee.

As told in Mark, Jesus' parable has been transformed into an allegory, where the vineyard is Israel, the tenants are Israel's leaders—the chief priests, the scribes, and the elders—the owner of the vineyard is God, the messengers are prophets, the son is Christ, the punishment of the tenants represents the destruction of Israel, and the other people are Christians—those who were "of Christ" (*Christou*, 9:41), many of whom were of Gentile origins.

From a literary point of view, the allegory stands midway between a parable, such as that of the seed (4:3-8), and its allegorical interpretation (4:14-20). In the allegory of the tenants (12:1-11), the allegorical interpretation is brought directly into the original parable. Instead of interpreting it from the outside, it transforms it from the inside.

The Vineyard (12:1b). First, the owner "planted a vineyard, put a hedge around it, dug a wine press, and built a tower." The owner then leased the vineyard to farmers and went away (12:12b).

It was all very simple and practical. The hedge was necessary to keep animals and marauders out. It could be made of thornbushes, thistles, and other scrub-brush from the area, cleared while planting the vineyard.

Digging the wine press meant removing the soil and preparing basins for trampling the grapes and collecting their juice. In the days of Isaiah, a winepress usually included two basins, square or circular, cut out of the rocky ground and joined by a channel. The upper basin was larger. It was used for treading the grapes. The lower, smaller basin was used for pressing the grapes, collecting the juice, and for the earliest stage of fermentation. The fermenting wine was then transferred to jars or skins, new skins for new wine (2:22).

---

[6] C. H. Dodd, *The Parables of the Kingdom* (New York: Charles Scribner's Sons, 1961) 5. On the same page, Dodd speaks of the parables as "the natural expression of a mind that sees truth in concrete pictures rather than conceives it in abstractions."

In New Testament times, a wine press often included only one basin with a sump built into it, a depression which served as a reservoir for collecting the juice. Such winepresses have been found at various sites in Judaea and Samaria. Recently, one was identified in the ruins of Qumran.[7]

The tower was built of field stones collected in the area. Rising some ten or fifteen feet in the midst of the vineyard, it provided shelter, storage space, and a vantage point.

A Series of Servants (12:2-5). In Isaiah's Song of the Vineyard, there is no question of the owner going on a journey, leaving the vineyard in the care of tenant farmers. The owner himself is the farmer, from beginning to end. When it came time to harvest the grapes, he expected to find good grapes, but the vineyard yielded only wild grapes. So he took away the hedge, gave the vineyard over to grazing, allowing it to be "overgrown with thorns and briers" (Isa 5:2b-6).

In Isaiah's Song, the problem that arose was with the vineyard itself, that is with "the house of Israel" (Isa 5:7). In the parable of the tenants, the problem was not with the vineyard but with the tenant farmers entrusted with its care.

The complex of images includes that of an earthly owner, an absentee landlord and his vineyard. But in view of the allusion to Isaiah 5:1-2, these clearly refer to God and Israel. It also includes the image of ordinary tenant farmers, but since their vineyard is the house of Israel, the image refers to those responsible for bringing God's vineyard to a fruitful harvest, namely the rulers and leaders.

When it was time, the owner sent a servant *(doulos)* to obtain some of the fruit of the vine. Taking the servant, the farmers beat him and sent him away with nothing (12:2-3). The Greek term translated as servant is *doulos,* which is very difficult to render in English. The *doulos* has some of the characteristics of a servant in that, like the *diakonos* (servant), the term refers to someone who serves. The *doulos,* however, has more of the characteristics of a slave, one totally at the service or disposition of a master *(kurios).*

---

[7] Father Roland de Vaux had identified the installation as a basin for levigating, storing, or dumping clay, as part of a potter's workshop. Recently, Father Jean Baptiste Humbert distinguished this later purpose from an earlier one when the installation served as a winepress. See J. B. Humbert, "L'espace sacre a Qumran. Proposition pour l'archeologie," "Annexe by Stephen Pfann," *Revue Biblique* (no. 2, April 1994) 161–214 (Annexe, 212–14).

Being *diakonos* describes the servant's relationship to those who are served. Being *doulos* describes the servant's relationship to the *kurios* in whose name he serves. Translating *doulos* as "slave" would consequently be more accurate, except for the term's historical associations with the horrors of the African slave trade.

In the parable of the tenants, the *doulos* is a prophet (see 2 Kgs 17:13-14), one defined by his relationship to the Lord *(kurios)* God, one who is totally in God's service and sent by God with a specific mission. When the *doulos*/prophet came to the tenants for some of Israel's harvest, the tenants beat him and sent him away empty.

Again the owner sent another servant *(doulos)* to them. The adverb "again" *(palin)* associates the mission of the second *doulos*/prophet with that of the first. His bad treatment by the leaders, however, escalates from a simple beating to hardened defiance and shameful treatment (12:4). The shameful treatment is left to the reader's imagination.

The owner of the vineyard sent yet another servant *(doulos)*. This time the tenant farmers killed him, as they beat or killed many others (12:5). The series of three, especially the third, is thus associated with the harsh treatment prophets often received at the hand of Israel's rulers.

As many commentators have noted, Mark keeps escalating the treatment of the servants, building up to a climax, which comes with the next and last messenger, not just a servant *(doulos)*, like those preceding, but "a beloved son," whom they also kill. The "beloved son" *(huios agapetos)* is a transparent reference to Jesus, God's "beloved Son." Many also have noted that the killing of the third *doulos* appears anticlimactic. Had Mark escalated the beating and shameful treatment further, reserving the killing for the beloved son, the parable would have been more effective.

That may be true, but only if the third *doulos*/prophet was part of the ordinary line of prophets, without a specific allegorical meaning. I suggest that the third *doulos*/prophet refers to John the Baptist. John prepared the way for Jesus' mission not only by preaching "a baptism of repentance for the forgiveness of sins" (1:4), but by his whole life. Like Jesus, John was also "handed over" (cf. 1:14) and put to death (6:17-29).

His Beloved Son (12:6-9). After sending three of his *douloi* to obtain some of the produce from the farmers, the owner had only one left to send, "a beloved son" *(huios agapetos)*. Thinking that they would respect his son, the owner sent him to the farmers. In the hope of inheriting the vineyard, they took him, put him to death, and threw him out of the vineyard.

Twice in the course of the Gospel, Jesus was declared God's beloved Son. The first was at his baptism (1:9-11), the second at the transfiguration (9:2-8).

Baptized by John, Jesus was associated with John (1:9). Indeed, he was a follower of John. As John announced, "One mightier than I is coming after me" (1:7), that is, "One of my followers is mightier than I." Jesus was a follower of John, but mightier than John. So it is that, on emerging from the water, Jesus saw the heavens torn open and the Spirit descending upon him. And a voice addressed him from the heavens: "You are my beloved Son; with you I am well pleased" (1:10-11).

In the parable of the tenants, Jesus is also associated with the *douloi*/prophets who preceded him, most especially with John the Baptist, the one who was killed. We must consequently think of Jesus as the Lord's *doulos*/prophet. As Jesus had told the disciples, whoever wished to be great *(megas)* among them would be their servant *(diakonos),* and anyone who wished to be the first *(protos)* among them would be the slave *(doulos)* of all. That is the way it was for the Son of Man, "who did not come to be served [*diakonethenai*] but to serve [*diakonesai*] and to give his life as a ransom for many," that is, to be the Lord's *doulos* on behalf of all (10:43-45).

At the baptism, the voice from heaven addressed Jesus. At the transfiguration, the voice addressed Peter, James, and John: "This is my beloved Son [*ho huios mou, ho agapetos*]. Listen to him" (9:7). Coming down from the mountain, Jesus told them not to tell anyone what they had seen until the Son of Man had risen from the dead. The discussion that followed focused on the teaching of the scribes concerning the coming of Elijah. In conclusion, Jesus told the three: "But I tell you that Elijah has come and they did to him whatever they pleased, as it is written of him" (9:13). Jesus was, of course, referring to John the Baptist (1:2, 6; see 2 Kgs 1:8).

Both at the baptism and at the transfiguration, Jesus was associated with John the Baptist but was also distinguished from him as God's beloved Son. It was quite natural, then, that Mark do the same in the allegory of the tenants. Like John the Baptist, Jesus was the Lord's *doulos* and so put to death. But Jesus was much more than the Lord's *doulos*. He was God's beloved Son.

After putting God's beloved son to death, the leaders threw him out of God's vineyard, Israel. Wanting nothing to do with Jesus, God's beloved Son and the *doulos* of the Lord, who gave "his life as a ransom for many" (10:45), they tried to separate themselves from the redemptive purpose of Jesus' death.

What then would the owner do? What would God do? He would come and put the tenants, the leaders and rulers, to death and give the vineyard to others. In Isaiah's Song of the Vineyard, God destroyed the vineyard itself. In the parable or allegory of the tenants, God's judgment is not on the vineyard but on the farmers, Israel's leaders. Israel remains but in the care of new leaders, those who were "of Christ," whom Jesus had called, constituted as the Twelve and sent on mission.

The Cornerstone (12:10-11). Appended to the parable are two verses from Psalm 118:

> The stone the builders rejected
>   has become the cornerstone.
> By the LORD has this been done;
>   it is wonderful in our eyes (Ps 118:22-23 [LXX]).

The same passage is referred to in Acts in a discourse of Simon Peter, summarizing the message of salvation through Christ. Addressing the Sanhedrin (Acts 4:5-6), Peter spoke of Jesus Christ the Nazorean, the one they had crucified. God had raised him from the dead. Christ is "the stone rejected by you, the builders, which has become the cornerstone. There is no salvation through anyone else" (Acts 4:11-12).

In 1 Peter, the passage from Psalm 118 is associated with two passages from Isaiah:

> See, I am laying a stone in Zion,
>   a stone that has been tested, . . .
> he who puts his faith in it shall not be shaken (Isa 28:16).

> Yet he shall be a snare, an obstacle and a stumbling stone
>   to both the houses of Israel,
> A trap and a snare
>   to those who dwell in Jerusalem;
> And many among them shall stumble and fall,
>   broken, shaved, and captured (Isa 8:14-15).

In the parable of the tenants, the quotation about the stone rejected which becomes the cornerstone makes a very important contribution. First, it points to Christ's resurrection as it does in Acts and 1 Peter. Unlike John the Baptist, who was put to death but not raised from the dead (see 6:14, 16, 29), Jesus was raised after three days (8:31; 9:31; 10:32-34). Second, it emphasizes Jesus' new role as the cornerstone, the foundation stone, on which the entire building rests.

Jesus' Response of the Sanhedrin (12:12)

The whole encounter (11:27–12:12) ends with the chief priests, the scribes and the elders seeking once again to arrest Jesus. As on the previous occasions, when they heard of Jesus cleansing the Temple, they were stymied by the crowd, whom they feared (12:12a; 11:18). What provoked their new effort was their realization that Jesus addressed the parable directly to them (12:12b).

It might appear that Mark was contradicting himself. While giving the purpose of Jesus' teaching in parables, he had quoted Isaiah 6:9. To those outside, everything came in parables, so that

> they may look and see but not perceive,
>   and hear and listen but not understand,
>   in order that they may not be converted and be forgiven (4:12).

For those inside, however, who were around Jesus and with the Twelve, and to whom "the mystery of the kingdom has been granted," he explained everything and they could understand (4:10-12, 34).

How is it then that the chief priests, the scribes, and the elders grasped immediately that Jesus addressed the parable of the tenants to them? As we indicated earlier, a parable is figurative speech that demands reflection for understanding. But what kind of reflection?

The reflection that is demanded includes two movements. First, the parable must be able to penetrate someone's world. For this, the listener need only pay attention. That is what the chief priests, the scribes, and the elders did, and so they realized that Jesus addressed the parable to them.

But there is a second movement. Once the parable has moved into someone's world, it also demands that those who hear it move into the parable's world. That is what the chief priests, the scribes, and the elders could not do. While they realized the parable was addressed to them, they did not allow it to be gospel for them and transform them into good tenants. In another part of the Gospel, with reference to the Pharisees, the same attitude is called "hardness of heart" (see 3:5).

With that, Jesus' encounter with the chief priests, the scribes, and the elders comes to an end. They left him and went away.

Jesus, the Pharisees and the Herodians:
Paying Taxes to Caesar (12:13-17)

No sooner had the chief priests, the scribes, and the elders gone away (12:12), when they sent some Pharisees and Herodians to trap Jesus in his speech (12:13).

The chief priests, the scribes, and the elders had challenged Jesus' authority to cleanse the Temple and make it a house of prayer for all peoples (11:15-19). The Pharisees and the Herodians now challenged Jesus' teaching concerning "the way of God" *(he hodos tou theou),* more specifically, his teaching on paying the tax to Caesar. According to "the way of God," was it lawful to pay the tax to Caesar or not (12:14)?

Earlier, responding to the chief priests, the scribes, and the elders, Jesus had turned their challenge around. He did the same thing to the Pharisees and the Herodians, leaving them utterly amazed (12:15-17).

Pharisees and Herodians. The Pharisees[8] are not new to the Gospel. Nor are the Herodians. What is new is their association with the chief priests, the scribes, and the elders (11:27), who sent them to ensnare Jesus in his speech (12:13).

The Pharisees made their first appearance in the first section of the Gospel (1:14–3:6) in four controversies with Jesus (2:13-17, 18-22, 23-28; 3:1-6). An introductory controversy, highlighting the Son of Man's authority to forgive sins (2:1-12), had provided a general setting for the next four controversies.

When Jesus was at table at the home of Levi, "some scribes who were Pharisees" questioned why Jesus ate with tax collectors and sinners (2:13-17). After that, people objected why the disciples of Jesus did not fast, unlike the disciples of John and disciples of the Pharisees (2:18-22). The Pharisees then protested that Jesus' disciples did something unlawful on the sabbath (2:23-28). Finally, in the synagogue, they tried to catch Jesus in the act of healing a man with a shriveled hand on the sabbath (3:1-6). It is at that point that the Pharisees went out and consulted the Herodians about how they might put Jesus to death (3:6).

In their next appearance, the Pharisees, accompanied by scribes from Jerusalem, questioned Jesus about his disciples' disregard for the tradition of the elders and eating with unclean hands (7:1-15). In the same section of the Gospel (6:6b–8:21), the Pharisees came testing Jesus, demanding a sign from heaven (8:11-13). In the section's conclusion (8:14-22), Jesus warned his disciples against the leaven of the Pharisees and the leaven of Herod (8:15).

The Pharisees were the guardians of legal observance, ritual purity, and tradition. The Sanhedrin, represented by the chief priests,

[8] Regarding the Pharisees, see Joachim Jeremias, *Jerusalem in the Time of Jesus* (Philadelphia: Fortress Press, 1969) 246–67.

the scribes, and the elders (11:27–12:12), constituted the Jewish governing and judicial body in Jerusalem. Both groups challenged Jesus' authority. Normally, the Pharisees would not have associated with the Herodians. To attack Jesus' authority, however, they did.

The Herodians are not so easily identified. In general, the Herodians were supporters of Herod and his political position, such as it was. Herod the Great had been a king. At his death, Rome denied the same title to his sons, Archelaus, Herod Antipas, and Philip. Still, one could pretend, as Herod Antipas did, when he offered Herodias' daughter half of the kingdom he did not have (6:23).

Herod held the title of tetrarch of Galilee and Perea, and like his father, King Herod, he owed his position to Caesar. The Herodians, who depended on Herod Antipas' largesse and patronage, supported him in his position. Many of them were surely present at the banquet Herod gave on his birthday "for his own military officers, and the leading men of Galilee" (6:21).

Like Herod, some of the Herodians may have been intrigued and somewhat attracted by John the Baptist and his preaching, not enough, however, to spare his life (6:20, 26-28). Like Herod, they must also have found Jesus' message of the kingdom of God quite disturbing.

No one would have described the Herodians as guardians of legal observance, ritual purity, and tradition. Their association with the Pharisees was purely pragmatic. For religious and personal reasons, the Pharisees wanted Jesus put to death. For political and personal reasons, the Herodians wanted the same. So it is that the two came together in a common cause.

The Sanhedrin, that is, the chief priests, the scribes, and the elders, had very different interests from the Pharisees and the Herodians. The Sanhedrin was centered on Jerusalem, the Temple, and the palace of the high priest. The Pharisees' sphere of influence was the synagogue. That of the Herodians was Herod's court. Differences notwithstanding, what the chief priests, the scribes, and the elders failed to do personally (11:27–12:12), they hoped to accomplish through the Pharisees and the Herodians (3:6).

The Challenge of the Pharisees and the Herodians (12:14). So the Pharisees and the Herodians were sent by the chief priests, the scribes, and the elders to ensnare Jesus in his speech. They greeted Jesus as "Teacher" *(Didaskale)*. Using the Hebraic form, they would have said "Rabbi," as Judas would do in the garden called Gethsemane (14:45). They might even have inflated the title to "Rabbouni" (see 10:51). Instead, they called him "Teacher," underlining Mark's catechetical purpose at this point.

Lacing the greeting with flattery, the Pharisees and the Herodians continued: "We know that you are a truthful man [*alethes*][9] and that you are not concerned with anyone's opinion." As a truthful person, Jesus did not adapt his teaching to what people expected to hear. Going further, they added: "You do not regard a person's status but teach the way of God in accordance with the truth." As a truthful person, Jesus taught in accordance with the truth.

The key statement in the greeting was that Jesus taught "the way of God," an expression familiar from wisdom literature, which often referred to "walking in the way of the Lord." The purpose of much of the wisdom literature was to teach people "the way of the Lord," to show and encourage them to walk, that is, live, in accordance with it, and to warn those who did not. Every teacher in Israel was expected to teach "the way of God."

Jesus and his followers were "on the way" (*en te hodo,* 8:3, 27; 9:33; 10:32, 52). Jesus called people to follow him on the way to his passion and resurrection in Jerusalem (see 8:31; 9:31; 10:32-34). Jesus called his followers to a way of life (see 8:34-38; 9:35–10:31; 10:38-45), one defined by the cross (10:34). He called them to offer their lives with Jesus, the Christ (8:29), the Son of Man, "who did not come to be served but to serve and to give his life as a ransom for many" (10:45). In Jesus' teaching, "the way of God" was extremely different from the teaching of the Pharisees and the Herodians.

With their flattery the Pharisees and the Herodians were preparing a trap, which they finally set with a double question: "Is it lawful to pay the census tax to Caesar or not? Should we pay or should we not pay?" The tax *(kenson)* refers to a poll tax, imposed on the inhabitants of Judea, Samaria, and Idumea. Recall that the Herodian family was Idumean.[10] The tetrarchy of Herod Antipas, however, did not include Idumea. Neither did it include Judea and Samaria, only Galilee and Perea, whose people were not subject to this tax.

The Herodians, as supporters of Herod, were, therefore, on safe ground in asking the question. The Pharisees, who resented Caesar's hegemony over Palestine, justified paying the tax as a practical

---

[9] The translation, "a truthful man," is that of the RNAB. The term "man," however, is not part of the Greek text, whose literal translation would read, "We know that you are truthful."

[10] Idumea was mentioned as one of the places from which people came to Jesus in Mark 3:7-12.

expedient. For the Pharisees, paying the tax was a religious question. For the Herodians, it was a political question.

If Jesus answered that it was not lawful to pay the tax, he would offend the Herodians, who supported it, at least in principle. If he said it was lawful, he would offend the Pharisees, who paid the tax, but resented it. The basic challenge, however, was not to make Jesus choose between offending the Pharisees or the Herodians. It was to make him choose between the kingdom of God and the kingdom of Caesar.

Jesus' Response (12:15-17). Jesus knew the hypocrisy of the Pharisees and the Herodians. He also knew they meant to trap him. So he confronted them: "Why are you testing me?" He even knew how they planned to trap him, and he skillfully set a trap of his own, one they did not recognize until they fell into it. "Bring me a denarius to look at," Jesus responded (12:15).

The denarius was a Roman silver coin, whose exchange value for a Roman gold coin, the aureus, was twenty-five to one. Issuing coins was an expression of independence.[11] Coins were issued by the tetrarchs and the procurators of Judea, but not gold and silver coins, which Rome reserved to itself. Rome also required that tax payments be paid in Roman coinage, hence the need for the money changers, whose tables Jesus had overturned in the Temple (11:15).

In asking for a denarius, Jesus issued a counterchallenge. By bringing the denarius, the Pharisees and the Herodians would show their subjection to Caesar, acknowledging Caesar's right to levy the tax, their readiness to pay it, and the practical irrelevance of Jewish law in the matter, at least for them. With that, the trap was sprung. But there was more.

At the time Jesus was teaching in the Temple, Tiberius (A.D. 14–37) had been emperor for some fifteen years. The denarius bore the image of Tiberius as the son of the god Augustus and the goddess Livia, with the abbreviation for the words "Tiberius Caesar Augustus, Son of the Divine Augustus" inscribed on the obverse, and the title "Pontifex Maximus," that is "Sovereign Pontiff" or "High Priest" on the reverse.[12]

A powerful symbol in itself, the coin became even more powerful when it was brought into the Temple. Introducing any image into the Temple was considered an abomination. A symbol of Roman

[11] Declaring their independence, the Jews issued coins during their revolts against Rome in A.D. 66–70 and 132–35.

[12] The full inscription, which was in Latin, would have read, "Tiberius Caesar Divi Augusti Filius Augustus." As abbreviated, it read, "Ti Caesar Divi Aug F Augustus."

power was a desolating abomination (13:14; see Dan 9:27), profaning the Temple. None of this would have been lost on Mark's Christian readers. But there was even more.

That the symbol of Roman power proclaimed Tiberius as the son of a god and a goddess was sacrilegious. But that the coin carried the title Pontifex Maximus announced Tiberius' religious sovereignty over the Jewish high priest. Jesus was thus showing the Pharisees and the Herodians that they were at odds with the Sanhedrin which sent them to ensnare him in his speech.

When the Pharisees and the Herodians produced the coin, the trap was already sprung. When Jesus asked whose image and inscription were on the coin (12:16), they could hardly answer, like the Sanhedrin had done, that they did not know (11:33). They said, "Caesar's," inviting Jesus' response, "Repay to Caesar what belongs to Caesar and to God what belongs to God" (12:17a).

By bringing the coin that bore Caesar's image and inscription into the Temple, they were not paying God what belonged to God. Jesus had done his part by overturning the tables of the money changers. It was time for them to do their part.

So it was that the Pharisees and the Herodians were outdone by the teacher who was truthful, showed no concern for their opinion, had no regard for their status, but taught the way of God in accordance with the truth. "They were utterly amazed at him" (12:17b).

With that, both the Pharisees and the Herodians leave Mark's story of "the beginning of the gospel of Jesus Christ [the Son of God]."

Jesus and the Sadducees:
The Resurrection of the Dead (12:18-27)

No sooner had the Pharisees and the Herodians made their exit, the Sadducees made their entrance. This is the first time they appear in the Gospel. It would also be their last. The Pharisees and the Herodians failed to ensnare Jesus in his speech. Jesus' response left them in dismay with the symbol of Caesar's power still in their hand. It was time for the Sadducees to try.

The Sanhedrin had challenged Jesus' authority for cleansing the Temple (11:27–12:12). The Pharisees and the Herodians challenged his teaching concerning the way of God in the matter of paying taxes to Caesar (12:13-17). The Sadducees, "who say there is no resurrection," now challenged his teaching concerning the resurrection of the dead (12:18-27).[13]

---

[13] The passage includes the basic Greek terms for resurrection, the noun *anastasis,* from *ana* (again) and *stasis* (standing), meaning "resurrection"

The Sadducees (12:18). We know very little about the Sadducees.[14] What we do know comes from the New Testament and Flavius Josephus,[15] a prominent Jew who became a Roman historian. The Sadducees left no writings of their own. We do not even have a record of their traditions, unlike the Pharisees, whose traditions were preserved in early rabbinic literature, such as the Mishnah.[16]

Less a religious sect than a social class, the Sadducees belonged to Judea's priestly aristocracy[17] and lay nobility,[18] whose positions were tied to inherited wealth. In the Sanhedrin, they were represented among the chief priests and among the elders. The Pharisees, on the other hand, who owed their position to education and acquired wealth, were represented among the scribes.

For the Sadducees, the center of religious life was the Temple, so that, when the Temple was destroyed, they disappeared as a recognizable group with influence in Jewish life. The Pharisees, however, who operated away from the Temple and for whom the center of religious life was the synagogue, became key players in the restructuring of Judaism.

Politically, the Sadducees upheld the status quo, including Roman rule. Religiously, they based their views exclusively on the Torah, the Pentateuch, and rejected innovative teachings such as were propounded by the Pharisees as "the tradition of the elders" (see 7:1-13).

The Resurrection. One of the innovative beliefs the Sadducees rejected was the resurrection of the dead, a belief espoused by the Pharisees.[19] For the Pharisees, the resurrection of the dead referred

---

(12:18, 23), the verb on which it was based, *anistemi,* meaning "to rise" (12:23, 25), as well as the verb *egeiro,* also meaning "to rise" (12:26).

[14] Concerning the Sadducees, see J. Jeremias, op. cit., 228–32 and Marcel Simon, trans. by James H. Farley, *Jewish Sects at the Time of Jesus* (Philadelphia: Fortress Press, 1967) 22–27.

[15] *Jewish Wars* 2, 119, 164–65; *Antiquities* 13, 171.

[16] The Mishnah was compiled *circa* A.D. 200, under the guidance of Judah the Patriarch *(hanasi).* One of the oldest tractates in the Mishnah is that of "The Fathers," *(Abot),* many of whose traditions come from early Judaism when Pharisees were closely associated with the synagogue. For an introduction to the Mishnah and "The Fathers," see Jacob Neusner, *Introduction to Rabbinic Literature,* Anchor Bible Reference Library (New York: Doubleday, 1994) 97–128, 570–90.

[17] On the priestly aristocracy, see J. Jeremias, op. cit., 181–98.

[18] On the lay nobility, see J. Jeremias, op. cit., 222–32.

[19] While defending himself before the Sanhedrin, Paul, whose background was Pharisee, took advantage of this difference in belief between the Pharisee and the Sadducee members of the Sanhedrin (Acts 23:6-10).

to the general resurrection at the end of time, and that is also what the Sadducees had in mind when they challenged Jesus in the Temple.

In traditional Jewish circles, the notion of resurrection was equivalent to what others referred to as immortality. The notion of immortality presupposed the Greek distinction between the perishable, mortal body and the imperishable, immortal soul. In the Old Testament, the notion of immortality is found only in the Wisdom of Solomon 1–6.

The notion of resurrection arose from the Semitic view of the human being, which did not presuppose the distinction between body and soul. In the Semitic view, one could be more or less alive. Death was the lowest possible level of living existence. The dead were in a place called in Hebrew, *She'ol,* in Greek, "Hades," where they had no sense of time, space, or relationship. It is from there that God would raise them. In the Old Testament, the notion of personal resurrection is found in the book of Daniel 12:1-3 and 2 Maccabees 7.

Mark had already introduced the notion of resurrection in Jesus' prophetic announcements of the passion of the Son of Man, who would rise after three days *(meta treis hemeras anastenai,* 8:31; *anestesetai,* 9:31; 10:34). Jesus also referred to the Son of Man's rising from the dead as he and the disciples were coming from the mount of transfiguration. The disciples were to tell no one what they had seen until the Son of Man had risen *(aneste)* from the dead (9:9). At the time, Peter, James, and John did not understand and questioned what rising from the dead *(ek nekron anastenai)* meant (9:10). The Sadducees now provided Jesus an opportunity to explain.

The Sadducees' Challenge (12:19-23). Like the Pharisees and the Herodians, the Sadducees addressed Jesus as "Teacher," signaling Mark's catechetical intent. The Sadducees presented their challenge in three parts. First, they referred to what Moses wrote in the Torah: "If someone's brother dies, leaving a wife but no child, his brother must take the wife and raise up descendants for his brother" (12:19). The passage cites the law of levirate referred to in Genesis 38:8 and Deuteronomy 25:5-6.

They then presented a hypothetical case in which a woman was married to seven brothers consecutively, each of whom died leaving her childless, before she herself died (12:20-22). The case recalls a story in the book of Tobit about the young woman named Sarah whom Tobiah was to marry. Tobiah had heard that the woman had "already been married seven times, and that her husbands died in their bridal chambers" (Tob 6:14).

The Sadducees concluded with a question: "At the resurrection [*anastasis*] [when they arise] whose wife will she be? For all seven had been married to her" (12:23). The trap seemed foolproof. Jesus either had to set aside the law of Moses (Deut 25:5-6) or recognize that the idea of the resurrection was nonsense.

The Sadducees rejected the reality of the resurrection because it was not part of Moses' teaching in the Torah. Questioning Jesus, they went further and tried to show that the resurrection was incompatible with Moses.

The dilemma they presented to Jesus was based on a very limited understanding of the nature and manner of the resurrection. For the Sadducees, resurrection implied that people would return to the same state of being before dying. For them, death was merely an interruption. Those who would rise would resume their former life and their former relationships, including that of marriage. With a different understanding of the resurrection, the dilemma would collapse, and belief in the resurrection would no longer be incompatible with Moses.

Paul encountered a similar situation at Corinth, where some rejected the fact of the resurrection because of their inadequate view of resurrection: "But someone may say, "How are the dead raised? With what kind of body will they come back?" (1 Cor 15:35). Paul responded with a series of analogies (1 Cor 15:36-58). For example, "What you sow is not brought to life unless it dies. And what you sow is not the body that is to be but a bare kernel of wheat, perhaps, or of some other kind" (1 Cor 15:36-37). The resurrection of the dead "is sown corruptible; it is raised incorruptible. . . . It is sown a natural body; it is raised a spiritual body" (1 Cor 15:42-44).

Jesus' Response (12:24-27). Like the challenge of the Sadducees, Jesus' responded in three parts. Jesus began with a rhetorical question with a double focus: "Are you not misled because you do not know the scriptures or the power of God?" (12:24). The question invited the Sadducees (and Mark's readers) to ask themselves, "How? How are we misled?"

Jesus then dealt with the Sadducees' understanding of the manner of the resurrection: "When they," that is, the wife and her seven consecutive husbands, "rise from the dead, they neither marry nor are given in marriage, but they are like the angels in heaven" (12:25). In the resurrection, those who rise will have an entirely new manner of being and very different relationships, akin to that of the angels. In 1 Corinthians, Paul had spoken of being raised with a spiritual body (15:42-44).

Jesus concluded by responding to the Sadducees' position on the fact of the resurrection, showing that the resurrection was actually in the Book of Moses, in reality, if not in word: "As for the dead being raised, have you not read in the Book of Moses, in the passage about the bush, how God told him, 'I am the God of Abraham, [the] God of Isaac, and [the] God of Jacob'? He is not the God of the dead but of the living" (12:26-27a). In Jesus' response, Abraham, Isaac, and Jacob were among the living. Since they had died, that meant they were in some sense risen, at least in relation to God, for whom there is no past, present, and future.

Jesus thus showed the Sadducees how little they understood the Scriptures. They were indeed "greatly misled" (12:27b).

The Sadducees' challenge and Jesus' challenging response had to do with the notion of resurrection itself, as referring to the general resurrection at the end of time on God's great day of judgment. It did not address the nature and meaning of Jesus' resurrection as the Son of Man (8:31; 9:9-10, 31; 10:34). But for Jesus' own resurrection to be meaningful, one needed first to understand the meaning of resurrection in general and to accept its possibility.

Jesus and the Scribes:
The First of All the Commandments (12:28-44)

Jesus drove the sellers and buyers from the Temple, overturned the tables of the money changers and the seats of those selling doves, and blocked those carrying things through the Temple area (11:15-19). People had turned the house of God into a marketplace, an agora. Many used it as shortcut, convenient for moving goods. Cleansing the Temple, Jesus declared it not only "a house of prayer," but "a house of prayer for all peoples," including the Gentiles. Those responsible for it made it "a den of thieves" (11:15-19).[20]

So provocative an action should normally have provoked a reaction. Years later, when Paul entered the Temple, word spread that he had brought Greeks into the Temple. The mere rumor was enough to cause a riot. The Roman garrison quickly swept down from the fortress, took charge, and arrested Paul (Acts 21:27-36).

But now, when Jesus and the Twelve took over the Temple area, the crowd did nothing. Nor did the Romans intervene. No one,

---

[20] The quotation, "My house shall be called a house of prayer for all peoples," is from Isaiah 56:7. Read in the Markan context, its reference to "all peoples" *(pasin tois ethnesin)*, literally, "for all the Gentiles," suggests that Temple business had taken over the Temple court of the Gentiles. The quotation, "You have made it a den of thieves," is from Jeremiah 7:11.

absolutely no one, reacted to Jesus' cleansing of the Temple. When evening came, Jesus and the Twelve left the city with no difficulty (11:19), as they did the day before (11:11).

Instead of reacting, several groups responded by challenging the authority of Jesus. For all its drama, Mark transformed the cleansing of the Temple into a rabbinical dispute. The response came the next day as a triple challenge while Jesus was walking in the Temple area. The chief priests, the scribes, and the elders questioned Jesus' authority over the Temple (11:27–12:12), some Pharisees and Herodians tried to undermine Jesus' teaching authority (12:13-17), and some Sadducees made fun of his teaching on the resurrection (12:18-27). All failed. After them came a scribe, whose attitude was quite different.

One of the Scribes (12:28-34)

Coming forward, the scribe overheard the various disputes. He saw how Jesus challenged the chief priests, the scribes, and the elders in return, how Jesus' response amazed the Pharisees and Herodians, and how well he answered the Sadducees (12:28a).

This is not the first time scribes figure in the Gospel. When Jesus began teaching in the synagogue at Capernaum, people were astonished. Unlike the scribes, Jesus taught with authority (1:21-28). Later, some of the scribes challenged Jesus' authority to forgive sins (2:7). Some scribes who were Pharisees also questioned Jesus' eating with sinners and tax collectors (2:16).

Next, we hear of the scribes who came from Jerusalem. Jesus had returned home, and a crowd, coming from Galilee, Judea, and Jerusalem, as well as Idumea, Transjordan, and the region of Tyre and Sidon, gathered around him (3:20; see 3:7-8). Jesus' relatives thought he was out of his mind. The scribes from Jerusalem thought he was possessed by Beelzebul (3:22-30). Later, the Pharisees with some scribes who came from Jerusalem asked Jesus why his disciples did not follow the tradition of the elders but ate bread with unclean hands (7:1-15).

Until now, the scribes either were from Galilee (1:21-28; 2:7, 16) or came from Jerusalem to Galilee (3:22-30; 7:1-15). This time, it is Jesus who had come from Galilee to Jerusalem.

Having heard how well Jesus answered his challengers, the scribe seems to have been impressed. Unlike the chief priests, the scribes, and the elders, he did not question Jesus' authority. And unlike the Pharisees and Herodians, and the Sadducees, he did not try to undermine or ridicule Jesus' teaching.

As an interpreter of the Law, the scribe asked Jesus a simple, straightforward, but very basic question about the Law: "Which is the first of all the commandments?" (12:28b). The scribe was testing Jesus' interpretation of the Law, as understood in Jewish tradition, like an eminent teacher would have tested a student or a young scribe.

"Hear, O Israel!" (12:29-31). Jesus did not answer the questions asked by the chief priests, the scribes, and the elders, the Pharisees and the Herodians, and the Sadducees. Recognizing them as challenges, he responded with challenges of his own. But he did answer the scribe with the first of all the commandments:

> "Hear, O Israel! The Lord our God is Lord alone! You shall love the Lord your God with all your heart, with all your soul, with all your mind, and with all your strength" (12:29-30).

Jesus answered with Deuteronomy 6:4-5, addressing Israel directly, "Hear, O Israel!" calling Israel to hear the ancient profession of monotheistic faith and commanding it to love the Lord their God (see Luke 10:27). The same verses were used at the beginning of the Jewish prayer known as the *Shema*.[21] For Israel, the *Shema* represented both a creed and a way of life.

As the first, the commandment to love God included all the others. As an extremely succinct summary of the Law, it was the key to all the commandments. Fulfilling the first commandment meant fulfilling all the others.

Jesus, however, immediately added a second commandment, going beyond the scribe's actual question: "You shall love your neighbor as yourself." Such was the second of all the commandments. Concluding, Jesus spoke of the two commandments as one: "There is no other commandment greater than these" (12:31).

The second commandment comes from Leviticus 19:18, summarizing the Law's many negative prohibitions with a single positive command. In Leviticus, the law commanding the children of Israel to love their neighbor was closely associated with the laws governing their relationship to the Lord their God (Lev 19:1-37).[22]

---

[21] The Hebrew name, *Shema,* meaning "Hear," comes from the prayer's first word, *Shema Israel* ("Hear, O Israel!").

[22] The main theme of Leviticus 19 is that of holiness. The Israelites were to be holy as the Lord their God was holy (see Lev 19:2). Loving one's neighbor as oneself, indeed fulfilling all the commandments, was part of being holy as the Lord their God was holy.

By including the second commandment together with the first, Jesus showed himself not only a good interpreter of the Law, but a real master. Very likely, Jesus was not the first to bring the two commandments together. For Jesus, however, there was no fulfilling the first without fulfilling the second.

Jesus showed love of neighbor when he cured a demoniac (1:21-28), forgave and healed the paralytic (2:1-12), ate with tax collectors and sinners (2:13-17), cured both Jews and Gentiles (3:7-12) and welcomed them to his home (3:20) to the dismay of his relatives and the chagrin of scribes who came from Jerusalem. Jesus also showed love of neighbor when he defended the word of God against the teaching of Pharisees and scribes who set it aside in favor of their tradition (7:1-15).

"Well Said, Teacher" (12:32-33). The scribe had asked Jesus, "Which is the first of all the commandments?" Going beyond the scribe's question, Jesus added the second commandment, joining love of neighbor to love of God. The scribe had tested Jesus with a question. Jesus tested him with the answer. The scribe was pleased with Jesus' answer. Addressing Jesus as *didaskale,* "teacher," the scribe accepted Jesus as an equal.

Repeating Jesus' answer, the scribe gave even greater emphasis to the *shema*'s monotheistic profession of faith and related the two commandments even closer. As Jesus had done, he too went a step further. Jesus had responded with the words of Deuteronomy: "The Lord our God is Lord alone." The scribe focused Jesus' response on the oneness of God: "He is One and there is no other than he." The Lord God alone is Lord for all human beings. There is no other.

The scribe's emphasis on God's oneness had implications for the commandment to love one's neighbor. In relation to God as Lord of the Israelite and Jewish people, the neighbor included other Jews along with strangers living in their midst. In relation to God as Lord of all human beings, the neighbor included all human beings, Gentiles as well as Jews. Was the scribe able to go that far?

Jesus responded with the first commandment, "You shall love the Lord your God with all your heart, with all your soul, with all your mind, and with all your strength," adding to it the second among all the commandments, "You shall love your neighbor as yourself." Most would have said there was no commandment greater than the first. For Jesus, there was no commandment greater than both the first and the second.

The scribe presented the two commandments as one: "to love him," that is, the One besides whom there is no other, "with all your heart, with all your understanding, with all your strength, and to love your neighbor as yourself." The scribe then went a step further than Jesus had gone. Not only was there no commandment greater than the twofold commandment of love, the twofold commandment itself was "worth more than all burnt offerings and sacrifices."

If so, Temple business, with people buying, selling, exchanging money, and anything else connected with burnt offerings and sacrifices that interfered with loving God and one's neighbor, could not be tolerated. The Temple had to be cleansed of everything that prevented it from being a house of prayer for all peoples.

"Not Far from the Kingdom of God" (12:34). Hearing Jesus' response, the scribe had greeted him as his equal. Now, hearing the scribe's response, Jesus saw that he answered with understanding. The scribe had risen to the test. Concluding the exchange, Jesus said to him: "You are not far from the kingdom of God."

Those who preceded the scribe, that is, the chief priests, the scribes, and the elders, the Pharisees and the Herodians, and the Sadducees, received no such response. Rejecting Jesus' authority over the Temple and his authority as a teacher, they remained very far from the kingdom of God. The scribe was an exception, even among scribes.

The scribe answered with understanding. Responding to Jesus' teaching, he addressed Jesus not as *Rabbi,* but as *Didaskale,* a Greek title, suggesting that Jesus was a teacher for Gentiles as well as Jews. He also confessed his faith in the One who was God for all human beings. In effect, the scribe saw that God's house had to be "a house of prayer for all peoples" (11:17).

The scribe was "not far from the kingdom of God." He was like the rich man who lacked only one thing to enter the kingdom of God (10:17-22). It was very hard "for those who have wealth to enter the kingdom of God" (10:23-25). As we are about to see it was also very hard for scribes to enter the kingdom of God (12:35-40). The scribe who came to Jesus in the Temple, however, was not far.

What was still lacking for the scribe to come still closer and enter the kingdom of God? We know already that anyone who wanted to enter the kingdom of God had to accept it like a child (10:15). We know also that it was very difficult, actually impossible, for someone with wealth to enter the kingdom of God and be saved. For God, however, all things were possible (10:23-27).

For a scribe, what did it mean to accept the kingdom of God like a child? What did it mean for one who was rich in scriptural knowledge and tradition? Did it have something to do with the commandment to love one's neighbor? Could the scribe recognize Gentiles as well as Jews as his neighbor? Was he prepared to love his Gentile neighbor as himself?

The exchange between Jesus and the scribe was now over. After that, "no one dared to ask him any more questions."

Jesus and the Scribal Interpretation of the Son of David (12:35-37)

Until now, people came to Jesus with questions, beginning with the chief priest, the scribes, and the elders (11:27–12:12), and ending with the scribe who "answered with understanding" (12:28-34). It was now time for Jesus to ask questions. He addressed them to the crowds, that is, to everyone who could hear.

The questions brought to Jesus were meant to challenge his authority, to ridicule his teaching or test his knowledge. Jesus' questions were meant to teach. The scribe had recognized Jesus as a true *didaskalos,* as an authentic teacher. Jesus would now show how great a *didaskalos* he was. Doing so, he would also show why the scribe, while not far, was not yet in the kingdom of God.

The key lay in Jesus' identity as the Davidic Messiah. The Messiah was the Son of David. But was he merely the Son of David, or was he more than that? If he was the Messiah for all peoples, that would have implications for love of neighbor.

What did it mean for Jesus to be the Messiah? What was his mission? Peter had declared that Jesus was the Christ, that is, the Messiah (8:29). At the time, however, Peter could not accept that as the Messiah, Jesus was "the Son of Man," who "must suffer greatly and be rejected by the elders, the chief priests, and the scribes, and be killed, and rise after three days" (8:31-32).

Later a blind beggar, whose name was Bartimaeus, cried out to Jesus as the Son of David (10:46-49). At the time, he was still blind. Then, receiving his sight, Bartimaeus followed Jesus on the way to Jerusalem, the city of the Son of Man's death and resurrection (10:50-52; see 10:32-34). Jesus was the Son of David, the Davidic Messiah. But what did it mean for Jesus to be the Son of David? Somehow it had to do with his passion and resurrection.

When Jesus made his royal entry into Jerusalem, "those preceding him as well as those following" cried out:

> "Hosanna!
>> Blessed is he who comes in the name of the Lord!
>> Blessed is the kingdom of our father David that is to come!
> Hosanna in the highest!" (11:9-10).

Jesus, the Son of David, was coming not in the name of David, but in the name of the Lord, announcing not a restoration of the old kingdom of David but a kingdom that was yet to come.

Jesus was now teaching the crowd about the Davidic Messiah. First, he raised a question concerning the teaching of the scribes: "How do the scribes claim that the Messiah is the son of David?" (12:35). His question was prompted by what David said, inspired by the Holy Spirit, in one of the Psalms:

> The LORD says to you, my lord:
> "Take your throne at my right hand,
> while I make your enemies your footstool" (Ps 110:1).[23]

Since David himself called the Messiah "lord," how then could the Messiah be David's son?

Jesus did not deny that as the Messiah he was the Son of David. As the Son of David, he was the Messiah for the Jews. But Jesus was also David's lord. As such, he transcended his Davidic origins and was the Messiah not only for David's people, but for all peoples. Jesus, the Son of David, was also the Son of God (see 1:1).

The passage in Mark echoes the primitive creed in Paul's greeting to the Romans. Paul was "set apart for the gospel of God, . . . the gospel about his Son, descended from David according to the flesh, but established as Son of God in power according to the spirit of holiness through resurrection from the dead, Jesus Christ our Lord" (Rom 1:1, 3-4).

Jesus' Denunciation of the Scribes (12:38-40)

Addressing the crowd, Jesus began by showing how he was David's son as well as David's lord and how that affected the commandment to love one's neighbor. As David's Lord, Jesus was the Son of God, the Son of the One beside whom there was no other, the Son of One who was Lord of all peoples. Jesus was consequently the Messiah for the Gentiles as well as for the Jews.

That meant the term "neighbor" could no longer be restricted to one's people alone. It applied to all human beings. Its scope would not be defined by the covenant, uniting the twelve tribes of Israel.

---

[23] The early Christians turned to Psalm 110 to express Jesus' eternal priesthood and messianic sovereignty over all peoples, kings, and nations. Besides Mark 12:36, the New Testament refers or alludes to Psalm 110 in 1 Corinthians 15:25; Acts 2:34-35; Hebrews 1:13, 5:6, 8:1, 10:12-13; and 1 Peter 3:22.

Its limits would be those of creation, uniting all human beings. Everything else fell short of the kingdom of God, including the scribe who was "not far from the kingdom of God."

As a body, however, the scribes were very far from the kingdom of God. And Jesus now warns the crowd against them: "Beware of the scribes, who like to go around in long robes and accept greetings in the marketplaces, seats of honor in synagogues, and places of honor at banquets" (12:38-39).

Jesus had quoted Leviticus 19:18: "You shall love your neighbor as yourself" (12:31), and the exceptional scribe had responded wholeheartedly. The scribes Jesus has just described, however, took only the last part of the commandment to heart, showing great love for themselves, going about with great display, seeking honors and recognition. But they had no time for love of neighbor. As Jesus went on to indicate: "They devour the houses of widows and, as a pretext, recite lengthy prayers" (12:40).

The expression, "the houses of widows," refers to their belongings and whatever money they might have. In the early Jewish and New Testament world, widows had no rights and depended on their oldest son, or their own father. In the event they did not have a son or their father had died, they depended on the charity of the community, whether Jewish or Christian. As such, widows were symbolic of all who were poor and helpless.[24]

Instead of seeing to the needs of the widows, the scribes exploited them religiously, devouring everything they had, down to the last little coin. In the commandment, love of neighbor was measured by love of self. Among the scribes, however, love of neighbor was swallowed up by love of self. That is why Jesus warned the crowd against them, that is, against imitating their behavior. That is also why "they would receive a very severe condemnation."

Jesus, the Disciples, and a Poor Widow (12:41-44)[25]

Jesus had now dealt with a series of challenges (11:27–12:12, 13-17, 18-27), and had answered a question, testing his understanding

[24] Having no rights of her own, a widow had to pester the judge to get a hearing (Luke 18:1-8). A widow's social position helps us understand why she would spend so much time and effort to find a single coin (Luke 15:8-10), also the significance of Jesus raising a widow's only son (Luke 7:11-17), as well as why widows are singled out in Acts 6:1-7. See E. LaVerdiere, *The Breaking of the Bread* (Chicago: Liturgy Training Publications, 1998) 114–18.

[25] For a recent article reviewing the commentaries of Swete (1898), Taylor (1952), and Nineham (1963), as well as an important article by Addison

of the Law (12:28-34). When no one dared ask him any more questions, he began teaching the crowd, raising questions about the Messiah (12:35-37) and issuing warnings not to imitate the scribes (12:38-40).

After that, Jesus sat down and watched the crowd put money in the Temple treasury. Many rich people were putting in large sums of money. We already know how difficult it was for the rich to enter the kingdom of God (10:17-27). The disciples understood that. Speaking for all of them, Peter had declared: "We have given up everything and followed you" (10:28).

By contrast, a poor widow put in two *lepta*. The *lepton*, a Greek bronze coin, was the smallest one issued, the equivalent of the Roman *quadrans*. Two *lepta* amounted to extremely little, enough, perhaps, to buy a little bread, but no more. Having given everything, the widow was like the disciples (10:28-30) and the scribe who was "not far from the kingdom of God" (12:34).

Noting the contrast, Jesus called his disciples and brought it to their attention. The two small coins the widow gave amounted to more than all the others gave. Why? Because the others, that is, the rich, gave from their surplus, while she gave from her need, everything she had, her whole life.

Until now Jesus had been teaching the crowds. He was now teaching his disciples. The contrast between the rich, giving large sums from their surplus wealth, and the poor widow, who gave all she had, held a lesson for the disciples. But what was that lesson?

Examining the story in itself (12:41-44), we are tempted to view the widow as an example to be imitated. Jesus would be telling the disciples to contribute everything they had, including what they needed to live. Taking the previous story into consideration, however, we see the widow as one who was exploited, whose possessions had been swallowed up by the scribes (12:40). In this context, her penury becomes a warning. The disciples must not allow the scribes to do the same to them.

Jesus, however, neither commends the widow's generosity nor laments the state to which she has been reduced. Nor does he warn the disciples against allowing themselves to be exploited as she was

---

Wright, "The Widow's Mites: Praise or Lament?—A Matter of Context," *Catholic Biblical Quarterly* 44 (1982) 256–65, see Elizabeth Struthers Malbon, "The Poor Widow in Mark and Her Poor Rich Readers," *Catholic Biblical Quarterly* 53 (1991) 589–04. Wright interpreted the passage in light of its immediate context (12:39-40). Malbon interpreted it in light of broader Markan contexts.

exploited. The widow's behavior, however commendable, or her condition, however lamentable, is not the point of the story.

The story's interpretation depends on how we view Jesus' denunciation of the scribes (12:38-40), who loved themselves at the expense of their neighbor (see 12:28-34), who could not see that Jesus, as David's lord, was the Messiah for all human beings (12:35-37), including the poor widow who had just given her all (12:41-44). Jesus had not warned the crowds against being exploited by the scribes, but against imitating their arrogance and exploiting others as they did.

The poor widow is presented as one of those whose possessions had been devoured by the scribes. Given the context of 12:38-40, she exemplifies what the scribes had done to widows, under the pretext of reciting lengthy prayers. Jesus had warned the crowds against acting like the scribes. He was now warning the disciples against the same. Jesus' disciples must never do to a poor widow what the scribes were doing.

Like the scribe who came to Jesus, the disciples were not far from the kingdom of God. Fulfilling the dual commandment, loving God as well as neighbor, was "worth more than all burnt offerings and sacrifices" (12:28-34). To actually enter the kingdom, however, they had to avoid the behavior of the scribes (12:38-40) and recognize all peoples (see 12:35-37), including a poor widow (12:41-44) as their neighbor.

Jesus' Discourse on the Mount of Olives (13:1-37)[26]

The previous section of the Gospel (8:22–10:52) told how Jesus came to Jerusalem from Bethsaida, passing through the villages of Caesarea Philippi (8:27), Galilee (8:30), Capernaum (8:33), the district of Judea by the Jordan (10:1), and Jericho (10:46). On the way, he taught his disciples what it meant to be the Christ. He also taught them what it meant to be his followers.

The section began with Jesus healing a blind man at Bethsaida (8:22-26). It ended with Jesus curing another blind man, whose name was Bartimaeus, as Jesus and the disciples were leaving Jericho (10:46-52).

The new section then begins with Jesus and the disciples approaching Jerusalem from the Mount of Olives and going into the

---

[26] For a good introduction to Mark 13 as an eschatological and apocalyptic discourse, see Adela Yarbro Collins, *The Beginning of the Gospel, Probings of Mark in Context* (Minneapolis: Fortress Press, 1992) 73–91.

Temple area (11:1-11). At the close of the previous section, we heard Bartimaeus cry out: "Jesus, Son of David, have pity on me. . . . Son of David, have pity on me" (10:47-48). Jesus was now entering Jerusalem as the Son of David. King David had once fled Jerusalem over the Mount of Olives (2 Sam 15:30-31). As Son of David, Jesus was returning, not, however, as a conqueror, triumphant on horseback, but modestly, astride a young colt (Zech 9:9).

For those accompanying Jesus, his entry into Jerusalem celebrated the restoration of David's fallen kingdom. From Mark's point of view, Jesus' entry announced the fulfillment of the kingdom of David in a future eschatological kingdom, "the kingdom of our father David that is to come" (11:9-10).

The section ends with Jesus and the disciples leaving the Temple area (13:1-2) and returning to the Mount of Olives (13:3-4). There, sitting on the Mount of Olives, Jesus gave his farewell discourse on the kingdom of David that was to come and how, as the Son of Man, he would eventually return in glory (13:5-37).

On entering Jerusalem for the first time, Jesus went directly into the Temple and looked around, but since it was already late, he returned to Bethany with the Twelve (11:11). Setting out the next day, Jesus was hungry. Seeing a fig tree in leaf, he went up to it, but finding it without figs, he cursed it (11:12-14). When they came to Jerusalem, Jesus went into the Temple, cleansed it of those selling and buying there, and declared it a house of prayer for all peoples (11:15-19). Returning again the third day, the disciples saw that the fig tree had withered to its roots (11:20-25).

Each event and every act was symbolic, announcing what it meant for Jesus to be the Son of David. Many expected Jesus to restore the ancient kingdom of David. But Jesus, David's son, was also David's Lord (12:35-37). Those preceding and following him said it well: "Blessed is the kingdom of our father David that is to come!" (11:10). It was no longer time for figs (11:12-14, 20-25). The Temple would be a house of prayer for all peoples (11:15-19). The kingdom of David would be fulfilled in the kingdom of God.

As the Christ, Jesus did not come as a political savior, but as the Son of Man, one who would suffer, die, and rise again after three days (see 8:31; 9:30-31; 10:32-34, 45). As the Son of David, Jesus did not come as an earthly ruler, but to announce his coming in power and glory as the heavenly Son of Man (13:26).

Associated with Jesus as the Christ, the title, "Son of Man," looked to Jesus' passion and resurrection (8:22–10:52). Associated with Jesus as the Son of David, the title "Son of Man," looked to Jesus' final return in glory (see 11:1–13:37).

Leaving the Temple Area (13:1-2)

While walking in the Temple area, Jesus was challenged by the chief priests, the scribes, and the elders, the Pharisees and the Herodians, and the Sadducees, and he had challenged them in return (11:27–12:27). Following a hopeful exchange with a scribe (12:28-34), Jesus taught the crowds, challenging scribal claims concerning the Christ as the Son of David (12:35-37). He also warned the crowds against behaving like the scribes (12:38-40). Concluding, he warned his disciples against the same (12:41-44). With that, Jesus and his disciples left the Temple area (13:1-2).

Earlier, entering the Temple area and looking around, Jesus saw that it was already late and so returned to Bethany with the Twelve (11:11). It was indeed very late for the Temple, as Jesus showed in two symbolic, prophetic acts: the cursing of the fig tree and the cleansing of the Temple (12:12-25). How late it was for the Temple would now become even more clear.

Leaving the Temple for the last time, one of Jesus' disciples marveled at the Temple's huge stones and imposing structures: "Look, teacher, what stones and what buildings!" (13:1). As on previous occasions, the title, "teacher" *(didaskale),* reflects the Gospel's catechetical interest.[27]

The disciple was not exaggerating. The stones and buildings he admired were those of the Herodian rebuilding of the Second Temple, begun around 20 B.C. and still in progress at the end of Jesus' life.[28] Even today, people who approach the site and visit the excavations conducted there since the late 1960s stand in awe before its great stones, imposing retaining walls, grand entrances, and various other structures. Even the ruins are magnificent: "What stones and what buildings!"

---

[27] Jesus was addressed as "teacher" *(didaskale)* by the disciples, fearing they would perish in a storm at sea (4:38), by a man whose son was possessed by a mute spirit (9:17), by John, telling Jesus the Twelve had tried to prevent someone from driving out demons in his name because he was not following them (9:38), by a rich man who wanted to know what he had to do to inherit eternal life (10:17, 20), by James and John requesting to sit one at Jesus' right and the other at his left when he came into his glory (10:35), also by the Pharisees and Herodians (12:14), the Sadducees (12:19), and one of the scribes (12:32). In each case, Jesus' response held an important catechetical message for the Markan community. The same is true here in 13:1, while introducing Jesus' eschatological discourse.

[28] Referring to approximately A.D. 26–28, John's Gospel refers to the Temple as having been under construction for forty-six years. It would not be completed until about seven years before its destruction in A.D. 70.

Jesus told the disciple to take a good look at the buildings. For all their magnificence, the time was coming when they would all be destroyed: "Do you see these great buildings? There will not be one stone left upon another that will not be thrown down" (13:2). The Temple would be utterly destroyed.

So it is that Jesus announced the destruction of the Temple, as Micah had done in the course of his prophetic mission (742–687 B.C.). For all their injustice, Israel's religious and political leaders felt secure so long as the Temple, the sign of the Lord's presence, remained in their midst. Micah announced the Temple's destruction as a divine judgment on them (Mic 3:11-12). About a hundred years later, Jeremiah did the same, warning that the Temple and all Jerusalem would be destroyed unless the people repented of their evil deeds and lived according to the law (Jer 26:1-6, 18-19).

Jesus now took a similar prophetic stance, for reasons revealed in the symbolic cursing of the fig tree (11:12-14, 20-25) and the cleansing of the Temple (11:15-19). As in the case of Micah and Jeremiah, Jesus' announcement was a warning and did not presuppose the Temple had already been destroyed. The full significance of Jesus' announcement is spelled out in the discourse on the Mount of Olives.[29]

The Eschatological Discourse (13:3-37)

Jesus had entered Jerusalem from the Mount of Olives (11:1-11). Leaving Jerusalem, he now returned to the Mount of Olives. While he was sitting there, opposite the Temple, four of his disciples, Peter, James, John, and Andrew, the first to be called (1:16-20), approached him in private (13:3). Whenever the disciples approached Jesus and he taught them in private *(kat' idian)*, it was in view of a future disclosure.[30] That disclosure was made in Mark's Gospel in the form of Jesus' farewell discourse.

[29] During the First Jewish War (A.D. 66–73), Roman legions would destroy the Temple (A.D. 70), along with the city of Jerusalem. Jesus' prophetic announcement, however, as given in Mark 13:2, does not presuppose this destruction. Nor do any references to the Temple in the discourse itself.

[30] That Jesus' teaching in private *(kat' idian)* was in view of future disclosure is quite clear from Mark 4:34, the conclusion of the discourse on parables: "Without parables he did not speak to them, but to his own disciples he explained everything in private [*kat' idian*];" and from the story of the transfiguration, for which Jesus "took Peter, James, and John and led them up a high mountain apart [*kat' idian*] by themselves" (9:2). Coming down from the mountain, Jesus told them to tell no one what they had seen "except when the Son of Man had risen from the dead" (9:9). See also 6:31, 32; 7:33; 9:28.

The disciples had two questions: "Tell us, when will this happen, and what sign will there be when all these things are about to come to an end?" (13:4). The two questions are quite different. The first asks when "this" *(tauta),* that is, the destruction of the Temple (see 13:2), will happen. The second asks what sign *(to semeion)* there would be, not when the Temple would be destroyed, but when "all these things" *(tauta panta)* were "about to be fulfilled" *(syntelesthai).*

The first question was a historical question, asking about the time of the Temple's destruction. Jesus would not answer this question. The second question was an eschatological question, asking about the final fulfillment of "all these things," including the Temple's destruction. Jesus' discourse would focus on this question, warning the disciples against false signs, giving them the true sign, and even describing its fulfillment. He would not, however, say when the sign would appear. The two questions were very closely related, with the first implying the second.

Jesus' entry into Jerusalem from the Mount of Olives (11:1-11a) and his going into the Temple (11:11b, 12-14, 15-19, 20-25) had introduced Jesus' teaching in the Temple area (11:27–12:44). At his departure, the disciples' amazement at the Temple's magnificence (13:1-2) and the setting on the Mount of Olives (13:3-4) introduced Jesus' final discourse, responding to the disciples' questions (13:5-37).

This is the second great discourse of Jesus in Mark's Gospel. The first was Jesus' discourse in parables, where Jesus gave the meaning of one of the parables and explained why he taught "in parables" (4:1-34). That first discourse, which was initiated by Jesus, was addressed to the crowd. Responding to a question from his disciples, Jesus also had special teaching for them (4:10-25). As we have seen, the second great discourse was initiated by the disciples (13:1-4) and addressed entirely to them (13:5-37).[31]

Because of its focus on historical teleology and the endtime, the discourse is aptly described as eschatological. Because of its focus on cataclysmic events associated with the endtime and its cosmic imagery, it is also described as apocalyptic. What these terms mean in this particular case, however, must be determined by a close look at Mark 13.

---

[31] In relation to Jesus' two great discourses (4:1-34; 13:3-37), another discourse, which is on the tradition of the elders, the commandments, and the word of God, may be considered a close third (7:1-23). Initiated by the Pharisees and some scribes (7:1-5), the discourse begins with Jesus addressing them (7:6-13). He then addressed the crowd (7:14-15) and, at home away from the crowd, he responded to a question raised by his disciples (7:17-23).

The discourse can be divided into four parts. In the first part, Jesus warns the disciples not to be misled by anyone or anything and to watch out for themselves. There surely would be persecutions (13:5-13). In the second part, Jesus speaks of the great sign as a time of unprecedented tribulation leading to the fulfillment of "all these things" (13:14-23). In the third part, Jesus describes the fulfillment itself, with its climax in the coming of the Son of Man in the clouds with great power and glory (13:24-27). In the fourth and final part, Jesus once again warns the disciples about being misled, this time in relation to the coming of the Son of Man (13:28-37).

"See That No One Deceives You" (13:5-13)

Jesus began the discourse with a series of warnings (13:5-13). The disciples must not be misled by impostors or alarmed by rumors of war and natural disasters. None of these were signs of the end (13:5-8). Nor must they become discouraged because of persecution. They must persevere to the end (13:9-13).

The opening imperative, "see" *(blepete),* sets the tone for the whole discourse (13:5, 9, 23, 33), just as the imperative, "hear" *(akouete),* did for the discourse on parables (4:3, 9, 12, 23, 24, 33). In Mark 13, the imperative, "see," is equivalent to "watch out," "look out," "beware," "take care," "be watchful" (see also 12:38), warning the disciples, first against being misled, then against discouragement.

Jesus' warnings responded to apocalyptic tendencies in the community. Many must have thought that "all these things" *(tauta panta)* were signs of the end if not the actual beginning of the end. Stressful times prove fertile ground for apocalyptic thinking. Many of the themes and images in Mark 13 are quite common in the apocalyptic literature of the time. For all these, however, Jesus' discourse in Mark 13 does not represent a full-blown apocalyptic stance. On the contrary, much of it is a warning not to interpret apocalyptically all the things that had been happening.

Throughout the discourse, Jesus addresses the future. That future, however, does not begin with the time Mark wrote the discourse in the late 60s, but with the time Jesus gave the discourse, according to Mark, just before his passion and resurrection around the year 30. For Jesus and the disciples who were with him on the Mount of Olives, all the events were in the future. For Mark and his community, much of what Jesus referred to was in the past, some of it was happening, and some of it was imminent and threatening.

The same had been true of the apocalyptic section of the book of Daniel (chapters 7–12). The four symbolic beasts in Daniel's dream all referred to the future. That future, however, was not in relation to the time of writing, around 165 B.C., but to the time of the Babylonian Empire, when Daniel is said to have the dream.[32] The first beast referred to the Babylonian Empire (Dan 7:4), the second to the kingdom of the Medes (Dan 7:5), the third to the Persian Empire (Dan 7:6), the fourth to Alexander and the Seleucid dynasty, including Antiochus IV Epiphanes (Dan 7:7-8, 23-25), who was reigning (175–163 B.C.) when the book of Daniel was written.

Jesus began by warning the disciples not to be deceived by many who would come in his name saying, "I AM" *(ego eimi)*. Some had already come, driving out demons in Jesus' name (see 9:38). Now some would come in his name claiming to be "I AM," as Jesus had revealed himself, when he came to the disciples on the sea as they were fighting a strong headwind (6:45-52). Many would be deceived by these impostors (13:5-6).

Those coming in Jesus' name were related to Jesus in some way, but they may not have been associated with the community of the Twelve. Speaking to Jesus earlier, John referred to someone who was driving out demons in Jesus' name but was not following them (9:38; see also 4:10). Jesus' response, that no one who did a mighty deed in his name could at the same time speak ill of him or be against them (9:39), suggests that the deceivers (13:5-6) were themselves deceived.

Jesus then warned them not to be alarmed when they heard of wars and rumors of wars. Such things had to happen in the course of history. They did not indicate the end (13:7). Yes, "nation will rise against nation and kingdom against kingdom. There will be earthquakes from place to place and there will be famines" (13:8a).

Wars, earthquakes, and famines would happen as they had been happening throughout the course of history. The Christians in Mark's community could look back on their own history and see that these things had been happening all along. They were not, however, meaningless. They *(tauta)* represented the beginning *(arche)* of the labor pains *(odinon),* leading to birth and new life (13:8b).

All these things were part of "the beginning [*arche*] of the gospel [*tou euaggeliou*] of Jesus Christ [the Son of God]" (1:1). Jesus' life, mission, and ministry announced the coming of God's kingdom. With it would come a new age, not, however, without pain.

---

[32] The book says Daniel had the dream in the first year of King Belshazzar of Babylon (Dan 7:1). Belshazzar had barely succeeded the Babylonian king Nabonidus when Cyrus, the king of Persia, conquered Babylon in 539 B.C.

Jesus then warned the disciples about persecutions (see 10:30). They would be handed over to courts, beaten in synagogues, arraigned before governors and kings because of Jesus, in view of witnessing to him. Again this was not the end. Before the end came, "the gospel must first be preached to all nations." When they were led away and handed over,[33] they should not worry about how they would witness. They would be given what to say. The Holy Spirit would speak through them (13:9-11).

From Jesus' point of view, all these things were in the future. From Mark's point of view, many of these things were in the past, beginning with the passion and death of Jesus and the Christian community's early history. It is as though Mark had read Luke's Acts of the Apostles. He certainly was familiar with many of the events that would be told there. Mark's purpose here, as in the whole Gospel, is to show that these things were not the end but the beginning of the Gospel.

There would even be terrible divisions within families, with members of the family persecuting other members, brother against brother, father against child, and even children rising up against their parents and having them put to death (13:12). Entering the family of rebirth, the family of God, would not be without cost. Persecutions would come, but so would "eternal life in the age to come" (10:28-30). They would be hated by others on account of Jesus' name, but if they persevered steadfastly through the whole ordeal *(eis telos)*,[34] they would be saved (13:13).

In this first part of the discourse (13:5-13), Jesus warned the disciples about things that for Mark's community had already happened, were happening, and would continue to happen. Through Mark, Jesus told the community not to misinterpret such things but to be strong in the face of them, even in the midst of persecution, counting on the Holy Spirit to speak through them. They should continue their mission to the nations, considering persecution as a great missionary opportunity to witness to Jesus as "the beginning of the gospel" continued.

---

[33] They would be handed over (13:9, 11, *paradidomi*) as Jesus had been handed over (9:31; 10:33) and before him John the Baptist had been handed over (1:14).

[34] The expression, *eis telos,* refers to the end of their personal and community ordeal, not to the end of the world. For that the expression would be *eis to telos.*

The Great Tribulation (13:14-23)

What the early Christians and the Markan community had already experienced—messianic impostors, wars, reports of war, earthquakes, famines, persecutions, deadly family conflicts—were but little tribulations compared to the great tribulation that lay ahead. Until now they had experienced but the beginning *(arche)* of the birthpangs. The climax of the birthpangs was yet to come.

In the second part of the discourse (13:14-23), Jesus described the sign *(to semeion)* that "all these things" *(tauta panta)* were "about to come to an end" (13:4). He also indicated what Christians should do and not do in these days.

The second part is very closely related to the previous one, and in some ways the two may be considered as one,[35] ending as it began with a warning about false messiahs (13:5-6, 22-23). Presenting them as two distinct units highlights the difference between the small, eschatological tribulations that for the Markan community have already been happening (13:5-13) and the great, apocalyptic tribulation that was still to come (13:14-23).

Since the small tribulations were already part of history, their date could easily be ascertained. No one, however, could know the time of the future great tribulation (13:14-23) which would signal the return of the Son of Man in glory (13:24-27).

The great sign of the end would be the presence of "the desolating abomination standing where he should not" (13:14a). The expression, "the desolating abomination" *(to bdelugma tes eremoseos),* is taken from the book of Daniel (9:27; 11:31; 12:11), where it refers to the desecration of the Temple in 167 B.C. by the Seleucid ruler Antiochus IV Epiphanes, who set up an altar of Zeus over the altar of burnt offering. Daniel refers to that time as "unsurpassed in distress" (Dan 12:1).

In an aside to the reader, Mark alerts the reader, "let the reader understand" (13:14b). Readers who were familiar with the book of Daniel and with traditions like the one found in 2 Thessalonians 2:3-5 ought to be able to do so. From Daniel 7–12, we see how what took place in the Temple had significance for the whole of history and how the Temple itself was symbolic of the entire created universe. We also see how the desecration of the Temple was viewed as tantamount to its destruction (Dan 9:26-27).

---

[35] See Augustine Stock's discussion of the structure of Mark 13 in *The Method and Message of Mark* (Wilmington, Del.: Michael Glazier, 1989) 324–28.

In Mark, therefore, the "desolating abomination" (13:14) symbolizes the Temple's destruction (13:2; *tauta*, 4a) and "all these things" (*tauta panta*, 4b) that would accompany the fulfillment of history and creation (13:24-25).

Jesus' reference to the "desolating abomination" in the book of Daniel does recall a past event, but it refers to a new event, which still lay in the future, in relation both to Jesus and to the writing of Mark's Gospel.

In Daniel, the desecration was future in relation to the prophet Daniel, but had already taken place when the book was written. The book of Daniel consequently focused on God's saving intervention, which still lay in the future. There was no need to warn his readers about an event that had already taken place.

For Mark's Gospel, both the desecration and God's saving intervention lay in the future. Mark's purpose was, therefore, both to warn the community concerning the future tribulation and to situate it positively as a sign of the coming of the Son of Man and ultimate salvation.

For Mark, the desecration itself would also be different from the event described in the book of Daniel. In Daniel, the "desolating abomination" was an altar replacing the Temple's own altar of sacrifice. In Mark, it would be a person, standing in the place of Christ and presenting himself as I AM. The "desolating abomination" would come as an Antichrist usurping the place of God.

As in the past (13:6), some would cry out: "Look, here is the Messiah [*Christos*]." They were not to be believed (13:21). As in the past, false Messiahs and false prophets would continue to perform signs and wonders in order to deceive the elect, if this were possible. If some in the community were misled by the small tribulations, what would it be like in the great tribulation? They must be vigilant. Through Peter, James, John, and Andrew, Jesus had warned them ahead of time (13:22-23).

After giving the sign, "the desolating abomination standing where he should not," Jesus described what people should do. Those in Judea must immediately flee to the mountains, without stopping for anything whatsoever (13:14c-16). It would be extremely difficult for pregnant women and nursing mothers, for anyone encumbered at all. They must pray that this will not happen in winter, when flight would be more difficult (13:17-18).

The time described by Daniel may have been of "unsurpassed in distress since nations began until that time" (Dan 12:1), but the time announced by Jesus "will have tribulation such as has not been since the beginning of God's creation until now, nor ever will be"

(13:19). God's chosen, the elect, would be saved. It is for their benefit that God shortened the days of tribulation. Otherwise, no one
would have been saved (13:20).

The Coming of the Son of Man (13:24-27)

After the great tribulation (13:14-23), they would see " 'the Son of
Man coming in the clouds' with great power and glory" (13:26), before whom even the great lights of heaven would pale (13:24-25). At
his coming, the Son of Man would send his angels to gather the
elect from the entire universe (13:27). From the literary and theological point of view, the third part of the discourse represents a
very creative, biblical synthesis of several prophetic passages.

The cosmic prelude to the coming of the Son of Man (13:24-25) recalls Isaiah 13:10; 34:4; Ezekiel 32:7-8; and Joel 2:10; 3:4; 4:15. All
of these passages refer to divine judgment, the day of the Lord, and
the presence of the Lord, stretching the human imagination and the
possibilities of language to their limits. All turn to cosmic imagery,
trying to imagine the unimaginable. And all of them are poetic, trying to express the inexpressible. But at the same time, all of them
are based on human experience.

The passages from Isaiah come from two oracles, one against
Babylon (13:1-22) and one against the nations, in particular Edom
(34:1-15).

This is how it would be on the day of the Lord (13:6-16), when divine judgment comes to Babylon. The approach of the day of the Lord
is comparable to the great tribulation in Mark, the climax of the
pangs of labor. As the day draws near, all hands fall helpless, the bows
of young men fall from their hands, hearts melt in terror, and "pangs
[*odines*, see Mark 13:8] . . . take hold of them, like a woman in labor
they writhe" (Isa 13:7-8). As the day of the Lord actually comes, to lay
waste the land and destroy the sinners with it (Isa 13:9),

> The stars and constellations of the heavens
>   send forth no light;
> The sun is dark when it rises,
>   and the light of the moon does not shine (Isa 13:10).

Related images are found also in the general judgment against
the nations (Isa 34:1-4), introducing the oracle against Edom (Isa
34:5-15):

> The heavens shall be rolled up like a scroll,
>   and all their host shall wither away,

> As the leaf wilts on the vine,
>> or as the fig withers on the tree (Isa 34:4).

For a Christian reader, the leaf wilting and the fig withering evoke Jesus cursing of the fig tree, where the whole tree withered to its very roots (11:12-14, 20-21).

The passage from Ezekiel comes from a lament over the destruction of Pharaoh, the king of Egypt (Ezek 32:1-16). The snuffing out of Pharaoh's life was comparable to extinguishing the heavenly luminaries. As in Isaiah 13, the cosmic imagery (Ezek 32:7-8) comes as the climax of devastation on the land and its people (Ezek 32:3-6).

> When I snuff you out I will cover the heavens,
>> and all the stars I will darken;
> The sun I will cover with clouds,
>> and the moon shall not give its light.
> All the shining lights in the heavens
>> I will darken on your account,
> And I will spread darkness over your land,
>> says the Lord GOD (Ezek 32:7-8).

In the case of Isaiah and Ezekiel, poets turned to cosmic imagery to express judgment on Israel's enemy nations. In Joel, the judgment is directed against the people and land of Israel. In Joel 1:1–2:17, the principal image is that of an army of locusts. After devastating the land (1:1-20), the army of locusts descends on the city (2:1-17).

> They assault the city,
>> they run upon the wall,
>> they climb into the houses;
> In at the windows
>> they come like thieves.
> Before them the earth trembles,
>> the heavens shake;
> The sun and the moon are darkened,
>> and the stars withhold their brightness (Joel 2:9-10).

The second part of the book of Joel gives the meaning of the great plague of locusts (2:18–4:21). After the plague would come salvation. The land, the city, and the people would be restored, and they would thrive (2:18-26). Even the tree would bear its fruit, "the fig trees and the vine give their yield" (Joel 2:22; see Mark 13:28-31). The purpose of the plague is given in Joel 2:27:

> And you shall know that I am in the midst of Israel;
>> I am the LORD, your God, and there is no other;
>> my people shall nevermore be put to shame.

The remainder of the book (3:1–4:21) describes the effects of God's saving presence. The cosmic imagery is now directly related to the outpouring of the spirit and the wonders God would work in the heavens and on the earth:

> The sun will be turned to darkness,
>   and the moon to blood,
> At the coming of the day of the LORD,
>   the great and terrible day.
> Then everyone shall be rescued
>   who calls on the name of the LORD;
> On Mount Zion there shall be a remnant,
>   as the LORD has said,
> And in Jerusalem survivors
>   whom the LORD shall call (Joel 3:4-5).

Describing the day of the Lord, when the nations would gather in the Valley of Jehoshaphat (Joel 4:2),[36] the cosmic imagery speaks how it would be for the nations and God's people on the day of the Lord:

> Sun and moon are darkened,
>   and the stars withhold their brightness.
> The LORD roars from Zion,
>   and from Jerusalem raises his voice;
> The heavens and the earth quake,
>   but the LORD is a refuge to his people,
>   a stronghold to the men of Israel (Joel 4:15-16).

From the literary and theological point of view, Joel comes closest to Mark 13:24-27, where the cosmic images (13:24-25) are related both to the great tribulation (13:14-23) and to the coming of the Son of Man (13:26-27).

Like the cosmic prelude (13:24-25), the coming of the Son of Man (13:26) is also presented in biblical terms, this time from the book of Daniel.

> One like a son of man coming,
>   on the clouds of heaven;
> When he reached the Ancient One
>   and was presented before him,
> He received dominion, glory, and kingship;
>   nations and peoples of every language serve him.
> His dominion is an everlasting dominion
>   that shall not be taken away,
>   his kingship shall not be destroyed (7:13-14).

[36] The word "Jehoshaphat" means "Yahweh judges." The "Valley of Jehoshaphat" is thus a symbolic name for the "Valley of the Lord's Judgment."

In Mark 13:26, we read, "And then they shall see 'the Son of Man coming in the clouds' with great power and glory." The Son of David comes as the Son of Man to transform the kingdom of David into the universal kingdom of God.

When the Son of Man comes, "he will send out the angels and gather [his] elect from the four winds, from the end of the earth to the end of the sky" (13:27). The ingathering of the people is related to Daniel, where the Son of Man has dominion over all nations and peoples. It is also related to Joel where the nations are called to decision and judgment (Joel 4:1-16) and salvation is granted God's elect (Joel 4:17-21).

The theme, however, is most closely related to Deuteronomy, promising that "though you may have been driven to the farthest corner of the world, even from there will the Lord, your God, gather you; even from there will he bring you back" (Deut 30:4; see also Zech 2:6, 10).

In the third part of the discourse, the Son of Man, the transcendent Son of David, "comes in the name of the Lord" and inaugurates "the kingdom of our father David that is to come" (11:9-10). We need to remember that Jesus was speaking of the "end" (13:7), of ultimate fulfillment (13:4). The Temple would indeed be destroyed (13:2). In the fulfillment, however, it would not be restored but replaced by the Son of Man. The very person of Jesus, the Son of Man, I AM (13:6), would himself be the place of God's dwelling.

The theme would be spelled out still further in Jesus' interrogation before the Sanhedrin, which accused Jesus of saying that he would destroy the Temple made with hands and within three days build another not made with human hands (14:58). Then when the high priest asked Jesus if he was the Messiah *(Christos),* the Son of the Blessed One, Jesus answered, "I am [*Ego eimi*];

> and 'you will see the Son of Man
> > seated at the right hand of the Power
> and coming with the clouds of heaven'" (Mark 14:62 [see Mark 13:26; Dan 7:13]).

So it is that, with a rich set of biblical allusions, references, and expressions, Mark created a new christological and eschatological synthesis, using apocalyptic imagery to portray the unimaginable. No other passage in all of Mark is so rich with biblical tradition. At the same time, no other passage reaches beyond every existing precedent to present God's new and definitive coming. In Mark 13:24-27, the old is completely at the service of the new.

"Be Watchful! Be Alert!" (13:28-37)

The fourth and last part of the discourse (13:28-37) returns to the theme of watchfulness, which dominated the first (13:5, 9) and second (13:23) parts. Now, however, the focus is not so much on the desecration of the Temple and the great tribulation (13:14-23) as on the return of the Son of Man (13:24-27).

The first part of the discourse opens with a little parable. The disciples must learn a lesson from the fig tree (13:28a). They already had learned a lesson from a fig tree when Jesus cursed it, because it was no longer time for figs, and the fig tree withered to its roots. This would be a new lesson. The first lesson was about destruction and the end of an era. By contrast, the new lesson spoke of new life. "When [the] branch [of the fig tree] becomes tender and sprouts leaves, you know that summer is near" (13:28b).

The parable does apply to the things that would happen, beginning with the desecration of the Temple: "In the same way, when you see these things happening" (13:29a). This time, however, the emphasis is not on the end (13:14-23) but on the beginning (13:24-27): "know that he is near, at the gates" (13:29b). The sign of the end, including the great tribulation, was also the sign of the beginning. Hence the paradoxical images of spring and new life. Jesus sees the dissolution of the old creation (see Gen 1:1–2:4) as a prelude to the new creation effected in the return of the Son of Man.

After the parable (13:28-29), Jesus solemnly assured the disciples that these things would surely take place: "Amen, I say to you, this generation will not pass away until all these things have taken place. Heaven and earth will pass away, but my words will not pass away" (13:3-31).

The passage recalls some of Jesus' teaching earlier in the Gospel: "Amen, I say to you, there are some standing here who will not taste death until they see that the kingdom of God has come in power" (9:1). With time, however, when all who had been standing there had died, some questioned the truth of Jesus' words. Hence his response: "Whoever is ashamed of me and of my words in this faithless and sinful generation, the Son of Man will be ashamed of when he comes in his Father's glory with the holy angels" (8:38).

On that occasion, Jesus' mini-discourse (8:34–9:1) was followed by the transfiguration (9:2-8), showing how his words had been fulfilled. In Jesus' farewell discourse, his words of reassurance are followed by categorical statements that, though these things would surely happen, there was no knowing when they would happen: "But of that day or hour, no one knows, neither the angels in heaven, nor the Son, but only the Father" (13:32). All the more reason to be vigilant: "Be watchful! Be alert! You do not know when the time [*ho kairos*, the critical moment] will come" (13:33).

This last part of the discourse closes with another parable, focusing directly on the need for watchfulness when someone does not know the hour. The parable tells of a man traveling abroad. On leaving home, the man placed his servants (*douloi,* see 10:43-45) in charge, ordering the gatekeeper to be on the watch (13:34). The reference to the gatekeeper recalls an image in the previous parable: "when you see these happenings, know that he (the Son of Man) is near, at the gates" (13:29).

The lesson is that they should watch. Like the slaves *(douloi)* of the household, they did not know when the lord *(ho kyrios)* of the house was coming, "whether in the evening, or at midnight, or at cockcrow, or in the morning." The times indicated correspond to the Roman division of the night into four watches. They also correspond to the critical events of Jesus' last night with the disciples, especially that of the Last Supper, "when it was evening" (14:17), of Peter's denial and repentance at cockcrow (14:66-72), and the gathering of the whole Sanhedrin "as soon as morning came" (15:1).

Jesus' concluding words also point ahead to the passion: "May he not come suddenly and find you sleeping. What I say to you, I say to all: 'Watch!'" (13:36-37). In the place named Gethsemane, Jesus would ask Peter, James, and John to keep watch. When Jesus returned, he found them asleep. He said to Peter, the gatekeeper (13:34): "Simon, are you asleep? Could you not keep watch for one hour?" (14:37).

Jesus' warning to Peter, Andrew, James, and John was meant for all. In Mark's Gospel they were being addressed to the Markan community as part of "the beginning of the gospel of Jesus Christ [the Son of God]" (1:1). Jesus had assured the disciples: "this generation will not pass away until all these things have taken place" (13:30). It may be that the saying originally referred to the generation of Jesus and his disciples. Mark applied it to his community, indeed to all who would read his Gospel: "Heaven and earth will pass away, but my words will not pass away" (13:31).

"Watch!"

X

The Passion and Resurrection of the Son of God

Mark 14:1–16:8

The story of the passion-resurrection (Mark 14:1–16:8) is the sixth and last section of "the beginning of the gospel of Jesus Christ [the Son of God]" (1:1).[1]

In the first section (1:14–3:6), we saw how Jesus proclaimed the good news of God (1:14-15) and called Simon, Andrew, James, and John to follow him in his mission (1:16-20). In the second (3:7–6:6a), we saw how Jesus welcomed large crowds from Gentile as well as

---

[1] For an excellent, short commentary on the passion in Mark, but excluding Mark 16:1-8, see Donald Senior, C.P., *The Passion of Jesus in the Gospel of Mark* (Wilmington, Del.: Michael Glazier, 1984). Senior's purpose in the commentary is to present Mark's message in the story of the passion. Readers will appreciate Senior's scholarship, spiritual insight, and pastoral sensitivity.

For a detailed commentary on Mark 14:26–15:47 and how it compares with the passion in Matthew, Luke, and John, see Raymond Brown, *The Death of the Messiah* (New York: Doubleday, 1994) 2 vols. Brown's purpose in the commentary was *"to explain in detail what the evangelists intended and conveyed to their audiences by their narratives of the passion and death of Jesus"* 1:4. An up-to-date bibliography on the passion narratives in general and on the passion narrative of Mark is provided in 1:94-100. Readers will appreciate Brown's attention to the linguistic, historical, and theological aspects of the narrative.

Jewish territories (3:7-12) and established his followers as the Twelve (3:13-19). In the third (6:6b–8:21), we saw how Jesus went about as an itinerant teacher (6:6b) and sent the Twelve on mission to both Jews and Gentiles (6:7-30).

Together, the three sections make up the first part of the Gospel (1:14–8:21), a story of Jesus and his followers, confronting hardness of heart among Pharisees (3:1-6), lack of faith in Jesus' native place (6:6-6a), and the blindness of his disciples (8:14-21). This first part of the Gospel ends with Jesus asking the Twelve: "Do you still not understand?" (8:21).

In the fourth section (8:22–10:52), we saw what it meant for Jesus to be the Christ, how, as the Son of Man, the Christ had to suffer, die and rise after three days. We saw also what this demanded of his followers.

In the fifth section (11:1–13:37), we saw what it meant for Jesus to be the Son of David, how as the Son of Man, David's Son would return "with great power and glory" and gather the elect from "the end of the earth to the end of the sky." Once again, we also saw what this demanded of Jesus' followers.

We have now reached the sixth and last section climax of the Gospel, the story of Jesus' passion and resurrection (14:1–16:8). Like the previous five sections, Mark's account of the passion and the resurrection is a story of Jesus' followers as well as of Jesus. Together with the fourth and fifth sections, the passion-resurrection[2] makes up the second part of the Gospel (8:22–16:8).

The fifth section (11:1–13:37) ended with a warning: "What I say to you, I say to all: Watch!" (13:37). The warning was directed to the disciples and all who would follow them, from Jesus' passion and resurrection to his return in glory.

As the passion-resurrection opens, the chief priests and the scribes look for a way to arrest Jesus by treachery (14:1-2). Soon Judas would offer to hand Jesus over to them (14:10-11). But Jesus had already warned his disciples: "Watch!"

As the story ends, the women are fleeing from the tomb, trembling and bewildered: "They said nothing to anyone, for they were afraid" (16:8). Everyone had to be vigilant.

---

[2] In faith, liturgy, and theology, the passion and resurrection of Jesus constitute a single mystery. To emphasize their unity in the one mystery, I use the expression, "the passion-resurrection." I do the same when referring to their story as a literary unit in Mark 14:1–16:8. To refer to the events of the passion and resurrection, I use the separate terms, "the passion" and "the resurrection."

A Century of Scholarship

From early patristic times to the nineteenth century, many thought Mark's Gospel was an abbreviation of Matthew's. To know something about the gospel, therefore, people did not turn to Mark but to Matthew. For a long time, Mark drew very little interest.[3]

In the nineteenth century, the weight of opinion shifted. Many came to see Mark as an early, reliable, historical account, uncontaminated by theological tendencies. Even so, Mark did not receive much scholarly attention. The big change came in the twentieth century, which, from a scholarly point of view, has been the century of Mark.

A single book made the difference, Wilhelm Wrede's *Das Messiasgeheimnis in den Evangelien* (1901), in English, *The Messianic Secret*. Today, most of Wrede's interpretations and conclusions have been superceded. His main point, however, that Mark's Gospel is an interpretation of events and not a simple chronicle, proved unassailable. From the beginning of the century, a good part of the scholarly effort has been directed to the passion-resurrection (14:1–16:8), in part because of the prominence of this theme throughout the Gospel, but also because the story of the passion-resurrection stands out as a single literary unit.[4]

Some scholars have focused primarily on the difference between Mark's passion-resurrection and the rest of the Gospel (1:1 to 13:37). For these scholars, the unity and coherence found in Mark 14:1–16:8 shows that he relied on an earlier account of the passion, which had a history of its own. Their main concern is with how the account in Mark relates to the earlier account and to the passion tradition behind it.[5]

A major contribution of this approach has been to focus attention on the various settings for which traditional stories of the passion were developed and in which they were told. One of those settings was the Christian assembly and its liturgy.

---

[3] For a good discussion of the reasons, see R. H. Lightfoot, *The Gospel Message of St. Mark* (London: Oxford University Press, 1950) 1–6.

[4] Donald Senior put it well: "The passion is an extended, coherent narrative, unlike the more staccato structure of the rest of the gospel materials," *The Passion of Jesus in the Gospel of Mark,* 9.

[5] For works emphasizing the differences between Mark's story of the passion-resurrection (14:1–16:8) and Mark 1:1–13:37, see Etienne Trocme, *The Passion as Liturgy, A Study in the Origin of the Passion Narratives in the Four Gospels* (London: SCM Press, 1983), and Adela Yarbro Collins, *The Beginning of the Gospel, Probings of Mark in Context* (Minneapolis: Fortress Press, 1992).

Other scholars have focused on the literary and theological continuity between Mark's account of the passion (14:1–16:8) and the
previous parts of the Gospel (1:1–13:37). For them, the story of the
passion-resurrection contributes to the Gospel's many themes and
brings these to their climax. Their main concern is with how the
story of the passion-resurrection forms an integral part of Mark's
story of the Gospel. These scholars do not necessarily deny that
Mark relied on a traditional story of the passion-resurrection, but
they do not try to define or reconstitute it.[6]

A major contribution of this approach has been to focus attention
on Mark's message and how, as part of the whole Gospel, the story
of the passion-resurrection addressed the Markan community.
Mark's community, suffering a "passion" of its own, needed to hear
Mark's story of the passion-resurrection of Jesus.

In my study, I have found both approaches congenial and com-
plementary. Each leads to a better understanding of the passion-
resurrection and the Gospel as a whole. Mark may or may not have
been the first to write the story of Jesus' passion-resurrection, but
he certainly was not the first to tell it.[7]

From the very beginning, Jesus' death, burial, and resurrection
constituted the very heart of the gospel, as early tradition (see 1 Cor
15:3-5), the apostolic discourses in Acts 1–5, and Paul's letters clearly
attest. The story Mark told was one the readers already knew from
their evangelization and catechesis, a story associated with various
settings, including the Christian assembly, with the liturgy of baptism, and with the Eucharist.

On the other hand, no one had told the story of the passion-
resurrection precisely as Mark told it. Telling the story, Mark
brought the whole Gospel together in a new concluding synthesis,
inviting the community to join Jesus in his passion and resurrection.

---

[6] For works emphasizing the similarities between Mark's story of the
passion-resurrection (14:1–16:8) and Mark 1:1–13:37, see Werner H. Kelber,
editor, *The Passion in Mark: Studies on Mark 14–16* (Philadelphia: Fortress,
1976); Augustine Stock, O.S.B., *The Method and Message of Mark* (Wilmington, Del.: Michael Glazier, 1989); and Ernest Best, *The Temptation and the
Passion: The Markan Soteriology*, Second Edition (New York: Cambridge
University Press, 1990). In *The Passion of Jesus in the Gospel of Mark*, Donald Senior also sees the passion narrative in close continuity with the rest of
the Gospel.

[7] See John R. Donahue, S.J., "Introduction: From Passion Traditions to
Passion Narrative," in *The Passion in Mark*, edited by Werner H. Kelber, 1–20.

The Climax of Mark's Gospel

As the last section of the Gospel, Mark's story of Jesus' passion-resurrection (14:1–16:8) brings the whole Gospel to a climax. It is only now, with the story of the passion-resurrection, that we can appreciate fully Mark's prefatory title: "The beginning of the gospel of Jesus Christ [the Son of God]" (1:1). Jesus' passion, death, and burial were not the end but the beginning of the gospel.

The entire Gospel, each story of conflict, confrontation, challenge, or denunciation, every effort to destroy Jesus, was told with the passion and resurrection in mind. Even the prologue (1:2-13) pointed to the story of Jesus' passion and resurrection, with its portrayal of John the Baptist as Elijah (1:2-8) and of Jesus as God's "beloved Son" (1:9-11), driven into the desert by the Spirit, tested for forty days by Satan, while "he was among wild beasts, and the angels ministered to him" (1:12-13). John the Baptist prepared "the way of the Lord" (1:3) by his mission, his message, his ministry, and his death (6:14-29).

The first section of the Gospel (1:14–3:6) showed how Jesus (1:14-15) and his first disciples (1:16-20) came into conflict with scribes and Pharisees (2:1-12, 13-17, 18-22, 23-28; 3:1-6) as Jesus went about Galilee "proclaiming the gospel of God" (1:14). The most basic conflict of all, however, the one underlying all the others, was Jesus' conflict with unclean spirits (1:21-28). The first section ended with the Pharisees going out to take counsel with the Herodians against Jesus, looking for a way to put him to death (3:6). Later, the chief priests and the scribes would do the same, when Jesus cleansed the Temple (11:18), while he was teaching in the Temple (12:12), and at the beginning of the passion (14:1-2).

The second section (3:7–6:6a) showed how Jesus (3:7-12) and the community of the Twelve (3:13-19), including Judas who would betray him (3:19), came into conflict with Jesus' relatives, who thought Jesus was "out of his mind" (3:21). They also came into conflict with the scribes from Jerusalem, who considered him "possessed by Beelzebul" (3:22). But who were the true relatives of Jesus? And what constituted his true home? At issue were Jesus' identity and the nature of the Church, welcoming the Gentiles and transcending all blood relationships. This second section ended with the people of Jesus' native place taking offense at him (6:3).

The third section (6:6b–8:21) showed how difficult it would be for Jesus (6:6b) and the Twelve (6:7-13) to fulfill their mission. Earlier, in their first crossing of the sea, the disciples thought their little boat would flounder (4:35-41). In their second crossing, they ran into a strong, contrary wind (6:45-52). They did not understand that the breaking of the bread was for the universal community of the Twelve (6:34-44). They had to contend with the Pharisees, objecting that the disciples did not abide by "the tradition of the elders." Was their mission exclusively for the Jews? Was it also for the Gentiles? Eventually, "the breaking of the bread" would include both Gentiles and Jews, women as well as men (8:1-9). But as the third section of the Gospel ended, the Twelve were still blind to the demands of Jesus' mission (8:14-22).

The fourth section of the Gospel (8:22–10:52) showed how Jesus opened the eyes of the blind to recognize who he truly was (8:22-26; 10:46-52). Jesus was both the Christ and the Son of Man. As such he would have to suffer and die and after three days rise (8:31; 9:31; 10:32-34): "For the Son of Man did not come to be served but to serve and to give his life as a ransom for many" (10:45). The whole section shows the implications of Jesus' passion-resurrection for his followers, who, like Jesus, would suffer persecution (10:30). Their mission required they drink the cup he would drink and be baptized in the same baptism with which he was baptized (10:38-39). As the fourth section ends, Bartimaeus receives his sight and follows Jesus on the way (10:52) to the passion and resurrection (10:32-34).

The fifth section of the Gospel (11:1–13:37) showed how Jesus entered Jerusalem as the Messiah and how late it was for the Temple (11:1-11). Returning with the Twelve, he cursed a fig tree (11:12-14, 20-25) and cleansed the Temple of everything that prevented it from being a house of prayer for all peoples (11:15-19). Now it was not just the Pharisees and the Herodians (3:6), but the chief priests and the scribes who looked for a way to put him to death (11:18). After responding to a series of four challenges (11:27–12:12; 12:13-17, 18-27, 28-34) and issuing challenges of his own (12:35-37, 38-40, 41-44), Jesus announced the destruction of the Temple (13:1-2). In a farewell discourse, he related what the community had already experienced, and had yet to experience, to their universal mission and his final coming in glory (13:5-37).

With that we stand on the threshold of the passion and resurrection, the literary and theological climax of "the beginning of the gospel of Jesus Christ [the Son of God]" (1:1). As the passion unfolds, we shall see how every theme introduced in the Gospel reaches its climax in the passion-resurrection.

An Overview

Mark's story of the passion-resurrection, like an oriental rug or tapestry, is tightly knit, making it very difficult to divide into parts. Every unit, large and small, contributes to the whole.

We can distinguish the smaller units that make up the story as well as the seams joining them to one another. We recognize these seams from similar themes and various literary devices used earlier in the Gospel. At times, Mark announces a new unit at the end of the previous section. Sometimes, he introduces a new personage or set of personages, a new indication of time, or a change of place. All three, personages, time, and place, to which the story is very attentive, also contribute a great deal to the story's internal coherence.

Sometimes Mark uses a genitive absolute, a grammatical device for connecting a distinct event with the one preceding. Quite often, he interrupts a story midstream to tell another story, after which he resumes the first story, giving us a "Markan sandwich."

But these smaller units are so integrated in the entire story of the passion-resurrection as to conceal any major seams that would enable us to divide the story into two or more major parts. The change in personages, for example, does not necessarily mean a change of place. Nor does a change of place mean a change of time. In the passion-resurrection, the various units are not just attached to one another but interwoven, requiring the passion and resurrection be read as a literary whole.

For that reason, modern commentators have all but given up looking for major divisions in the story. Instead, they provide convenient divisions for purposes of presentation.[8] And that is what I have done, dividing the story into three parts, like a drama in three acts.

—The first part (Act I) begins with the plot to destroy Jesus and ends with his arrest at Gethsemane (14:1-52).

—The second (Act II) includes his trial and condemnation by the Sanhedrin and by Pilate (14:53–15:20).

---

[8] In a short but very insightful commentary, edited by John L. McKenzie, Rudolf Schnakenburg offered the following three-part division: (1) From the opponents' plot to Jesus' arrest (14:1-52); (2) the proceedings before the Sanhedrin and the trial before Pilate (14:53–15:15); (3) Passion, cross, and tomb (15:16–16:8); *The Gospel According to St. Mark* (New Testament for Spiritual Reading 3 & 4), (New York: Crossroad, 1981) 2:106. Introducing part 3 of the passion, he was quite explicit about the nature of the division: "The break we are making after the condemnation of Jesus in order to follow him now on his way to the foot of the cross is an artificial one for the sake of clarity" (2:146).

—The third (Acts III) begins with the crucifixion and ends with the women's visit to the tomb (15:21–16:8).

As we shall see, each part, or act, has a distinctive, internal structure which is quite different from the other two, giving some justification for our division in three acts.

Each of the three acts can also be subdivided into two scenes,[9] giving the following general outline:

Act I. Plot, betrayal, and arrest (14:1-52)
    Scene One. Introduction and Last Supper (14:1-31)
    Scene Two. Events at Gethsemane (14:32-52)
Act II. Trial, condemnation, and torture (14:53–15:20)
    Scene One. At the palace of the high priest (14:53-72)
    Scene Two. At the palace of Pilate (15:1-20)
Act III. Crucifixion, death, and resurrection (15:21–16:8)
    Scene One. Crucifixion and death at Golgotha (15:21-41)
    Scene Two. Burial and women's visit to the tomb (15:42–16:8)

Act I. Plot, Betrayal, and Arrest (14:1-52). The first part (Act I) of the passion and resurrection is the story of how Jesus was arrested. It begins with the plot to arrest Jesus (14:1-2). It ends with his arrest at Gethsemane (14:43-52).

The chief priests and the scribes were seeking how, "arrest[ing] [*kratesantes*] Jesus by treachery," they might put him to death (14:1). The key word is "arrest," in Greek, *krateo,* which can also be translated as "take hold of" or "seize." With the complicity of Judas, the chief priests, the scribes, and the elders sent a crowd to arrest Jesus (14:43-52). The verb, *krateo,* is used four times in the story of Jesus' arrest (14:44, 46, 49, 51).[10]

Scene One (14:1-31) features two meals. The first meal was in Bethany at the home of Simon the leper. In the course of the meal, a woman anointed Jesus for his burial (14:3-9). The second meal, the Last Supper, in which Jesus ate the Passover with his disciples, was at a home in "the city." In the course of the meal, Jesus revealed the Lord's Supper (14:12-26a).

---

[9] The idea of dividing the story of the passion-resurrection comes from Raymond Brown: "The use of 'Act' and 'Scene' to designate the divisions reflects my understanding of the Gospel accounts as dramatic narratives," *The Death of the Messiah,* 1:ix.

[10] Although the verb, *krateo,* was used ten times previously in the Gospel (11:31; 3:21; 5:41; 6:17; 7:3, 4, 8; 9:10, 27; 12:12), it does not appear in the passion-resurrection beyond part one (14:1-52).

Scene Two (14:32-52) is set in a place named Gethsemane at the Mount of Olives. It features two episodes. In the first, popularly called "The Agony in the Garden," Jesus again warns the disciples to be watchful and gives them a final catechesis on prayer (14:32-42). In the second, Judas arrives, Jesus is arrested, and his disciples abandon him (14:43-52).

The unity of Act I comes from its dominant story line, telling how

—the chief priests, the scribes, and the elders conspired against Jesus (14:1-2), how
—Judas, "one of the Twelve," offered to hand Jesus over to them (14:10-11), how
—Jesus announced his betrayal at the Last Supper (14:17-21), how
—Jesus also announced Peter's denial (14:27-31), and how
—a crowd coming from the chief priests arrested Jesus at Gethsemane (14:43-52).

Were this the whole story, however, Jesus would be presented as the tragic victim, albeit knowing and accepting, of a plot to destroy him. Such a story would not have been gospel.

To transform the story into gospel, Mark repeatedly interrupts the main story line with other stories, showing how Jesus was not the tragic victim of a plot against him but the Anointed One (14:3-9), a heroic figure sending his disciples to prepare his Last Supper (14:12-16), offering his life "for many" (14:22-26), and teaching his disciples to pray, "*Abba,* Father," that they might not undergo the test (14:32-42).

These stories, whose background is catechetical and liturgical, do not represent a second story line but are quite distinct from one another. Their purpose is to interpret the main story line, give it a Christian point of view, and transform it into gospel.

The combination of the main story line and the interpretive passages tells the first part of the passion as a multi-layered Markan sandwich, for which we have no precedent in Mark. So far, we have seen several Markan sandwiches, all of them simple.[11]

Here, in the climax of the Gospel, Mark's multi-layered sandwich seems quite appropriate. Instead of interrupting the story once to tell another story, Mark interrupts the story of the passion-resurrection repeatedly by a succession of stories, transforming it from a tragedy

---

[11] For a fine and fairly recent study of Markan sandwiches, see James R. Edwards, "Markan Sandwiches: The Significance of Interpolations in Markan Narratives," *Novum Testamentum* XXXI, 3 (1989) 193–216.

into a gospel story, the passion of Jesus Christ [the Son of God] (see 1:1).

Act II. Trial, Condemnation and Torture (14:53–15:20). The second part (Act II) of the passion and resurrection is the story of Jesus' two trials, the trial before the Sanhedrin (14:53-72) and the trial before Pilate (15:1-20).

The two trials, the first held the same night Jesus was arrested, the other early the next morning, suggest a division in two scenes. Scene One opens as Jesus is led to the palace of the high priest (14:53). It ends in the palace courtyard with Peter's denial of Jesus (14:66-72). Scene Two opens as the Sanhedrin hands Jesus over to Pilate (15:1). It ends inside the praetorium, Pilate's palace in Jerusalem, with the soldiers mocking Jesus as "King of the Jews" (15:16-20).

The company of disciples (14:12, 32) and the body of the Twelve (14:17) were present throughout the first part of the passion-resurrection (Acts I). But when Jesus was arrested, they all left him and fled (14:50, 51-52). As Act I comes to an end, so does the story of Judas, "one of the Twelve" (14:10, 20, 43).

The only disciple to reappear in Act II is Peter, who has a secondary role. But Peter has his own story line (14:27-31, 37-38, 14:54; 15:66-72), weaving the two acts together and contributing to the continuity of the story. Peter's role, however, is limited to Scene One (14:53-72). As the scene ends, so does Peter's active role in the passion-resurrection.

In Act II, the main focus is on Jesus and those who tried to destroy him, and the chief concern is christological. Scene One shows Jesus as the Messiah, the Son of the Blessed One (14:61), who would appear as "the Son of Man / seated at the right hand of the Power / and coming with the clouds of heaven" (14:62). Scene Two shows Pilate referring to him ironically as "the king of the Jews" (15:2, 9, 12). Later, that is also how the soldiers mocked him: "Hail, King of the Jews!" (15:18).

The chief priests, the scribes (14:1-2, 10-11), and the elders (14:43), also contribute to the continuity between Act I and Act II, as representing the Sanhedrin in Act I, and as the Sanhedrin's full contingent in Act II (14:43-65; 15:1-15). Besides Jesus, only the chief priests and the scribes have an active role in all three acts (see 15:31-32a).

Act III. Crucifixion, Death, and Resurrection (15:2–16:8). The third part (Act III) of the passion and resurrection tells the story of Jesus' crucifixion and death as well as his burial and the women's visit to the tomb.

At the end of Act II, the soldiers were introduced, leading Jesus into the praetorium, where they mocked him as "king of the Jews" (15:16-20). In Act III, the soldiers continue to play a part, especially at the beginning, pressing into service a passerby, Simon, a Cyrenian, to carry Jesus' cross (15:21), and taking Jesus to Golgotha, where they crucified him (10:22-27).

Later, one of the soldiers, the centurion, who was responsible for carrying out the execution and so stood facing Jesus as he breathed his last, declared: "Truly this man was the Son of God!" (15:39).

The chief priests and the scribes make their last appearance in the midst of the crowd of bystanders (15:29-30, 35-36) mocking the crucified Jesus. Their own mockery echoes that of the soldiers in the praetorium: "Let the Messiah, the King of Israel, come down now from the cross that we may see and believe" (15:31-32a). The soldiers had mocked Jesus as the "King of the Jews" (15:18).

This third part is characterized by the rapid succession of events, a large cast of diverse characters, and a series of precise indications of time, distinctive even in the passion-resurrection, which is noted for its attention to specific times.

Jesus was crucified at the third hour, that is, at 9:00 a.m. (15:25). At the sixth hour, 12:00 noon, darkness came over the whole land and remained until the ninth hour, 3:00 p.m. (15:33). It is at the ninth hour that Jesus breathed his last (15:34-38). Jesus was placed in the tomb when it was evening, on the day of preparation, the day before the sabbath (15:42-47). The following evening, when the sabbath was over, the women bought spices (16:1). Then, "very early when the sun had risen, on the first day of the week" the women went to the tomb (16:1-8).

Scene One in Act III presents the crucifixion and the death of Jesus on Golgotha. Scene Two presents the events at the tomb, the burial of Jesus (15:42-47) and the women's visit to the tomb (16:1-8). The women, who were first mentioned at the end of the crucifixion (15:40-41), are named again at the end of Jesus' burial (15:47), and immediately after that as they go to buy spices (16:1). They thus contribute to the unity of Act III as well as the literary continuity between Scene One and Scene Two.

The Passion As Gospel

The way we read Mark's story of the passion-resurrection matters. We must not read it, for example, with Jesus as the passive victim of a plot to destroy him. That would turn the story into bad news. As gospel, good news, the story shows how Jesus actually gave his life for others. Nor must we read the passion-resurrection as a story of Jesus' alone. Jesus' followers also have a role.

The passion-resurrection, like the rest of the Gospel, is first and foremost a story of Jesus, and that is how it should be read. But, like the rest of the Mark's Gospel, it is also a story of Jesus' followers, and his followers play an extremely important part in all three Acts. The primary focus on Jesus must not obscure their role.

In the passion-resurrection, Jesus, the Son of Man, heroic and unflinching, represents an ideal to which we are called but can never fully attain. Jesus' followers represent the Markan community, the intended readers, and all who would share their experience in the future. We understand the challenge of the passion-resurrection for his followers, also their good will, and their weakness.

Earlier in the Gospel, just about every summary, every episode, every story of Jesus was followed up by their implications for Jesus' followers. We saw it at the very beginning, when a great summary of Jesus' mission (1:14-15) was followed immediately by the call of his disciples (1:16-20). We saw it again and again, throughout the Gospel, to the very end of Jesus' discourse on the Mount of Olives (13:1-37), and the threshold of the passion-resurrection.

The same is true in the passion-resurrection, where the story of Jesus is paralleled by the story of his followers. The story of the passion is not just a story of Jesus. It is the story of Jesus together with his followers. In terms that evoke baptism, we would say that the story of Jesus' passion is the story of Christ dying. It is also the story of his followers challenged to die with Christ.

As a story of Jesus and his followers, the passion-resurrection is thus a very baptismal story. This should not come as a surprise. Recall the dialogue between Jesus and the sons of Zebedee: "Can you drink the cup that I drink or be baptized with the baptism with which I am baptized?" Jesus asked. When they answered that they could, Jesus responded: "The cup that I drink, you will drink, and with the baptism with which I am baptized, you will be baptized" (10:38-39).

Jesus' question and response presented the passion in terms of the Eucharist and Christian baptism. As part of the Gospel, the story of the passion is then told with baptism and the Eucharist in mind. For Christians, dying with Christ in baptism becomes a daily challenge, to which they recommit themselves every time they drink Christ's eucharistic cup.

Mark's community needed to remember their baptism, which for them was "the beginning of the gospel" (1:1). They needed to renew their baptismal commitment in the Eucharist. Hence the importance of the Eucharist and its prominent place in the passion-resurrection (14:12-26, 35-36).

The story of Christ dying includes that of Christ being buried. It also includes the story of his followers, challenged to be buried with Christ. In this respect, recall the young man, wearing a garment symbolic of Jesus' burial, but slipping out of that garment, his baptismal garment, when he was seized (14:51-52) as Jesus had just been seized (14:43-50).

Mark's story of the passion-resurrection concludes with the announcement of Jesus' resurrection. Those who would follow Christ in Galilee, fulfilling the challenges of their baptism, wear the garment of his risen life and will one day follow him into glory.

In light of these observations, I suggest that the liturgical context of the pre-Markan tradition or traditions of the passion was that of a baptismal and eucharistic liturgy of initiation. I do not believe that we can reconstitute such a liturgy from Mark's account. But it certainly seems that Mark intended to evoke such a liturgy in telling the story of the passion-resurrection. Remembering their baptism and eucharistic initiation, in which they participated in the mystery of Christ's death and resurrection, Mark's readers should understand the nature and purpose of the passion they were now suffering.[12]

Act I. Plot, Betrayal, and Arrest (14:1-52)
Scene One
Preparation and Last Supper (14:1-31)

Jesus concluded his farewell discourse on the Mount of Olives (13:3-37) with a solemn warning: "What I say to you, I say to all: 'Watch!'" (13:37). Jesus told the disciples to watch because the feast of Passover and Unleavened Bread[13] was two days away, and the

---

[12] The body of the Gospel prepared us to read the passion of Jesus in this light. As Senior indicated, "The passion of Jesus is also the passion of the community," *The Passion of Jesus in the Gospel of Mark,* 39; see 37–39.

[13] The feast of Passover, adopted by Israel in its early nomadic years, originated as a pastoral feast at which young lambs were offered in sacrifice. The feast of Unleavened Bread, adopted after Israel settled on the land, originated as an agricultural feast celebrating the wheat harvest. The Israelites celebrated these two, originally distinct, feasts at the same time, in memory of their liberation from slavery in Egypt. Mark presents them as one feast, the feast *(he heorte)* of Passover *(to pascha)* and Unleavened Bread *(ta azuma),* but retains the two names for their historic, symbolic, and theological value. See Roland de Vaux, *Ancient Israel: Its Life and Institutions* (New York: MacGraw-Hill, 1961) 484–92; also Baruch M. Bokser, "Unleavened

chief priests and the scribes[14] were looking for a way to have Jesus arrested and put to death (14:1).[15]

So begins Mark's story of the passion-resurrection (14:1–16:8), the climax of "the beginning of the gospel of Jesus Christ [the Son of God]" (1:1).

Act I tells how the chief priests and the scribes plotted to have Jesus arrested and put to death, how Judas, "one of the Twelve," betrayed him, and how Jesus was finally arrested. It also tells how the whole series of events, far from a tragedy, was gospel, the gospel of Jesus, the Messiah, who heroically gave his life that all might live.[16]

Scene One shows how the chief priests and the scribes, with the complicity of Judas, prepared the Passover and Unleavened Bread of Jesus and his disciples (14:1-2, 10-11), how Jesus and his disciples prepared the same (14:12-16), and how Jesus ate the Passover with the Twelve (14:17-26), including Judas, the one who betrayed him (14:18-21), and Peter, the one who denied him (14:26-31).

Bread and Passover, Feasts of," *The Anchor Bible Dictionary* (New York: Doubleday, 1992) 6:755–65.

[14] The chief priests entered the Gospel in Jesus' first announcement of the passion and resurrection of the Son of Man (8:31). From the very first, they were associated with the scribes (8:31; 10:32; 11:18; 11:27), sometimes also with the elders (8:31; 11:27).

The scribes entered the Gospel much earlier, at first on their own, in the story of Jesus healing a paralytic (2:1-12), but also together with the Pharisees (2:16-17). The Gospel also introduced some scribes who came from Jerusalem, protesting (3:22-30) how, coming home, Jesus received a large crowd (3:20) who came from Galilee, Judea, Jerusalem, Idumea, Transjordan, and the region of Tyre and Sidon (3:7-8). Later, some scribes from Jerusalem reappeared, together with the Pharisees, protesting that Jesus' disciples were eating their meals with unclean hands (7:1-13). Later yet, when Jesus was teaching in the Temple, a scribe approached him asking about the first of the commandments (12:28-34).

From the beginning of Jesus' ministry, the crowd compared the scribes unfavorably with Jesus, who taught "as one having authority and not as the scribes" (1:22). At the end of his ministry, while teaching in the cleansed Temple, Jesus challenged the scribes regarding their teaching on the Messiah as David's son (12:35-37) and warned the crowds against behaving like the scribes (12:38-40).

[15] Jesus' warning was related to the eschatological discourse. But it was also related to the approaching passion.

[16] For a good article on Mark 14:1-52, see John Paul Heil, "Mark 14, 1-52: Narrative Structure and Reader-Response," *Biblica* 71 (1990) 305–32. Heil's analysis of the literary structure of Mark 14:1-52, our Act I, is similar to the one presented in this commentary.

Two Days Before the Feast (14:1-11)

It was now two days before the feast of Passover and Unleavened Bread. By ancient reckoning, that could mean the day before, long commemorated in the Christian calendar as Spy Wednesday. Everyone, including the chief priests and the scribes, Jesus and a woman who anointed him, and Judas, one of the Twelve, was preparing the Passover.

By themselves, the events "two days before the feast" form a Markan sandwich (14:1-2, 3-9, 10-11). The story opens with the chief priests and the scribes conspiring against Jesus (14:1-2). The scene suddenly shifts to Bethany, where Jesus is at table in the home of Simon the leper. That is where the woman anointed him. Judas was there (14:3-9). As Judas leaves, the scene returns to the chief priests, with Judas offering to hand Jesus over to them (14:10-11).[17]

The Conspiracy (14:1-2). The chief priests and the scribes had been seeking to put Jesus to death (*apolesosin,* see 3:6) from the moment they heard about Jesus cleansing of the Temple. They feared Jesus because the whole crowd (*pas ho ochlos*) was enthralled by his teaching (11:18; 12:12). That is why they wanted him killed.

Later, when the chief priests, the scribes, and the elders challenged Jesus' authority, and Jesus publicly challenged them in return, they looked for a way to arrest (*kratesai*) him. Jesus had told a parable about tenants who killed the owner's son, the heir to the vineyard that was leased to them (12:1-11). There was no mistaking Jesus' intent. They knew, everyone knew, the parable referred to them. They wanted Jesus arrested, but they feared the crowd (12:12).

The chief priests and the scribes were caught in a dilemma. Fearing Jesus because he was popular with the crowd (*ho ochlos),* they wanted him killed (11:18). But fearing the crowd (*ho ochlos)* because it knew the parable was about them, they were unable to arrest him (12:12).

Now, with the feast of Passover and Unleavened Bread two days away, the chief priests and the scribes were still looking for a way

---

[17] For the structure and meaning of Mark 14:1-11 as a Markan sandwich, see James R. Edwards, "Markan Sandwiches: The Significance of Interpolations in Markan Narratives," *Novum Testamentum* XXXI, 3 (1989) 193–216, in particular 208–09. Edwards found and studied nine sandwiches in the Gospel of Mark, including 3:20-35; 4:1-20, 5:21-43; 6:7-30; 11:12-21 and four in the passion-resurrection narrative: 14:1-11, 17-31, 53-72; 15:40–16:8; see 197–98. Several of the sandwiches are part of a considerably more complex structure.

to arrest Jesus (*kratesantes,* see 12:12) and put him to death (*apokteinosin,* see 11:18). Because of the feast, however, their dilemma was even greater.

On the one hand, they could not arrest Jesus during the feast, for fear the people *(ho laos)* might riot on his behalf. On the other, they absolutely had to arrest him during the feast, for fear the people *(ho laos)* might rally to Jesus and riot against them. The only way out of the dilemma was to arrest Jesus by treachery *(en dolo).*

The shift from "the crowd" *(ho ochlos)* to "the people" is significant. When Jesus cleansed the Temple and confronted the chief priests and the scribes, their concern was with the crowd *(ho ochlos),* that anonymous multitude referred to over and over again throughout the Gospel. "The crowd" appears thirty-eight times in Mark's Gospel beginning with Jesus' cure of the paralytic (2:1-12), where those who brought the paralytic were "unable to get near Jesus because of the crowd" (2:4).

Now that the feast was approaching, however, they were concerned about the people *(ho laos),* God's Passover people, who had come to Jerusalem to celebrate their liberation from Egypt. Mark refers to the people *(ho laos),* that is, the Jewish, Israelite people, the people of God, only one other time in the Gospel, in a quotation from Isaiah:

This people [*laos*] honors me with their lips,
    but their hearts are far from me;
In vain do they worship me,
    teaching as doctrines human precepts (7:6-7; Isa 29:13, LXX).

Ironically, the chief priests and the scribes were planning to arrest and put Jesus to death on the feast of the people's deliverance from slavery and death. The feast was celebrated by sacrificing the Pasch and ridding one's life of everything associated with the previous harvest. Unwittingly, the chief priests and the scribes were preparing the new Passover, in which Christ, handed over, would offer his life in sacrifice. They were also preparing the new feast of Unleavened Bread,[18] in which Christians banished the leaven of the Pharisees and the leaven of Herod (see 8:15) from their lives.

[18] In New Testament times, the principal way to leaven bread was by retaining dough from the previous day's batch and mixing it with the new batch. Having fermented overnight, the dough had a leavening action on the new batch, producing a kind of sourdough bread. When Jews, including Jesus and his disciples, celebrated the new harvest, they allowed no mixture of dough made from the previous year's harvest. Hence the feast of Unleavened Bread.

The Anointing at Bethany (14:3-9). The scene suddenly shifts. While the chief priests and the scribes were plotting against Jesus, Jesus was in Bethany, where he stayed with the Twelve after spending the day in Jerusalem at the Temple (11:11-12, 15, 19-20, 27). The contrast is very striking. While others were seeking to arrest him, Jesus was reclining at table, a free man,[19] in the house of Simon the leper (14:3a). As a leper, Simon was considered unclean.

Jesus, who made lepers clean (1:40-45), who dined with tax collectors and sinners (2:13-17), and who set aside "the tradition of the elders" and "declared all foods clean" (7:1-23), was dining with Simon the leper. Whether or not Simon had already been cured is irrelevant. What matters is that the story introduces Simon as a leper. To the very end, Jesus was pursuing his mission on behalf of outcasts, unafraid of those plotting against his life.

While Jesus was reclining at dinner, a woman (*gyne*) came with an "alabastron" of ointment, a small but delicate jar, ordinarily, but not necessarily, made of alabaster, containing very precious perfumed oil, genuine nard made from a rare Indian plant (14:3b). Those present at the dinner estimated the value of the ointment at three hundred denarii, close to a year's wage for an average laborer (14:5).

The woman broke the alabastron and poured the ointment on Jesus' head, a symbolic and extremely significant gesture. Parallel stories in John 12:1-8 and Luke 7:36-50 have the woman anoint Jesus' feet. In Mark she anoints him on the head, evoking the prophetic anointing of a king.[20] So it is that the prophet Samuel poured oil on Saul's head, anointing him king of Israel (1 Sam 10:1) and that the prophet Elisha sent a young prophet to anoint Jehu (2 Kgs 9:6).

For the early Christians, for whom Jesus' teaching and way of life represented something radically new (1:27), the feast was especially significant, representing separation from everything in their former way of life that stood in the way of being Christians. Their baptismal self was not an old garment patched with a piece of new, unshrunken cloth (2:21). Their new wine required new wineskins (2:22).

[19] In the Hellenistic, Jewish, and Roman world of the time, only free, adult men reclined at a dinner. Recall how at Herod's birthday party, Herodias was not present at the dinner. Her daughter, who provided unseemly entertainment after the dinner, during the drinking feast, had to leave the banquet room to consult her mother (7:22-25).

[20] Mark 14:3-9 and the parallel stories in John 12:1-8 and Luke 7:36-50 have roots in the same basic tradition. All three emphasize the extravagance of the woman's gesture.

Breaking the jar indicated the anointing was absolutely unique and definitive. There would never be another anointing such as this. Jesus was the one and only Christ, the Anointed One, who would rule in the kingdom of God.

Like Peter (8:29), the woman proclaimed Jesus as the Christ, the Anointed One. What Peter did with words the woman did with a symbolic, prophetic act. Unlike Peter, however, who did not accept that Jesus, the Christ, as the Son of Man had to suffer, die, and rise again (8:31-33), the woman's prophetic act anticipated the anointing of Jesus' body for burial (14:8).

When some of those present protested her gesture as wasteful extravagance, Jesus defended both her (14:6) and what she did (14:8). The woman's gesture associated Jesus' mission as the Christ with his death and burial. Those who protested rejected the woman's symbolic proclamation that, as the Christ, Jesus had to die, be buried, and rise again.

Earlier in the Gospel, Peter had taken Jesus aside and rebuked him (8:32) for announcing that he had to suffer greatly, be rejected, and be killed, but would rise after three days (8:31). Later, out of fear, the disciples avoided so much as thinking about a similar announcement (9:31). Instead they discussed which among them was the greatest (9:32-34). Later yet, James and John, the sons of Zebedee, avoided the implications of the passion as the way of Christ (10:32-34) by focusing on Jesus' glorious destiny (10:35-40).

Now, when the woman anointed Jesus (14:3) in view of his burial (14:8), proclaiming him the Christ who was to suffer, die, and be buried, some of those at the dinner protested her prophetic gesture. Peter (8:32), the disciples (9:32-34), and James and John (10:35-40) had rejected Jesus' prophetic announcement. Now, rejecting the woman's prophetic announcement, some who were at the home of Simon the leper declared the ointment should have been sold and the money given to the poor.

To follow Christ and have treasure in heaven, Jesus' disciples did have to sell what they had and give the proceeds to the poor (10:21-22; see also 10:23-31). But giving to the poor presupposed and flowed from the following of Christ, even to his passion and resurrection (10:32-34). There was no escaping the implications of the passion, but for that, you first had to accept the passion.

The poor would be with them always (14:7). Giving to the poor would always be part of following Christ to his passion, burial, and resurrection. And that is why what the woman did would be told in memory of her, "wherever the gospel is proclaimed to the whole world" (14:9).

The Betrayal (14:10-11). Again the scene shifts, taking up the narrative line begun in 14:1-2, with Judas breaking off his relationship to Jesus and going to the chief priests and the scribes.

When Jesus formed *(epoiesen)* the Twelve (3:13-19), he included Judas Iscariot, the one "who betrayed him" (3:19). Like the others, Jesus called Judas to "be with him" and be sent "to preach and to have authority to drive out demons" (3:14-15).

Judas was with Jesus when Jesus cursed the fig tree (see 11:11, 12-14, 20-25), cleansed the Temple (11:15-18), and challenged the chief priests, the scribes, and the elders while he was teaching in the Temple (11:27–12:12). Judas knew that the chief priests and the scribes were looking for a way to arrest Jesus (11:18) and put him to death (12:12).

As "one of the Twelve," he was also "with Jesus," dining at the home of Simon the leper (14:3-9). When the "woman came with an alabaster jar of perfumed oil, costly genuine spikenard, . . . broke the alabaster jar and poured it on his head" (14:3), some indignantly protested that the perfume could have been sold and the money given to the poor (14:4-5). When Jesus defended her act of messianic faith and proclaimed it gospel, Judas left the dinner and offered to betray him.

Cleansing the Temple, Jesus had driven out those selling and buying there (11:15). Ironically, the chief priests and Judas, "one of the Twelve," were selling and buying the life of Jesus (14:11a), I AM (14:62), the life of one who would replace the Temple three days after it was destroyed (14:58). Unwittingly, the conspirators and the betrayer were furthering God's plan of salvation.

At that point, Judas began looking for an opportune time *(eukairos)* to hand him over (14:11b). Judas, one of the Twelve, had now joined the chief priests and the scribes in preparing the Passover, which would be Jesus' Last Supper with the Twelve. "The opportune time" would be "the first day of the Feast of Unleavened Bread, when they sacrificed the Passover Lamb" (14:12).

The First Day of the Feast (14:12-72)

For two days, the chief priests and the scribes had been preparing Jesus' final Passover (14:1-2). So had Judas, one of the Twelve, seeking an opportune time and place to betray him (14:10-11).

Jesus, too, had been preparing the Passover, at the home of Simon the leper, where a woman anointed him in view of his burial (14:3-9). The woman's symbolic gesture, confessing Jesus as the Christ, would be told wherever the gospel *(to euaggelion)*[21] is proclaimed "to the whole world" (14:9).

Now it was the "first day of the Feast of Unleavened Bread," the day, Mark says, when they sacrificed the Passover *(to pascha)*. There seems to be a mistake. In the Jewish reckoning of time, where the day began at sundown, the Feast of the Unleavened and the Passover began in the early evening. By that reckoning, the sacrifice took place the previous afternoon, which was the day before the feast.

In the passion, however, Mark follows the popular Roman reckoning of time, where the day began at dawn, in today's reckoning, at six o'clock in the morning.[22] With this reckoning, the Feast of the Unleavened Bread began, not at sundown, but the previous morning, and the Passover sacrifice as well as the Passover supper took place on the same day, "the first day of the Feast of Unleavened Bread."

The remainder of Act I, Scene One (14:17-31), and all of Scene Two (14:32-52) unfold on this first day of the feast, beginning with Jesus sending his disciples to prepare the Passover (14:12-16). Later, when evening came *(opsias genomenes)*, Jesus came with the Twelve and shared the Passover with them (14:17-21, 22-26). Then, after singing hymns of praise, they left for the Mount of Olives, where Jesus announced all would be scandalized on his behalf, including Peter, who would deny him (14:27-31).

The setting for Scene Two is a place called Gethsemane, somewhere on the slope of the Mount of Olives. While Jesus was praying and exhorting the disciples to be watchful (14:32-42), Judas came with an armed crowd *(ochlos)* and arrested Jesus (14:43-52).

Disciples Prepare the Passover (14:12-16)

On the first day of the Unleavened Bread, when they sacrificed the Passover, the disciples said to Jesus, "Where do you want us to go and prepare for you to eat [*phages*] the Passover?"[23] This was to be Jesus'

[21] Mark refers to "the gospel" in 1:1; 10:29; 13:10 ("to all nations"), and here in 14:9. "The gospel" refers to a message that is to be preached. Since the gospel message is in story form, the gospel is preached (announced, proclaimed) by telling the story.

[22] That Mark followed the popular Roman system becomes clear from chapter 15. The new day, the second day of the Feast of Unleavened Bread, began "as soon as morning came" (15:1). Jesus was crucified at "nine o'clock in the morning [*hora trite*, the third hour]" (15:25), darkness came over the whole earth at "noon [*horas hektes*, the sixth hour]" until "three in the afternoon [*horas enates*, the ninth hour]" (15:33), when Jesus died (15:34-37). See Adela Collins, *The Beginning of the Gospel* (Fortress Press: Minneapolis, 1992) 101–02.

[23] For Mark's presentation of the Last Supper, see Vernon K. Robbins, "Last Meal: Preparation, Betrayal, and Absence, Mark 12–25," in *The Passion*

Passover, not theirs. The disciples were trying to avoid the implications of Jesus' passion-resurrection, as some had done at the house of Simon the leper (14:4-5) and after each prophetic announcement of the Son of Man's passion-resurrection (8:31-32; 9:30-34; 10:32-37).

Each time Jesus responded. There was no way his followers could avoid the passion-resurrection (14:6-8; 8:33; 9:35-37; 10:38-40). Now, concluding his instructions to the disciples, Jesus pointedly answered, "Make the preparations for us [*hemin*] there" (14:15b). This would be their Passover as well as his.

The story of the preparations for the Passover of Jesus and his disciples is the second interpretive event (see 14:3-9) interrupting the main story line (14:1-2, 10-11). Like the dinner at the house of Simon the leper (14:3-9), it transforms what would have been the tragedy of Jesus into the gospel of Jesus.

The story is patterned on the preparations for Jesus' messianic entry into Jerusalem (11:1-7a). After a brief introduction (14:12; 11:1), Jesus gives the disciples instructions, sending them forth and telling them what to expect (14:13-15; 11:2-3), and the disciples fulfill Jesus' instructions (14:16; 11:4-7a).

In both cases, Jesus' instructions begin the same way: "He sent two of his disciples and said to them, 'Go into the city'" (14:13a). For the entry into Jerusalem, Jesus told them, "'Go into the village opposite you'" (11:2a). Jesus then described what they would find. In the village, they would find a colt tethered on which no one has ever sat (11:2). In the city, a man would meet them, carrying a jar of water (14:13).

Mark obviously wants to evoke the liturgical interpretation or celebration of Jesus' solemn entry into Jerusalem, a unique historical event (11:2-10). In the present case, the preparations (14:13-16) are for the Passover meal which would be Jesus' Last Supper (14:17-21), also a unique historical event, as well as for the Lord's Supper (14:22-25), an event repeated regularly in the life of the community.

After his solemn entry, Jesus returned to Bethany with the Twelve (11:11). After the Last Supper, Jesus and the Twelve went to the Mount of Olives (14:26). The Mount of Olives is where Jesus began his processional entry into Jerusalem (11:1) and where he gave his final discourse to Peter, James, John, and Andrew (13:3).

---

in Mark, Studies on Mark 14–16, edited by Werner H. Kelber (Philadelphia: Fortress, 1976) 21–40. For the Eucharist in Mark's Gospel, see E. LaVerdiere, *The Eucharist in the New Testament and the Early Church* (Collegeville: The Liturgical Press, 1996) 46–64.

While evoking the liturgical celebration described in 11:2-10, Mark's primary concern in 14:13-16 is not so much liturgical as catechetical, as it was in the final discourse, indeed, wherever Jesus is addressed as "Teacher" *(didaskale).*[24] Besides the reference to Jesus as "Teacher," the catechetical concern is also shown from the disciples' taking the initiative (14:12b).

That is how it was when Jesus and his disciples left the Temple for the Mount of Olives: "Look, teacher, what stones and what buildings!" (13:1). In both cases, the disciples' question or observation raises an issue that had become significant in the Markan community. Jesus' response provides an authoritative catechetical response.

Ordinarily, it is the disciples who address Jesus as "Teacher" *(didaskale).* This time, it is Jesus who calls himself "the Teacher" *(ho didaskalos).* In the city, someone *(anthropos)*[25] carrying a jar of water would meet them. They were to follow this person into a house and say to the master, "The Teacher [*ho didaskalos*] says, 'Where is my guest room where I may eat the Passover with my disciples?'" (14:13-14). The disciples would speak in the name of Jesus, their teacher.

This is the only time in the Gospel that Jesus referred to himself as "the Teacher," the one with a new teaching and who taught with authority, unlike the scribes (1:22, 27). This is also the only time Jesus referred to his disciples as "my disciples." Jesus obviously had something extremely important to teach his disciples.

While others were preparing to arrest Jesus and put him to death, the disciples would prepare Jesus' *(mou)* guest room *(katalyma)* where, eating the Passover with his disciples, Jesus would offer them his body and blood. The Greek word rendered as "guest room," is *katalyma.* Actually, the term *katalyma* refers to any place where hospitality is offered to people on a journey. In this case, it refers to a large upper room *(anagaion)* furnished and ready (14:15).[26] This

---

[24] Jesus is addressed or referred to as "Teacher" at times in a question (4:38; 5:35; 10:17), an affirmation (9:17, 38; 10:20, 35), a combination of both (12:14, 19-23, 32-33), even in an exclamation (13:1). In each case, the question, affirmation, or exclamation invites some catechesis on Jesus' part for Mark's readers.

[25] Very often, the word *anthropos,* which can refer to a woman as well as a man, is translated as "a man." For a man to be carrying a water jar would be quite extraordinary, and so the two disciples would recognize the person easily. Note, however, that the disciples do not need to find or recognize the person. Rather, it is the person with the jar of water who will meet them.

[26] See E. LaVerdiere, "Mary's Son, God's Firstborn," *Church* (Winter 1994) 9.

would be Jesus' *kataluma,* the place where he would offer Passover hospitality.

Jesus' Passover would be with his disciples. Hospitality, like the Passover meal, always involved more than one person. The two disciples would make the preparations for their Passover with Jesus (14:15b), not only for the Passover of Jesus (14:12b).

The disciples followed Jesus' instructions. They "went off, entered the city, and found it just as he had told them." The two prepared the Passover in a large upper room for Jesus and his disciples (14:16). In the story of Jesus' passion and resurrection, apart from the liturgical interpretation or celebration of the Last Supper, there was no need to describe in detail how the two fulfilled Jesus' instructions (compare 11:4-7).

At Table with the Betrayer (14:17-21)

The upper room, Jesus' *kataluma,* was ready, and so were the preparations for the meal. When evening came, Jesus came with the Twelve (14:17). While they were reclining at table and eating, Jesus made a solemn announcement: "Amen, I say to you, one of you will betray me, one who is eating with me" (14:18). With that Mark picks up the main narrative line (14:1-2, 10-11, 17-21), after interrupting it for the second time (14:3-9, 12-16).

The Passover meal has begun. No doubt, many things could have been told about such a meal. The order of the meal, for example, and the various kinds of food could have been indicated, as well as the name and the place of each guest. But this was not an ordinary Passover, and none of these were important. Two events made this Passover meal different from every other Passover meal: Jesus' announcement that "one of the Twelve" would betray him, and Jesus' gift of himself as food and drink.

The first event focuses on Jesus' Last Supper with the Twelve, one of whom was the betrayer. Judas had already severed his relationship to Jesus when he left Jesus and the others at the house of Simon the leper and went off to the chief priests (14:10). Now Judas was back, "one of the Twelve," but no longer was "with the Twelve" (4:10). The intimacy of the setting contrasts with Judas' treachery, as does the Passover celebration of liberation.

After Jesus announced the betrayal, the others became distressed. Each began to declare, asking, "Surely it is not I?" (14:19). Jesus did not indicate which of them was the betrayer. In 14:17-21, the identity of the betrayer remains somewhat open. We know, of course, about Judas (14:10-11; see also 3:19), but the disciples did not. Besides, there would be others after Judas who would betray them. Jesus had warned them of these in his farewell discourse (see 13:9-12).

Instead of identifying which of the Twelve would betray him, Jesus reinforced his earlier statement. The betrayer was one of the Twelve, one who was dipping with him into the common dish (14:20). But that could have been any one of them. All were dipping with him into the common dish.

Jesus knew one of the Twelve was betraying him. He also knew the Son of Man had to go as it was written (see 8:31; 9:31; 10:32-34). The story evokes Psalm 41:10, "Even my friend who had my trust, who shared my table, has scorned me." Knowing, however, and accepting the prophetic necessity of his death did not make it less tragic. Woe to the one by whom he was betrayed! It would be better if that person had never been born!

The Lord's Supper (14:22-26)

Not far away, the chief priests and the scribes were still plotting Jesus' death (14:1-2), and Judas was still looking for an opportune time to hand him over to them (14:10-11). As "one of the Twelve," Judas was present at the Last Supper, like the others, dipping into the common dish, enjoying Jesus' Passover hospitality (14:17-21). That alone was enough to make this Passover different from every other. But then the Supper would have been but another moment in the mounting tragedy of Jesus. And so, for the third time, Mark interrupts the main narrative line (14:1-2, 10-11, 17-21) with an independent story (14:22-26), once again (see 14:3-9, 12-16) transforming what would have been the tragedy of Jesus into the gospel of Jesus.

This time the independent story was a liturgical story, a narrative connecting the Lord's Supper,[27] as celebrated in the Markan community and elsewhere, with Jesus' historic Last Supper, celebrated "on the first day of the Feast of Unleavened Bread, when they sacrificed

---

[27] For the Eucharist in Mark's Gospel, see Vernon K. Robbins, "Last Meal: Preparation, Betrayal, and Absence, Mark 14:12-25," in *The Passion in Mark*, edited by Werner H. Kelber, 21–40; Jerome Kodell, *The Eucharist in the New Testament*, Zacchaeus Studies: New Testament (Wilmington: Michael Glazier, 1988) 83–92, and E. LaVerdiere, "In the Following of Christ: The Eucharist in Mark's Gospel," *Emmanuel* 100 (April 1995) 132–42. For a general study of the accounts of the institution in the New Testament, see P. Benoit, "The Accounts of the Institution and What They Imply" in J. Delorme, et al., *The Eucharist in the New Testament* (Baltimore: Helicon Press, 1965) 71–101; and Edward J. Kilmartin, *The Eucharist in the Primitive Church* (Englewood Cliffs, N.J.: Prentice-Hall, Inc., 1965) 22–73.

the Passover Lamb" (14:12). Quoting the formula, Mark drew on the community's lived, liturgical experience and brought it to bear on the story of the passion.

A little phrase, "and while they were eating" *(kai esthionton auton)* connects the liturgical narrative with the meal already in progress (see 14:18a). The narrative itself is in two parts, the first regarding the bread (14:22), the second regarding the cup (14:23-25).

Primitively, the two parts represented distinct formulas, one spoken at the beginning of the supper, the other after the supper (see 1 Cor 11:23-25; Luke 22:19-20). Together, the formulas recalled what Jesus did and said at the Last Supper as seen through the lens of the passion-resurrection and the Lord's Supper.

In the Markan liturgical tradition, the two formulas had become a single two-part formula, leaving no trace of an intervening meal. In the process, the two parts also became much more symmetrical. Compare, for example, Jesus' words in 1 Corinthians 11:24-25 with the corresponding words in Mark 14:22, 24:

1 Corinthians 11:24-25:

"This is my body that is for you. . . . This cup is the new covenant in my blood."

Mark 14:22, 24:

"This is my body. . . . This is my blood of the covenant, which will be shed for many."

The cup formula in Mark (14:23-25) is much more extensive than the corresponding bread formula (14:22). It even includes an "Amen" saying, related to the previous "Amen" saying announcing Jesus' betrayal:

"Amen, I say to you, I shall not drink again the fruit of the vine until the day when I drink it new in the kingdom of God" (14:25).

"Amen, I say to you, one of you will betray me, one who is eating with me" (14:18b).

Together, the two sayings show how the Lord's Supper was inseparable from Jesus' Last Supper.

He Took Bread (14:22). The significant elements at the early Christian Eucharist were bread and the cup. Following Jewish tradition, Jesus blessed God before breaking the bread and giving it to the participants.

Bread was the staple food in the ancient Mediterranean world, so much so that "bread" could refer to the entire meal, to one or several loaves, or even to food in general. In early Judaism, taking bread, pronouncing a blessing, breaking the bread, and giving it to those at table constituted an important ritual observed at the beginning of a family or community meal.

At a family meal, it is the father who took the bread, blessed God, broke the bread, and gave it to the family, various members of the household, and any guests. At a community meal, it was the "head" of the community who performed the ritual. Among the Essenes at Qumran, it was the priest.

At the Last Supper, it was Jesus, "the Teacher," who broke bread for the disciples. At the Lord's Supper, the Lord Jesus Christ broke bread through a disciple who was commissioned to act and speak in his name.[28]

As part of the liturgical formula, recalling, solemnly and deliberately, what Jesus did and said at the Last Supper, each expression evokes the entire Christian meal celebrated as "the Lord's Supper" (1 Cor 11:20). The formula includes five verbs: taking *(labon),* having blessed *(eulogesas),* he broke *(eklasen),* he gave *(edoken)* to them, and he said *(eipen).*

As participles, the first two verbs, taking and having blessed, are subordinate to the main indicative verbs, he "broke," "gave," and "said." Taking the bread is in view of breaking and giving it once the blessing has been offered. Breaking the bread is for the purpose of sharing it.

Having taken and given the bread to the disciples, Jesus commands them to take *(labete)* the bread that he took, broke, and gave to them. He then declares that this bread, taken, broken, and given to them, is his body: "This is my body" *(touto estin to soma mou).*

In the context of Mark's story of the passion-resurrection, Jesus' body *(to soma mou)* is the body *(to soma mou)* the woman anointed in view of Jesus' burial (14:3, 8), the body Joseph of Arimathea would lay in a tomb (15:45-46), the body of Jesus, the Christ, who as Son of Man suffered and died and rose after three days (8:31; 9:31; 10:32-34; 16:6).

In the context of Mark's Gospel, Jesus' action recalls the two previous occasions when Jesus took bread, spoke a blessing *(eulogesen)* or gave thanks *(eucharistesas),* broke the bread, and gave it to his disciples to set before the people (6:41; 8:6).

---

[28] A parallel for this is found in Mark 14:13-15, where the two disciples, sent to prepare the Passover Jesus would eat with his disciples, are told to speak in the name of Jesus, "the Teacher" (14:14).

After the first occasion, the disciples resisted crossing the sea from the Galilean, Jewish shore to Bethsaida on the Gentile shore (6:45-52). When Jesus came across the sea to them as I AM and calmed the wind, they were overwhelmed. That was because they had not understood about the loaves (6:52).

After the second occasion, they still did not understand. Having only one bread with them in the boat, they thought they had no bread. Jesus had to warn them against the leaven of the Pharisees and the leaven of Herod (8:14-22). The bread Jesus took, broke, and gave to them was meant for all. The one bread they had in the boat was more than sufficient.

At the Last Supper, we finally learn what the disciples did not understand. The bread Jesus took and broke, after blessing God or giving thanks, and gave to them was his body, the same body the woman anointed in view of his burial. There was no separating the breaking of bread from the death and burial of the Anointed One, who rose after three days.

Then He Took a Cup (14:23-25). The major symbol in the second part of the liturgical formula (14:23-25) is the cup, not as a static object, but as an event. Just as the bread was taken, and after blessing God, broken, and given to the disciples, so the cup was taken and given to them, after Jesus gave thanks.

The cup contained "the fruit of the vine" (14:25), that is, wine, which, unlike bread, was not taken at ordinary meals in the ancient Mediterranean world. Wine was taken only on special occasions at a formal dinner.

At a Jewish family or community dinner, the cup was preceded by a blessing. Reflecting that usage, Paul asked the Corinthians: "The cup of blessing that we bless, is it not a participation in the blood of Christ?" (1 Cor 10:16).

Again the blessing was spoken by the father of the family or the "head" of the community. Among the early Christians, blessing was frequently replaced by giving thanks, especially among Christians of Gentile background, who, apart from the religious heritage of those whose background was Jewish, became members of the community by special grace.

At the Last Supper, it was Jesus, "the Teacher," who gave thanks. At the Lord's Supper, it was the Lord Jesus Christ who gave thanks through a disciple commissioned to give thanks in his name.

The act of blessing was traditionally Jewish. Blessed by God, Jews and Christians bless God in return. They also bless one another. The purpose of God's blessing is that people may fulfill all the potential that is theirs from their creation and birth. The purpose of blessing God is that he manifest himself as God. When Jesus broke bread on the Galilean shore, he blessed God (6:41). At the Last Supper, that is also what he did before breaking and giving the bread (14:22).

Giving thanks is quite different. Thanksgiving *(euCHARIStia)* is the Christian response to grace *(CHARIS)*. Graced by God, Christians thank God, that is, they reflect the grace back to God. The early Christians did not thank one another. They thanked God for the grace others represented. So, St. Paul to the Philippians: "I give thanks to my God at every remembrance of you, . . . who are all partners with me in grace" (Phil 1:3-7).

When Jesus broke bread on the Bethsaida shore, he gave thanks to God (8:6). At the Last Supper, that is what Jesus did before giving the cup (14:23).

As part of the liturgical formula, each expression introducing the cup evokes the entire thanksgiving event. The formula includes four verbs: taking *(labon),* having given thanks *(eucharistesas),* he gave it *(edoken)* to them, and said *(eipen).*

As participles, the first two verbs, "taking" and "having given thanks," are subordinate to the main indicative verbs, "he gave it to them" and "he said." Taking is in view of giving, and giving presupposes giving thanks. Like the bread, the cup is for sharing. Mark makes this very plain. After Jesus gave the cup to the disciples and before he said anything to them, Mark indicated that "they all drank from it."

That "they all drank from it" is not part of the liturgical text but an important link with an earlier part of Mark's Gospel. When James and John came to Jesus and asked to sit one at his right and one at his left when he came into his glory, Jesus asked them in return: "Can you drink the cup that I drink or be baptized with the baptism with which I am baptized?" They responded they could, and Jesus told them they would, but to sit at his right or at his left was not for him to give (10:35-40).

Now at the Last Supper, James and John, indeed all the disciples, drank from the cup that Jesus would drink, a cup symbolic of Jesus' passion. At the Last Supper, the disciples committed themselves to solidarity with Christ, the Son of Man who "did not come to be served but to serve and give his life as a ransom for many" (10:45). And, as Mark pointedly reminds his readers, that is what Christians continue to do whenever they celebrate the Lord's Supper.

Having taken and given the cup to his disciples, who all drank from it, Jesus declared that "This is my blood of the covenant, which will be shed for many." "Blood" in biblical terms means life, just as "body" means person.

The cup Jesus offered was a sharing of his life with those who received it, joining them to one another and to him as did the covenants of old. That is how Moses inaugurated the Israelite covenant with God, but with the blood of sacrificial animals (Exod 24:1-11). The Christian covenant was in the blood of Christ which was shed, not for one, but "for many," that is, for all human beings.

At the end of the meal, Jesus and the disciples sang a hymn, no doubt a hymn of praise, an Alleluia hymn, as was customary at the Passover meal, and they went out to the Mount of Olives (14:26; see 11:1; 13:3).

At the Mount of Olives (14:27-31)

It is from Bethany on the Mount of Olives that Jesus and the disciples, together with a large crowd, processed into Jerusalem (11:1). While staying in Jerusalem, that is also where they returned at the end of each day (11:11, 12, 15, 19, 27). It is while sitting on the Mount of Olives opposite the Temple that Jesus gave his final, eschatological address to Peter, James, John, and Andrew (13:3). It is also where Jesus went with the disciples after the Last Supper (14:26).

Once there, Jesus announced that all of them would be scandalized *(skandalisthesesthe)* on his behalf (14:27). True, they all drank the cup that Jesus drank (14:23; 10:38-39). But like those in the parable who were sown on rocky ground, they had no root. When tribulation *(thlipsis)* and persecution *(diogmos)* came, they would be scandalized *(skandalizontai)* because of the word (4:16-17). Like those in Jesus' native place, who were scandalized *(eskandalizonto)* by his wisdom and the mighty deeds he wrought (6:3), they would be scandalized by the events of the passion (14:27).

Like Judas' betrayal of Jesus, it was all according to the Scriptures:

"Strike the shepherd,
    that the sheep may be dispersed" (Zech 13:7).

But, after he was raised up *(egerthenai)* he would go before them in Galilee (14:28; see 16:7), as he had gone before them to Jerusalem and his passion and resurrection (10:32-34).[29] They would not be left as sheep without a shepherd (see 6:34).

Peter protested that even if all would be scandalized *(skandalis-thesontai)*, he would not be (14:29). Jesus responded with a solemn

---

[29] See Bas van Iersel, " 'To Galilee' or 'In Galilee' in Mark 14,28 and 16,7?" *Ephemerides Theologicae Lovanienses* 58 (1982) 365–70.

"Amen" saying, the last of four in the passion narrative: "Amen, I say to you, this very night before the cock crows twice you will deny me three times" (14:30; see 14:9, 18, 25).

Peter protested even more vehemently. He was ready to die with Jesus rather than deny him. After Jesus had announced that one of the Twelve would betray him, all responded: "Surely it is not I?" (14:19). Now, after Jesus announced that all would be scandalized by the events of the passion, they joined Peter, affirming their willingness to die rather than deny him (14:31).

Act I, Scene Two
The Events at Gethsemane (14:32-52)

Act I, Scene One of Mark's story of the passion-resurrection includes the plot to destroy Jesus (14:1-2), Judas' offer to betray him (14:10-11), and the Last Supper with Jesus announcing the betrayal (14:17-21). The scene ends after the Supper, at the Mount of Olives, with Jesus announcing Peter's denial (14:27-31). Together these stories form the passion's main story line.

Inserted into this story line are several distinct stories, interrupting and interpreting it, transforming it from what would have been the tragedy of Jesus into the gospel of Jesus. These interpretive stories include a dinner at Bethany in the home of Simon the leper (14:3-9), Jesus' preparations for the Passover (14:12-16), and the Lord's Supper (14:22-26).

After the Lord's Supper (14:22-26a), Jesus and the Twelve went out to the Mount of Olives (14:26b), and Jesus spoke to them of what was about to happen. Their faith would be shaken. All would be scandalized on his account. It is written, "I will strike the shepherd, / and the sheep will be dispersed" (Zech 13:7). This, however, would not be the end for them! Once Jesus was raised up, he would go before them in Galilee (14:27-28).

Hearing Jesus, Peter protested. Even if all were scandalized, he would not be scandalized. Unlike the others, his faith would not be shaken. Responding, Jesus announced Peter's upcoming, triple denial, and Peter protested even more. Even if he had to die with Jesus, he would not deny him. And the others all spoke in the same way (14:29-31).

Peter's reaction brings to mind the time Jesus announced the death and resurrection of the Son of Man. Taking him aside, Peter rebuked him (8:31-32). This time, Peter was protesting his allegiance to him unto death. As on that other occasion, all the others reacted very much as Peter did (14:31b; see 9:31-34; 10:32-37).

Scene Two continues at the Mount of Olives in a place called Gethsemane (14:32a). The Gethsemane scene includes two very significant events, one showing Jesus at prayer and exhorting his disciples (14:32b-42), the other telling the story of his arrest, when Judas came with an armed crowd from the chief priests, the scribes, and the elders (14:43-49).

Judas came to Gethsemane later, when Jesus had finished praying and was speaking to his disciples (14:43). The story presupposes Judas had left Jesus and the Twelve at the end of the Supper or while they were on their way to the Mount of Olives. The disciples who came with Jesus to Gethsemane stayed until his arrest, when "all left him and fled" (14:50), just as Jesus had said they would (14:27). Peter, however, would follow Jesus at a distance (14:54) as far as the courtyard of the high priest. That is where he would deny Jesus (15:54, 66-72). That, however, is for Act II. The events at Gethsemane end with the story of a young man following Jesus, who fled like the others had fled (14:51-52).

Prayer at Gethsemane (14:32-42)[30]

The story of Jesus' prayer at Gethsemane (14:32-42) is the fourth in the series that transforms the tragedy of Jesus into the gospel of Jesus (see 14:3-9, 12-16, 22-26, 32-42). Jesus had just announced how all would abandon him (14:27-31). The next story would tell how he was arrested and how all in fact did abandon him (14:43-52). Between these two stories, Jesus prays that God's will be done and instructs his disciples to watch and pray that they might not undergo the test (14:34, 37, 38; see 13:9, 18, 32-37).

The introduction shows Jesus and his disciples coming to Gethsemane and Jesus giving them a simple instruction, "Sit here while I pray" (14:32). From this point on, the body of disciples remains in the background as the story focuses on three of them, Peter, James, and John, whom Jesus took with him (14:33-42).

[30] For a basic literary, redactional, and theological study of Mark 14:32-42, see J. Warren Holleran, "The Synoptic Gethsemane," *Analecta Gregoriana* 191 (Rome: Universita Gregoriana Editrice, 1973) 5–68, 107–45, 206–11. For Mark's message in the passage, see also David M. Stanley, S.J., *Jesus in Gethsemane* (New York: Paulist Press, 1980) 131–45. See also Werner H. Kelber, "The Hour of the Son of Man and the Temptation of the Disciples (Mark 14:32-42)," *The Passion in Mark, Studies on Mark 14–16,* op. cit., 41–60. For a recent study of the passage as a part of the New Testament passion narratives, see Raymond Brown, S.S., *The Death of the Messiah: from Gethsemane to the Grave: a Commentary on the Passion Narratives in the Four Gospels* (New York: Doubleday, 1994) 1:146–234.

Three times Jesus withdrew even from these three, and three times he returned to them. At the beginning of the story, the emphasis is on Jesus' own prayer and his interior state (14:33-34a, 35-36, 39). But as the story progresses, the emphasis shifts to the disciples, Jesus' instructions to them, and their inability to follow these (14:34b, 37-38, 40-42). For the disciples, Jesus' prayer in distress provides a challenging model, one they were unable to follow.

The farewell discourse on the Mount of Olives had ended with a general, eschatological exhortation regarding the return of the Son of Man and the events that would accompany it: "What I say to you, I say to all: 'Watch!'" (13:37). As the passion began, that exhortation received a more immediate, historical objective: the chief priests and the scribes were seeking to arrest Jesus and put him to death (14:1-2).

At Gethsemane, the same eschatological theme remains in the background as Jesus exhorts Peter, James, and John to be watchful, to watch and pray that they might not undergo the test (14:37-38): The betrayer was at hand (14:42). Jesus' historical message to the disciples was also Mark's eschatological message to his community.

A Place Called Gethsemane (14:32-34). They then came to a piece of land or field *(chorion)* called Gethsemane.[31] John's Gospel refers to Gethsemane as a "garden" *(keros),* across the Kidron valley from Jerusalem (John 18:1). According to Luke, it was Jesus' custom *(kata to ethos)* to go to this "place" *(topos)* on the Mount of Olives (Luke 22:39-40). And Mark presupposes this was the case, at least according to tradition, since when Judas came, he knew exactly where to find Jesus (14:43; Luke 22:47).

Gethsemane was the place Jesus went for a final period of extended prayer. Gethsemane was also the place he was arrested. "Sit here while I pray," he told his disciples, before withdrawing from them. This is the third time in Mark's Gospel that Jesus goes apart to pray in solitude.

The first at the beginning of Jesus' ministry in Galilee, on leaving the house of Simon and Andrew after curing Simon's mother-in-law

---

[31] For the name "Gethsemane" *(gat shemanim,* "press of olives") and the present site called either "The Garden of Gethsemane" or "The Garden of Olives," see Holleran, *The Synoptic Gethsemane* 8–10; and Donald A. D. Thorsen, "Gethsemane," *The Anchor Bible Dictionary* (New York: Doubleday, 1992) 2:997–98. The tradition associating Gethsemane with the garden area and the church cared for by the Franciscans goes back to the fourth century. Although any first-century olive trees on the site would have been cut down during the seige of Titus (A.D. 69–70), the place remains very evocative of the events it commemorates.

(1:29-31) and many others who gathered at the door (1:32-34): "Rising very early before dawn, he left and went off to a deserted place [*eis eremon topon*], where he prayed" (1:35). The second was after the breaking of the bread (6:34-44). After making the disciples leave by boat for the other side and dismissing the crowd (6:45), "he went off to the mountain to pray" (6:46).

At Gethsemane, Jesus separated himself from his disciples in two stages, first, from the larger body, which, after Judas' departure, was reduced to eleven (14:32), and then, even from the three (14:34). Taking with him Peter, James, and John (14:33), the same who were with him at the raising of Jairus' daughter (5:37) and at the transfiguration (9:2), Jesus became deeply troubled *(ekthambeisthai)*[32] and distressed *(ademonein,* 14:33).

Then, after speaking to Peter, James, and John of his intense, interior suffering—"My soul is sorrowful even unto death"—Jesus withdrew even from them. On leaving them, Jesus told them to remain *(meinate)* and be watchful *(gregoreite,* see 14:34). Jesus' message to the chosen three, like his farewell discourse, was intended for all (13:37). At the Lord's return, no one should be found sleeping (13:35-37).

"Abba, Father" (14:35-36).[33] Having advanced a little, Jesus was now alone. Falling to the ground, he prayed. The narrator, who had just described Jesus' personal suffering (14:33), now describes Jesus' personal prayer that "if it were possible the hour might pass by him" (14:35).

Jesus' prayer, "if it were possible [*ei dynaton estin*]," recalls the time Jesus cured a boy who was possessed by a mute spirit. The boy's father pleaded with Jesus: "If you can do anything [*ei ti dyne*], have compassion on us and help us." "'If you can!' [*To Ei dyne*]" Jesus

---

[32] The crowd would react the same way *(exethambethesan)* on seeing Jesus when he came down from the mountain after the transfiguration (9:15). So would the women *(exethambethesan)* on entering the tomb of Jesus and seeing the young man on the right side clothed in dazzling white (16:5-6).

[33] There has been an enormous amount of research and reflection on Jesus' *Abba* prayer. A chief figure in that research has been Joachim Jeremias. See Jeremias' *The Prayers of Jesus* (Naperville: Alec R. Allenson, Inc., 1967) 11–65. More recently, Joseph A. Fitzmyer has reviewed the work of Jeremias and others and pushed it even further, philologically, historically, and theologically. A synthesis of his research and conclusions can be found in "*Abba* and Jesus' Relation to God," *A cause de l'evangile, etudes sur les Synoptiques et les Actes offertes au P. Jacques Dupont, O.S.B. a l'occasion de son 70e anniverssaire,* Lectio Divina 123 (Paris: Cerf, 1985) 15–38.

responded. "Everything is possible [*panta dynata*] to one who has faith" (9:22-23). But there is a difference between Jesus' response to the boy's father and his prayer at Gethsemane. The boy's father asked if Jesus could do anything. At Gethsemane, Jesus did not ask if God could do anything, but "if it were possible."

Jesus' prayer also recalls the time he told his disciples that it was easier for a camel to pass through the eye of a needle than for one who was rich to enter the kingdom of heaven. "Then who can [*dynatai*] be saved?" they asked. "For human beings," Jesus answered, "it is impossible [*adynaton*], but not for God. All things are possible [*panta dunata*] for God" (10:25-27).

Again, there is a difference. At Gethsemane, Jesus was not asking if God was capable or had the power to make the hour *(he hora)* pass by him (14:35), but if it were possible in God's salvific plan. He was asking if it was necessary *(dei,* 8:31) that he be handed over *(paradidotai,* see 9:31; also 10:33) into the hands of sinners. Such was Jesus' intimate, personal prayer as he faced the fulfillment of his mission.

Later, he himself would announce: "The hour [*he hora*] has come. Behold, the Son of Man is to be handed over [*paradidotai*] to sinners" (14:41). His prayer had been answered. The hour would not pass him by. As he had told the Twelve, "The Son of Man did not come to be served but to serve and to give his life as a ransom for many" (10:45).

Just before, when the narrator described Jesus' interior suffering (14:33), Jesus followed up with a description of his own, one that was more personal (14:34). Now that the narrator has described his prayer, Jesus does the same, following up the narrator's description with his own personal prayer: "Abba, Father, all things are possible to you. Take this cup away from me, but not what I will but what you will" (14:36). The hour *(he hora)* to which Jesus had referred and the cup *(to poterion)* are one.[34] Both refer to his passion and death. The hour was now upon Jesus, so he prayed that the cup be taken away from him.

---

[34] In John's Gospel, Jesus embraced "the hour" as his own: "'Woman, how does your concern affect me? My hour [*he hora mou*] has not yet come'" (John 2:4). Later, he would reflect, "Yet what should I say? 'Father, save me from this hour'? But it was for this purpose that I came to this hour" (John 12:27). "This hour" was "his hour," and the Father's will was his own. He did the same with the cup: "Shall I not drink the cup that the Father gave me?" (John 18:11). In Mark, Jesus prayed that this cup might pass by him. In John, this cup was his cup, given to him by the Father.

Earlier, Jesus spoke of all things being possible for God (10:25-27). The narrator just spoke of him praying that "if it were possible the hour might pass by him" (14:35). Jesus, however, was not praying merely to an all-powerful God *(theos),* for whom everything was possible, nor merely to the Lord *(kyrios)*[35] of history, present to his people and guiding them to salvation. Jesus was praying to *Abba,* his Father.[36] Was not Jesus the Father's Son? Was he not the Father's "beloved Son," one in whom the Father was well pleased (1:11; see also 9:7)? At Gethsemane, Jesus addressed God with the title "*Abba,* Father" *(Abba, ho pater),* the title proper to their personal relationship. All things were possible to his Father.

Jesus was indeed the Son of God. But he was also the Christ, the Son of Man (see 1:1). As such it was necessary that Jesus give his life as a ransom for the many (10:45). Jesus, the beloved Son, was being handed over by one who was not merely God, as he was for the entire universe, or Lord, as he was for his people. He was being handed over by his personal Father, one whom Jesus intimately addressed as *Abba.* He was being handed over so that Jesus' *Abba* might become the *Abba* of all who found life in and through Jesus.[37]

Praying as the Son to *Abba,* Jesus asked that this cup, the cup of his approaching passion, would be taken away from him. In this, however, he prayed that his Father's will, not his own, be done.

---

[35] In the New Testament, as in the Septuagint, the Greek word, *theos,* corresponds to the Hebrew word, *elohim;* the Greek word, *kyrios,* corresponds to the word, *yahweh,* the name of God first revealed to Moses. Like *elohim, theos* is a more generic and impersonal name, appropriate to the creator as revealed in the created universe. Like *yahweh, kyrios* is a personal name, appropriate to one who reveals himself personally and is present to those to whom he reveals himself.

[36] Regarding the historicity of Jesus' prayer, here is Fitzmyer's conclusion: "There is no evidence in the literature of pre-Christian or first-century Palestinian Judaism that '*abba*' was used in any sense as a personal address for God by an individual—and for Jesus to address God as '*abba*' or 'Father' is therefore something new. The *earliest* attestation of such usage remains that given by Paul in an otherwise Greek letter (Ga 4, 6), written in the mid-fifties of the first century, and it may be an echo of the tradition about a prayer uttered by Jesus himself, later recorded in Mark 14:36" ("*abba* and Jesus' Relation to God") 28.

[37] In Galatians and Romans, Paul referred to Christians as addressing God as *Abba:* "As proof that you are children, God sent the spirit of his Son into our hearts, crying out, 'Abba, Father!'" (Gal 4:6); "You received a spirit of adoption, through which we cry, *Abba,* 'Father!' The Spirit itself bears witness with our spirit that we are children of God" (Rom 8:15-16).

Earlier in the Gospel, Jesus had asked James and John if they could drink the cup that he would drink. They said they could, and he said they would. (10:38-39). Then at the Last Supper, Jesus took the cup, gave thanks, and gave it to the Twelve, "and they all drank from it" (14:23). This was his "blood of the covenant" which would be shed for many (14:24). Now at Gethsemane, Jesus showed the disciples that the cup of Jesus' passion and death was not to be sought, only to be accepted, if it was the Father's will.

"Watch and Pray" (14:37-40). When Jesus returned to Peter, James, and John, he found them asleep (*heuriskei autous katheudontas,* 14:37a). Finding the disciples asleep recalls the parable in Jesus' eschatological discourse about a man traveling abroad and ordering the gatekeeper to watch (*gregore,* 13:34). Applying the parable, Jesus had warned his disciples, "Watch [*gregoreite*] therefore; you do not know when the lord of the house is coming, whether in the evening, or at midnight, or at cockcrow, or in the morning. May he not come suddenly and find you sleeping [*heure humas katheudontas*]. What I say to you, I say to all, 'Watch!' [*gregoreite*]" (13:35-37). At Gethsemane, after telling the three, Peter, James, and John, to watch (*gregoreite,* 14:34), Jesus had just found them asleep (14:37a).

Jesus began by speaking to Peter (14:37b), the one who protested that if all had their faith shaken, his would not be, the one, also, who was prepared to die with Jesus rather than deny him (14:27-31). "Simon," he said, "are you asleep? Could you not keep watch for one hour [*mian horan gregoresai*]?" Jesus addressed Peter, not as Peter, but, pointedly, as Simon. Peter was the name Jesus gave Simon when he constituted the Twelve (3:16). Simon was Peter's pre-apostolic name.

Then, speaking to all three, Jesus warned them, "Watch and pray[38] that you may not undergo the test [*eis peirasmon*]. The spirit is willing but the flesh is weak" (14:38).

Watching "for one hour" could mean "for the duration of one hour." In this case, it would mean that Simon had not been able to watch even for that span of time. The assumption would then be that Jesus himself had just spent one hour in prayer. In Matthew, where the disciples are asked to keep watch "with" Jesus (*gregoreite met' emou,* Matt 26:38) and Peter is asked if he could not keep watch "with" Jesus for one hour (*mian horan gregoresai met' emou,* Matt 26:40), that seems to be the case. In Mark, however, there is no

[38] In 14:37, when Jesus is addressing Peter, the verbs, "are you asleep" and "watch" are in the singular. In 14:38, the verbs "watch" and "pray" are in the plural, addressing all three disciples.

question of keeping watch with Jesus, only of keeping watch (14:34) and keeping watch for one hour (14:37).

Watching "for one hour," however, could also refer to a particular hour, answering the question, "Which hour?" instead of "How long?" Instead of indicating the length of time in prayer, "for one hour" would then refer to the object of Jesus' prayer, the hour of Jesus' passion (14:35, 41). In praying *for* the hour of his passion, Jesus had prayed *regarding* the hour of his passion (14:35).

Since even Peter was not able to watch with respect to that "one hour," that is, the hour of Jesus' passion, Jesus exhorted them to watch and pray not to enter into *(hina me elthete)* the test *(eis peirasmon)* of their own passion. Unable to watch for Jesus' passion, they would surely be overwhelmed by their own.

Jesus' Gethsemane prayer and exhortation evokes several themes from the Lord's Prayer (Matt 6:9-13; Luke 11:2-4). These include the address to God as Father and the petition that the Father's will be done (14:36), as well as the petition to be spared the test (14:38). An additional theme may have been referred to earlier, after the disciples came upon the withered fig tree Jesus had cursed: "When you stand to pray, forgive anyone against whom you have a grievance, so that your heavenly Father may in turn forgive you your transgressions" (11:25; see Matt 6:14). As told by Matthew and Luke, the Gethsemane story surely has the Lord's Prayer in mind, since both gospels adjusted their respective wording to reflect their distinctive wording of the Lord's Prayer more closely.

Although Mark's Gospel does not include the Lord's Prayer, the four parallels just noted seem more than coincidental. Mark must have known an early version of the Lord's Prayer. If so, Mark provides a wonderful insight into the prayer's petition not to enter, or be brought into, the test *(peirasmos),* that is, into the final eschatological test.

The spirit is willing. At the Lord's Supper, the disciples did drink the cup that Jesus drank (14:23), as Jesus told James and John they would (10:38-39). Even so, the flesh is weak. The disciples would not be able to survive the final test. The disciples must therefore watch and pray that they not enter that test. Indeed, "If the Lord had not shortened those days, no one would be saved; but the for sake of the elect whom he chose, he did shorten those days" (13:20).

Simon had not been able to keep awake even for that one hour the hour of Jesus' passion. His spirit was willing, as he showed in 14:27-31, but the flesh was weak. At the Last Supper, all had drunk the symbolic cup of Jesus' passion. Now that the passion was upon them, Peter and the others were not even able to remain awake. This is the second time Jesus told them to watch *(gregoreite,* 14:34, 38).

Withdrawing from the eleven with Peter, James, and John, Jesus had told them to sit while he prayed (14:32-33). Then, telling the three to remain and keep watch, he advanced a little further and prayed (14:34-36). Now, returning and finding them asleep, he told them to watch and to pray (14:37-38). For the Markan community, the terms, "watch" and "pray," evoked Jesus' exhortation to the four, Peter, James, John, and Andrew, in his eschatological discourse on the Mount of Olives (13:18, 34, 35, 37).

Jesus then withdrew a second time *(palin)*. For this second time, Mark simply recalled the first *(palin)*, saying that Jesus repeated the same prayer. Then, when Jesus returned to the disciples for the second time *(palin)* and found them asleep, Mark provides an excuse for them: "for they could not keep their eyes open and did not know what to answer him" (14:39-40; cf. 9:32-34).

"The Hour Has Come" (14:41-42). When Jesus "returned a third time" (14:41), the story does not even mention that Jesus had withdrawn from them. All the emphasis is on his return and his final message to them: "Are you still sleeping [*katheudete*] and taking your rest?" This was the third time Jesus returned to them and the third time he found them asleep (14:41, see 37, 40).

"It is enough," Jesus said, meaning, "It is settled." Jesus would drink the cup. It was his Father's will. The hour of the passion, the test, was upon him. Jesus then directed their vision toward the future: "Behold [*idou*], the Son of Man is to be handed over [*paradidotai*] to sinners" (14:41), that is, to be handed over to sinners but by God, his Father, to whom he prayed as *"Abba."*

"Get up [*egeiresthe*]," he told them, "let us go [*agomen*]." The time for watching was over. Again Jesus focused their vision toward the future: "See [*idou*], my betrayer is at hand [*eggiken*]" (14:42). The one through whom Jesus was about to be handed over by God was near. The critical time *(ho kairos)* had come. The kingdom of God was at hand *(eggiken,* 1:15).

Betrayal, Arrest, and Abandonment (14:43-52)

Suddenly, while Jesus was still speaking, Judas arrived, accompanied by a crowd with swords and clubs from the chief priests and the scribes and the elders (14:43). So begins the concluding episode in the events at Gethsemane, bringing the major themes of Act I to a close.

The plot of the chief priests and the scribes to arrest Jesus by treachery has apparently succeeded (14:44-49; see 11:18; 12:12; 14:1). Thanks to Judas, who offered to betray him (14:10), they arrested Jesus at the Mount of Olives (14:26) in a place called Gethsemane, where Jesus went with his disciples to pray (14:32). There would be no riot among the people (14:2). Judas, one of the Twelve (14:10, 20, 43) had found an opportune time (14:11).

At the same time, however, Jesus, the Christ, had been anointed in view of his burial (14:3-9). All was not as it appeared. Following Jesus instructions, the disciples had prepared the Last Supper, his definitive Passover (14:12-16). At the Supper, Jesus took bread, blessed God, broke the bread, and offered it as his body. He also took the cup, gave thanks, and gave it to the disciples. This was the blood of his covenant which would be shed for many (14:22-25). Joining him in solidarity, "they all drank from it" (14:23).

Arriving at Gethsemane, Jesus had told the disciples to watch (14:34, 37) and pray (14:38) that they might not undergo the test (14:38). Unable to do so, instead of watching, they slept (14:37, 40, 41) while Jesus prayed (14:32, 35, 36, 39). Jesus was ready to be handed over (14:21). He accepted the will of his Father (14:36). For all their promises, however, the disciples were not ready to remain with him. And so, as it was written (14:27, 49), the shepherd would be struck (14:27a, 44-49) and the sheep would be dispersed (14:27b, 50-52).

Judas Arrives (14:43). The introductory verse shows Judas arriving at the place called Gethsemane (14:43). Jesus and the other disciples had been there for some time. Judas, one of those Jesus had appointed to be with him, to be sent forth to preach, and to have authority to drive out demons (3:14-15; 6:7-13), was now at the head of an armed band from the chief priests, and the scribes, and the elders, the three groups represented in the Sanhedrin.[39] Mention of the "swords" *(meta machairon)* announces the action of

---

[39] This is the first time in the passion narrative that all three of the groups forming the Sanhedrin, "the chief priests, the scribes, and the elders," are mentioned together. The previous time they were mentioned was when they approached Jesus while he was walking in the Temple area (11:27; see also 8:31). After the cleansing of the Temple (11:18) and at the beginning of the passion (14:1), only "the chief priests and the scribes" were mentioned (see also 10:33). When Judas offered to betray Jesus, he went off "to the chief priests" (14:10).

Mentioned each time, "the chief priests" were the primary group. After them "chief priests and the scribes" were the primary grouping. Mention of all three, "the chief priests, the scribes and the elders," points to the complicity of the Sanhedrin as such, the principal Jewish authoritative body in Jerusalem. Later, when Jesus was brought before Pilate, the Sanhedrin would be named explicitly (15:1).

an anonymous bystander and Jesus' response to those who came with swords and clubs to arrest him (14:47-49).

After introducing Judas (14:43), the story is told in three small segments. The first tells how Judas betrayed Jesus by a kiss (14:44-46). The second shows Jesus refusing to resist the arrest (14:47-49). In the third, Jesus' followers run away in flight (14:50-52). Each segment is told in three parts, as shown by the following outline:

Introduction: Judas arrives (14:43)
    Segment 1. Jesus betrayed by a kiss (14:44-46)
      a. A signal prearranged (14:44)
      b. The kiss of Judas (14:45)
      c. Jesus arrested (14:46)
    Segment 2. Not with swords and clubs (14:47-49)
      a. A bystander takes up the sword (14:47)
      b. Jesus' response (14:48-49a)
      c. The scriptures fulfilled (14:49b)
    Segment 3. The flight of his followers (14:50-52)
      a. All left him and fled (14:50)
      b. A young man arrested (14:51)
      c. Flight of the young man (14:52)

The whole scene is tightly knit into a single unit, with several key words repeated. The most important of these is the verb "arrest" (or "seize," *krateo*), appearing in each of the three segments (14:44, 46, 49, 51). Each of the segments also has a key word of its own: "to kiss" (segment 1); "sword" (segment 2); "to flee" (segment 3).

Jesus Betrayed by a Kiss (14:44-46). Judas had arranged to identify Jesus for the crowd which came from the chief priests, the scribes, and the elders. The crowd, quite obviously, did not know Jesus. They could not even distinguish him from his disciples, who had accompanied him to Gethsemane. Judas had to identify him for them. Before coming, or on the way, Judas arranged with them to identity Jesus with a kiss, a friend's sign of affection.

For this, the story quotes Judas directly: "The man[40] I shall kiss is the one; arrest [*kratesate*] him and lead him away securely" (14:44). Telling the crowd to "arrest" Jesus, Judas introduces the scene's major theme, fulfilling his bargain with the chief priest and the scribes who wanted to arrest (14:1; see 12:12) Jesus. Judas was not privy to Jesus' prayer that ultimately Jesus' will was that his Father's be done. There really was no need to take Jesus away "se-

[40] Instead of "the man" (RNAB), the Greek text says simply "the one" *(hon)*.

curely," that is, under close guard. Judas was but an instrument. Jesus had no intention to escape. He was being handed over by God. On arriving, Judas immediately went up to Jesus and said, "Rabbi," and with that he kissed him (14:45). Jesus knew what Judas was doing, and Judas knew that Jesus knew. Addressing Jesus as "Rabbi," Judas presented himself as a faithful disciple. When Judas spoke to the crowd, the term he used for "kiss" *(phileo)* indicated an ordinary kiss. Describing the action, however, the story says he kissed Jesus very affectionately or warmly *(kataphileo)*, as befitted "one of the Twelve."[41] It is quite striking that Jesus did not respond to Judas' greeting and gesture. Blatant hypocrisy does not need a response.

As Judas kissed Jesus with a show of affection, those who accompanied him from the Sanhedrin laid hands on Jesus and arrested him *(ekratesan auton)*. With that, Judas' role in the passion comes to an end. Jesus has been arrested by treachery *(en dolo kratesantes,* 14:1). The plot of the chief priests and the scribes has succeeded, at least in their eyes. All they needed now was to have him put to death *(auton . . . apokteinosin,* 14:1). For this, they would have to try him, present him to Pilate, and have him condemned.

Not with Swords and Clubs (14:47-49). In the first segment, in which Jesus was betrayed by a kiss (14:44-46), the prearranged signal served as an introduction (14:44) for Judas' greeting and display of affection display as the body (14:45), and the arrest of Jesus as the conclusion (14:46). The second segment has the same kind of development, with the action of a bystander as the introduction (14:47), Jesus' reply to those who arrested him as the body (14:48-49a), and the announcement that the Scriptures had to be fulfilled as the conclusion (14:49b).

The action of the unnamed bystander seems out of place. Where does this anonymous bystander come from? He was not one of the Twelve nor one of the crowd who arrested Jesus. To understand his role, we must appeal to narrative, not historical, logic.

[41] Noting the difference between the verbs *phileo* and *kataphileo,* F. W. Belcher suggested that the second verb, conveying "a sense of intense emotion" indicates that Judas' kiss was "a kiss of repentance." In relation to this, he interprets Judas' instruction to "lead him away securely" as to "lead him away without doing him harm." See "A Comment on Mark xiv. 45," *Expository Times* 64 (1952–1953) 240. Belcher's suggested interpretation seems to be a desperate attempt to "save" Judas, "the one who betrayed him" *(ho paradidous auton,* 14:44), the one of whom Jesus said at the Last Supper: "But woe to that man by whom the Son of Man is betrayed. It would be better for that man if he had never been born" (14:21).

The unnamed bystander plays a symbolic, literary role in the story, one that evades historical criticism. Drawing the sword, he acted like those who came with swords and clubs to arrest Jesus. Striking the servant *(ton doulon)* of the high priest, he struck at someone who represented the high priest. And cutting off the servant's earlobe *(to otarion),* he mutilated him, rendering him unfit to fulfill his office in the Temple. In all this, the bystander's action was misdirected. It was not the high priest or his servant who was to be handed over, but Jesus, the Son of Man.[42]

Jesus had not responded to Judas' hypocritical address and display of affection. Nor did he respond to the bystander's effort. Like Judas' gesture, it spoke for itself. Instead, Jesus responded to those who arrested him: "Have you come out as against a robber, with swords and clubs, to seize me? Day after day [*kath' hemeran*][43] I was with you teaching in the temple area, yet you did not arrest [*ekratesate*] me" (14:48-49a).

All this was that the Scriptures might be fulfilled. The hour *(he hora)* had indeed come. The Son of Man was to be handed over into the hands of sinners (14:41b). Jesus would not resist arrest. Even their treating him as a robber was that the Scriptures might be fulfilled (14:49b).

Abandoned by His Followers (14:50-52). The second segment (14:47-49) showed how the part of the quotation from Zechariah 13:7 was fulfilled: "I will strike the shepherd" (14:27b). The third shows how the rest of the quotation was fulfilled: "and the sheep will be dispersed" (14:27c).

Like the second, this third segment shows the same kind of development as the first, with the flight of the disciples as an introduction (14:50), the example of a young man who was following as the body (14:51), and the flight of the young man as the conclusion (14:52).

As Jesus announced, "But that the scriptures may be fulfilled" (14:49b), "they all [*pantes*] left him and fled" (14:50). We recall that

[42] See Benedict T. Viviano, O.P., "The High Priest's Servant's Ear: Mark 14:47," *Revue Biblique* 96 (1989) 71–80.

[43] A. W. Argyle has suggested that *kath' hemeran* would be better translated as "by day," that is, "in the day-time," as opposed to "in the nighttime," rather than as "each day," "day after day," or "daily." See A. W. Argyle, "The Meaning of *kath' hemeran* in Mark xiv. 49," *Expository Times* 63 (1951–1952) 354. The suggestion would carry more weight if Mark were contrasting Jesus' teaching "by day" with the crowd's arresting him "by night." Such a contrast, however, is neither expressed nor implied.

all *(pantes)* had drunk from the cup Jesus gave them in the liturgy of the Last Supper (14:23), also that Jesus had announced how all *(pantes)* would have their faith shaken (14:27). Responding to Jesus, all *(pantes)* had joined Peter in protesting their willingness to die with him rather than deny him (14:31). Now all *(pantes)* abandoned Jesus and fled.

The term "all" *(pantes)* relates the disciples, abandoning Jesus to the commitments they made earlier and their protests to be with him at all costs. Now they abandoned him *(aphentes auton)*. We recall, too, that, unlike Jesus, they had not been able to watch and pray (14:34, 37, 38, 40-41).

The key term in this segment is the verb "to flee" *(pheugo)*. Abandoning Jesus, all fled *(ephugon)*, including a young man who was following with them (14:51-52). The young man *(neaniskos)* was following with them *(synekolouthei)*. The imperfect of the compound verb, *synakoloutheo*, suggests that the young man was following Jesus along with the other disciples, who fled when Jesus was arrested, thereby fulfilling the Scriptures.

In Mark, as in the other Gospels, "to follow" is usually expressed by the verb *akoloutheo* (see 1:18; 2:14; 8:34). The compound with *syn*, that is, *synakoloutheo*, may mean "to accompany" Jesus, but its normal meaning is "to follow" Jesus "with" the others who were following him, in this case, with the remnant of the Twelve (see 4:10).

Like the anonymous bystander who took the sword (14:47), the certain *(tis)* young man comes on the scene quite suddenly, provoking a great deal of speculation and discussion among scholars. Like the unnamed bystander, the young man plays a symbolic, literary role in the story, if not a historical one.[44]

The incident must be taken seriously. In a Gospel that from the beginning has associated the story of Jesus' followers and disciples with that of Jesus, the incident of the young man comes at the conclusion of the story of the arrest of Jesus, together with the flight of all who had been with Jesus (14:50).

In the first part of the Gospel, after giving a summary of Jesus' mission and ministry (1:14-15; 3:7-12; 6:6b), Mark gives a story of

---

[44] After a thorough review of various positions concerning the young man's identity, both historical and symbolic, Raymond Brown, having found no way of testing the incident's historicity, concluded: "To modern sensibilities the creation of an especially disgraceful incident without historical basis might seem unlikely; but it is best to practice modesty in every sense by leaving this young wrapped in mystery, if naught else," *The Death of the Messiah,* I:310 (see 294–304, 309–10).

the disciples (1:16-20; 3:13-19; 6:7-30), showing how they were associated with Jesus in his mission and challenged by its demands. In the second part of the Gospel, the same pattern continues, presenting Jesus as the Son of Man who was to suffer, die, and rise again (8:31; 9:30-31; 10:32-34), and showing how the disciples were either unable or unwilling to meet the challenge of his passion-resurrection (8:32; 9:32-34; 10:35-37). As we have seen, the disciples were also associated with Jesus in all of Act I of the passion-resurrection.

Besides the disciples, Mark also referred to others who were following Jesus, providing a precedent for the distinction between all who fled (14:50) and the young man following him (14:51): "They were on the way, going up to Jerusalem, and Jesus went ahead of them [*en proagon autous*]. They were amazed, and those who followed [*hoi de akolouthountes*] were afraid. Taking the Twelve aside again, he began to tell them what was going to happen to him" (10:32).

The young man is described as having a linen cloth *(sindon)* wrapped around his naked body *(epi gymnou)*. This is not the first time Mark describes people by their clothing.[45] In ancient cultures, such as those represented by Mark's Gospel, clothing acts as a personal, proper symbol, akin to one's personal, proper name. As such, it does more than identify a person. It expresses or announces a person's identity.[46]

In this case, the linen cloth associates the young man with Jesus in his burial. "Having bought a linen cloth" *(sindona),* Joseph of Arimathea took Jesus down from the cross, "wrapped him in the linen cloth [*te sindoni*] and laid him in a tomb that had been hewn out of the rock" (15:46). As such, the young man is a symbol of the baptized, one who has accepted to be baptized with the same baptism with which Jesus was baptized (10:38-39). Up to this point, others have suggested a similar interpretation, presenting the young man as a symbol of the baptized Christian.[47]

[45] E. LaVerdiere, "Robed in Radiant White," *Emmanuel* 90 (April 1984) 138–42.

[46] Identifying someone is very different from revealing someone's identity. The purpose of Judas' prearranged kiss was simply to identify Jesus, that is, to distinguish Jesus from his disciples for people who did not know him. The linen cloth, however, did far more. Like John the Baptist's clothing in 1:6, and Jesus' clothing in the transfiguration in 9:3, it expressed and revealed his identity for someone who knew him.

[47] For a baptismal interpretation and a discussion of the literature concerning the incident, see Albert Vanhoye, "La fuite du jeune homme nu (Mc 14,51-52)," *Biblica* 52 (1971) 401–06; also Robin Scroggs and Kent I. Groff, "Baptism in Mark: Dying and Rising with Christ," *Journal of Biblical Lit-*

Who then is the young man? He is one who followed Jesus as the disciples did, one who was baptized with the same baptism as Jesus, like Peter, committing himself to be with Christ even if he had to die with Christ (14:31). But when they seized him (14:51) as they seized Jesus (14:44, 46, 49), he fled (14:52) as they all fled (14:50).[48]

Abandoning the linen cloth, the young man abandoned his baptismal identity and his commitment to die and be buried with Christ to live with Christ that one day he might rise with Christ (see Rom 6:3-11; Eph 2:5-6; Col 2:13; 3:1). Like the disciples who abandoned Jesus, he forsook his new life as a baptized person. In putting on Christ, the young man put off his previous identity, like the blind beggar, Bartimaeus, whom Jesus called and who "threw aside his cloak [*apobalon to himation autou*], sprang up, and came to Jesus" (10:49-50).

In baptism, the young man did as Paul wrote to the Colossians, who had "taken off the old self [*apekdysamenoi ton palaion anthropon*] with its practices" and "put on the new self [*endysamenoi ton neon*], which is being renewed, for knowledge, in the image of its creator" (Col 3:9-10).

As the beginning of a life process, baptism did not guarantee salvation. One had to persevere to the end (13:13). The young man did not. Having taken off the old self *(ton palaion anthropon),* he had put on the new *(ton neon),* covering his naked body. Now, having put off the new *(ton neon),* he was totally naked. Being neither his former self nor his new self, the young man was truly nobody.

---

erature 92 (1973) 531–48. Both, however, use the term "young man" and the reference to his clothing merely to make a connection with the young man in 16:5. Clothing does more than identify someone. It expresses the person's identity, and it is on this basis that the baptismal interpretation should be made. Besides, both of the articles find positive baptismal meaning in the fact that, when they seized him *(kratousin),* the young man left the cloth behind and fled *(ephugen)* naked (14:52). For Vanhoye, the young man's naked flight symbolizes the liberation of the baptized: *"comme un condition de liberation"* (405). For Scroggs and Groff, the young man's nakedness symbolizes his taking off the garment of his former person (541). The story requires closer attention to the literary context of the symbol of clothing, as well as of the seizing of the young man and his naked flight.

[48] For an interpretation approaching the one presented here, see J. P. Heil, "Mark 14:1-52: Narrative Structure and Reader-Response," *Biblica* 71 (1990) 329–30; also Augustine Stock, *The Method and Message of Mark* (Wilmington, Del.: Michael Glazier, 1989) 373–75.

Act II. Trial, Condemnation, and Torture (14:53–15:20)
Scene One
At the Palace of the High Priest (14:53-72)

Act I of Jesus' passion-resurrection told how the chief priests and the scribes arrested Jesus with the help of Judas, "one of the Twelve," who betrayed him (14:10, 20, 43; see 3:19). They had him arrested (14:1, 44, 46, 49; see 12:12) "by treachery" (14:1) at the Mount of Olives (14:26) in a place called Gethsemane (14:32), where Jesus went with the disciples after the Last Supper (14:17-26a).

Act I also showed how the arrest of Jesus was a gospel event. Betrayed and arrested, Jesus was bearing our infirmities (see Isa 53:4), fulfilling his mission (14:12-16, 22-26a), in accord with his Father's will, that the Scriptures might be fulfilled (14:21, 27, 49). Such was his personal prayer (14:35-36).

Throughout the ordeal, the disciples proved very weak (14:27-31, 37-38, 40), and when Jesus was arrested, they all abandoned him (14:50-52). Like them, Mark's readers also had to watch and pray, as Jesus prayed (14:36), that they might not undergo the test (14:38; see Matt 6:13; Luke 11:4).

Act I presented the passion as a series of alternating scenes in which the story line (14:1-2, 10-11, 17-21, 27-31, 43-52) is interrupted by independent stories (14:3-9, 12-16, 22-26, 32-42), transforming what would have been the tragedy of Jesus into the gospel of Jesus. That pattern continues in Act II, opening with a "gospel" story, Jesus' trial before the Sanhedrin (14:53-72), before resuming the "tragic" story line with Jesus' trial before Pilate (15:1-20).[49]

Act I ended with the arrest of Jesus (14:43-52). Abandoned by his disciples (14:50-52), Jesus was now alone with those who came from the chief priests, the scribes, and the elders to arrest him (14:43). Act II tells how the chief priests, the scribes, and the elders tried Jesus, found him guilty of blasphemy (14:53-72), and had him condemned to death by Pilate (15:1-20). Such had been the intention of the chief priests and the scribes from the beginning (14:1; see 11:18).

Like Act I, Act II is easily divided into two scenes, the first unfolding during the night of Passover at the palace of the high priest (14:53-72), the second the next morning at the palace of Pilate (15:1-20).

[49] For a literary analysis of Mark 14:53–15:20, together with 15:21–16:8, see John Paul Heil, "The Progressive Narrative Pattern of Mark 14,53–16,8," *Biblica* 73 (1992) 331–58; the article complements his earlier article, "Mark 14, 1-52: Narrative Structure and Reader-Response," *Biblica* 71 (1990) 305–32.

In Scene One (14:53-72), Jesus proclaims his identity as the Christ, the Son of the Blessed One, who will appear as "the Son of Man, / seated at the right hand of the Power / and coming with the clouds of heaven" (14:61-62; see 13:26). In the same scene, Peter denies his identity as a follower of Jesus (14:66-71), but unlike Judas, who betrayed him, and the other disciples, who abandoned him, Peter immediately repented (14:72).

In Scene Two (15:1-20), at the palace of Pilate, Jesus is once again presented as a victim, not just of the Sanhedrin but of the Roman authority represented by Pilate, the Roman prefect of Judea. In the same scene, the crowd chooses a criminal, Barabbas, "who had committed murder in a rebellion" (15:8), over Jesus, "the king of the Jews" (15:9, 12, see 15:2, 18).

Scene One, the story of Jesus and Peter at the palace of the high priest (14:53-72), includes a brief general introduction (14:53) and two episodes. The second episode is introduced in 14:54, showing how Peter denied Jesus when a maid and some bystanders confronted him and how Peter immediately repented (14:55-72). The first is introduced in 14:55, presenting Jesus' trial before the high priest and the entire Sanhedrin (14:56-65).[50]

The structure of the scene is like the story of Jesus, his family, and the scribes at the home in Capernaum (3:20-35), which also has a brief general introduction (3:20) and two episodes. The second is introduced in 3:21, shows Jesus responding to his mother and brothers who remained outside (3:31-35). The first is introduced in 3:22, and has Jesus responding to the scribes from Jerusalem (3:23-30).[51]

---

[50] The literary structure of 14:53-72 is often described as an "intercalation," that is, as resulting from a historical, redactional process in which one story that was originally independent has been inserted into another story, both of which were traditional. For a critique, see R. Brown, *The Death of the Messiah*, I:426–28.

Describing the structure as a "sandwich" refers more simply to a pattern of presentation, whether rhetorical or literary, in which two events are related to one another. The "two stories" may actually have been conceived together from the very beginning, whether in the tradition or in the writing of the gospel, as one story in two related scenes. This does not preclude that the combined story was created from traditional elements. The fact that the sandwich, 14:54 (55, 56-65) 66–72, has a common introduction (14:53) suggests this was the case.

[51] After their respective general introductions, both stories show the familiar ABB'A' pattern. A (14:54) introduces Peter; A' (14:66-72) tells the story of his denial. Within the story of Peter, B (14:55) introduces the trial of Jesus and B' (56-65) tells its story. In the same way, A (3:21) introduced and A' (3:31-35)

They Led Jesus Away (14:53)

Those who came from the chief priests, the scribes, and the elders (14:43) led Jesus away (14:53a). Judas had arranged to identify him with a kiss. They were to arrest him *(kratesate auton)* and lead him away *(apagete)* securely (14:44). Arriving at Gethsemane, Judas went over to Jesus and kissed him, and they arrested him *(ekratesan auton,* 14:45). They now led Jesus away *(apegagon)* for judgment.[52]

They led Jesus away to the high priest *(ton archiera,* singular), the chief of the chief priests *(hoi archiereis,* plural), the leader of the Sanhedrin, the highest authority in cultic matters and in everything related to Jewish life in Judea.[53] The high priest held supreme authority over the Temple, which Jesus had cleansed (11:15-19), in which he taught (11:27–12:41), and whose destruction he announced (13:1-2).

---

told the story of Jesus and his family. Within that story, B (3:22) introduced and B' (3:23-30) told the story of Jesus and the scribes.

This pattern is different from the usual Markan sandwich, such as the story of Jairus' daughter and the woman with a hemorrhage (5:21-43), where the pattern is ABA' rather than ABB'A'. The story of Jairus' daughter, opening and closing the sandwich, is told in two movements (A, A'; 5:21-24, 35-43). The story of the woman with the hemorrhage (B, 5:25-34) is inserted at a natural break in the story of Jairus' daughter.

[52] The verb *apagein* is a quasi-legal term for leading away one who has been arrested for judgment, or who has been judged and condemned for execution. See *"apagein"* in William F. Arndt, F. Wilbur Gingrich, and Frederick W. Danker, *A Greek-English Lexicon of the New Testament and Other Early Christian Literature,* 2nd ed. (Chicago: The University of Chicago Press, 1979) 79.

[53] For the office and *de facto* position of the high priest, see J. Jeremias, *Jerusalem in the Time of Jesus* (Philadelphia: Fortress Press, 1969).

In Jesus' time, the high priest exercised political authority by virtue of a series of Roman *senatus consulta,* granted between 48 and 44 B.C., by Julius Caesar:

I, Julius Caesar, have decided as follows with the advice of the council. It is my wish that Hyrcanus, son of Alexander, and his children shall be ethnarchs of the Jews and shall hold the office of high priest of the Jews for all time in accordance with their national customs; and whatever high-priestly rights or other privileges exist in accordance with their laws, these he and his children shall possess by my command. . . . And if . . . any question shall arise concerning the Jews' manner of life, it is my pleasure that the decision shall rest with them (Josephus, *Jewish Antiquities* XIV, 192–95, 199).

See Miriam Pucci Ben Zeev, "Caesar and Jewish Law," *Revue Biblique* 102 (January 1995) 28.

The high priest's personal and official servant *(doulos)* was among those who came to arrest Jesus and lead him away for judgment. When they arrested Jesus, a bystander struck the servant and severed part of his ear, making him ritually unfit to serve in the Temple (14:47).

When those who arrested Jesus led him to the palace of the high priest, all *(pantes)* the chief priests, and the elders, and the scribes came together *(synerchontai,* 14:53b). Later, the whole *(holon)* Sanhedrin would try to obtain testimony against Jesus (14:55). Eventually, all *(pantes)* would condemn him to death (14:65). When Jesus was arrested, all *(pantes)* his disciples left him and fled (14:50). When he was led to the palace of the high priest, all who had planned his arrest gathered to condemn him (14:53).

Peter Followed Him at a Distance (14:54)

Jesus, betrayed, arrested, and abandoned by all (14:43-52), was now at the palace of the high priest, and all the chief priests, the elders, and the scribes had come together. The scene was set for Jesus' trial before the Sanhedrin. There would be witnesses, and allegations. Jesus would be interrogated, and he would proclaim his identity. At the end, he would be condemned and subjected to mockery (14:55-65).

Before presenting the trial, however, an additional personage needed to be introduced, Peter, who would play a very significant role in the scene. Peter followed *(ekolouthesen)* Jesus at a distance *(makrothen)* into the high priest's courtyard. Peter followed Jesus, like the young man had followed Jesus. But, unlike the young man, who was arrested (14:51), Peter followed at a distance (14:54a). Peter, the same who was willing to die with Jesus rather than deny him (14:31; see 14:29), followed Jesus at a safe distance and only as far as the courtyard of the high priest (14:54b).

As Jesus' trial began, Peter, still at a distance, was seated with the guards *(meta ton hypereton),* warming himself at the fire (14:54c).[54] The same guards would greet Jesus with blows (14:65) once the Sanhedrin condemned him as deserving to die (14:64). The trial of Jesus was at the same time the trial of Peter. For him too there would be witnesses and allegations. He too would be interrogated, but, instead

---

[54] As John Paul Heil observed, "Although Peter is still following Jesus even into the courtyard of the high priest, he is no longer 'with' *(meta)* Jesus as befits one of the Twelve (3,14), but is sitting 'with' *(meta)* the guards, warming himself 'before' *(pros)* the fire rather than standing ready to die 'with' (14,31) Jesus 'before' *(pros)* the high priest (14,53)," "The Progressive Narrative Pattern of Mark 14,53–16,8," *Biblica* 73 (1992) 338.

of proclaiming his identity as one who was with Jesus, he denied it, denying Jesus at the same time. At the end, he would remember what Jesus had said to him and break down in tears (14:66-72).

Intended for the disciples and the members of Mark's community, the story of Jesus' trial is told within that of Peter's denial. To understand Jesus' trial and its implications, they had to see and hear it with Peter's denial in the background. The story suggests that many in Mark's community were following Christ from a safe distance.

The Chief Priests and the Entire Sanhedrin (14:55)

After introducing Peter's denial (14:54), Mark introduces[55] the story of Jesus before the Sanhedrin (14:55) with a summary of the trial proceedings: "The chief priests and the entire Sanhedrin kept trying to obtain testimony against Jesus in order to put him to death" (14:55a).[56] How they kept trying *(ezetoun)* is told in the actual trial (14:56-64).

---

[55] As J. Donahue indicated (see "Temple, Trial and Royal Christology, Mark 14:53-65," *Passion in Mark, Studies on Mark 14–16*, op. cit., 62), the trial has a double introduction (14:53, 55). The first (14:53), however, is a general introduction for the whole scene (14:53-72), including the denial and repentance of Peter (14:54, 66-72) as well as the trial of Jesus (55-65). The second (14:55) is a particular introduction just for the trial (14:55-65).

[56] In recent years, much of the research on the trial of Jesus has focused on historical issues, in particular on the discrepancies between the gospel accounts and the Rabbinic legal prescriptions for trials such as that of Jesus. For the legal and political issues involved in Jesus' "trial" before the Sanhedrin, see R. Brown, *The Death of the Messiah*, I:311–97, with an extensive bibliography on the subject (315–27), a discussion of Roman governance (331–38) and of Jewish self-governing bodies, including the Sanhedrin (339–72), an evaluation of the evidence that Jewish authorities took against Jesus (372–83), and of the responsibility and/or guilt for the death of Jesus (383–97).

For the trial in Mark, see J. Donahue, "Temple, Trial and Royal Christology (Mark 14:53-65)," in *The Passion in Mark, Studies on Mark 14–16*, 61–79; also *"Are You the Christ?" The Trial Narrative in the Gospel of Mark*, SBL Dissertation Series 10 (Missoula: University of Montana, 1973), which includes an excellent survey of research on the trial narrative in Mark, relating redaction criticism to other methodological approaches, 5–51. For a more recent study of Jesus' Jewish trial in Mark but as seen as one of four New Testament passion narratives, see R. Brown, *The Death of the Messiah*, 1:498–586, especially 426–28, 438–48, 467–70, 488–89, 494–500, 573–77, where Brown deals specifically with Mark.

The chief priests, who were part of the Sanhedrin, were acting with the whole Sanhedrin.[57] Introducing Scene Two, Jesus' trial before Pilate, Mark would refer to the "whole Sanhedrin" as comprising the chief priests with the elders and the scribes (15:1). From the beginning, the story announces that all their efforts to obtain testimony against Jesus failed (14:55b). The key word in the introduction is "testimony" *(martyria)*, statements from witnesses that would allow them to put Jesus to death *(eis to thanatosai auton).*

The Trial of Jesus Before the Sanhedrin (14:56-65)

The story of the trial is then told in three segments. First, there were false witnesses *(pseudomartyreo),* whose testimony did not agree against Jesus (14:56-59). Then, there was the high priest, who tried to make Jesus testify against himself (14:60-62). Finally, dispensing with witnesses, they condemned Jesus for his testimony and they began to mock him (14:63-65).

False Testimony (14:56-59). Many were giving false testimony *(epseudomartyroun)* against him, but their testimony *(martyriai)* did not agree (14:56). This opening statement (14:56) introduces and summarizes the first segment of the trial. The body of the segment focuses on a particular false allegation regarding the destruction of the Temple (14:57-58). The segment ends by concluding, "Even so their testimony did not agree" (14:59).

Throughout the segment (14:56-59), the storyteller emphasizes two things. First, those who came forward as witnesses testified falsely *(epseudomartyroun,* 14:56, 57). Second, their testimony *(hai martyriai, he martyria,* 14:56, 59) did not agree.

The false testimony brought against Jesus evokes Psalm 27 and 35, lamenting the suffering and oppression of a just one.[58]

> Do not abandon me to the will of my foes;
> malicious and lying witnesses have risen against me (Ps 27:12).

---

[57] For a study of "the Sanhedrin in Jerusalem, as it appears in the gospels, Josephus, and rabbinic literature," see Anthony J. Saldarini, "Sanhedrin," *The Anchor Bible Dictionary* (New York: Doubleday, 1992) V:975–80.

[58] See also Psalms 37:32; 38:13; 54:5; 71:10; 86:14; Wisdom of Solomon 2:12-20; 5:1-7, especially 5:3; Proverbs 6:17; and the story of Susanna, Daniel 13:52-59. As R. Brown noted, "the evangelists are depicting the trial of Jesus in an atmosphere colored by Psalms and other OT passages describing the plots against the righteous, wherein the wicked 'stand up,' give false testimony to accuse the righteous man of things he knew not, and seek to put him to death," *The Death of the Messiah,* I:434.

> Malicious witnesses come forward,
> accuse me of things I do not know (Ps 35:11).

Both psalms also anticipate and celebrate the just one's divine vindication.

> But I believe I shall enjoy the LORD's goodness
> in the land of the living.
> Wait for the LORD, take courage;
> be stouthearted, wait for the LORD! (Ps 27:13-14).

> But let those who favor my just cause
> shout for joy and be glad.
> May they ever say, "Exalted be the LORD
> who delights in the peace of his loyal servant."
> Then my tongue shall recount your justice,
> declare your praise, all the day long" (Ps 35:27-28).

Even with false testimony they might have been able to condemn Jesus to death (14:55), on condition that the testimony agreed. Since the testimony did not agree, the chief priests and the whole Sanhedrin failed to get the testimony they needed to put Jesus to death (14:55).

The body of the segment is a specific allegation concerning the Temple: "We heard him say, 'I will destroy this temple *(naos)* made with hands and within three days I will build another not made with hands'" (14:58).[59] The allegation highlights the story's principal theme, which is christological.

Jesus never actually said that he would destroy the sanctuary *(naos),* the inner sanctum, the most sacred structure among the Temple buildings. On coming out of the Temple *(hieron)* for the last time, when the disciples had been so impressed with its great stones and buildings, he announced that not even one stone would be left upon another and that all will be thrown down (13:1-2). Never, however, did he suggest that he personally would destroy the Temple *(hieron),* let alone the sanctuary *(naos).*

In the context of Mark's Gospel, the accusation recalls Jesus' announcement about the utter destruction of the Temple (13:2). Peter, James, and John asked him when this would happen and what sign there would be when all these things would come to an end (13:3-4). Jesus warned them not to be deceived (13:5-8), and to watch out

[59] See J. Donahue, "Temple, Trial, and Royal Christology," 66–71; R. Brown, *The Death of the Messiah,* I:438–54; J. P. Heil, "The Progressive Narrative Pattern of Mark 14,53–16,8," 339.

for themselves, for they would be handed over, even by family members (13:9-13).

After that would come a time of unprecedented tribulation, inaugurated by "the desolating abomination standing where he should not," desecrating the Temple, destroying it as God's dwelling (13:14-23). But after the days of tribulation, they would see the "'Son of Man coming in the clouds' with great power and glory." At his coming, even the great lights in the heaven, the sun and the moon, would pale, and the stars would fall from the sky (13:24-27).

The Temple would indeed be destroyed, in the great tribulation, when people would say to the disciples, "Look, here is the Messiah" *(Christos),* and false messiahs *(pseudochristoi)* would arise (13:21-22). Already there were those coming in Jesus' name and claiming to be "I AM" (13:6).

When Jesus spoke of the destruction of the Temple, he meant far more than the destruction of a set of buildings, however great. Somehow, some in the Sanhedrin had heard of his response to the disciples (13:1-2). And somehow, they had twisted what he said into a revolutionary threat that he himself would destroy the Temple.

In a sense they were right. Not that Jesus personally would take revolutionary action against the Temple and its holy of holies *(naos).* The Temple *(hieron)* and its sanctuary *(naos),* however, would be destroyed in Jesus' person.[60] At the moment of Jesus' death, this would be symbolized with the rending of the veil of the sanctuary from top to bottom (see 15:38). The new sanctuary would also be built in Jesus' person, all within three days *(dia trion hemeron).*[61]

[60] Since the Temple sanctuary would be destroyed and rebuilt in Jesus' passion-resurrection, it was quite true to say that he would both destroy and rebuild it. Since Jesus had announced his passion-resurrection (8:31; 9:31; 10:32-34), it was consequently true that he also had announced the destruction and rebuilding of the sanctuary.

[61] All three of Jesus' prophetic announcements of the passion and the resurrection spoke of his rising "after three days" *(meta treis hemeras,* 8:31; 9:31; 10:34). The ancient Antiochene creed in 1 Corinthians 15:3-5 indicated that Christ rose "on the third day" *(te hemera te trite).* The allegation against Jesus (14:58) refers to "within three days" *(dia trion hemeron).*

The expression, "on the third day," is very traditional, with rabbinical roots interpreting "the third day" as the day God saves his people (see G. R. Beasley-Murray, "Jesus and Apocalyptic: With Special Reference to Mark 14,62," in *L'Apocalypse johannique et l'Apocalyptique dans le Nouveau Testament,* edited by J. Lambrecht, *Ephemeridium Theologicarum Lovaniensium* LIII [Leuven: University Press, 1980] 415–29, 424).

The Temple and its sanctuary, made with hands, would be destroyed, and a new one, not made with hands, would be built in the passion-resurrection of Jesus, the definitive event in the history of salvation, inseparable from the great tribulation and the manifestation of the Son of Man in glory.

In Mark's presentation, those who brought false witness against Jesus had no idea what they were saying. From their point of view, distorting Jesus' words, they gave false witness. From Mark's point of view, they could not have spoken more truly. So understood, the "false testimony" against Jesus plays an important role in the trial, introducing Jesus' interrogation by the high priest and Jesus' extraordinary christological proclamation (14:60-62).

Interrogation and Response (14:60-62). When the Sanhedrin failed to obtain consistent false testimony against Jesus (14:56-59), the high priest rose in the assembly *(eis meson)*. He himself would question Jesus. The exchange between the high priest and Jesus is extremely dramatic.

The high priest, the one holding authority over the Temple, rose to interrogate and judge Jesus in whose very person the sanctuary, made with hands, would be destroyed and a new sanctuary, not made with hands, would be built. Unwittingly, the high priest was ensuring the destruction of the Temple and paving the way for the new Temple, which would be a house of prayer for all peoples (11:17).

The high priest asked Jesus two questions in quick succession: "Have you no answer?" *(ouk apokrinen ouden);* "What are these men testifying against you?" (14:60). The first question presupposed that Jesus had remained silent until that point. With the second, the high priest suggests a reason for Jesus' silence. Either Jesus did not understand what they testified against him, or he did not grasp the gravity of their charges. Why else would Jesus not have responded? Jesus responded with more silence. Again Jesus answered nothing *(ouk apekrinato ouden).*[62]

Jesus' silence associates him with the suffering servant in Isaiah:

The Markan expression, "after three days," emphasizes the length of time between the passion and the resurrection for a Christian community undergoing a passion of their own.

This additional Markan expression, "within three days," joins the resurrection to the passion. Within three days, the Temple would be both destroyed and rebuilt.

[62] See J. C. O'Neill, "The Silence of Jesus," *New Testament Studies* 15 (1968–1969) 153–67.

Though he was harshly treated, he submitted
   and opened not his mouth;
Like a lamb led to the slaughter
   or a sheep before the shearers,
   he was silent and opened not his mouth (Isa 53:7).

Responding to Jesus' silence, the high priest questioned him again *(palin):* "Are you [*su ei*] the Messiah [*ho christos*], the son of the Blessed One [*ho huios tou eulogetou*]?" (14:61, RNAB).[63] The adverb, "again" *(palin),* connects the third question closely with the previous two, making them as a three-question sequence:

"Have you no answer?"
"What are these men testifying against you?"
"Are you the Messiah, the son of the Blessed One?"

The high priest was asking Jesus to testify on his own behalf, hoping he would give them the grounds to condemn him.

In the third question, the high priest included two titles: "the Christ" *(Messiah)* and "the Son of the Blessed One." The conjunction of these two titles can be understood in various ways.

One way would be to view them as two independent titles, with "the Christ," as the principal title and "the Son of the Blessed One" as additional title, given in simple apposition. So understood, what the high priest asked Jesus was, first, if he was "the Christ," and second, if he was "the Son of the Blessed One." His question would thus have represented two distinct questions: "Are you the Christ?" and "Are you the Son of the Blessed One?" This is how most translations interpret the question, as indicated by the comma separating the two titles.

Another way would be to view them as one single title, with the second term qualifying and defining the first. So understood, the high priest asked Jesus if he was "the Christ" in the sense of being "the Son of the Blessed One."[64] This second way corresponds more closely to the general context of Mark's Gospel.

For Mark, it was not enough to confess Jesus as "the Christ." Being the Christ could mean many things. It could refer to a political or revolutionary messianic role. It could also associate Jesus with King David, presenting him as a Davidic Messiah. Jesus' response to Peter's confession indicated that he was not the Christ in

---

[63] See Norman Perrin, "The High Priest's Question and Jesus' Answer (Mark 14:61-62)," *The Passion in Mark,* 80–95.

[64] See Joel Marcus, "Mark 14:61: 'Are You the Messiah-Son-of-God?'" *Novum Testamentum* XXXI, 2 (1989) 125–41.

a political or revolutionary sense. His teaching in the Temple showed that as the Christ he was much more than the Son of David (12:35-37; see 10:46-52). As we saw in Jesus' Messianic entry into Jerusalem and the Temple, his kingdom was not of this world (11:1-11).

The high priest raised the critical question of Jesus' identity. From the high priest's point of view, the question was meant to provoke Jesus to blasphemy. From Jesus' point of view, the question was an invitation to proclaim who he truly was. From Mark's point of view, the question brought to a first climax the Gospel's basic christological teaching, as announced in its prefatory title: "The beginning of the gospel of Jesus Christ [the Son of God]" (1:1).

With this question, Jesus broke his silence. "I am" *(ego eimi),* he said, responding to the high priest's "Are you?" Jesus was the Christ in the sense of being the Son of the Blessed One. As was revealed at his baptism and again at the transfiguration, he was God's beloved Son (1:11; 9:7). That is what made his Messianic mission different from every other, making it pleasing to God (1:11) and giving it divine authority (9:7). Jesus acted and fulfilled his Messianic mission by the authority of God present in and through him (11:33).

Going beyond the high priest's question, Jesus associated himself intimately with God, "I AM," as he did when he came to the disciples on the water (6:50) after he broke bread for the five thousand (6:34-44). On the Mount of Olives, he announced that many would come declaring to be "I AM." The disciples must not be deceived (13:6).

Earlier in the Gospel, Jesus announced that he was the Christ in the sense of being the Son of Man, one who would suffer, die, and rise again after three days (8:31; 9:31; 10:32-34). Now he announced that he was the Christ, in the sense of being the Son of the Blessed One, I AM, but also as the Son of Man: "and 'you will see the Son of Man / seated at the right hand of the Power / and coming with the clouds of heaven'" (Mark 14:62).

Jesus' response to the high priest recalls these words from his eschatological discourse: "And then they will see 'the Son of Man coming in the clouds' with great power and glory, and then he will send out the angels and gather [his] elect from the four winds, from the end of the earth to the end of the sky" (13:26-27). On that occasion, Jesus based his announcement on Daniel 7:13, which referred to "One like a son of man coming, / on the clouds of heaven." Responding to the high priest, he joined that earlier reference to Daniel 7:13 with Psalm 110:1, with the words: "The LORD says to you, my lord: / 'Take your throne at my right hand, / while I make your enemies your footstool.'"

Jesus associated his death and resurrection with the return of the Son of Man at the consummation of the ages, when he would come to judge all human beings. We now understand Jesus' silence when many gave false witness against him and when the high priest asked why he did not respond. The Sanhedrin and the high priest had no authority to judge him. They had no authority to judge the one who had ultimate authority over them, the one whom they would see seated at the right hand of the Power, coming with the clouds of heaven to judge them (14:62).[65]

Condemnation and Mockery (14:63-65). Jesus' announcement moved the high priest to tear his garments (14:63a), as Eliakim, the master of the palace, Shebnah the scribe, and the herald Joah had done when an Assyrian official blasphemously challenged the power of the God of Israel. When they reported the blasphemy to King Hezekiah, he too tore his garments (2 Kgs 18:37–19:1). So now the high priest.

From the point of view of Mark's Gospel, the high priest's action had an additional connotation. Throughout Mark, a person's clothing expressed that person's identity. Tearing his garments meant rending his very identity as high priest. With the coming of Jesus, the era of the high priest, like that of the fig tree and of the Temple (11:12-25), came to an end. At Jesus' death, the veil of the sanctuary would be torn in two from top to bottom, and the sanctuary made of hands would be no more (15:38).

Tearing his garments, the high priest addressed the Sanhedrin; "What further need have we of witnesses? You have heard the blasphemy. What do you think?" (14:63b-64a). He spoke truly. After Jesus' announcement, there was no further need of witnesses. Jesus' testimony was enough. From the high priest's point of view, however, Jesus blasphemed. His words were meant to incite the Sanhedrin to action and condemn Jesus as deserving to die (14:64b). Such had been their intention from the beginning (11:18; 14:1, 55).

Jesus' appearance before the Sanhedrin ended with a mockery scene (14:65), the first of three. The trial before Pilate would also close with a mockery scene (15:16-20), as would the crucifixion scene (15:29-32).

---

[65] As G. R. Beasley-Murray noted, "For the implication of the saying is clear: in that day the positions of judges and accused will be reserved; the members of the court will stand before the Son of Man and give account of their conduct towards him," "Jesus and Apocalyptic: With Special Reference to Mark 14,62," 426. Actually, the positions were already reversed, save that the Sanhedrin and the high priest were blind to it. Knowing his true relationship to his judges, Jesus had kept silent until asked about his identity.

They began by spitting at him. Then they blindfolded him, and they struck him, challenging him to prophesy. In their eyes, Jesus was not even a prophet, let alone the Christ who was the Son of the Blessed One. The guards, with whom Peter had been sitting, greeted him with blows. The end of Jesus' trial before the Sanhedrin contrasts with the end of Peter's "trial" down in the courtyard and out in the outer court. Peter would remember Jesus' prophetic words that before the cock crows twice he would deny Jesus three times. Instead of mocking Jesus, Peter would repent, breaking down in tears (14:72).

The Trial and the Denial of Peter (14:66-72)

At Gethsemane, while Jesus prayed (14:35-36, 39), Peter, together with James and John, had slept. Three times Jesus returned and found them sleeping (14:37, 40, 41). Jesus had warned Peter, "Watch and pray that you may not undergo the test" (14:38a).

The spirit was willing but the flesh was weak (14:38b), as Peter demonstrated when Jesus told the disciples that all would be scandalized (14:27-29), and again when Jesus announced that Peter himself would deny him that very night, not once, but three times, even before the cock crowed twice (14:30-31).

When Jesus was arrested (14:46), all abandoned him and fled (14:50). Among them, there was a young man who was following him. When they seized him as they had seized Jesus, he fled, abandoning his baptismal commitment (14:51-52). Peter abandoned Jesus at the palace of the high priest, while Jesus was being tried before the Sanhedrin (14:66-71). Unlike the young man, however, Peter repented (14:72).

Peter followed Jesus at a distance and only as far as the courtyard of the high priest. While Jesus was interrogated, falsely accused, and questioned about his identity, Peter was seated with the guards, warming himself by a fire (14:54), until he too was asked about his identity (14:66-67).[66]

Peter's denial took place in three moments, the first in the courtyard when a maid confronted him (14:66-68a), the second outside in the outer court when the same maid confronted him again (14:68b-

---

[66] For Peter's denial, see Max Wilcox, "The Denial-Sequence in Mark, XIV. 26–31, 66–72," *New Testament Studies* 17 (1970–1971) 426–36; Kim E. Dewey, "Peter's Curse and Cursed Peter (Mark 14:53-54, 66-72), *The Passion in Mark*, 96–114. For a study of the passage in Mark 14:66-72 in relation to the corresponding passage in Matthew, Luke, and John, see R. Brown, *The Death of the Messiah*, I:587–626.

70a), and the third a little later when bystanders challenged him (14:70b-71).

The contrast with Jesus' trial is extraordinary. While Jesus was confronted by the Sanhedrin and the high priest, Peter was confronted by the high priest's maid and some bystanders. While Jesus proclaimed his identity as the Christ who was the Son of God, Peter denied his identity as a follower of Jesus, the Nazarene.

When one of the high priest's maids *(paidiske)* saw Peter warming himself, she eyed him closely and said: "You too were with [*meta*] the Nazarene, Jesus" (14:66-67). At the time, Peter had distanced himself from Jesus (14:54). The one who was called to be with Jesus *(meta autou)* as one of the Twelve (3:14) was now with *(meta)* the guards who greeted Jesus with blows (14:65).

The maid's statement could be understood as a simple observation that she had observed Peter in Jesus' company. In the context of the Gospel, however, her words recall the time Peter was fishing with his brother Andrew, and Jesus called him to fish for human beings (1:16-20). It also recalls his further call to be one of the Twelve, indeed, to be the first among them (3:13-19), as well as the time Peter tried to deter Jesus from announcing the passion and resurrection of the Son of Man (8:31-33). Most of all, however, it recalled his commitment to be with Jesus even unto death if that were necessary (14:27-31).

Peter denied *(ernesato)* that he was with the Nazarene, Jesus: "I neither know [*oute oida*] nor understand [*oute epistamai*] what you are talking about" (14:68a). Denying Jesus meant denying having any relationship to him.

In this first denial, Peter tried to avoid denying that he actually was with Jesus. He simply answered the maid that he had no knowledge or understanding of what she said. For Mark, however, Peter's evasive response amounted to an actual denial. Having no knowledge of his relationship to Jesus presupposed that there was no relationship.

When Peter rebuked Jesus for his announcement that the Son of Man had to die and after three days rise again (8:31-32), Jesus rebuked him in return: "Get behind me [*opiso mou*], Satan. You are thinking not as God does, but as human beings do" (8:33). Later, in his prayer at Gethsemane, Jesus would show what it meant to think as God does (14:35-36).

After rebuking Peter, Jesus spoke to the crowd with the disciples: "Whoever wishes to come after me [*opiso mou*] must deny himself [*aparnesastho heauton*], take up his cross, and follow me" (8:34). Denying oneself meant giving up all claim to one's person for personal goals, and allowing God to claim one's whole self for Christ's mission and the kingdom of God. Peter and the others had done that, leaving everything behind and following Jesus (10:28).

In his relationship to Jesus, as one who was of Christ *(Christou)*, he had a new identity (9:41). But now, confronted by the maid of the high priest, Peter denied his relationship to Christ and with it his new identity. Denying Christ meant denying himself as one who was of Christ.

After denying his relationship to Jesus, Peter went outside *(exo)* to the outer court (14:68b). Outside *(exo)*, he further distanced himself from Jesus. He was now like Jesus' relatives who came to the home in Capernaum (3:21) but remained outside *(exo,* 3:32) instead of joining the crowd (3:7-8) inside (3:33).

Peter was also with those outside *(exo)* to whom everything came in parables, that, looking and seeing, they might not perceive, and hearing and listening, they might not understand (4:10-12). From the Gospel's point of view, therefore, Peter spoke truly when he told the maid he did not know or understand what she was referring to. At this point, many manuscripts indicate: "Then the cock crowed" (14:68c).

Jesus had said Peter would deny him three times before the cock crowed twice (14:30; see 14:72). Historically, Jesus may have referred to cockcrow as a time of day, that is, around three o'clock in the morning (see 13:35). The statement would then have meant that Peter would deny Jesus three times late that very night. For all his promises, it would take less than two days (the second cockcrow) before Peter denied him.

What could be an addition, "Then the cock crowed" (14:68c), at least at the level of tradition, understands Jesus' statement as referring literally to the cock crowing twice. That is surely the way Mark understood Jesus' announcement of Peter's denial, since the Gospel later refers to the cock crowing a second time (14:72).

Outside in the outer court, the same maid saw Peter and again *(palin)* started saying to the bystanders *(tois parestosin):* "This man [*houtos*] is one of them [*ex auton*]" (14:69). This second time, the maid confronts Peter with his relationship not so much to Jesus but to the Twelve. Peter, she said, was one of them. Once again *(palin),* Peter denied knowing or understanding what she said (14:70a).

A short time later, it was the bystanders *(hoi parestotes)* who again *(palin)* confronted Peter: "Surely you are one of them [*ex auton*]; for you too are a Galilean" (14:70b). This third time, the bystanders confronted Peter with his relationship both to the Twelve and to Jesus, the Nazarene.

This time, cursing and swearing, he responded directly: "I do not know [*oida*] this man [*ton anthropon touton*] about whom you are talking" (14:71). On the previous occasions, Peter denied knowing or understanding what the maid was saying. This time, Peter denied knowing Jesus, the one the bystanders were talking about.

Peter's Repentance (14:72). As soon as Peter denied knowing Jesus for the third time, the cock crowed a second time (14:72a; see 14:68c). And "Peter remembered [*anemnesthe*] the word [*to hrema*] that Jesus had said to him, 'Before the cock crows twice you will deny me three times'" (14:72b). Memory is very important in the Gospel tradition. It recalls the past, but looks to the future, and is transforming of the present.

Remembering, Peter repented. As Matthew 27:3-5 (see Acts 1:16-18) indicated, Judas did not repent. He regretted what he had done. Repentance has to do with the future, about which one can do something. Regret has to do with the past, which one cannot undo. What Peter remembered is what Jesus said, that is, the reality *(to hrema)* to which Jesus referred. Everything had happened as Jesus had indicated and as Peter had vowed they would not (14:30-31).

With that Peter "broke down [*epibalon*] and wept [*eklaien*]" (14:72c), leaving us to ponder what precisely made him break down and cry. Was it the confrontation with his past? Or was it gratitude for Jesus' promise, that even though all would be scandalized and Peter would deny him, not once, but three times, once Jesus was raised up, he would go before them anew in Galilee (14:28)?

Peter now leaves the Gospel as an active participant, but he would be referred to by the young man in the tomb, commissioning the women: "But go and tell his disciples and Peter, 'He is going before you to (in) Galilee; there you will see him, as he told you'" (16:7).

Act II, Scene Two
At the Palace of Pilate (15:1-20)

Act II, Scene One (14:53-72) of Mark's story of the passion and resurrection is situated at the palace of the high priest, where two trials unfolded simultaneously, that of Jesus, the Christ (14:53, 55-65), and that of Peter, the follower (14:54, 66-72).

Jesus' trial took place up in the palace, where he was interrogated by the high priest, the chief priests, and the entire Sanhedrin. Peter's trial took place in the courtyard, where he was interrogated by one of the high priest's maids and some of the bystanders.

At his trial before the Sanhedrin, Jesus proclaimed his identity as "the Messiah, the son of the Blessed One" (14:61), the Son of Man who would be seen "seated at the right hand of the Power / and coming with the clouds of heaven" (14:62). For that, the Sanhedrin charged Jesus with blasphemy and condemned him to death. After condemning him, some of the Sanhedrin "began to spit on him." They also blindfolded him, struck him, and asked him to prophesy (14:65).

At his trial before the maid and some of the bystanders, Peter denied his identity as a follower of Jesus. Peter denied Jesus three times, withdrawing further and further away from him. After Peter's third denial, a cock crowed for the second time, and Peter remembered what Jesus said to him at the Mount of Olives: "Before the cock crows twice you will deny me three times" (14:72; see 14:30). Remembering Jesus' words, Peter broke down and cried.

Scene Two (15:1-20) is situated at the palace of Pilate, the Roman prefect. As the scene opens, the chief priests, the elders, and the scribes bind Jesus, lead him away *(apenegkan,* aorist form of *apophero),* and hand him over to Pilate (15:1; see 14:53). The scene ends with the soldiers leading Jesus out *(exagousin)* for crucifixion (15:20).

With this second scene, we return to the passion's main narrative line, which presents Jesus as a knowing but passive victim of a plot to destroy them (see 14:1-2, 10-11, 17-21, 27-31, 43-52). As we showed earlier, the passion keeps interrupting this narrative line with distinct, interpretive events, showing Jesus as an active participant in the passion (14:3-9, 12-16, 22-26, 32-42, 53-72). In this way, the passion-resurrection according to Mark transforms what would otherwise be a tragedy into a gospel message. Jesus did not lose his life. He gave it, in accord with his Father's will (14:36, 39), for the salvation of all (14:24).

After a short introduction, providing a transition from Jesus' trial before the Sanhedrin to his trial before Pilate (15:1), this second scene unfolds in three sections.

In the first, Pilate interrogates Jesus, presumably in an outer court before the palace (15:2-5).[67] The interrogation by Pilate roughly parallels that by the high priest (14:60-62). At the end, how-

---

[67] When Pilate handed Jesus over to be crucified (15:15), the soldiers led him away inside *(eso)* the palace (15:16). Mark thus assumes that the interrogation itself took place outside the palace proper, in the outer court, where the governor sat in judgment on a raised platform, called in Greek a *bema,* in Latin, a *tribunal.*

ever, unlike the high priest and the Sanhedrin (14:63-64), Pilate has not passed judgment on Jesus, let alone pronounced sentence.

In the second section, Pilate refers to Jesus but Jesus himself does not have an active role. In this section, Pilate deals with the crowd, which is demanding Barabbas' release and Jesus' condemnation. Like the interrogation, the crowd scene takes place in the outer court before the palace (15:6-15). Again the section ends without Pilate judging Jesus guilty of a crime. On the contrary, in Pilate's eyes, Jesus was innocent of anything deserving condemnation. But, wishing to please the crowd, Pilate sentences Jesus and hands him over to be crucified.

In the third section, the soldiers lead Jesus away into the palace, where they mock and torture him before leading him out for crucifixion (15:16-20). This is the second time Jesus is mocked and tortured. The first time was at the palace of the high priest (14:65).

"As Soon as Morning Came" (15:1)

Jesus' Last Supper (14:17-26) was held the previous evening (14:17). After the Supper, Jesus had gone with his disciples to the Mount of Olives (14:26) and to a place called Gethsemane (14:32), where Jesus prayed (14:33-42). That is where he was arrested (14:43-52). After his arrest, Jesus was taken to the palace of the high priest, where he was tried before the Sanhedrin (14:53-72). The trial lasted until cockcrow (14:72). Later, when morning came, the Sanhedrin handed Jesus over to Pilate (15:1).

We recall Jesus' warning to the disciples at the end of his discourse on the Mount of Olives: "Watch, therefore; you do not know when the lord of the house is coming, whether in the evening [*opse;* see 14:17, *opsias;* see also 6:47], or at midnight [*mesonyktion*], or at cockcrow [*alektorophonias*], or in the morning [*proi*]" (13:35). Cockcrow [*alektor phonesai*], a popular designation coinciding with the beginning of the fourth Roman watch (*circa* 3:00 a.m.; see also 6:48), is when Peter repented (14:72).

The trial before Pilate took place when morning *(proi)* came, some three hours later (*circa* 6:00 a.m.). For people who take electricity for granted and regulate their lives by the clock, it may seem unusual to hold a trial at that early hour. In old Jerusalem, however, where daily life was regulated mainly by the sun and public life began with its rising, it was quite normal.

The story suggests, even if only implicitly, that after the trial at the house of the high priest, the Sanhedrin dispersed around cockcrow. Later, "as soon as morning came," the entire Sanhedrin *(holon to synedrion),* including the chief priests, the elders, and the scribes reassembled at the palace of the high priest. They had already, however, completed their council session and consultation *(symbolion)* and condemned Jesus to death.

On several occasions, the gospel referred to the chief priests and the scribes (10:33; 11:18; 14:1), sometimes including the elders (8:31; 11:27; 14:43, 53). But this is the first time Mark actually specifies that they constituted the Sanhedrin,[68] wishing to emphasize that Jesus was condemned and handed over to Pilate by the most authoritative, religious body in Judaism.

The Sanhedrin had the authority to pass judgment on Jesus and condemn him to death, but did not have the authority to carry out the sentence. Only Pilate, the Roman prefect, could do that. That is why the chief priests, the elders, and the scribes, the whole Sanhedrin, bound Jesus, led him away, and handed him over to Pilate.[69]

Just as the Sanhedrin was the highest religious authority in Jerusalem, Pilate, as the imperial prefect, was the highest civil authority in Jerusalem. Pilate (A.D. 26–36) was the fifth of seven prefects[70] between A.D. 6 and 41, when the monarchy was temporarily restored at the accession of Herod Agrippa (A.D. 41–44).

By condemning Jesus to death and handing him over to Pilate, the Sanhedrin fulfilled the prophetic announcement Jesus made earlier on the way to Jerusalem: "The Son of Man will be handed over to the chief priests and the scribes [see 14:53], and they will condemn him to death [see 14:64] and hand him over to the Gentiles" (10:33).

Jesus Before Pilate (15:2-5)

The high priest's concerns were primarily religious, but also political. There was no separating the religious from the political in

---

[68] For the nature and composition of the Sanhedrin, see Joachim Jeremias, *Jerusalem in the Time of Jesus* (Philadelphia: Fortress Press, 1969) 222–26.

[69] For the background and position of Pontius Pilate, see Raymond Brown, *The Death of the Messiah* (New York: Doubleday, 1994) I:693–705; also Daniel R. Schwartz, "Pontius Pilate," in *The Anchor Bible Dictionary* (New York: Doubleday, 1992) 5:395–401.

[70] Roman governors had the Latin title *praefectus* (in Greek *eparchos*) from A.D. 6–41. Only after Herod Agrippa did they have the title "procurator." In the New Testament, but outside the Gospels, Pilate is mentioned in 1 Tim 6:13: "Christ Jesus, who gave testimony under Pontius Pilate for the noble confession."

the Palestinian Judaism of that time. The high priest's interrogation of Jesus, therefore, focused primarily on Jesus' religious identity and claims: "Are you the Messiah, the son of the Blessed One?" (14:61). The high priest's use of the title "Messiah," however, had clear political implications. On the basis of Jesus' answer, the high priest and the Sanhedrin accused Jesus of blasphemy, condemned him to death, and brought him to Pilate.

Pilate's concerns, very different from those of high priest and the Sanhedrin, were primarily political. But again, there was no separating the political from the religious in first-century Jerusalem. Accordingly, Pilate's interrogation focused on Jesus' civil identity and political claims: "Are you the king of the Jews?" (15:2a).

Without preamble, the trial before Pilate begins somewhat abruptly. Pilate asks: "Are you the king of the Jews?" (15:2a). We would like to know how the Sanhedrin actually accused Jesus before Pilate. It is not likely they would have denounced Jesus for claiming personal divinity or for blaspheming. For the Sanhedrin, such claims may have been cause for condemning someone to death, not, however, for Pilate.

Could the Sanhedrin have denounced Jesus for claiming to be "the king of the Jews"? Again, not very likely. That would have been treading on dangerous ground, suggesting that someone, if not Jesus, might indeed be "the king of the Jews." In the rest of the proceedings, Pilate himself would refer to Jesus as "the king of the Jews" (15:9, 12), trying to set a trap for the crowd and mocking the chief priests. It is unlikely the Sanhedrin would have provided a title so easy to use against them.

The gospel does not say what prompted Pilate to ask Jesus if he were "the king of the Jews." But then, the story of the trials is not a chronicle but a literary diptych, with two trial scenes, one Jewish, one Roman, side by side.

The Jewish trial raises the question of Jesus' religious identity as the Messiah. Jesus shows how his messianic role transcends not only Judaism but all of history. The Roman trial raises the question of Jesus' political identity as the king of the Jews. Jesus accepts the title king but not as Pilate understands it.

The kingship of Jesus was first broached by Peter when he confessed Jesus as the Christ, that is "the Messiah" (8:29). Jesus then announced that as the Christ he was the Son of Man who "must suffer greatly and be rejected by the elders, the chief priests, and the scribes, and be killed, and rise after three days" (8:31; see also 9:31; 10:32-34). At that, Peter "took him aside and began to rebuke him" (8:32).

Later, Bartimaeus, a blind beggar beside Jesus' way to Jerusalem called out to Jesus with the title "son of David" (11:47-48). While teaching in the Temple, Jesus himself then raised the question, "How do the scribes claim that the Messiah [the Christ] is the son of David?" David himself refers to the Messiah as his "lord." How then could the Messiah be David's son? (12:35-37).

As king, Jesus was very different from what people expected of the son of David. His kingdom was not an earthly kingdom but an eschatological kingdom, as the crowd accompanying him sang at his entry into Jerusalem:

> Blessed is he who comes in the name of the Lord!
> Blessed is the kingdom of our father David that is to come!
>   (Mark 11:9-10)

The nature of Jesus' kingly role is described later in the great eschatological discourse:

> And then they will see "the Son of Man coming in the clouds" with great power and glory, and then he will send out the angels and gather [his] elect from the four winds, from the end of the earth to the end of the sky (Mark 13:26-27).

Jesus would rule as king in the kingdom of God. From the beginning of his ministry, Jesus had been proclaiming God's kingdom (1:14-15).

When the high priest asked Jesus if he was "the Messiah, the son of the Blessed One," he was testing Jesus for personal claims of messianic and divine kingship. Jesus' response (14:62), recalled his announcement in 13:26-27. For it, he was judged blasphemous. When Pilate asked if Jesus was "the king of the Jews," he was asking whether he was an earthly king, the political king of the Jews. That is why Jesus answered so evasively: "You say so" (15:2b). Jesus accepted the title Pilate gave him, but not as Pilate understood it.

Only now, after Pilate's opening question and Jesus' evasive answer, does the story refer to accusations by the chief priests, but very vaguely. The chief priests accused Jesus of many things (*polla,* 15:3). None of these "many things" are actually specified. Nothing is said about Jesus claiming to be "the king of the Jews." Pilate, however, again *(palin)* asked the same question: "Are you the king of the Jews?" (15:2a). Jesus' silence (see also 14:60-61) amazed Pilate: "Have you no answer?" (15:4b).

Concluding his interrogation, Pilate tried to make Jesus aware of "how many things" *(posa)* they were accusing him of (15:4c). But beyond Jesus' first answer, "You say so," he had no further response, reinforcing Pilate's amazement (*thaumazein,* 15:5).[71] We saw something of the same amazement when the Pharisees and the Herodians tried to trap Jesus over the issue of paying taxes (12:13-17). Hearing Jesus' response, "Repay to Caesar what belongs to Caesar and to God what belongs to God," they were utterly amazed (*exethaumazon,* 12:17).

For us, Jesus' silence, first before the Sanhedrin (14:61), and now before Pilate, evokes the silent suffering of the servant of the Lord:

> Though he was harshly treated, he submitted
> and opened not his mouth;
> Like a lamb led to the slaughter
> or a sheep before his shearers,
> he was silent and opened not his mouth (Isa 53:7).

Pilate Before the Crowd (15:6-15)

The interrogation of Jesus is over. From Jesus before Pilate, the scene shifts to Pilate before the crowd. In the first section, the chief priests were in the foreground, accusing Jesus of many things (15:3-4). In the second, the crowd replaces them in the foreground. The chief priests remain in the background, stirring up the crowd (15:11). Jesus himself does not seem to be present when Pilate appears before the crowd.

Jesus' interrogation by Pilate ended without Pilate pronouncing judgment on Jesus. The same is true in the second section. Pilate does not judge Jesus guilty of any crime (see 15:9-10). He does, however, sentence him to death by crucifixion.

After some introductory background regarding a Roman custom on the occasion of "the feast," that is, Passover (15:6), the section includes a two-part exchange between Pilate and the crowd (15:7-15). With the title, "the king of the Jews," Pilate tries to use the crowd in an effort to mock the Sanhedrin. At the same time, however, the Sanhedrin uses the crowd in their effort to have Pilate condemn Jesus to death.

In the first part, Pilate asks the crowd if they want him to release "the king of the Jews." Stirred up by the chief priests, the crowd presses Pilate to release Barabbas instead (15:7-11). In the second, the crowd pushes Pilate to sentence Jesus to death by crucifixion (15:12-15).

---

[71] As Raymond Brown indicated, Pilate is amazed "that Jesus holds himself aloof from the charges" (*The Death of the Messiah,* I:735).

On the Occasion of the Feast (15:6). "On the occasion of the feast [*kata de heorten*]," that is, "the Feast of the Unleavened Bread, when they sacrificed the Passover lamb" (see 14:12), Pilate used "to release to them one prisoner whom they requested" (15:6).[72] Outside the passion accounts in the New Testament, there is no evidence, biblical or extrabiblical, of such a custom.

There is, however, a good deal of evidence in the ancient world in general for the release of prisoners on the occasion of various feasts or festivals. In the Old Testament, Johoiachin, king of Judah, benefited from such a custom when released by Evil-merodach [Amel-Marduk], king of Babylon, in the inaugural year of his reign (561 B.C.), very likely during the festival that accompanied his accession to the throne (2 Kgs 25:27-30; Jer 52:31-34). The custom was also fairly common in the Hellenistic and Roman world.

As described by Mark, the custom was a Roman custom, which Pilate himself had been observing. In John's Gospel, Pilate refers to it as a Jewish custom (John 18:39), that is, a Roman custom already being observed in Jerusalem when Pilate became prefect. The fact that the custom was Roman explains why there is no reference to it in ancient Jewish literature.[73]

Again, as described by Mark, the custom was to release a single prisoner whom the people selected. Outside the New Testament, the custom was not so limited. Several, or even many prisoners were released on the occasion of a feast or festival. As a measure of largesse, a governor intended to please the people over which he ruled, but the choice of prisoners was not left to them. The custom also excluded certain prisoners from consideration. It is unlikely that a murderer or someone trying to overthrow the state would have been released.

Very likely, therefore, Mark refers to a well-known custom, prevalent in the Roman world in New Testament times, and adapts it for the trial scene of Jesus. The adaptation heightens the drama, un-

[72] Concerning the custom of a paschal pardon, see Robert L. Merritt, "Jesus Barabbas and the Paschal Pardon," *Journal of Biblical Literature* 104 (1985) 57–68.

[73] Pilate's statement in John, "But you have a custom that I release one prisoner to you at Passover" (John 18:39), does not indicate that the custom was specifically Jewish, only that it was a custom observed in Jerusalem or Judea. Since the custom was that the Roman governor release a prisoner, the custom would have been a Roman custom. Since the custom was observed in Jerusalem, before the arrival of Pilate, Pilate could easily refer to it as their custom. If so, there would be no disagreement between John and Mark, who refers to a custom observed by Pilate.

derlines the contrast between two prisoners, Jesus and Barabbas, and focuses on the crowd's choice to have Barabbas released instead of Jesus. Other criminals would be crucified with Jesus (15:27), but not Barabbas.

A Man Called Barabbas (15:7). After presenting the custom, the story introduces Barabbas (15:7),[74] who, like Jesus, seems not to have been present during the exchange. All the attention focuses on the crowd and Pilate himself.

Barabbas is described as one who "was then in prison along with the rebels who had committed murder in a rebellion" (15:7). Mark does not actually say that Barabbas actually committed murder *(phonos),* but that would not have been a significant factor in his arrest or release. Suffice that he was with *(meta),* that is, in solidarity with, those who rebelled and with their rebellion. For Mark, therefore, the crowd demanded that a killer be released and an innocent man be killed.

There is a lot of discussion concerning the identity of Barabbas, for whom there is no mention outside the New Testament or, within the New Testament, before or after the trial of Jesus before Pilate. Naturally, readers of the New Testament are curious about his identity.

Many explore the etymology of his name in search of possible clues. In Aramaic, *bar* means "son of," and *abba,* whose Greek form is *abbas,* means "father." Some see a play on words, between Jesus, the Son of the Father, who addressed God in prayer as *Abba,* and Barabbas, "the son of the father." Since Matthew gives Barabbas' full name as Jesus Barabbas (Matt 27:16-17), the crowd would have chosen between two men named Jesus, Jesus (Christ), the Son of the Father, and Jesus (Barabbas), the son of the Father.

The name, Jesus—in Greek, *Iesous,* from the Hebrew name, Joshua—was fairly common in both Old and New Testament times. Recall, for example, Jesus ben Sirach, the author of the Book of Sirach, in Latin, Ecclesiasticus (Sir 50:27).

For Mark, however, who does not include Barabbas' full name, and who shows no interest in the etymology of the name Barabbas, such etymological speculation has to be set aside. When Mark is interested in the etymology of a name, he explains it. That is what he did with Bartimaeus, a name, as Mark notes, meaning "Son of Timaeus" (10:47).

[74] Concerning Barabbas, see Raymond Brown, *The Death of the Messiah,* I:796–800.

The Crowd Came Forward (15:8-10). When "the crowd came forward" before Pilate, Jesus had already been taken away from the outer court. The crowd came to Pilate to request the release of a prisoner on the occasion of the feast (see 15:6) according to Pilate's custom (15:8). The story gives no indication the crowd knew that Jesus had been handed over to Pilate and was in his custody (15:1), nor that Jesus had been interrogated about being the king of the Jews. At this point in the story, therefore, the crowd did not have Jesus in mind.

While interrogating Jesus, Pilate's first and principal question was: "Are you the king of the Jews?" (15:2). For the reader, the question came very abruptly. We know the charges the Sanhedrin levied against Jesus in their own assembly, not, however, how they charged him before Pilate.

Now, responding to the crowd's request, Pilate's first and principal question was: "Do you want me to release to you the king of the Jews?" (15:9). For the reader, the question to the crowd comes just as abruptly as the question to Jesus. The reader knows about Pilate's earlier question whether Jesus was "the king of the Jews," but how was the crowd to know? Besides, Pilate did not refer to Jesus by name. How could they answer without knowing the identity of "the king of the Jews?"

While interrogating Jesus, Pilate may have used the title, "the king of the Jews," derisively, even with sarcasm, amused that the Sanhedrin had handed over "the king of the Jews" to him. Speaking to the crowd, he continued to speak with sarcasm, now baiting the crowd, who did not know about "the king of the Jews."

For Mark, the storyteller, and his readers, Pilate was simply acting on Jesus' response. When Pilate asked Jesus if he was the king of the Jews, Jesus answered: "You say so" (15:2). And that is what Pilate again did when asking the crowd: "Do you want me to release to you the king of the Jews?" (15:9). But would the crowd accept one whom Pilate called their king? Would they ask for his release?

Of itself, the crowd might have accepted Pilate's offer. But the chief priests, who had handed Jesus over out of envy, stirred up the crowd to have Pilate release Barabbas instead of Jesus, "the king of the Jews" (15:12).

Pilate Again Said to Them in Reply (15:12-15). Pilate's exchange with the crowd now moves into a final phase. Twice already Pilate had referred to Jesus as "the king of the Jews." The first time, interrogating Jesus, Pilate initiated the dialogue: "Are you the king of the Jews" (15:2). The second time, the crowd initiated the dialogue, and Pilate responded to their request: "Do you want me to release to you the king of the Jews?" (15:9). This third time, Pilate again *(palin)* responds to the crowd (15:12a), now stirred up by the chief priests to choose Barabbas instead of Jesus (15:11).

With regard to the release of a prisoner, Pilate had left the decision to the crowd. The crowd chose Barabbas. In the matter of Jesus' sentence, he again left the decision to the crowd: "Then what [do you want] me to do with [the man you call] the king of the Jews?" (15:12b).

According to some manuscripts Mark's original text may have been shorter, without the verb, "do you want *[thelete]*" (see 15:9). Omitting the verb, "do you want," does not alter the sense of the question. Without it, the translation would read, "Then what will I do with [the man you call] the king of the Jews?"

According to a few of the same manuscripts and some others, the original text may have been even shorter, without the expression, "the man you call *[hon legete]*" (see Matt 27:22, "Jesus called Messiah *[ton legomenon Christon]*"). This time, omitting the expression does make a difference.

Read without the expression, the translation would read: "Then what will I do with the king of the Jews?" Again with sarcasm, Pilate would continue to bait the crowd, applying pressure on them. Would they ask Pilate to condemn one he called "the king of the Jews"?

Read with the expression, Pilate would not only continue to bait the crowd, but would apply considerable pressure on them as well as on the chief priests, ever in the background. Would they ask Pilate to condemn one whom they themselves called "the king of the Jews"?

There is a progression in the three questions concerning the title, "the king of the Jews." From what Jesus might say (15:2a), the story moves to what Pilate said (15:2b, 9), and from there to what the crowd said (15:12), all in question form, and all told with extraordinary irony.

The crowd shouted again *(palin):* "Crucify him" (15:13). The adverb, "again," indicates that in asking for Barabbas' release they had been shouting. From the very beginning, Pilate abdicated control to the crowd. Pilate now asks, "Why?" that is, "Why crucify him?" Pilate sees no reason to crucify him. He himself could find no evidence against "the king of the Jews." "What evil has he done?" he asked (15:14a).

The crowd did not respond. "They only shouted louder, "Crucify him" (15:14b). This is the first time crucifixion *(stauroo)*[75] is referred

---

[75] For the phenomenon of crucifixion in first-century Palestine, see Joseph Fitzmyer, "Crucifixion in Ancient Palestine, Qumran Literature, and the New Testament," *Catholic Biblical Quarterly* 40 (1978) 493–513.

to in Mark's Gospel. Until now, the Gospel referred to efforts to destroy *(apollumi)* Jesus (3:6) or to kill *(apokteinein)* him (8:31; 9:31; 10:34; 14:1). Crucifixion was a form of public execution the Romans used, but only for people who were not Romans. Asking that "the king of the Jews" be crucified, the crowd was calling for the form of execution that the Romans in Palestine reserved mainly for them.

Jesus was never actually named in the whole exchange between Pilate and the crowd. Mark, of course, knew, and so did his readers, that the one referred to as "the king of the Jews" was Jesus. The crowd, however, was simply responding to questions about "the king of the Jews." Only now, at the end of the session, is Jesus named. Wishing to satisfy the crowd, which was stirred up by the chief priests, Pilate released Barabbas to them. And, after having Jesus scourged, he handed him over to be crucified.

Jesus Is Mocked for the Second Time (15:16-20)

As Jesus announced on the way *(en te hodo)* to Jerusalem, the Son of Man would be handed over to the chief priests and the scribes, and they would condemn him to death and hand him over to the Gentiles who would mock him, spit upon him, and scourge him. After that they would put him to death (10:32-34).

We have already seen how Judas Iscariot, one of the Twelve, went off to the chief priests to hand Jesus over to them (14:10-11). In that, Judas was accompanied by a crowd with swords and clubs who had come from the chief priests, the scribes, and the elders (14:43-46). We have also seen how the chief priests, the elders, and the scribes condemned Jesus to death (14:53-65) and handed him over to Pilate, the Roman prefect, who handed Jesus over to be crucified (15:1-15). With that, the Son of Man's way *(hodos)* to Jerusalem became the way *(hodos)* of the cross.

Act II, Scene Two of the passion (15:1-20) now moves into its third and final section, with the Gentiles mocking Jesus, spitting upon him, and scourging him (15:16-20). Earlier, in Scene One, Jesus had been mocked by some of the chief priests, the elders, the scribes, and the guards at the palace of the high priest: "Some began to spit on him. They blindfolded him and struck him and said to him, 'Prophesy!' And the guards greeted him with blows" (14:65). This time, he is mocked by the Roman soldiers.

As the section opens, the soldiers are leading Jesus inside the palace (15:16a). Until now, the scene was situated at the palace but in an outer court. As it ends, the soldiers are leading Jesus out to crucify him (15:20b).

An introductory verse describes the setting, which is inside the palace, that is, the praetorium. It also presents the personages, Jesus and the soldiers, the whole cohort (15:16). The body of the section describes how Jesus was mocked as the king of the Jews, clothed in royal, indeed imperial, purple, crowned with thorns, and given mock homage (15:17-19). The concluding verse shows how, after mocking Jesus, they stripped him of the purple, royal cloak, dressed him in his own clothing, and led him away for crucifixion (15:20).

The Soldiers Led Him Away (15:16). With the introduction, the action moves into the palace. Called "the king of the Jews" (15:2, 9, 12), Jesus would be acclaimed as "the king of the Jews" (15:17-19). For such a royal acclamation, the palace was the most fitting setting. The palace setting itself would thus contribute to the mockery of Jesus as "the king of the Jews."

The introduction (15:16) recalls how those who arrested Jesus (14:43-46) led him *(apegagon)* to the high priest *(pros ton archieria,* 14:53), that is, into the palace *(eso eis ten aulen)* of the high priest (14:54). Now the soldiers led Jesus away *(apegagon)* into the palace *(eso tes aules)* of Pilate, that is, the praetorium *(praitorion).*

At the palace of the high priest, all *(pantes)* the chief priests and the elders and the scribes came together, the whole *(holon)* Sanhedrin. Now the soldiers called together the whole *(holon)* cohort.

Pilate, like his predecessors, had his official residence in Caesarea Maritima, the Roman capital of Palestine. During the feast, however, when large crowds gathered in Jerusalem and there was greater risk of a disturbance, Pilate took temporary residence in Jerusalem. The palace in question was very likely the palace of Herod situated by Jerusalem's Jaffa Gate.

Mark explains that the palace *(aule),* the governor's residence, was also the praetorium *(praitorion),* his administrative and judicial office. Traditionally a praetorium was associated with the residence of a praetor, a general officer in a Roman army. Later, when military leadership in a province was associated with a governor, the Latin military term, *praetorium,* Hellenized as *praitorion,* was retained.[76]

After leading Jesus inside the palace, the soldiers "assembled the whole cohort" (15:16b). Pilate had five cohorts at his disposal. Mark's account presupposes that one of those cohorts was with him in Jerusalem.

---

[76] For the term, "praetorium," its location in Jerusalem, and historical background, see Raymond Brown, *The Death of the Messiah,* I:705–10.

They Clothed Him in Purple (15:17-20). Mocking Jesus, the soldiers clothed Jesus in purple and, weaving a crown of thorns, they placed it on him (15:17). The emperor himself wore a purple cloak, the color of royalty. Mockingly, they clothed Jesus in a purple cloak.[77] Throughout Mark's Gospel, we have noted the significance of clothing as expressing someone's identity, beginning with the garments of John the Baptist, identifying him as Elijah (1:6; see 2 Kgs 1:8). The purple cloak identifies Jesus as a king.

The irony of the statement, "they clothed him in purple," is apparent. For the soldiers, the garment was meant to ridicule Jesus and the title given him. For Mark and his readers, it expressed Jesus' true identity. So did the crown of thorns. Jesus inaugurated the kingdom of God and became king through his passion. For this, any crown would have served. The crown of thorns, however, pointed directly to the passion.

Having clothed Jesus in purple and crowned him with thorns, they then began to salute him: "Hail, King of the Jews" (15:18). Again the irony is obvious. Not only was Jesus truly the king of the Jews, they were actually ensuring that through the passion he would rule as king of the Jews, indeed as the king of all in the kingdom of God.

While saluting him, "Hail, King of the Jews" (15:18), they kept striking him on the head with a reed and spitting on him. They also knelt before him in homage, as subjects did approaching a king in the Hellenistic world. It is as one who gave his life for the life of the world that Christians give him homage.

While mocking Jesus, they proclaimed Jesus' true identity as king. Stripping him of the purple cloak, they stripped him of the mockery, not of his identity as king. They then dressed him in his own clothes, the clothes of Jesus, the king of the Jews, whom Pilate handed over to be crucified. And they led him out to crucify him.

---

[77] T. E. Schmidt associates the mocking of Jesus and his subsequent crucifixion with a Roman triumphal procession, "Mark 15:16-32: The Crucifixion Narrative and the Roman Triumphal Procession," *New Testament Studies* 41 (1995) 1–18. The study may not be convincing in every detail, but I find the overall suggestion very helpful. For the mockery scene, see pp. 6–9.

Act III. Crucifixion, Death, and Resurrection (15:21–16:8)
Scene One
Crucifixion and Death at Golgotha (15:21-41)

Act I of Jesus' passion-resurrection showed how the chief priests, the scribes, and the elders arrested Jesus by treachery with the help of Judas, "one of the Twelve," who betrayed him with a kiss (14:1-52). Judas' opportunity came during the night of Passover, after the Last Supper, in a place called Gethsemane (14:32), where Jesus was praying with his disciples. When they arrested Jesus, all his disciples left him and fled (14:50-52).

It could have been a tragedy, the story of a great teacher (1:22), a powerful prophet (6:15; 8:28), "the king of the Jews" (15:2, 9, 12, 18, 27), whose gospel of the kingdom (1:14-15) led to his arrest and destruction (3:6). Mark presented it as a gospel event. Betrayed and arrested, Jesus did not resist. Instead, he took on our infirmities (see Isa 53:4), according to the Scriptures (14:21, 27, 49) and fulfilled the will of his Father. Such was his prayer (14:36).

From a literary point of view, Act I consists of a series of alternating episodes in which the story line of the passion (14:1-2, 10-11, 17-21, 27-31, 43-52) is interrupted and interpreted by independent stories (14:3-9, 12-16, 22-26, 32-42). In this way, Mark transformed what would have been the tragedy of Jesus into the gospel of Jesus.

Act I tells the story of the arrest of Jesus in two scenes. Scene One is an introductory scene whose high point is the Last Supper (14:17-26). It sets the stage for Jesus' arrest, (14:1-31). Scene Two, situated at Gethsemane, tells of Jesus' arrest while he was at prayer (14:32-52).

Act II showed how the chief priests, the scribes, and the elders tried Jesus and found him guilty of blasphemy (14:53-72) and brought him to Pilate for condemnation (15:1-20). The chief priests, the scribes and the elders feared the crowd (11:18; 12:12; 14:2). Pilate was swayed by it. Wishing to please the crowd, Pilate handed Jesus over to be crucified (15:15).

Like Act I, Act II (14:53–15:20) is divided into two scenes. Scene One is situated at the palace of the high priest, where Jesus was tried by the Sanhedrin (14:53-72). The same scene tells of Peter's denial down in the courtyard, where he was tried by one of the maids of the high priest and some of the bystanders (14:66-72).

Interrogated by the high priest, Jesus proclaimed his identity as the Messiah and the Son of the Blessed One, "I AM," who would come on the clouds of heaven as the eschatological Son of Man

(14:61-62). Questioned by the maid, Peter denied his identity as a follower of Jesus the Christ (14:67-71; see 1:16-20; 8:31-33).

Scene Two was situated at the palace of Pilate, to whom the Sanhedrin handed Jesus over (15:1-20). Pilate asked Jesus if he was "the king of the Jews" (15:2; see 15:9, 12). Jesus answered, "You say so," and then remained silent. In Scene One, the high priest and the entire Sanhedrin mocked Jesus as a prophet (14:65). In Scene Two, Pilate's soldiers mocked him as the "King of the Jews!" (15:16-19).

The alternating pattern, so prominent in Act I, continues but is quite different in Act II. In place of a succession of short episodes, Act II contains two major episodes, both of which belong to the main story line. The first contains "tragic" elements but is basically a "gospel" story (see 14:3-9, 12-16, 22-26, 32-42), in which Jesus proclaims his identity and Peter, after denying Jesus, repents of his denial (14:53-72). The second contains "gospel" elements but is basically a "tragic" story (see 14:1-2, 10-11, 17-21, 27-31, 43-52). It tells of Jesus' trial and condemnation by Pilate (15:1-20).

Act III of Jesus' passion-resurrection tells of Jesus' crucifixion (15:21-32), death (15:33-41), burial (15:42-47), and a visit to the tomb by some women who had followed Jesus from Galilee (16:1-8). It opens with Jesus' "way of the cross" (15:21; see 15:20b). It ends with a group of women fleeing the tomb, "saying nothing to anyone, for they were afraid" (16:8).

Like Acts I and II, Act III can be divided into two scenes. The first unfolds from the third to the ninth hour at a place called Golgotha (15:21-41). The second begins in the evening, the day before the sabbath, and continues in the morning, when the sabbath was over, at the tomb of Jesus (15:42–16:8).

As the climax of the passion-resurrection according to Mark, Act III moves quickly, presenting the sequence of events simply and objectively, with no description of how Jesus suffered or how others reacted to his suffering. The passion-resurrection is not a matter of feeling and emotion. Its significance transcends every other consideration.

None of the disciples who played a role in Acts I and II have a part in Act III. The disciples and Peter are referred to by a young man in the tomb (16:7), but they have no role in the actual story. The chief priests and the scribes, who were prominent from the start (14:1-2), make their final appearance in Scene One (15:31-32). Of those who had a role in the passion to this point, only Pilate, who was introduced in Act II, reappears in Scene Two in the story of the burial of Jesus.

Act III contains many new personages, including a certain Simon, the Cyrenian who carried Jesus' cross (15:21), two revolutionaries, who were crucified with Jesus (15:27), Joseph of Arimathea, a distinguished member of the council *(bouleute),* who laid him in a tomb (15:43), and a young man (see 14:51-52), who proclaimed the resurrection of "Jesus of Nazareth, the crucified" (16:5-7).

A major role is given to a group of women, mentioned at the end of Scene One: Mary Magdalene, Mary the mother of the younger James and Joses, Salome, and many others who came up with him to Jerusalem. These women had followed Jesus in Galilee and ministered to him (15:40-41; see also 15:47; 16:1-8).

The alternation of "gospel" and "tragic" stories, much attenuated in Act II, just about disappears in Act III, where every personage is symbolic and every episode laden with "gospel" symbolism. A remnant of the tragic line may be seen in Scene One, the story of Jesus' crucifixion (15:21-32) and death (15:33-41), but it is all but overwhelmed by transparent irony, with references to Scripture and traditional gospel expressions.

Scene One (15:21-41) presents Jesus' crucifixion (15:21-32) and death (15:33-41). Crucified as "The King of the Jews," Jesus died as the "Son of God" (15:39). The scene ends by introducing the group of women who followed Jesus in Galilee and all the way to Golgotha (15:40-41).

Scene Two (15:42–16:8) tells of Jesus' burial (15:42-47) and the women's visit to the tomb (16:1-8). Jesus was buried by Joseph of Arimathea, a distinguished member of the council, "who was himself awaiting the kingdom of God" (15:43). Some of the women (see 15:40-41) were there, watching where Jesus was laid (15:47). After the sabbath, they went to the tomb, where they were greeted by a young man proclaiming Jesus' resurrection and giving them a message for the disciples and Peter (16:5-7).

As envisioned by Mark, Scene Two (14:42–16:8), the passion-resurrection (14:1–16:8), and "the beginning of the gospel of Jesus Christ [the Son of God]" (1:1) ended with the women running away from the tomb, saying "nothing to anyone, for they were afraid" (16:8; see 14:51-52).

The ending did not provide the Gospel with closure, leaving its readers wondering and pondering. That is because the story was not over. Mark told only the beginning of the Gospel. The continuation, in which the disciples and Peter would again play a great part, still lay in the future.

The Gospel would continue in the life of the Church through the Markan community and those who would follow them. The fear and the silence of the women spoke to the Christians in Mark's community, who said "nothing to anyone, for they were afraid" (16:8).

The Way of the Cross (15:21)

Mocking Jesus, the soldiers had dressed him in royal purple. They also wove a crown of thorns and placed it on his head (15:17). When they finished mocking him, "they stripped him of the purple cloak, dressed him in his own clothes, and led him out to crucify him" (15:20). So ended the trial at the palace of Pilate and the mockery by the soldiers in the praetorium.

The last statement, "they led him out to crucify him," also introduces the way of the cross.[78] Mark did not dwell on Jesus' way of the cross,[79] as popular piety in the Christian West has done since the thirteenth century. Today's spirituality of the way of the cross was inspired and influenced by a long tradition of pilgrimages to Jerusalem for Holy Week.[80]

For Mark, Jesus' way *(hodos)* of the cross began when he set out for the villages of Caesarea Philippi. That is when Jesus first announced that, as the Christ, the Son of Man "must suffer greatly and be rejected by the elders, the chief priests, and the scribes, and be killed, and rise after three days" (8:31). That is also when he told the crowd: "Whoever wishes to come after me must deny himself, take up his cross [*arato ton stauron autou*], and follow me" (8:34).

Jesus' way of the cross is set out throughout 8:22–10:52, where Mark relates it to the opening of the eyes in faith (8:22-26; 10:46-52), the following of Christ (8:34-38), baptism and the Eucharist (10:38-39), and many other aspects of Christian life. For Mark, the

---

[78] In the Synoptics, the way of the cross features the part played by Simon of Cyrene. See Brian K. Blount, "A Socio-Rhetorical Analysis of Simon of Cyrene: Mark 15:21 and its Parallels," *Semeia* 64 (1993) 171–98.

[79] Like Mark, Matthew and John did not dwell on Jesus' way of the cross (Matt 27:32; John 19:17). Only Luke told of Jesus' way of the cross in greater detail (Luke 23:26-32), in keeping with Luke-Acts' interest in the journey theme. After mentioning Simon of Cyrene, Luke also tells of those who followed Jesus, notably some women, on his way of the cross. He also included the two revolutionaries who were led away with him to be crucified.

[80] The tradition of pilgrimages to Jerusalem can be traced to the 4th century. The most famous account is that of Egeria, who came on pilgrimage *circa* 384 (381–84), arriving two weeks before Easter. The earliest account is that of the Pilgrim of Bordeaux, who came in 333, while the Church of the Holy Sepulchre was still under construction. Begun in 326, the Church of the Holy Sepulchre, commemorating the resurrection of Jesus (the *Anastasis*) was dedicated in the year 335. See *Corpus Christianorum, Series Latina* CLXXV. *Itineraria et Alia Geographica* (Turnholti: Brepols, 1965); for the Pilgrim of Bordeaux, 1–26; for the journal of Egeria *(Itinerarium Egeriae)* 37–90.

way of the cross was a life journey, a journey to Jerusalem to Christ's passion and resurrection (10:32-34). Jesus' entry into Jerusalem and his teaching in the Temple (11:1–13:37), as well as the events of Jesus' passion, burial, and resurrection (14:1–16:8), are also part of Mark's way of the cross.

At this point in the way of the cross, with Jesus being led to Golgotha for crucifixion, Mark says extremely little about Jesus. Instead he speaks of a certain Simon, a Cyrenian,[81] whom they pressed into service to take up the cross of Jesus *(hina are ton stauron autou)*. Mark does not say why Jesus did not personally carry the cross.[82] In light of 8:34, Mark introduces Simon, who was pressed into service to carry the cross of Jesus, as a personal symbol of a follower who was forced to carry his or her cross.

The way Mark introduced Simon as "a passerby, Simon, a Cyrenian" *(paragonta tina Simona Kyrenaion),* shows he did not expect his readers to know Simon personally.[83] By adding, however, that Simon was "the father of Alexander and Rufus," he shows that he expected his readers to know Simon's two sons.

Alexander and Rufus may even have been members of the Markan community. But all we know for certain about them is that they enabled Mark's intended readers and the Markan community to situate Simon, the Cyrenian, who carried the cross of Jesus.

[81] Cyrene, now Shahhat in Libya, was the capital of the Roman province of Cyrenaica on the northern coast of Africa. The designation "Cyrenian" could refer either to the province or to its capital. Acts 6:9 mentions Cyrenian and Alexandrian Jews, along with Jews from Cilicia and Asia, among the members of the Synagogue of Freedmen in Jerusalem. Cyrenians also had an important role in the development of the early Church. They were among the first to preach the gospel to Greeks (Gentiles) as well as Jews in Antioch (Acts 11:19-20). Later, Lucius of Cyrene is mentioned among the prophets and teachers at Antioch, together with Barnabas, Symeon who was called Niger, Manaen who was a close friend of Herod, the tetrarch, and Saul (13:1).

[82] John may have had Mark or the Markan tradition in mind when he wrote: "So they took Jesus, and carrying the cross himself he went out to what is called the Place of the Skull, in Hebrew, Golgotha" (John 19:17).

[83] Like Mark, Matthew and Luke did not expect their readers to know Simon. Introducing him, Luke stayed close to Mark: "a certain Simon, a Cyrenian" *(Simona tina Kyrenaion,* 23:26). Matthew introduced Simon as "a Cyrenian [man] named Simon" *(anthropon Kyrenaion onomati Simona,* 27:32).

The Crucifixion (15:22-27)

As he did for "the way of the cross," Mark describes the crucifixion very simply, without dwelling on Jesus' sufferings, which must have been terrible. Nor does he describe the personal reactions of those who crucified him. Avoiding any such considerations, he eliminated anything that could have distracted from the significance of Jesus' suffering. The mockery scene itself, the third in Mark's passion, focuses on Jesus' mission as savior, Messiah, and King of Israel (15:29-32; see 14:65; 15:17-20), rather than on the insults made to him.[84]

The Place of Golgotha (15:22). They bring Jesus to the place of Golgotha, which, as Mark explains, means "Place of the Skull" (15:22). Having led Jesus out to crucify him (15:20b), they bring him to Golgotha. Throughout the crucifixion, Mark uses the historic present: "they lead Jesus out," "they bring him to the place of Golgotha," "they crucify him," "they divide up his clothes," "they crucify two revolutionaries." As Mark tells it, the sequence of events becomes extremely vivid, as though the crucifixion were taking place before our very eyes.

Golgotha is a Greek transliteration of the Aramaic name *Gulgulta'*, meaning Skull. In Hebrew, the name would be *Gulgulit*. As Mark indicates, the place of Golgotha *(Golgotha topos)* can be translated as "Place of the Skull" *(Kraniou Topos)*. In the Latin Vulgate, the Greek *Kraniou Topos* is translated as *Calvariae locus,* from which our English name "Calvary" is derived.

The place of Golgotha was an outcropping of rock left in a long abandoned quarry outside the walls of Jerusalem. In the Hellenistic and Roman world, as in the biblical world, executions and burials were not allowed inside the city walls. Some ten years after Jesus' crucifixion, King Agrippa (A.D. 41–44) built a new wall, enlarging the walled city and including Golgotha and the area surrounding it within the city. Today Golgotha stands within the entrance of the Church of the Holy Sepulchre, a short distance from the great rotunda of the Resurrection (the *Anastasis*) built by Constantine.

Of itself, Golgotha may or may not have looked like a skull. Its use as a place of execution, however, may have reminded people of a skull. Hence the name, Place of the Skull.

---

[84] For a redactional study of Jesus' crucifixion and death, see Theodore J. Weeden, Sr., "The Cross as Power in Weakness (Mark 15:20b-41)," *The Passion in Mark, Studies on Mark 14–16,* edited by Werner H. Kelber (Philadelphia: Fortress Press, 1976) 115–34. For a historical critical study of Mark in relation to the other Gospels and a comprehensive bibliography, see Raymond Brown, *The Death of the Messiah* (New York: Doubleday, 1994) 2:884–1198.

Wine Mixed with Myrrh (15:23). Once at Golgotha, before crucifying Jesus, they gave him drugged wine, wine mixed with myrrh, an aromatic, bitter gum resin (15:23a). As we read in the book of Proverbs:

> Give strong drink to one who is perishing,
>   and wine to the sorely depressed;
> When they drink, they will forget their misery,
>   and think no more of their burdens (31:6-7).

It was customary, indeed common wisdom, to give one who was dying some drugged wine to alleviate the suffering. In light of Proverbs 31:6-7, offering a strong drink would have been an act of mercy. Mark's account, however, obviates any show of compassion on the part of those who put Jesus to death. Instead Mark may have had Psalm 69:22 in mind: "Instead they put gall in my food, / for my thirst they gave me vinegar" (see John 19:28-30).

Jesus, however, did not take the drugged wine (15:23b). We recall the solemn pronouncement he made at the Last Supper: "Amen, I say to you, I shall not drink again the fruit of the vine until the day when I drink it new in the kingdom of God" (14:25). Paradoxically, by refusing the drugged wine, Jesus was accepting the conditions of the prayer he spoke at Gethsemane, namely, to drink fully the cup of the passion if that were his Father's will.[85]

They Crucified Him (15:24a). After that, they crucify Jesus. The statement could hardly be more stark—"Then they crucified him" (15:24a)—with not the least effort to describe the crucifixion. Even the manner of crucifixion is left out. One need not have been nailed to the cross. One could have been attached to the cross by ropes. From Mark alone, we would not know for sure that Jesus was nailed to the cross.

We first learn about the nails from John, after Jesus' resurrection, in the story of Thomas: "Unless I see the mark of the nails in his hands and put my finger into the nailmarks and put my hand into his side, I will not believe" (John 20:25; see also 20:27). Luke seems to have implied the use of nails when the risen Lord appeared to the community assembled in Jerusalem: "Look at my hands and my feet, that it is I myself" (Luke 24:38).

After they crucify Jesus, they divide up his garments, leaving us to understand they stripped Jesus anew. We recall that after mocking

---

[85] See Augustine Stock, O.S.B., *The Method and Message of Mark* (Wilmington, Del.: Michael Glazier, 1989) 399.

him, they "stripped him of the purple cloak" and "dressed him in his own clothes" before they "led him out to crucify him" (15:20b). They "divided his garments by casting lots for them to see what each should take" (15:24b).

By noting how and why they divided Jesus' garments, Mark invites us to see Jesus' crucifixion in light of Psalm 22:

> Indeed, many dogs surround me,
>   a pack of evildoers closes in upon me;
> They have pierced my hands and my feet;
>   I can count all my bones.
> They look on and gloat over me;
>   they divide my garments among them,
>   and for my vesture they cast lots (Ps 22:17-19).[86]

But if Mark wanted to refer to Psalm 22, why did he not quote, or at least allude to, the "many dogs," the "pack of evildoers," surrounding him (Ps 22:17)? In the prologue, had he not presented Jesus' baptismal life as among wild beasts (see 1:13)? Why did he not refer to the piercing of his hands and his feet (Ps 22:18)? Why refer to their dividing his garments?

A person's garments were symbolic of the person's person. What would the soldiers do with Jesus' garments? Could it be Mark was suggesting, ironically, that they wanted to put on Christ (see 10:46-52; 14:51-52; 16:5-7)? In that case, they would be like Simon of Cyrene, modeling, unwittingly and ironically, what it meant to be a follower of Christ.

The Third Hour (15:25). Returning to Jesus' crucifixion, Mark notes that "it was nine o'clock in the morning when they crucified him" (15:25). By indicating the time, literally "the third hour," which corresponds to 9:00 a.m., Mark may have been influenced by the Christian hours of prayer on the anniversary of Jesus' crucifixion and death.

The *Didache* refers to the Christian practice of praying three times a day (*Didache* 8:3). On Good Friday these may have corresponded to the third, the sixth, and the ninth hours. If so, the Markan community may have been commemorating the corresponding event, as presented by Mark. If so, Mark told the story of Jesus' crucifixion and death through the lens of its commemoration in Christian prayer and contemplation.

---

[86] The text of Psalm 22:19 is actually quoted in John 19:24.

The Inscription (15:26). Mark adds that there was an inscription giving the charge against Jesus: "The King of the Jews" (15:26). Such an inscription was a normal part of the process of crucifixion, which was a public event. While carrying the cross, the one condemned carried the inscription around his neck. On the cross, he continued to wear the inscription until he was taken down.

From the point of view of those who condemned Jesus, the charge was meant in mockery, both of Jesus and of those who arrested him and demanded his crucifixion. As we read in John's Gospel, the chief priests protested the inscription: "Do not write 'The King of the Jews,' but that he said, 'I am the King of the Jews'" (John 19:21). From the point of view of Mark and his Christian readers, however, the charge was no charge at all. It was a proclamation. By offering his life and dying on the cross Jesus was "The King of the Jews."

The Two Revolutionaries (15:27). The mention of the inscription is part of the crucifixion account. At the same time, it acts as a transition, announcing the third mockery of Jesus. The same is true for the indication that "with him they crucified two revolutionaries, one on his right and one on his left" (15:27). The two revolutionaries who were crucified "with him" *(syn auto)* are part of the crucifixion scene. At the same time, associating Jesus with the two revolutionaries also announces the mockery that follows (15:29-32).

As part of the crucifixion scene, the revolutionaries evoke the request of the apostles James and John: "Grant that in your glory we may sit one at your right and the other at your left" (10:37). In response, Jesus asked: "Can you drink the cup that I drink or be baptized with the baptism with which I am baptized?"

Like Simon of Cyrene, and like the soldiers who divided Jesus' garments by casting lots to see what each should take, the two revolutionaries crucified with Jesus *(syn auto)* indicate what it means to be a follower of Christ. Jesus' followers take up their cross in view of being crucified with him.

The Mockery (15:29-32)

The remainder of the story of the crucifixion of Jesus describes the third and climactic mockery of Jesus (15:29-32).[87] After interrogat-

---

[87] Verse 15:28 would read, "And the scripture was fulfilled that says, 'And he was counted among the wicked.'" The verse is absent from the best manuscripts. As Bruce M. Metzger indicates in *A Textual Commentary on the Greek New Testament* (New York: United Bible Societies, 1971), "The

ing Jesus, the chief priests, the elders, and the scribes joined the high priest and his palace guard in mocking Jesus: "Some began to spit on him. They blindfolded him and struck him, 'Prophesy!' And the guards greeted him with blows" (14:65). At the palace of the high priest, they mocked Jesus as a prophet.

Then, after Pilate interrogated Jesus and "handed him over to be crucified," the soldiers, the whole cohort at the praetorium, mocked Jesus. They clothed him in purple, placed a crown of thorns on his head, saluted him as "the King of the Jews." Spitting on him, they knelt down before him in homage (15:16-20). At the palace of Pilate, they mocked Jesus as the King of the Jews.

The third mockery comes after Jesus' crucifixion. In a sense, it began at the end of the crucifixion proper, with the mention of the inscription and of the two revolutionaries crucified with Jesus (15:26-27). This third time, those who mock Jesus include those simply passing by, once again the chief priests and the scribes, and the two revolutionaries who were crucified with him. At the palace of Jesus, before the throne of the cross, they mocked Jesus as the savior.

Those Passing by (15:29-30). As told by Mark, the mockery was conducted in orderly fashion. First came those passing by, who "reviled him, shaking their heads and saying, 'Aha! You who would destroy the temple and rebuild it in three days, save yourself by coming down from the cross'" (15:29-30). Those passing by *(hoi paraporeuomenoi)* and wagging their heads *(kenountes tas kephalas),* like the soldiers who divided Jesus' garments (15:24), are described in terms of Psalm 22:

> But I am a worm, hardly human,
>> scorned by everyone, despised by the people.
> All who see me mock me;
>> they curl their lips and jeer;
>> they shake their heads at me (Ps 22:7-8).

Their mockery may also evoke Psalm 35, a prayer for salvation against unjust enemies:

> Lord, how long will you look on?
>> Save me from roaring beasts,
>> my precious life from lions! . . .

_____

earliest and best witnesses of the Alexandrian and the Western types of text lack ver. 28. It is understandable that copyists could have added the sentence in the margin from Lk 22.37, whence it came into the text itself," 119.

Do no let lying foes smirk at me;
  my undeserved foes wink knowingly. . . .
They open wide their mouths against me.
They say, "Aha! Good! Our eyes relish the sight!" (Ps 35:17, 19, 21).

Those passing by did not only revile Jesus, they actually blasphemed him *(eblasphemoun auton)*. We recall that before the Sanhedrin Jesus himself was condemned as deserving to die for blaspheming (14:64). We also recall that some in the Sanhedrin testified falsely, alleging, "We heard him say, 'I will destroy this temple made with hands and within three days I will build another not made with hands'" (14:59). Those passing by now use the same false testimony, taunting Jesus to save himself by coming down from the cross.

They surely meant to mock Jesus. For Mark and his Christian readers, however, their taunt was full of irony. By remaining on the cross to the end, Jesus was fulfilling the false testimony used to condemn him. We also recall Jesus' words to the crowd and his disciples: "For whoever wishes to save his life will lose it, but whoever loses his life for my sake and that of the gospel will save it" (8:35). At the cross, the mocking taunt of those passing by had serious implications for all those who came after Christ, denied themselves, took up his cross, and followed him (8:34).

The Chief Priests and the Scribes (15:31). After those passing by came the chief priests and the scribes, who mocked Jesus among themselves (see 15:31). In their mockery, they continued with the same theme of salvation: "He saved others; he cannot save himself. Let the Messiah, the King of Israel, come down now from the cross that we may see and believe." Pilate had called Jesus, "the King of the Jews," that is, the king of the people of Judea, situating him politically. The chief priests and the scribes refer to him as "the king of Israel," situating Jesus in biblical perspective and the history of salvation.

The chief priests and the scribes referred to Jesus' great saving acts in the course of his gospel ministry when he silenced and expelled unclean spirits and healed people of various illnesses, some of them long-standing. In the synagogue at Capernaum, there had been a demoniac (1:21-28), in the home of Simon and Andrew, there was Simon's mother-in-law (1:29-31), and at the gate many others whom Jesus healed (1:32-35). Later, away from Capernaum, there was a leper whom Jesus told to go and show himself to the priests (1:40-45), and a paralytic back in the synagogue at Capernaum (2:1-12).

Even more important, there had been Jairus' daughter and a woman afflicted with hemorrhages for twelve years (5:21-43). Jesus asked Jairus to have faith (5:36). After curing the afflicted woman, he said to her: "Daughter, your faith has saved you" (5:34). Later, to the father of a boy possessed by a violent demon, he said: "Everything is possible to one who has faith" (9:23).

The chief priests and the scribes did not understand. Faith, faithful trust in God, leads to salvation. By remaining on the cross, Jesus gave the finest possible example of faith. Jesus had saved others through faith, through their own faith and the faith of those close to them. He himself would be saved by remaining faithful to the end on the cross.

That is how he also showed himself the Messiah, the Christ and the King of Israel. On the cross, Jesus was fulfilling his mission. As the chief priests and the scribes said in mockery, Jesus had saved others. They were referring to his ministry. They could not see that Jesus, suffering faithfully on the cross, surpassed all his previous acts of salvation.

Those Crucified with Jesus (15:32). After the chief priests and the scribes, even those who were crucified with Jesus mocked him. Like the others, "they kept abusing him" (15:32b). Those who were crucified with Jesus symbolize the challenge of all those who come after Jesus, deny themselves, take up their cross (8:34), all those who save themselves by losing their lives for the sake of Jesus and the gospel (8:35).

For that symbolism, however, one has to see and accept crucifixion as integral to the following of Christ. For those who do not, the two revolutionaries become a symbol of Christians, who may be in the midst of their passion but do not recognize that it is their passion.

Such Christians may be crucified with Christ, but they do not grasp the significance of their suffering. Like the young man who abandoned his Christian garment when Jesus was arrested (14:51-52), and like Simon of Cyrene who was forced to carry Jesus' cross (15:20), they reflect the situation of many in the Markan community.

Those following Jesus must drink his cup and be baptized with his baptism (10:38-39; 14:23-24). They must be crucified with Christ (15:32). With Jesus, the Christ, they must serve and give their life as a ransom for many (10:43-45).

The Death of Jesus (15:33-41)

"It was nine o'clock in the morning [*hora trite*] when they crucified" Jesus (15:25). For us, that would be nine o'clock in the morning, Good Friday. For the early Christians, it was the hour of morning prayer (see *Didache* 8:3), the anniversary of Jesus' death, when they united themselves with Jesus as he was crucified.

At the sixth hour *(hora hecte),* "darkness came over the whole land" (15:33). For us, that would be twelve noon, Good Friday. For the early Christians, it was the hour of midday prayer, the anniversary of Jesus' death, when they joined him as he defeated the power of darkness.

At the ninth hour *(hora enate),* when the darkness lifted, "Jesus cried out in a loud voice," praying, *"Eloi, Eloi, lema sabachthani?"* (15:34), "and breathed his last" (15:37). For us, that would be three o'clock in the afternoon, Good Friday. For the early Christians, it was the hour of afternoon prayer, the anniversary of Jesus' death, when they joined Jesus in his cry of confidence, praying with him the words of Psalm 22.[88]

When Jesus cried out, *"Eloi, Eloi, lema sabachthani?"* some of the bystanders responded mockingly, "Look, he is calling Elijah" (15:35). Prolonging the mockery, one of them offered Jesus a sponge soaked with wine (15:36). But Jesus completed his cry, *"Eloi, Eloi,"* and breathed his last (15:37).

With Jesus' death, the veil of the sanctuary tore from top to bottom (15:38), and the centurion confessed Jesus as the Son of God (15:39).

The story of Jesus' death concludes with a reference to some women who were looking on from a distance (15:40). These women had followed Jesus in Galilee and ministered to him (15:41a). Besides them, there were "many other women who had come up with him to Jerusalem" (15:41b).

Like the crucifixion (15:22-32), Jesus' death (15:33-41) is dramatically told, as a symbolic, rapid-fire sequence of events, with very little elaboration. But at the same time, the story of Jesus' death is quite different from that of the crucifixion.

In the story of Jesus' crucifixion (15:21-32) the primary focus was not on Jesus, but on the soldiers, who crucified him (15:22-26), and those who mocked him as the Messiah (the Christ), the Savior-King of Israel (15:29-32). The story focused also on Simon of Cyrene (15:21) and two revolutionaries (15:27, 32b), presenting these as symbols of those who would follow Jesus, take up the cross (8:35),

[88] The hours Mark gives for the crucifixion, the coming of the darkness, and Jesus' final cry refer, at least in general, to the sequence of events in Jesus' passion. But to account for the specific hours noted, the third, the sixth, and the ninth, we should turn to the celebration of the passion in the early Church rather than to the historical event.

be baptized with the baptism of Jesus' passion, and drink the cup of his suffering (10:38-39).

In the story of Jesus' death (15:33-41), the primary focus is on Jesus himself and the cosmic and historic events accompanying his death. There are bystanders mocking Jesus (15:35-36), but their voice is all but overwhelmed by that of Jesus crying out in a loud voice, confident to the end (15:34, 37).[89] The cosmic and historic events include the darkness that came over the whole earth (15:33), the rending of the sanctuary veil (15:38), and the climactic confession by the centurion (15:39).

As the climax of the passion, the story of Jesus' death is linked with the whole passion and all that led up to it. With Jesus' death, the plot to destroy him seems to have succeeded. But once again, as we shall see, what might have been the tragedy of Jesus is transformed into gospel.

Jesus' death is linked in a special way with the crucifixion in the same temporal sequence, from the third hour (15:25), to the sixth (15:33), to the ninth (15:34). They are also linked with the offer of wine. Just before Jesus was crucified, they gave him wine drugged with myrrh (15:23). Just before Jesus died, they "soaked a sponge with wine, put it on a reed, and gave it to him to drink" (15:36).

Jesus' death, which ends by introducing a group of women (15:40-41), is also related to Jesus' burial (15:42-47) and the visit to the tomb (16:1-8). Some of the same women will be present later at Jesus' burial, that evening, the day before the sabbath (15:47). When the sabbath was over, some of the same women will return to the tomb, early in the morning on the first day of the week (16:1-8).

Darkness over the Earth (15:33). They crucified Jesus at the third hour (15:25). "With him they crucified two revolutionaries, one on his right and one on his left" (15:27). The crucifixion of the two evokes the request of James and John that one might sit at Jesus' right and the other at his left when he came into his glory (10:37). The time had come for Jesus to enter into his glory.

When they crucified Jesus, they mocked him as the Christ, the king and savior of Israel (15:29-32). Earlier, at the palace of the high priest, the chief priests, and the elders and the scribes had mocked him as prophet (14:65). At the palace of the Roman governor, Pilate, the soldiers had mocked Jesus as King of the Jews (15:17-20).

Jesus was a king, "the anointed one," in Hebrew, "the Messiah," in Greek, "the Christ." Jesus was anointed at the beginning of the pas-

---

[89] Jesus' crying out in a loud voice with Psalm 22 forms an *inclusio* (15:34, 37) framing the bystanders' mockery (15:35-36).

sion at the home of Simon the leper (14:3-9) by a woman who came with "an alabaster jar of perfumed oil, costly genuine spikenard" and poured it on his head (14:3). What the woman did was in view of Jesus' burial (14:8). Jesus was the "King of the Jews," as the inscription announced (14:26). Anointed, tried, and crucified, he was about to enter his kingdom.

It was now the sixth hour, twelve noon, and darkness came over the whole land. The darkness would remain until the ninth hour, three in the afternoon, when Jesus died (15:33). With Jesus' death, the darkness was lifted. The same is reported in Matthew 27:45 and Luke 23:44.

In itself, daytime darkness could have been a natural phenomenon, not uncommon at Passover time, when the prevailing winds in the eastern Mediterranean shift from west to east. The east winds, at first barely perceptible and extremely dry, are laden with particles of desert dust, at times so thick they obscure the sun.[90] In Deutero-Isaiah, these east winds are described as "the breath of the Lord" (Isa 40:7).

Mark also may have wanted to evoke an eclipse of the sun, though an eclipse could not have occurred naturally at Passover time (see 14:12), whose yearly celebration was set by the vernal equinox.

While using such images, however, Mark meant more than a natural event. The darkness filled the whole land from the sixth to the ninth hour. It began once Jesus was crucified and lasted the whole time Jesus was on the cross until the time of his death. Evoking natural phenomena, the darkness is surely symbolic, recalling Jesus' words in the eschatological discourse on the Mount of Olives:

> "But in those days after that tribulation
> the sun will be darkened,
>   and the moon will not give its light,
> and the stars will be falling from the sky,
>   and the powers in the heavens will be shaken" (Mark 13:24-25).

In the context of Mark's Gospel, the reference to the darkness that descended over the whole earth (15:33) evokes the whole statement (13:24-25) from Jesus' eschatological discourse along with its prophetic background in Isaiah 13:10; Ezekiel 32:7; and Joel 2:10. Mark thus associates Jesus' crucifixion with the great tribulation (see 13:14-23). The darkness that came once Jesus was

[90] In Arabic, the phenomenon is referred to as the *khamsin*. In Italy, a comparable phenomenon, with winds coming from North Africa, is called the *sirocco*.

crucified announces the eschatological moment when history and all of creation would be plunged into darkness (see 13:24-25).

The darkness also evoke these words from the prophet Amos:

> On that day, says the Lord GOD,
>   I will make the sun set at midday
>   and cover the earth with darkness in broad daylight.
> I will turn your feasts into mourning
>   and all your songs into lamentations.
> I will cover the loins of all with sackcloth
>   and make every head bald.
> I will make them mourn as for an only son,
>   and bring their day to a bitter end (Amos 8:9-10).

Jesus' crucifixion was a cosmic event! Even the sun hid its face, mourning for "an only son" (Amos 8:10), God's only son (see 1:1, 11; 9:8), preparing the reader for the centurion's confession: "Truly this man was the son of God!" (15:39).

With the crucifixion of Jesus, the sun was indeed darkened! But the darkness would lift at the ninth hour, three in the afternoon, when Jesus died. The sixth hour was the hour of darkness. The ninth hour, when Jesus died, was the hour of salvation.

Jesus Cried Out in a Loud Voice (15:34). At the ninth hour, the darkness that came over the whole land lifted, and Jesus cried out *(eboesen),* as John the Baptist once cried out, "a voice of one crying out [*boontos*] in the desert" (1:3; see Isa 40:3). Jesus cried out in a loud voice *(phone megale),* as unclean spirits cried out in the presence of Jesus (1:26; 5:7).

John's cry was to "prepare the way of the Lord." The unclean spirits' cried out in defiance and defeat before Jesus, "the Holy One of God" (1:24), the "Son of the Most High God" (5:7). Jesus' cry announces his triumph over the forces of evil and the fulfillment of his mission.[91]

In a loud voice *(phone megale),* strong, firm, and clear, Jesus cried out the opening words of Psalm 22. Mark gives the verse in Aramaic: *Eloi, eloi lema sabachthani* (Ps 22:2).[92] Some years later, the

---

[91] Focusing on the words the historical Jesus cried out before he died, many commentators interpreted Jesus' cry as one of despair. The same commentators also saw the psalm's opening words apart from their function as a title for the psalm. Focusing on Mark's literary point of view, we see Jesus' words as a gospel proclamation. In relation to the rest of the psalm, they also become a prayer of deep trust.

[92] On four previous occasions, Aramaic expressions were attributed to Jesus: *"Talitha koum"* (5:41), *"qorban"* (7:11), *"Ephphata"* (7:34), *"Abba"*

Gospel of Matthew would have Jesus crying the same words, but in their original Hebrew.[93]

In Jesus' cry, the opening words of Psalm 22 are meant to evoke the entire psalm.[94] As such, the cry does not portray Jesus as abandoned by God but as abandoning himself into the arms of God.

The psalm begins with a lamentation (Ps 22:2-22). God seems very far away: "My God, I call by day, but you do not answer" (Ps 22:3). Still, the psalmist turns to God in trusting faith:

> Yet you are enthroned as the Holy One;
>   you are the glory of Israel.
> In you our ancestors trusted;
>   they trusted and you rescued them.
> To you they cried out and they escaped;
>   in you they trusted and were not disappointed (Ps 22:4-6).

Scorned and despised, mocked and humanly abandoned, the psalmist is confident that God will hear his cry:

> But you, LORD, do not stay far off;
>   my strength, come quickly to help me.
> Deliver me from the sword,
>   my forlorn life from the teeth of the dog.
> Save me from the lion's mouth,
>   my poor life from the horns of wild bulls (Ps 22:20-22).

With verse 23, what began as a lamentation becomes a song of praise and thanksgiving. The psalmist is at peace:

> Then I will proclaim your name to the assembly;
>   in the community I will praise you:
> "You who fear the LORD, give praise!
>   All descendants of Jacob, give honor;
>   show reverence, all descendants of Israel!
> For God has not spurned or disdained
>   the misery of this poor wretch,

(14:36). This is the first time Jesus quotes Scripture in Aramaic. Aside from these, Mark's Gospel includes three other Aramaic terms, *Boanerges* (3:17), *Hosanna* (11:9, 10), and *Golgotha* (15:22). Except for *Hosanna,* Mark always provides a translation in Greek.

[93] The Hebrew in Matthew is very close to the Aramaic in Mark, with *Eli Eli* replacing *Eloi Eloi* and *lama* instead of *lema.*

[94] For a commentary on Psalm 22, see Carroll Stuhlmueller, *Psalm I (1–72),* Old Testament Message, vol. 21 (Collegeville: The Liturgical Press, 1983) 144–51.

Did not turn away from me,
　　but heard me when I cried out" (Ps 22:23-25).

In a second song, the psalmist's praise and thanksgiving look beyond Israel to include the Gentiles:

All the ends of the earth
　　will worship and turn to the LORD;
All the families of nations
　　will bow low before you (Ps 22:28).

In the conclusion, the psalm looks to the future to include all generations to come:

The generation to come will be told of the Lord,
　　that they may proclaim to a people yet unborn
　　the deliverance you have brought (Ps 22:32).

It only appeared that God had abandoned Jesus. Through the opening words of Psalm 22, *Eloi eloi, lama sabachthani,* we see Jesus' death as a triumph. Jesus' cry is a prayer of lamentation, trusting faith, praise, and thanksgiving. It is also a proclamation. In dying, Jesus was vindicated.[95] His victory would be celebrated in song by all peoples, Jew and Gentile. In the story of Jesus' death, the cry, evoking the whole of Psalm 22, announces the centurion's profession of faith in Jesus the Son of God.

Jesus' cry and Psalm 22 also responded pastorally to the situation in Mark's community. The community had to accept the passion they were experiencing as Jesus accepted his own passion. The community was not abandoned by God. The passion challenged them to abandon themselves into the hands of God as Jesus did in his dying prayer.

Psalm 22, which had a liturgical setting in Israelite worship, must have retained a liturgical setting in early Christian worship. Evoked in the passion story, Psalm 22 helped the early Christians to understand and appreciate Jesus' passion and death. Conversely, the psalm itself, even apart from the passion, must have been read in its light. Psalm 22 situated the passion in biblical tradition, and the passion gave new meaning to Psalm 22.[96] That may explain the persistence of the Aramaic, which was used in the liturgical prayer

[95] See Donald Senior, *The Passion of Jesus in the Gospel of Mark* (Collegeville: The Liturgical Press, 1984) 123–24.

[96] Other references to Psalm 22 can be found in Mark 15:24 (see Psalm 22:19) and Mark 15:29 (see Psalm 22:8).

of the Markan community, at least at early stages of the community's development.[97]

As Mark did each time he quoted Jesus in Aramaic, he added a translation in Greek for the benefit of his Greek-speaking readers. Mark seems to be quoting from memory, approximating the version of the LXX. In our modern translations, the Aramaic is retained and the Greek is rendered in English: "My God, my God, why [*eis ti*] have you forsaken me?"

Rendering Jesus' Aramaic *lema* (why), by the Greek, *eis ti* (for what purpose), provides a precious interpretation of Jesus' intent. For Mark, Jesus' "why" is not a protest. Jesus is not questioning the will of God (see 14:36). Jesus is asking God to disclose the purpose for abandoning him to death, the purpose why he has been handed over (9:31).[98] The answer would be given at the moment of Jesus' death when the veil of the sanctuary was torn in two and a centurion would proclaim his identity as the Son of God (15:38-39).

"Look, He Is Calling Elijah" (15:35-36). Some of the bystanders *(ton parestoton)*[99] heard Jesus cry out in a loud voice, *"Eloi, Eloi, lema sabachthani"* (15:34). "Look," they said, "he is calling Elijah" (15:35). It is not that they misheard or misunderstood Jesus' words. Had Jesus cried out in Hebrew, *"Eli, Eli,"* that might have been possible, but in Mark, Jesus cried out in Aramaic, *"Eloi, Eloi,"* whose sounds do not suggest Elijah. Besides, after crying out, *"Eloi, Eloi,"* Jesus continued with *"lema sabachthani,"* all in a loud voice *(phone megale)*. As Mark indicates, the bystanders heard Jesus' cry. They must then have recognized the beginning of Psalm 22 and understood its implications in Jesus' prayer.[100]

The bystanders did not misunderstand. They heard Jesus' cry, "My God, my God, why have you forsaken me?" (15:34). When they said Jesus was calling for Elijah, it was in deliberate mockery.

At the palace of the high priest, some of the chief priests, the elders, the scribes, and the guards mocked Jesus as a prophet (14:65). At the palace of Pilate, the soldiers mocked him as King of the Jews (15:16-20). When they crucified Jesus, those passing by, the chief

[97] For the other Aramaic terms and phrases in Mark, see above, note 5.

[98] See John Paul Heil, "The Progressive Narrative Pattern of Mark 14,53–16,8," *Biblica* 73 (3, '92) 348–49.

[99] The perfect participle of the verb *paristemi* ("to stand by") has two forms, the one used here *(paristos)* and the one used for "one of the bystanders" *(parestekos)* when Jesus was arrested at Gethsemane (14:47).

[100] I base this conclusion on the literary viewpoint of Mark's Gospel, not on what the historical bystanders might have understood.

priests, their scribes, and those crucified with him, mocked Jesus as the savior, the Christ, the King of Israel (15:29-32). Finally, when Jesus was abandoning himself into the hands of God, the bystanders mocked him for his prayer of praise and thanksgiving, and his absolute confidence in God (15:35-36).

But in doing that, why did the bystanders refer to Elijah? To grasp their mockery and their reference to Elijah, we must distinguish the point of view of the bystanders, as presented by Mark, from the point of view of the narrator telling the story.

Some interpreters have pointed out that in early Jewish tradition, Elijah was seen as the patron of people in dire need.[101] On that basis, it may be that the bystanders meant to mock Jesus as a hopeless case. They certainly did not expect Elijah to come to his rescue.

From the narrator's point of view, there was surely more to their mockery. When Jesus came down from the mountain of the transfiguration, accompanied by Peter, James, and John, he had spoken to them of Elijah, who was expected to come and restore all things (9:12a) before the Son of Man had risen from the dead (9:9). At the time, Jesus raised a rhetorical question, "how is it written regarding the Son of Man that he must suffer greatly [*polla pathe*] and be treated with contempt [*exoudenethe*]?" (9:12b).

Ironically, the bystanders, treating Jesus with contempt, were fulfilling Jesus' prophetic announcement as it was written in Psalm 22:1-18 and in Isaiah's Song of the Suffering Servant, describing both his suffering and triumph (Isa 52:13–53:12; see 53:3).

Mocking Jesus, the bystanders did not know that Elijah had already come (9:13) in the person and mission of John the Baptist. "Clothed in camel's hair, with a leather belt around his waist" (1:6), John came as Elijah, God's messenger sent (1:2a; see Mal 3:1, 23) ahead of Jesus (1:2a; see 1:7 and Exod 23:20). He was sent to prepare his way (1:2b; see Isa 40:3), restoring all things (9:12a) before Jesus suffered greatly, was treated with contempt (9:12b).

In the person of John the Baptist, Elijah did not come to help those in dire, physical need. He came to prepare Jesus' way of suffering and death by his own suffering and death (see 6:14-29; 9:13).

One of the bystanders "ran, soaked a sponge with wine, put it on a reed, and gave it to him to drink" (15:36a). The bystander's mocking gesture of mercy was meant to prolong Jesus' misery and with

---

[101] See, for example, D. E. Nineham, *Saint Mark,* The Pelican Gospel Commentaries (Baltimore: Penguin Books, 1963) 429, and Josef Schmid, *The Gospel According to Mark,* The Regensburg New Testament, trans. by Kevin Condor (New York: Alba House, 1963) 296.

it their mockery. Interpreting his own gesture, he said, "Wait, let us see if Elijah comes to take him down" (15:36b). Like the other bystanders, he did not realize that Elijah had come as John the Baptist, and that his mission included his own death preparing the way for that of Jesus. Ironically, he was also fulfilling Psalm 69:22, "for my thirst they gave me vinegar."[102]

When they crucified Jesus, they mocked him as one who saved others but could not save himself (15:31): "Let the Messiah, the King of Israel, come down now from the cross that we may see and believe" (15:32). Jesus did not come down from the cross. Dying on the cross, Jesus fulfilled his mission. Nor would Elijah take him down. Elijah's coming in the person and mission of John the Baptist was to prepare Jesus' mission, not to abort it.

Jesus' prophetic announcement and the Scriptures were fulfilled. Suffering greatly, the Son of Man was treated with contempt (9:12b). Jesus completed his triumphant cry, continuing to evoke Psalm 22 in a loud voice *(phone megale)*. With that, Jesus breathed his last (15:37).

"Jesus . . . Breathed His Last" (15:37). The entire Gospel has been building up to this point. Then, with a few, simple words, it was over: "Jesus gave a loud cry and breathed his last" (15:37). It is hard to imagine that the story of Jesus' final moment could have been more stark. Immediately following it, we sense a great silence. Further elaboration would have detracted from the event. The implications of Jesus' death, however, were awesome.

Jesus' death was followed by two major, symbolic events, giving the effects of Jesus' death for the history of salvation:

> The veil of the sanctuary was torn in two
>   from top to bottom (15:38).

> When the centurion who stood facing him
>   saw how he breathed his last he said,
> "Truly this man was the Son of God!" (15:39).

Together with Jesus' death (15:34-37), the two constitute the theological climax of the passion, indeed, of the whole gospel. Jesus had asked: "My God, my God, why have you forsaken me?" The two events provide the answer.

Apart from Jesus' death, neither event would make sense. Apart from one another, the same would be true. The tearing of the veil of

---

[102] Like Psalm 22, Psalm 69 is a psalm of lamentation to which the early Christians frequently referred in telling the story of Jesus' passion.

the sanctuary is intimately related to the centurion's confession. Together, the two events proclaim the meaning of Jesus' death.

The tearing of the veil of the sanctuary shows the effect of Jesus' death for Israel, the chosen people, its long history, and its central institution, the Temple, and its priesthood. The Temple, with its Holy of Holies, was a symbol for everything Israel stood for as a people set apart. When Jesus died, the veil of the sanctuary was torn from top to bottom, putting an end to the sanctuary (15:29) which was made with human hands (14:58).

The centurion's proclamation, "Truly this man was the Son of God," shows the effect of Jesus' death for the Gentiles, once separated from the sanctuary by the veil, now invited into the sanctuary together with the Jews. Dying, Jesus opened the way for the Gentiles to pray in the Temple Jesus rebuilt in three days (15:29), one not made with human hands (14:58).

The tearing of the veil of the sanctuary marked the end of an era in the history of salvation. The centurion's proclamation marked the beginning of a new era, in which the house of God would "be called a house of prayer for all peoples" (11:17; see Isa 56:7).

The Veil of the Sanctuary (15:38). Scholars have long debated about which veil the story refers to. Was it the veil separating the Holy of Holies from the Holy Place, the one described in Exodus 26:31-33?

> You shall have a veil woven of violet, purple and scarlet yarn, and of fine linen twined, with cherubim embroidered on it. It is to be hung on four gold-plated columns of acacia wood, which shall have hooks of gold and shall rest on four silver pedestals. Hang the veil from clasps. The ark of the commandments you shall bring inside, behind this veil which divides the holy place from the holy of holies (see also Exod 36:35-36).

Or was it the veil at the entrance to the Holy Place, the one described in Exodus 26:36-37, separating the entire sanctuary from the surrounding areas where the people gathered?

> For the entrance of the tent make a variegated curtain of violet, purple and scarlet yarn and of fine linen twined. Make five columns of acacia wood for this curtain, have them plated with gold, with their hooks of gold; and cast five bronze pedestals for them (see also Exod 36:37-38).

In the story of Jesus' death, Mark does not specify. For an answer, we look to the larger gospel context.

From the point of view of the Temple's relation to Israelite and Jewish history, the veil in question seems to be the one at the entrance of the Holy of Holies, where only the high priest entered, and only once a year. The tearing of the veil would thus dissolve the distinction between Israel's priestly caste and the people. Christological considerations lead to the same conclusion, since in dying and rising, Jesus replaced the entire Temple, including its Holy of Holies, with his very person.

From the point of view of the Temple's relation to the rest of the human race, that is, to the Gentiles, and their place in the history of salvation, the veil in question seems to be the one separating the whole sanctuary from the surrounding areas. Ecclesiological considerations lead to the same conclusion, since Jesus' dying and rising, the climax of his mission opened the sanctuary to the Gentiles.

We recall that the two veils described in Exodus 26 and 36 were meant for a tent, which would be God's special Dwelling while Israel wandered in the desert. For the building of the Temple by Solomon, 2 Chronicles refers only to one veil, the one separating the Holy of Holies from the Holy Place (2 Chr 3:14). For the entrance to the Holy Place, Chronicles does not refer to a veil but to doors (2 Chr 4:22), as 1 Kings does both for the entrance to the Holy of Holies and for the entrance to the Holy Place (1 Kgs 6:31-35).

It may be, therefore, that Mark may not have distinguished one veil from the other as described for the Dwelling in Exodus. The veil of the sanctuary would then be symbolic of the entire old sanctuary. When Jesus entered the Temple for the first time, it was indeed late for the Temple (11:11).

Now, torn in two from top to bottom, the veil proclaimed the end of the old sanctuary and proclaimed the new, as announced by Jesus in the symbolic cleansing of the Temple when he returned to Jerusalem with the Twelve (11:15-19). As the new Temple, a house for all peoples, Jesus welcomed both Jews and Gentiles.

The Centurion Facing Him (15:39). In the tearing of the veil of the sanctuary, Jesus' question, "My God, my God, why [*eis ti*] have you forsaken me?" received a first answer. The reason Jesus was handed over (9:31) was to destroy the Temple, bringing it to fulfillment in his very person. The centurion's confession, proclaiming Jesus as the Son of God (15:39), completes the answer. The reason Jesus was given over to suffering and death was to rebuild the Temple in his person as "a house of prayer for all peoples" (11:17).

The centurion was the one responsible for carrying out Jesus' execution. In the event of a crucifixion, the centurion personally stood facing the person who was crucified, assuring that the death sentence was duly executed. By duty, he had to remain in that position until the person died. Later, when Joseph of Arimathea asked for the body of Jesus, the same centurion would be summoned to testify to his death (15:43-44).

The centurion, therefore, saw how Jesus breathed his last (15:39). But there is seeing, and there is seeing. Not everyone who has eyes to see is able to perceive. But those who do are converted and their sins are forgiven (see 4:12).

The centurion saw *(idon)* as no one else had seen. In the crucifixion, the chief priests and the scribes mocked Jesus, "Let the Messiah, the king of Israel, come down from the cross that we may see [*idomen*] and believe" (15:32). As Jesus cried out, *"Eloi, Eloi,"* some bystanders alerted people, "Look" *(ide),* and one of them mockingly offered Jesus some wine to drink, saying, "Wait, let us see [*idomen*] if Elijah comes to take him down" (15:36).

The centurion saw how *(houtos)* Jesus breathed his last. Seeing, his eyes were opened in faith. Others thought they would believe if they saw Jesus come down or be brought down from the cross. The centurion believed from seeing Jesus remain and die on the cross, hence the importance of the adverb, "truly" *(alethos),* in his confession: "Truly this man was the Son of God."

Seeing, the centurion understood Jesus' prayer of confidence with Psalm 22. That is why he proclaimed Jesus as the Son of God. He understood the purpose of Jesus' death, inviting him and the Gentiles, along with the Jews, to worship in the Temple rebuilt in the person of Jesus.

The centurion's confession of faith was based on how *(houtos)* Jesus died. In the climax of his life as Jesus of Nazareth, Jesus was revealed as the Son of God.

Earlier in the Gospel, Jesus opened the eyes of a blind man at Bethsaida (8:22-26). At first, the man could see something, but his sight was distorted, like Peter's faith when he confessed Jesus as the Christ but did not accept that, as the Christ, Jesus had to suffer and die (8:27-33).

Later, a blind beggar, Bartimaeus by name, cried out to Jesus as "Son of David." Jesus gave him sight that he might follow him on the way to the passion (10:46-52).

Seeing how Jesus died, the centurion saw everything distinctly (see 8:25). Jesus had regularly presented himself as *the* Son of Man, a title intimately related to his human identity (see 2:11, 28; 8:31 *passim*).

Others proclaimed Jesus as the Christ (8:29) and the Son of David (10:47-48), titles describing Jesus' mission in history as savior and king. In the trial before the Sanhedrin, the high priest asked Jesus if he was the Christ, the Son of the Blessed One (14:61). Pilate asked Jesus if he was the King of the Jews (15:2). He also referred to him as the King of the Jews (15:9, 12). In mockery, the soldiers addressed him as King of the Jews, and the inscription stating with the charge against Jesus read "The King of the Jews."

At Jesus' baptism and in the transfiguration, a heavenly voice addressed Jesus as God's beloved Son (1:11; 9:7). Unclean spirits identified him as "the Holy One of God" (1:24) and "Son of the Most High" (5:7). The centurion, a Gentile, is the first human being to proclaim Jesus the Son of God, a title, like Son of Man, that tells Jesus' very identity.

The centurion proclaimed Jesus the Son of God after seeing how Jesus breathed his last. Mark presents the centurion, his faith, and his proclamation as a major challenge to his readers, who were scandalized by the cross and thought it spelled the end. For those who thought it was the end of the gospel, Mark presented the centurion as one who saw it was "the beginning of the gospel of Jesus Christ [the Son of God]" (see 1:1).

"Women Looking on from a Distance" (15:40-41). The story of Jesus' death ends with a brief appendix (15:40-41). Some women were present, observing everything from a distance (15:40a). The mention of the women is very significant. Among Jesus' followers, only the women followed him all the way to the crucifixion and, along with the centurion, witnessed how he died.

When Jesus was arrested, all his disciples abandoned him and fled (14:50), as did the young man who followed him until that point. In the passion, the young man represented the baptized Christian who had left everything to put on Christ (14:51-52). Peter continued to follow, but at a distance *(apo makrothen)* as far as the courtyard at the palace of the high priest (14:54), where he sat with the guards and eventually denied that he was with Jesus and the Twelve. In the end, Peter broke down and wept (14:66-72).

Just as Peter followed at a distance *(apo makrothen),* the women observed everything from a distance *(apo makrothen).* The indication, "from a distance," adds an ominous note. They may have followed beyond the other disciples, including Peter, but like the others, they would eventually flee, overwhelmed by the young man's message in the tomb (16:8).

Among the women, three are named, Mary Magdalene, Mary the mother of the younger James and of Joses, and Salome (15:40b). Like Peter, James, and John, who had a special role among the Twelve, these three women were singled out from the others. They would have an important role in the remainder of the gospel.

Two of them, Mary Magdalene and Mary the mother of Joses, would be present at Jesus' burial and observe where he was laid (15:47). After the sabbath, all three would return to the tomb on the first day of the week (16:1-2).

The three women had followed Jesus in Galilee, where, like Simon's mother-in-law, they ministered to him (15:41a; see 1:29-31). The three were part of a larger group of women who observed Jesus' crucifixion and death from a distance (15:40a).

Like Bartimaeus (10:46-52), the women had joined Jesus on the way to Jerusalem (15:41b) for his passion and resurrection. In Jerusalem, Jesus would be handed over to the chief priests and the scribes, condemned to death and handed over to the Gentiles, who would mock him, spit upon him, scourge him, and put him to death (10:32-34). The women stayed with him all the way. Their test would come three days later, when Jesus would rise (10:34b).

Act III, Scene Two
The Burial of Jesus (15:42-47)
and the Women's Visit to the Tomb (16:1-8)

Scene One told of Jesus' crucifixion (15:21-32) and death (15:33-41). After Jesus "gave a loud cry and breathed his last" (15:37), Mark tells how "the veil of the sanctuary was torn in two from top to bottom" (15:38) and how the centurion announced, "Truly this man was the Son of God!" (15:39). Mark then added that there were women observing *(theorousai)* from a distance, women who followed him in Galilee and ministered to him. Among those women were Mary Magdalene, Mary the mother of the younger James and of Joses, and Salome (15:40-41).

Scene Two now tells of Jesus' burial (15:42-47) and the women's visit to the tomb (16:1-8). When Joseph of Arimathea buried Jesus and "rolled a stone against the entrance to the tomb," two of the women, Mary Magdalene and Mary the mother of Joses, saw *(etheoroun)* where Jesus was laid (15:47). When the sabbath was over, the same two women, Mary Magdalene and Mary the mother of James, went to the tomb, accompanied by Salome (see 15:40). When they got there, they saw *(theorousin)* that the stone had been rolled away from the entrance (16:4).

The scene begins with the burial of Jesus, the day before the sabbath, when it was already evening the day Jesus died (15:42-47). It continues when the sabbath was over, early in the morning with the women's visit to the tomb (16:1-7). It ends with the women fleeing from the tomb (16:8), as the disciples and a certain young man *(neaniskos tis)* had done when Jesus was arrested (14:50-52). For the disciples and the young man, the test came with the arrest of Jesus at Gethsemane (14:43-52). For Peter, it came with Jesus' trial at the palace of the high priest (14:53-72). For the women who followed Jesus, it came with the proclamation of the resurrection (16:1-8).

At the end of the story of Jesus' death, everyone went away, leaving Jesus alone, hanging on the cross, with no one to bury him. Normally, it would have been for Jesus' disciples to bury him, but they had already fled (14:50). Nor did any of those who mocked him (15:35-36) remain, not even the women watching from a distance (15:40-41).

But "when it was already evening, . . . the day before the sabbath," a new personage appears, "Joseph of Arimathea, a distinguished member of the council" (15:42-43a). Joseph of Arimathea, a stranger, would see to Jesus' burial.

Several others have a role in the story of Jesus' burial, including Pilate (15:43b-45), who tried Jesus and handed him over to be crucified (15:1-15), and the centurion (15:44-45), who saw to Jesus' execution and proclaimed him the Son of God (15:39). Two women also have a role, Mary Magdalene and Mary the mother of Joses (15:47), who were among those who looked on from a distance when Jesus died (15:40-41). None of them, however, actually took part in the burial.

The women's visit to the tomb (16:1-8), after the sabbath was over (16:1), is even simpler than the story of the burial (15:42-47). Gone is Joseph of Arimathea. Gone too are Pilate and the centurion. Only some of the women who looked on from a distance when Jesus died (15:40-41) and observed where he was laid (15:47) continue to have a role in the story.

The only other personage in the story is the young man in a white robe (16:5-7), a symbolic counterpart for the young man in the linen cloth who fled when Jesus was arrested (14:51-52). The young man in the tomb, proclaiming the resurrection of the crucified one, transforms what would have been the end of a tragedy into gospel.

The Burial of Jesus (15:42-47)[103]

In Mark's story of Jesus' crucifixion, death, and resurrection (15:21–16:8), the story of Jesus' burial serves three major functions.

---

[103] For Mark's story of Jesus' burial, see Raymond E. Brown, S.S., "The Burial of Jesus (Mark 15:42-47)," *The Catholic Biblical Quarterly* 50 (1988) 233–45. Brown shows that Mark's account of the burial is much

In relation to Jesus, it serves a narrative function; in relation to the followers, a thematic, baptismal function; in relation to Mark's readers, an apologetic function.

In relation to Jesus, the burial completes the story of his crucifixion and death on the cross. Crucified (15:22-32), Jesus died on the cross (15:33-41). After he died, his body could be taken down from the cross. In relation to the visit to the tomb (16:1-8), Jesus' burial also serves a transitional function. The stone that was rolled before the entrance of the tomb (15:46) would be found rolled away from the entrance (16:4). Having seen where Jesus was laid (15:47) the evening before the sabbath (15:42), two women (see 15:40-41) would return to the tomb when the sabbath was over (16:1).

In relation to Jesus' followers, the burial furthers Mark's baptismal theme. Those who were called to follow Jesus on his journey to Jerusalem, where he would be put to death (10:32-34), also had to follow him to his burial. Being baptized with the baptism with which Jesus was baptized (10:38-40) meant both dying with Christ and being buried with Christ (see 14:50-51; Rom 6:3-4).

Jesus' body, wrapped in a linen cloth *(sindon),* recalls the young follower who wore nothing but a linen cloth *(sindon)* about his body (14:51). The stone that Joseph rolled against the entrance to the tomb (15:46b) is symbolic of the obstacles preventing Jesus' followers from being buried with Christ.

In relation to Mark's readers, the burial story also serves some important apologetic functions. Apart from the story's apologetic intent, it would have been enough to say that Jesus was buried, both from a narrative point of view and in relation to baptism (see 1 Cor 15:3b-5).

But for Mark's readers, it was important to show that Jesus had really died and that the tomb was really empty. Otherwise, when they announced Jesus' resurrection, people could claim that Jesus had not really died or that the so-called empty tomb was not the tomb in which Jesus was buried.[104]

---

more plausible than that of Matthew and Luke, from both the Roman and the Jewish legal points of view. Joseph of Arimathea, a pious Jew, buried Jesus in a tomb adjacent to the place of crucifixion in view of fulfilling the Jewish law that a body should be buried before sundown (Deut 21:22-23), especially when the following day was the sabbath (15:42).

[104] Like Mark, Matthew had an apologetic intent but for another reason. For Matthew's readers, there was no question that Jesus had really died and that his tomb was actually empty. But it could be claimed that his body had been stolen by his disciples (see Matt 27:63-64). That is why the chief priests and the Pharisees asked Pilate that the tomb be secured. According

The story's apologetic intent is shown by Pilate's amazement that Jesus had already died, by Pilate's verification of the fact, by the centurion's confirmation, and Pilate's granting the corpse *(ptoma)* of Jesus to Joseph of Arimathea (15:44-45). It is also shown by the story of the women. Having seen where Jesus was laid, they would not have mistaken the tomb of Jesus for another that happened to be empty.

"When It Was Already Evening" (15:42). It was already evening, on the day of preparation, that is, the day before the sabbath (15:42). Mark started noting the precise time of day with the previous evening *(opsias),* when Jesus came with the Twelve for the Last Supper (14:17). Reckoning the day in the Roman way, from 6:00 a.m. to 6:00 a.m., that was the first day of the Feast of Unleavened Bread, when they sacrificed the Passover Lamb (14:12).[105]

Evening began around 6:00 p.m., before sunset (see 1:32). By the Roman reckoning, Passover had ended that morning, and Jesus was crucified the day after Passover, the day of preparation for the sabbath, which would begin the following morning, Saturday at 6:00 a.m.

Normally, the Romans left the body on the cross for several days as a warning to others and a deterrent. But they made an exception for Judea and Jerusalem because of a Jewish law recorded in Deuteronomy 21:22-23:

(21:22) If a man guilty of a capital offense is put to death and his corpse hung on a tree,

(21:23) it shall not remain on the tree overnight. You shall bury it the same day; otherwise, since God's curse rests on him who hangs on a tree, you will defile the land which the LORD, your God, is giving you as an inheritance.

In Jewish law, a corpse was not to be left exposed overnight. The law applied to every day of the week, not just the evening before the sabbath.

Since, by the Roman reckoning, it was the evening before the sabbath, there was no problem with Joseph of Arimathea buying a linen cloth for Jesus' burial. By the Jewish reckoning, he would have had to do that before sunset.

---

to Matthew, that was done. Their guard "went and secured the tomb by fixing a seal to the stone and setting the guard" (Matt 27:66).

[105] Had Mark used a Jewish reckoning for the day, from sunset to sunset, the Passover Lamb would have been sacrificed the previous day. By the Roman reckoning, the sacrifice and the Passover supper took place on the same day.

Joseph of Arimathea (15:43). In view of the Deuteronomic law, Joseph of Arimathea took it upon himself to see that Jesus was buried and not left exposed overnight. Normally, his disciples would have buried him, but they had all fled. As one who was "awaiting the kingdom of God," Joseph would have buried Jesus, even without knowing him. In some ways, Joseph of Arimathea may be compared to the scribe who asked Jesus about the first of all the commandments, while Jesus was teaching in the Temple. Jesus declared the scribe "not far from the kingdom of God" (12:28-34).

Unlike Matthew, Mark did not present Joseph as a disciple of Jesus (Matt 27–57). John presented him as one who was "secretly a disciple of Jesus for fear of the Jews" (John 19:38). Had Joseph been a disciple, it would be hard to explain why the women were not involved in the preparations for Jesus' burial.

Until now, the Jewish council *(boule)* in Jerusalem, that is, the Sanhedrin, was presented in a very bad light, with its members condemning Jesus of blasphemy (14:63-64), bringing Jesus before Pilate (15:1-2), and mocking him at the crucifixion (15:31-32). Describing Joseph of Arimathea as "a distinguished member of the council" *(euschemon bouleutes),* Mark showed that the whole council was not of the same mind. There were also those who were "awaiting the kingdom of God."

Joseph of Arimathea "courageously went to Pilate and asked for the body of Jesus" (15:43b). Given the role of the Sanhedrin in Jesus' death, Joseph of Arimathea was indeed a courageous person. The chief priests, the scribes, and the elders had Jesus arrested during the night of Passover (14:43-52). That same night they tried Jesus at the palace of the high priest (14:53-72). As soon as morning came, *circa* 6:00 a.m., with the whole Sanhedrin in council *(symboulion),* they handed Jesus over to Pilate (15:1).

The chief priests and the scribes had no scruple about arresting and trying Jesus on Passover, so long as a riot among the people could be avoided (14:1-2, 10-11). It took some courage *(tolmesas),* then, vis-à-vis other members of the council, for Joseph of Arimathea, a respected member of the council, to go to Pilate and request the body *(soma)* of Jesus.

"Pilate Was Amazed" (15:44-45). With Pilate's reaction, Mark's apologetic intent comes into play. Pilate had no objection to giving Joseph the body of Jesus, so long as Jesus was really dead. Amazed that Jesus "was already dead," he called for the centurion and asked if Jesus had already died (15:44).

The centurion was the one responsible for Jesus' execution. Seeing how Jesus died (15:34-37), he had also proclaimed Jesus' divine identity: "Truly this man was the Son of God!" (15:39). The high priest had asked Jesus, "Are you the Messiah, the son of the Blessed One?" Jesus had answered, "I am," and for that Jesus was charged with blasphemy (14:61-64). The centurion's proclamation now responded: Jesus was truly the Son of the Blessed One.

When the centurion confirmed that Jesus had died, Pilate gave the body *(ptoma)* to Joseph. Joseph had asked for the body *(soma)* of Jesus. The word *soma*, which is normally associated with a living person, evokes Jesus as a living person. The word *ptoma*, associated with something that had once been alive, emphasizes that Jesus, now lifeless, was really dead, and ready for burial.

"Having Bought a Linen Cloth" (15:46). Having bought a linen cloth *(sindona)*, Joseph took Jesus *(auton)* down from the cross, wrapped him in the linen cloth *(sindoni)* and placed him in a tomb which was hewn out of rock. The linen cloth, mentioned twice, recalls the linen cloth worn by the young man who was following Jesus when Jesus was arrested (14:51-52).

For Jesus, the linen cloth was a shroud. For the young man, it was a symbol of his baptismal commitment to die and be buried with Christ (see 10:38-39), of joining Jesus, the Son of Man, in offering "his life as a ransom for many" (10:45).

Mark did not say where Jesus' tomb was situated. From tradition and archeological evidence, however, we know it was adjacent to the place of execution, an ancient quarry, abandoned in the sixth century at the time of the deportation to Babylon. The abandoned quarry, which at the time was outside the walls of Jerusalem, provided a convenient place of burial for those executed on Golgotha. Golgotha, which was situated in the same quarry, was just a few yards away.[106]

For Jesus' burial, there was no reason to say that Joseph "rolled a stone against the entrance to the tomb" (15:46b). That could have been taken for granted. Mentioning it, however, prepares the story of the women's visit to the tomb, where the stone would be a major concern (16:3-4). A stone that had been rolled against the entrance could be rolled away from the entrance. For now, however, the stone seals Jesus in death. It also blocks the way for anyone to be buried with Christ.

[106] Today, Golgotha and the place of the tomb of Jesus are both within the Church of the Holy Sepulchre. The present line of the wall of Jerusalem, built by Agrippa I a few years after Jesus died, included Golgotha and the site of Jesus' burial within the walls.

"Mary Magdalene and Mary the Mother of Joses" (15:47).
Mary Magdalene and Mary the mother of Joses had been among
the women who observed how Jesus died, albeit from a distance
(*apo makrothen,* 15:40-41). As women who had followed Jesus in
Galilee and up to Jerusalem, they were present at the tomb, observing where Jesus was laid (15:47).

Their presence at the tomb, observing everything, contributes to
the story's apologetic intent. The same women would have a major
role in the following story, the last in Mark's Gospel. Having seen
where he was buried, they would be able to verify, "when the sabbath was over" (16:1), that the stone that had been rolled against
the entrance to the tomb (15:46) had been rolled away (16:4) and
that Jesus' body was no longer in the tomb (16:6).

The Women's Visit to the Tomb (16:1-8)

With the story of the women's visit to the tomb (16:1-8), the passion-resurrection according to Mark (14:1–16:8) comes to an end. So
does the second major part of the gospel (8:22–16:8). And so does
"the beginning of the gospel of Jesus Christ [the Son of God]" (1:1).

The story of the passion-resurrection began two days' time before
the Passover and the Feast of Unleavened Bread with the chief
priests and the scribes looking for a way to put Jesus to death (14:1-
2). It ends two days after Passover with a young man proclaiming that
Jesus of Nazareth, the one who was crucified, had been raised (16:6).

The first part of the Gospel (1:14–8:21) raised the question of Jesus'
identity. The second part reveals his identity together with his mission and what it means for Jesus' followers (8:22–16:8). It began with
a blind man who was brought to Jesus asking Jesus to touch him.
Jesus cured the blind man in two stages. At first he could see but his
vision was distorted. He could not see that Jesus had to be handed
over, that he had to die and rise again after three days. When Jesus
laid hands on his eyes a second time, he could see perfectly (8:22-26).

The second part of the Gospel ends with the story of the women,
who saw how Jesus died (15:40-41) and was buried (15:47) and how
the stone was rolled away from the tomb (16:4). But the women,
who followed Jesus in Galilee and to Jerusalem (15:40-41), were unable to see when it came to Jesus' resurrection and its implications
for their mission (16:5-8). Peter's sight was distorted regarding the
passion (8:31-33). In various ways, the disciples' sight was also distorted (9:30-34), and so was the sight of James and John (10:32-40).
The women's sight was distorted regarding the resurrection.

The women's visit to the tomb is the last story in "the beginning
of the gospel of Jesus Christ [the Son of God]" (1:1). The women may

have run away and said nothing to anyone, but this was not the end of the gospel, only the beginning, inviting Mark's readers to join in the continuation of "the beginning of the gospel of Jesus Christ [the Son of God]" (1:1). Jesus of Nazareth, the crucified one who was raised, was going before them to Galilee (see 10:32-34). Following him to and in Galilee, they would see him, just as he told them (16:6; see 14:28), unless, fleeing, they abandoned the way and said nothing to anyone. Why were they afraid?

"When the Sabbath Was Over" (16:1). It was now morning and the sabbath was over. So Mary Magdalene, Mary, the mother of James, and Salome were able to buy spices that they might go and anoint Jesus (16:1).

After Jesus' death, at his burial, and now, when the sabbath was over, Mary Magdalene is mentioned first. Then there is another Mary, now identified as the mother of James. At Jesus' burial, she was identified as the mother of Joses. At Jesus' death, she was the mother of the younger James and of Joses. For the women's visit to the tomb, there was also Salome, the one mentioned among those who saw how Jesus died (10:40).

Mark seems to have retained two traditional lists, one for Jesus' burial (15:47), and one for the visit to the tomb (16:1). The list of women who saw the crucifixion and how Jesus died (10:40) very likely represents an effort to harmonize the two lists, hence "Mary the mother of the younger James and of Joses" (see 15:47; 16:1), and Salome, mentioned together with Mary Magdalene as among those who followed Jesus in Galilee (10:41).

As women who ministered *(diakonoun)* to Jesus in Galilee, their intention was to minister to him to the very end. Having observed Jesus' burial, they knew that Joseph of Arimathea had not anointed Jesus' body. That explains why they bought spices with the intention of anointing Jesus (16:1).

But they were apparently not aware that Jesus had already been anointed by a woman while Jesus was at table at the home of Simon the leper (14:3). The woman anointed Jesus on the head, proclaiming him the Christ (Messiah). What Peter did with a word, she did with a symbolic act. Peter, however, had not accepted that, as the Christ, Jesus had to suffer before rising after three days (8:31-32). As Jesus declared, defending the woman's symbolic act, she anointed his body *(soma)* in view of his burial (14:8).

Buying spices to anoint Jesus, Mary Magdalene and the others did not know of the woman's symbolic act at the home of Simon the leper, but Mark's readers do. The women's intention to anoint Jesus alerts us that all will not go well for them. Buying spices in view of anointing Jesus is a mysterious omen of trouble yet to be disclosed.

"On the First Day of the Week" (16:2). The women came to the tomb, very early *(lian proi)* in the morning, when the sun had risen *(anateilantos tou heliou),* on the first day of the week *(te mia ton sabbaton,* 16:2). Unlike Mark and the reader, the women did not know that there was something special about "the first day of the week."

Earlier in the Gospel, Jesus had announced that the Son of Man had to *(dei)* "suffer greatly . . . and be killed, and rise after three days" *(kai meta treis hemeras anastenai)* (8:31; see also 9:31; 10:32-34). In the passion itself, Jesus was accused of saying: "I will destroy this temple made with hands and within three days [*dia trion hemeron*] I will build another not made with hands." In this, Mark is tributary to a very early tradition, referred to by Paul when he reminded the Corinthians: "Christ . . . , was raised on the third day [*te hemera te trite*] in accordance with the scriptures" (1 Cor 15:3-4).

There is a difference in meaning between "the third day" and "the first day of the week." The third day was associated with the very event of Jesus' resurrection. In early Judaism, the third day was recognized as the day God saved his people. The rabbis had collected all the places in Scripture referring to God saving his people on the third day.

In the *Midrash Rabbah,* they noted those references while commenting on God's testing Abraham, demanding he sacrifice his beloved son, Isaac. It is "on the third day" that Abraham got sight of the place of sacrifice from afar (Gen 22:4). As Abraham took the knife to slaughter his son, the Lord's messenger called out to him: "Abraham, Abraham! . . . Do not lay your hand on the boy" (Gen 22:10-12).

In saving Isaac, the firstborn of God's people, God saved the entire people. In the same way, the early Christians saw that by raising Jesus, the firstborn (see Col 1:15, 18; Rom 8:29), from the dead, God saved his entire people.

"The first day of the week" *(te mia ton sabbaton)* is not associated directly with the event of Jesus' resurrection, but with its proclamation and celebration. In all four gospels, the visit to the tomb took place "on the first day of the week" (16:2; Matt 28:1; Luke 24:1; John 20:1). For Luke, "the first day of the week" would be the day the disciples recognized Jesus in the breaking of the bread (Luke 24:13-35), the day they received their mission (Luke 24:36-53), and the day the Christians assembled for the breaking of the bread, celebrating the manifestation of the risen Lord (Acts 20:7-12).

The first day of the week was the day that Jesus' resurrection was revealed to his followers, transforming them into a new creation. Normally, the Greek expression for "the first day" should have been written with an ordinal numeral, *prote* ("first"), as we find it in translation. Instead, what we find in Greek is a cardinal numeral, *mia* ("one"), making for a very awkward expression in Greek, "the day one," instead of "the first day."

We would understand such an expression as a semitism preserved in a very early tradition, rendering a Hebrew equivalent. Instead of an ordinal, the Hebrew language uses a cardinal numeral for "first." Normally, however, such a semitism would have been corrected along the way. This did not happen until the second century in the alternative ending for Mark's Gospel, where we read *prote sabbatou,* literally, "the first [*prote*] day of the week" (16:9). To explain the expression's persistence, we must assume, therefore, that it must have some special significance. And it does.

The key is in the Septuagint, which translated the Hebrew for the first day of creation very literally with a cardinal numeral, "day one," instead of "first day." With the Septuagint for Genesis 1:5 in mind, New Testament references to "the first day of the week" present that day as the day of the new creation, the day Jesus' resurrection transforms those previously born of human generation into children of God (see John 1:12-13; Gal 3:26-29; Col 3:11). The first day of the week is also the day Christians remember, celebrate, and proclaim the new creation.

It is on the first day of the week that the women went to the tomb early in the morning just after sunrise (16:1). The night had passed. The sun had risen. Jesus' resurrection signals a new day, the first day of the new creation. For the women, however, who came to the tomb with the intention of anointing Jesus, the day of the new creation had not dawned. For Mark and his readers, it has, but not for everyone. Regarding Mary Magdalene and the others, we can see the irony. Regarding all those who do not experience the first day of the week as the day of the new creation, we feel an urgency to proclaim it.

"Who Will Roll Back the Stone for Us . . . ?" (16:3-4). We have already seen that Joseph of Arimathea "rolled a stone against the entrance of the tomb" (15:46). The women had observed him doing that. Now, on their way to the tomb, they remembered about the stone and were saying to one another, "Who will roll back the stone for us from the entrance to the tomb?" (16:3).

Intended for multiple burials, a tomb like that of Jesus had a track hewn in the rock in front of the entrance to the tomb. A large circular stone, resembling a millstone, could be rolled in the track against the entrance to the tomb. When the tomb had to be re-opened, the stone would be rolled back.

As the women approached the tomb, they looked up and "saw [*theorousin,* see 15:40, 47] that the stone had been rolled back" (16:4a). Explaining why the women themselves were not able to roll back the stone, Mark added that the stone was very large (*megas sphrodra,* 16:4b).

We sense that the stone must be symbolic. Mentioning it four times (15:46; 16:3, 4a, 4b), Mark underlined its importance. In this part, Mark's story is not so much about the empty tomb as about the rolling away of the stone.

The symbol of the stone is connected not with Jesus' resurrection but with his burial. The stone was not rolled against the exit from the tomb but against the entrance (*epi ten thuran,* 15:46) to the tomb. When the women came, they saw that the stone had been rolled away not from the exit but from the entrance (*ek tes thuras,* 16:3) to the tomb. For Jesus' resurrection, the stone was no obstacle. But rolled against the entrance to the tomb, it prevented anyone from entering.

Early in the morning, shortly after sunrise, on the first day of the week, the stone effectively blocked the way for the women to enter the tomb. The stone was very large. But when they came, they saw that the stone, large as it was, had already been rolled away (16:4).

In terms of Mark's story of the passion-resurrection, the stone was a baptismal symbol, blocking the way for someone effectively to be buried with Christ. The passion was a story not just of Jesus dying but of the challenge for the disciples to die with Christ. So also Jesus' burial and the visit to the tomb was not just a story of Jesus being buried, but of the challenge for the disciples to be buried with Christ. In this, the stone is a symbol for everything that blocks the way. It may be different for each, but for everyone it is a very large stone.

When the women came to the tomb, however, the stone had already been rolled away. All they needed to do was enter the tomb. But who could have rolled away the stone from the entrance to the tomb?

"A Young Man Sitting on the Right Side" (16:5-7). Seeing that the stone had been rolled away from the entrance, the women entered the tomb. Their only concern was that the stone be rolled away. Since that was already done, they entered the tomb with no trepidation.

In John's Gospel, when Mary Magdalene went to the tomb and saw that the stone had been removed, she ran off to Simon Peter and the other disciple Jesus loved with the news that the Lord had been taken away from the tomb (John 20:1-2). In Mark, Mary Magdalene, Mary, the mother of James, and Salome simply went in, as though that was normal, even in the case of one who had been executed.

On entering, they saw a young man *(neaniskon)* seated on the right *(kathemenon en tois dexiois)* clothed in a white robe *(stolen leuken,* 16:5).[107] Seeing that the stone had been rolled back did not amaze them. But seeing the young man, they were completely overwhelmed *(exethambethesan)*.

This is the second time a young man *(neaniskos)* figures in the passion-resurrection. The first was at Jesus' arrest, when a young man following him wore nothing but a linen cloth *(sindon),* a garment symbolic of Jesus' burial (15:46). When they seized the young man (14:51) as they had seized Jesus (14:43-49), he slipped out of the linen cloth and fled (14:52), as the disciples had fled (14:50).

We saw that the young man was symbolic of the young Christian committed in baptism to die with Christ and be buried with Christ. Abandoning his baptismal commitment, the young man left his identity behind. He was now naked, that is, nobody.

The young man *(neaniskos)* in the tomb is clothed with a white garment, the garment of the risen Lord, revealed at the transfiguration (9:3). Like the Lord, who would come seated at the right hand of the power *(ek dexion kathemenon tes dynameis,* 14:62), the young man was seated on the right in the tomb where Jesus' body had been laid.

James and John asked Jesus to be seated one on his right and one on his left, when he came into his glory (10:37). In response, Jesus asked if they could be baptized with the same baptism as he was baptized (10:38). When they answered that they could, Jesus told them they would, but as for sitting on his right and on his left, that was for those for whom it was prepared (10:39-40).

The young man was not seated in glory on Jesus' right. He was seated in the tomb, a memorial of his death and resurrection. Symbolic of the Christian, the young man represented Jesus of Nazareth, the crucified one, who was raised. Those who were of Christ (9:41) were baptized not only to die with Christ and be buried with Christ (see 8:34-37) but to live with Christ, one day to rise with Christ (see Rom 6:3-4).

In his very person, the young man in the tomb represented the person of Jesus of Nazareth, the crucified one who had been raised.

---

[107] See Steven R. Johnson, "The Identity and Significance of the *Neaniskos* in Mark," *Forum (Foundations and Facets)* 8/1–2 (March/June 1992) 123–39.

His message corresponded to what he represented. First, the young man told the women not to be amazed. They were seeking "Jesus of Nazareth, the crucified. He has been raised; he is not here. Behold, the place where they laid him" (16:6).

Vice versa, what the young man represented corresponded to his message. As the baptized Christian, the young man proclaimed the gospel of Jesus of Nazareth, the crucified one who had been raised. The young man was the evangelizer, representing the whole of Mark himself and "the beginning of the gospel of Jesus Christ [the Son of God]" (1:1).

Having announced the resurrection of Jesus of Nazareth, the crucified one, the young man continued with a special mission for the women. They were to "go and tell his disciples and Peter, 'He is going before you to [eis] Galilee; there you will see him, as he told you'" (16:7). The women were to tell those who fled when Jesus was arrested (14:50) and Peter, who denied him in the courtyard at the palace of the high priest (14:66-72) but broke down and wept when he remembered what Jesus had told him (14:72). As we shall see, instead of doing that, they too fled, saying nothing to anyone (16:8).

Jesus was going before them not only to but in Galilee,[108] as he had done from the moment they accepted to follow him (see 1:16-20; 15:40-41). He had also gone before them from Galilee to Jerusalem, to his passion and resurrection (10:32-34), and like the blind beggar, Bartimaeus whom Jesus healed, they had followed him on the way to Jerusalem (10:46-52).

With Jesus in Galilee, they may be blind or have badly distorted vision, but Jesus, who opened the eyes of the blind (8:22-26), would open their eyes as well. Following him on the way to Jerusalem, to his crucifixion, to his burial, and to the tomb, they would see him, just as he told them (see 14:27-28).

Mark may not have told particular stories in which Jesus appeared after his resurrection, but that is because the entire Gospel was an appearance story. For Mark, Jesus' appearing as risen Lord was not so much an event as a life process. To see Jesus the risen Lord, one has to follow him in Galilee and from Galilee to Jerusalem.

The women's mission, therefore, was to tell the disciples and Peter to go back to the start of the Gospel and live it anew. The young man's message to the reader is to reread the Gospel, now as the story of Jesus the crucified one who was raised and his followers. The reader is invited to reread "the beginning of the gospel of Jesus

---

[108] See B.M.F. van Iersel, "'To Galilee' or 'In Galilee' in Mark 14,28 and 16,7?" *Ephemerides Theologicae Lovanienses*. Tomus LVIII (1982) 365–70.

Christ [the Son of God]" (1:1) as the continuation of the gospel of Jesus Christ [the Son of God]. Their gospel was only beginning.

"They Went Out and Fled from the Tomb" (16:8). The women did not fulfill their mission. Instead, "they went out and fled from the tomb, seized with trembling and bewilderment. They said nothing to anyone, for they were afraid" (16:8). Like the disciples and the young man when Jesus was arrested (14:50-52), the women fled. The young man in the tomb had not succeeded in calming them. Hearing his message, they were even more overwhelmed.

Following the Last Supper, Jesus had announced:

> (14:27) All of you will have your faith shaken, for it is written:
> "I will strike the shepherd,
>   and the sheep will be dispersed."

> (14:28) But after I have been raised up, I shall go before you to Galilee.

Like the others, the women had their faith shaken. The shepherd had been struck, and they were among the sheep that were dispersed.

The message of the young man is carried by Mark and his Gospel, challenging all who follow Christ. The women, like the disciples and the young man in the passion, challenge us. Shall we too run away and say nothing to anyone, bewildered by the message and the mission of the gospel? Or shall we, like the young man in the tomb, proclaim the gospel of the resurrection of Jesus Christ, the crucified one? To do that we have also to heed the whole of his message: Jesus, the risen Lord, is going before us in Galilee. There we will see him!

XI

❧ ❧

An Alternate Ending

Mark 16:9-20

INTRODUCTION

Originally, the Gospel According to Mark ended with the women's visit to the tomb (16:1-8), bringing "the beginning of the gospel of Jesus Christ [the Son of God]" (1:1) to a very striking and extremely challenging conclusion.[1]

Coming out, the women fled *(ephugon)* from the tomb; for trembling *(tromos)* and amazement *(ekstasis)* took hold of them *(eichen gar)*. They said nothing to anyone, for they were afraid *(ephobounto gar,* 16:8).[2] Why were they afraid? Why did they not say anything to anyone?

To answer those questions, Mark's community had to reflect on why they themselves were afraid and did not fulfill their mission? In baptism, they died with Christ and were buried with Christ to live with Christ and continue his mission. At the Lord's Supper, they drank the cup that Christ drank and renewed their baptismal commitment (see 10:38-39; 14:22-25). Why then were they afraid to proclaim the gospel of Jesus of Nazareth, the crucified one, who was raised from the dead?

---

[1] See E. LaVerdiere, "The Passion-Resurrection According to Mark, Act III, Scene Two, the Burial of Jesus (15:42-47) and the Women's Visit to the Tomb (16:1-8)" *Emmanuel* (October 1996) 475–79, 482–88.

[2] In Mark's Gospel, trembling *(tromos)* and amazement *(ekstasis)* are associated with fear *(phobos, phobeomai,* see 5:33, 36).

A Problem

Until recently, the original ending of Mark's Gospel was seen as problematic. How could Mark possibly have ended "the beginning of the gospel" with a scene of followers fleeing from the tomb? How could he have ended the Gospel on a note of fear? And how could he have ended the whole Gospel with conjunction "because" *(gar)?*

Present at Jesus' burial, the women had watched Joseph of Arimathea wrap the body of Jesus in a linen cloth, lay him in the tomb, and roll "a stone against the entrance to the tomb" (15:46). When they came to the tomb (16:2), wondering who would roll back the stone for them (16:3), they saw that the stone, large as it was, had already been rolled back (16:4).

There is no question of the women mistaking another tomb for that of Jesus. Jesus' tomb was hewn out of the rock, and the stone rolled against its entrance was very large (15:46). Besides, the women had been looking on from a distance when Jesus breathed his last (15:37, 40). They were present when Pilate gave Jesus' body to Joseph of Arimathea (15:45), and they saw where the body was laid (15:47). The empty tomb was surely the tomb in which Jesus had been laid.

When the sabbath was over, the women bought spices, intending to anoint Jesus (16:1). The following morning they went to the tomb: "On entering the tomb they saw a young man sitting on the right side, clothed in a white robe, and they were utterly amazed. He said to them, 'Do not be amazed! You seek Jesus of Nazareth, the crucified. He has been raised; he is not here. Behold, the place where they laid him" (16:5-6). Hearing that, the women should have been overjoyed. Instead, they were overcome by fright.

The young man also gave the women a message for Jesus' disciples and Peter: "He is going before you to Galilee; there you will see him, as he told you" (16:7; see 14:28). Mark says nothing about how they would see him, except that it would be in Galilee, where Jesus was going before them. That is where and when they would see him.

The women had received an important commission. They were to proclaim the gospel of the resurrection to the disciples and Peter.[3] After that, we would expect the gospel to continue and tell how the women went and fulfilled their commission. Instead, they "said nothing to anyone, for they were afraid" (16:8). The silence of the women is matched by the silence of the Gospel concerning the appearances of Jesus.

---

[3] The women were to proclaim the gospel of the resurrection to the disciples and even to Peter. Peter is singled out from the other disciples in the story of the visit to the tomb as he was in the passion (see 14:27-31, 37, 54, 66-72).

How could any evangelist have ended a gospel with a scene of women running away and saying nothing to anyone? In John, Mary Magdalene "ran and went to Simon Peter and to the other disciple whom Jesus loved, and told them, 'They have taken the Lord from the tomb, and we don't know where they put him'" (John 20:2). In Matthew, "they went away quickly from the tomb, fearful yet overjoyed, and ran to announce this to his disciples" (Matt 28:8). In Luke, "they returned from the tomb and announced all these things to the eleven and to all the others" (Luke 24:9).

All the other gospels end with at least two appearances of Jesus.[4] But Matthew is the only one that situates an appearance in Galilee.[5] In doing so, Matthew presents the appearance as the climax of the entire Gospel. In Matthew, an angelic message parallels and develops the message of the young man in Mark: "Then go quickly and tell his disciples, 'He has been raised from the dead, and he is going before you to Galilee; there you will see him.' Behold, I have told you" (Matt 28:7).

To this point, the message stays fairly close to the message in Mark. But then, departing from Mark, Matthew shows how the women ran to announce this to the disciples and how Jesus himself met them on the way: "Do not be afraid. Go tell my brothers to go to Galilee, and there they will see me" (Matt 28:8-10).

The conclusion of Matthew's Gospel (Matt 28:16-20) then tells how the eleven disciples went to Galilee "to the mountain to which Jesus had ordered them" (Matt 28:16), and how "when they saw him, they worshiped, but they doubted" (Matt 28:17). Matthew's Gospel ends with a short, final discourse of Jesus, declaring, "All power in heaven and on earth has been given to me. Go, therefore, and make disciples of all nations . . ." (Matt 28:18-20).

With that, Matthew resolved the problems raised by the ending in Mark. The women fulfilled their mission and the disciples did see Jesus in Galilee. In this, we assume that Matthew, like us, found Mark's ending problematic. It may be, however, that he simply proposed another good ending for the Gospel.

---

[4] In the Gospels, the appearances of Jesus are told in John 20:14-18, 19-23, 24-29; 21:1-23; Matthew 28:9-10, 16-20; Luke 24:13-35, 36-53 (see also Acts 1:3-11).

[5] Luke does keep a reference to Galilee but in connection with Jesus' prophetic announcement of the passion and resurrection of the Son of Man: "Remember what he said to you while he was still in Galilee, that the Son of Man must be handed over to sinners and be crucified, and rise on the third day" (Luke 24:6b-7). In Luke, Jesus' appearances as risen Lord take place in or in the vicinity of Jerusalem (Luke 24:13-53).

Our problem with Mark's ending may come from our presuppositions and our expectations concerning what makes an appropriate
ending for a gospel. Perhaps those presuppositions are reinforced
by Matthew's story of an appearance in Galilee and the expectations fueled more generally by stories of appearances in Matthew
and the other gospels.

Until recently, Mark's ending gave rise to a lot of speculation.
Could it be that Mark left the Gospel unfinished?[6] Could it be that
he intended to add one or more appearances of Jesus but for some
reason never got to write them? Such appearances would have
counterbalanced the fear and the silence of the women. Could it be
that Mark completed the Gospel but the ending was somehow lost?

Today, such speculation smacks of scholarly desperation. Some of
the best and earliest manuscripts of Mark, including Codex Vati-
canus and Codex Sinaiticus, end with the women saying nothing to
anyone, "for they were afraid." So do some early translations of
Mark in languages such as Latin, Syriac, and Armenian.[7] Besides,
Luke and Matthew, for whom Mark was a major source, give no sign
that they knew any other ending. For them, Mark's Gospel ended
with the flight and the silence of the women (16:8).

Continuing their accounts beyond the story of the empty tomb,
both Luke and Matthew confronted the problems presented by
Mark 16:1-8 for their version of the gospel. Luke avoided contradicting Mark 16:8 by distinguishing the women named by Mark
from those who actually relayed the message. The messengers were
those who accompanied them (see Luke 24:9, 10b). In this Luke depended on Mark 15:41b: "There were also many other women who
had come up with him to Jerusalem."

Matthew was less subtle in his use and adaptation of Mark. While
retaining the women named by Mark as messengers, he transformed their fearful reaction into one of joy: "Then they went away
quickly from the tomb, fearful yet overjoyed, and ran to announce
this to the disciples" (Matt 28:8).

---

[6] Commenting on Mark 16:8, Vincent Taylor wrote: "The view that
ephobounto gar is not the intended ending stands." In support, he refers to
a long line of distinguished textual and literary critics, including Hort,
Swete, Moffatt, Burkitt, and Bultman. See Vincent Taylor, *The Gospel According to St. Mark* (New York: St. Martin's Press, 1963) 609.

[7] The Old Latin *(Vetus Latina)* codex Bobiensis ended Mark with 16:1-
8. The Latin Vulgate, however, continues with 16:9-20. The Sinaitic Syriac
manuscript also ended with 16:1-8, as did one hundred Armenian manuscripts. See Bruce M. Metzger, *A Textual Commentary on the Greek New
Testament* (New York: United Bible Societies, 1971) 122–23.

For all these reasons, it seems best to try to understand the women's flight from the tomb and their fearful silence (16:8) as the ending Mark really intended. With that, what was seen as a problem becomes a challenge.

A Challenge

Today, the consensus of scholarly opinion is that Mark both intended and actually did end the gospel with the flight of the women and their saying nothing to anyone because they were afraid. The change in scholarly opinion came from the development of new methodologies, in which established methodologies, such as form criticism, redaction criticism, and historical criticism, are complemented with literary and rhetorical approaches.

To appreciate Mark's ending as a challenge, we need to attend, not only to the women's flight from the tomb (16:8), but to its literary function in the story of their visit to the tomb (16:1-8) and to its relationship to the whole passion according to Mark (14:1–16:8). The women's visit to the tomb is an integral part of the passion narrative, bringing many of its themes to a climax.

We also have to see the visit to the tomb in relation to the entire Gospel. We have to place ourselves in the situation of Mark's community and hear the ending of the gospel as they heard it, as part of "the beginning of the Gospel of Jesus Christ [the Son of God]" (1:1).

What are we to make of the young man's message that Jesus was preceding the disciples and Peter in Galilee, where they would see him? The expectations raised by the young man somehow have to be fulfilled. Otherwise they cannot be seen as gospel or good news. But how are they fulfilled? What are we to make of the fear and the silence of the women? And what was Mark's message to his community? What was his intention?

Commenting on the passion and resurrection (14:1–16:8), I showed how these questions can be answered.[8] Introducing the alternate ending, I add a few more reflections concerning the young man's message and the reaction of the women. My purpose is to highlight the difference between Mark's original ending (16:1-8) and a new ending (16:9-20) appended to Mark in the second century.

The reaction of the women, their fear and silence, is very consistent with the gospel as a whole. Recall the reaction of the disciples when Jesus calmed the storm at sea (4:35-41). When "the wind ceased and there was a great calm" (4:39), Jesus asked them, "Why are you terrified? Do you not yet have faith?" (4:40). Mark adds that "they were

[8] E. LaVerdiere, *Emmanuel* (October 1996).

330 *The Beginning of the Gospel*

filled with great awe" *(ephobethesan phobon megan)* or more literally, "they feared a great fear" (4:41).

Again, when Jesus went to the disciples as the Lord, I AM, walking out to them on the sea (6:45-52), they were terrified *(etarachthesan)*. Jesus told them not to be afraid *(me phobeisthe,* 6:50). When "he got into the boat with them and the wind died down," they were beside themselves with astonishment *(existanto,* 6:51). They had not understood about the loaves, and their hearts were hardened *(he kardia peporomene,* 6:52).

In both cases, their reaction was to an extraordinary manifestation of Jesus' personal identity as the Lord and to its implications for their mission. The fearful reaction was also associated either with lack of faith or hardness of heart.

Recall also when Jesus began to teach the disciples "that the Son of Man must suffer greatly and be rejected by the elders, the chief priests, and the scribes, and be killed, and rise after three days" (8:31), Peter tried to stop him. Taking him aside, Peter began to rebuke him (8:31-32).

Later, when Jesus announced a second time that "the Son of Man is to be handed over to men and they will kill him, and three days after his death he will rise" (9:31), the disciples "did not understand the saying, and they were afraid [*ephobounto*] to question him" (9:32). Then when Jesus asked them what they were arguing about on the way (9:33), "they remained silent" *(esiopon),* because "they had been discussing among themselves on the way who was the greatest" (9:34).

In both instances, Jesus announced his approaching death and resurrection, and in both instances, Peter or the disciples rejected the message. They were unable to accept the implications of the passion for them as Jesus' followers. Peter spoke up and rebuked Jesus. On the other hand, the disciples were afraid and remained silent.

The same thing happened later when the disciples "were on the way, going up to Jerusalem, and Jesus went ahead of them" (10:32a). The disciples were filled with amazement *(ethambounto);* those following Jesus were afraid *(ephobounto),* just as the disciples had been afraid (see 9:32).

This time Jesus spoke of his passion in greater detail, emphasizing the passion over the resurrection for pastoral reasons (10:33-34). James and John then responded with a request: "Grant that in your glory we may sit one at your right and the other at your left" (10:37). Jesus answered with a question: "Can you drink the cup that I drink or be baptized with the baptism with which I am baptized?" (10:38). When they answered that they could, Jesus responded that they would: "The cup that I drink, you will drink, and with the baptism with which I am baptized, you will be baptized; but to sit at my right or at my left is not mine to give but is for those for whom it has been prepared" (10:39-40).

For James and John, and all the others, Jesus again spelled out the implications of his passion and resurrection for his followers. This time he used traditional sacramental images, relating his passion and resurrection to the baptismal and eucharistic life of Mark's readers.

In light of these passages, each of them critical for the life and mission of the Church, we should not be puzzled by the reaction of the women at the conclusion of the gospel. For them, the young man in the white robe represented Jesus, the risen Lord, announcing the resurrection of Jesus of Nazareth, the crucified one. Like the disciples they reacted with fear. Like Peter, like the disciples, and like James and John, the women could not accept the implications of the passion and resurrection for their own life. They were overwhelmed by their commission to go and tell the disciples and Peter, "He is going before you to Galilee; there you will see him, as he told you" (16:7).

Mark challenged his community with the fear of the disciples when Jesus calmed the storm (4:35-41), and again when he came to them on the sea, got into the boat, and the wind died down (6:45-52). It must be that, like the disciples, the community feared the implications of Jesus' cosmic lordship and resisted their mission to all peoples.

Mark also challenged the community with the reaction of Peter, of the disciples, and of James and John to Jesus' gospel of the passion and resurrection. It must be that, like them, the community could not face the implications of the passion and resurrection, indeed of their own baptism and of the renewal of their baptismal commitment when they celebrated the Eucharist. In Pauline terms, it was not easy to "eat this bread and drink the cup." As often as they did that, they proclaimed "the death of the Lord until he comes" (1 Cor 11:26).

At the very end of the gospel, Mark challenged the community with the flight of the women. The women fled like the disciples and a young follower when Jesus was arrested (14:50-52). He also challenged the community with the women's failure to fulfill their mission because they were afraid. It must be that the community, at least many in the community were also fleeing from their baptismal commitment. Mark challenged the community with the fear and silence of the women. Why was the community afraid? Why did they not fulfill their mission to proclaim the gospel of the passion and resurrection?

To understand the flight, the fear and the silence of the women, we have to reread the entire gospel, following Jesus in Galilee, as gradually he opens the eyes of the blind to see him. The eyes of Peter and the disciples had to be opened (see 8:22–10:52). It is the same for his followers today as it was for the early followers portrayed in the Gospel.

A New Ending (16:9-20)

Mark may have ended the Gospel with the silence of the women (16:8), challenging his own community's silence because they too were afraid, but in Catholic editions of Mark, the Gospel continues with a new ending (16:9-20). The new ending includes a series of three appearances (16:9-14), closely connected with the commissioning of the Eleven (16:15-18), Jesus' ascension (16:19), and the ensuing mission of the Eleven (16:20). This "longer ending," as it is commonly called, was written and appended to Mark sometime in the second century, when the four Gospels were collected.[9]

The "longer ending" was clearly not part of the original Gospel according to Mark. Nor did Mark, the author of "the beginning of the gospel," add it later. Had Mark done that, he surely would have provided a smooth transition from the original ending (16:1-8) to the new (16:9-20). As it is, there is no transition at all. Adapting the new ending to new circumstances, Mark would also have respected the style, the vocabulary, and the theology of the Gospel.

Instead, the author simply appended the longer ending (16:9-20) without trying to integrate it with the original ending (16:1-8) and through it with the rest of the Gospel. There is no effort at a literary transition. The style and the vocabulary are extremely different, and the theology is not consistent with the rest of the Gospel. The pastoral setting presupposed by the new ending is also very different. From the world of Mark, we move into an entirely different world facing a whole new set of challenges.

Even so, the longer ending is part of the canonical Gospel of Mark. The Council of Trent defined it as such, even if indirectly, in relation to the Council's list of the books of the New Testament "as contained in the old Latin Vulgate edition."[10] The Latin Vulgate for

[9] For monographs on Mark's new ending (16:9-20), see William R. Farmer, *The Last Twelve Verses of Mark* (London: Cambridge University Press, 1974); Joseph Hug, *La finale de l'evangile de Marc (Marc 16, 9–20)* (Paris: J. Gabalda, 1978; Paul L. Danove, *The End of Mark's Story, a Methodological Study* (Leiden: E. J. Brill, 1993).

[10] The Council of Trent issued two decrees concerning sacred Scripture in its Session 4 (April 8, 1546), one on the "acceptance of the sacred books and

Mark's Gospel included the longer ending (16:9-20), making the ending a canonical part of Mark's Gospel.[11]

An Alternate Ending

The "longer ending" seems to have been conceived not as an addition to 16:1-8 but as an alternate ending to be read in place of 15:47 and 16:1-8. The basic themes of this alternate ending are the early appearances of Jesus, the report of those who saw him, the tradition concerning them, the unbelief of many, the basis for belief, and the mission that flows from believing.

The basic themes of the original ending were very different. Focusing on the visit to the tomb, the original ending highlighted the stone rolled away from the tomb, the proclamation of Jesus' resurrection, the women's commission, their flight from the tomb, their frightened silence, and their failure to fulfill their commission.

As an alternate ending, the author very likely conceived of 16:9-20 as replacing 15:47–16:8 and to be read immediately after 15:46. The intended sequence for reading would then be:

> (15:46) Having bought a linen cloth, he took him down, wrapped him in the linen cloth and laid him in a tomb that had been hewn out of the rock. Then he rolled a stone against the entrance to the tomb.

> (16:9) When he had risen, early on the first day of the week, he appeared first to Mary Magdalene, out of whom he had driven seven demons. . . .

Since the author does not include a visit to the tomb, there would have been no point to Mark 15:47: "Mary Magdalene and Mary the

---

apostolic traditions," the other on the "acceptance of the Latin Vulgate edition of the Bible; rule on the manner of interpreting sacred scripture etc." See Norman P. Tanner, S.J., *Decrees of the Ecumenical Councils*, vol. two, *Trent to Vatican II* (Washington, D.C.: Georgetown University Press, 1990) 663–65.

The pertinent passage is in the first decree: "If anyone should not accept as sacred and canonical these entire books and all their parts as they have, by established custom, been read in the catholic church, and as contained in the old Latin Vulgate edition, and in conscious judgment should reject the aforesaid traditions: let him be anathema" (Tanner, 664).

[11] Another ending, called "the shorter ending" and an addition between verses 14 and 15, the Freer Logion (4th–5th century), are often included in modern editions of the Bible but are not contained in the Latin Vulgate. They are, therefore, not canonical, that is, not part of the sacred Scriptures. They do, however, attest to the difficulties posed by both the original ending and "the longer ending" of Mark.

mother of Joses watched where he was laid." Without Mark 15:47 and 16:1, and since Mary Magdalene is the only woman mentioned in 16:9 (see John 20:1-2, 11-18), nor would there been any point to Mark 15:40-41: "There were also women looking on from a distance. Among them were Mary Magdalene, Mary the mother of the younger James and of Joses, and Salome. These women had followed him when he was in Galilee and ministered to him. There were also many other women who had come up with him to Jerusalem."

Mary Magdalene is introduced as the one from whom Jesus had driven seven demons (see Luke 8:1-3), suggesting that until this point she had not been part of the story. At the same time, the author presupposes that we are familiar with Mary Magdalene from the other gospel accounts.

INTERPRETATION

The longer or alternate ending for Mark (16:9-20) unfolds in four sections, including three appearances: one to Mary Magdalene (16:9-11), another to two disciples (16:12-13), and yet another to the Eleven (16:14-18). The alternate ending then concludes with the ascension of Jesus and the mission of the Eleven (16:19-20).

The four sections were clearly conceived as a whole, building up from the first appearance to the second, to the third, and to the ascension and the mission of the Eleven. Each section also presupposes the previous section, and is chronologically linked to it. Jesus "first" (*proton,* 16:9) appeared to Mary Magdalene. "After this" (*meta de tauta,* 16:12) he appeared to the two disciples. "[But] later" (*hysteron* [*de*], 16:14), he appeared to the Eleven. "So then [*men oun*] . . . , after he spoke to them" (*meta to lalesai autois,* 16:19), the Lord Jesus was taken up to heaven.

Each of the four sections refers to an event known from one or more stories told in John, Matthew, Luke, or the book of Acts.

—The appearance to Mary Magdalene (16:9-11) refers primarily to the appearance described in John 20:11-18 (see also Matt 28:9-10). The identification of Mary Magdalene, however, as the one from whom Jesus had driven seven demons, comes from Luke 8:1-3.

—The appearance to the two disciples (16:12-13) refers to a story told in Luke 24:13-35, in which Jesus appeared to two disciples on the way to Emmaus.

—The appearance to the Eleven (16:14-18) refers to an event situated on the first day of the week when Jesus appeared to the Eleven while at table in Jerusalem. The story is told in Luke 24:36-

49. Similar stories are told in Acts 1:3-5, 6-8 (see also Acts 10:40-42), in John 20:19-25, and in Matthew 28:16-20.

—The ascension of Jesus and the mission of the Eleven (16:19-20) refers to an event told at the end of Luke and the beginning of Acts (Luke 24:50-53; Acts 1:9-11). A related story is also told in Matthew 28:16-20. The mission itself (16:20) is told in symbolic terms in Mark 6:6b–8:21. It is also the subject of Luke's second volume, the book of Acts.

The author of the alternate ending (16:9-20) assumed that his readers were familiar with the New Testament stories of the appearances of Jesus, his ascension, and the mission of the Twelve. In the gospels of John, Matthew, and Luke, as well as in Acts, those stories are rich in narrative details, regarding the setting, the personages, and the circumstances in which Jesus appeared to them.

Each story tells where and when the event took place. They also introduce the personages, describe their attitude, tell how Jesus appeared to them and how they reacted. Like an icon, each story puts us in touch with the event itself and draws us into the drama of its unfolding.

The author of the alternate ending, however, is not interested in any of those details. Instead of telling or retelling the stories, he simply refers to the events.

The author also takes many liberties with the stories, sometimes transforming them almost completely. Employing different terms and expressions from those used in the tradition and in the original stories, he shows no interest in their symbolic language and theology. Paradoxically, he shows no interest in the resurrection itself or in the historical appearances of Jesus.

His interest is pastoral, focusing not on the past but on the present and the lack of belief among his readers. But to respond to this contemporary challenge, he refers to the past and emphasizes the unbelief of those who were with Jesus, that is, the unbelief of the Eleven. He also describes the signs accompanying those who believed.

From these observations, we conclude that the alternate ending is not and should not be described as a series of appearance stories. It refers to the appearances but does not retell them, as Matthew and Luke did for the stories in Mark's Gospel, including that of the visit to the tomb. The purpose of the alternative ending, therefore, was not to supply for the lack of appearances of Jesus in the Gospel of Mark.

The alternate ending is very different from any story in the Gospel. It does not address the reader or the listener as a gospel story does, that is, by proclaiming the gospel, telling its story, and inviting them to join the first disciples in the life, mission, and the passion-resurrection of Jesus. The alternate ending is also almost completely bereft of theology in the traditional, biblical sense, where theology is expressed and communicated through stories, prophecy, and prayers.

Basically, the alternate ending is a work of apologetics. As such, it tries to convince any readers who may have been wavering that their belief in Jesus' resurrection and their mission as Christians was well-founded. The signs to which it refers indicate great interest in charismatic phenomena.

Together, the apologetic and the charismatic aspect of the alternate ending point to a setting in which Christians either were questioning their own faith in the resurrection of Jesus or had to defend it against skeptics and non-believers. For such a setting, the author found the original ending of Mark (16:1-8) and the other resurrection accounts quite inadequate.

To bolster the faith of his readers and help them to respond to outsiders, the alternate ending emphasizes extraordinary signs associated with those who believe. The signs are presented as proofs of the authenticity of their belief and of their mission.

The Appearance to Mary Magdalene (16:9-11)

The first section of the alternate ending refers to Jesus' appearance to Mary Magdalene (16:9-11). As in John 20:11-18, there is no reference to the other Mary who accompanied her (see Matt 28:1, 9-10). Nor is there any reference to Mary Magdalene having made a previous visit to the tomb (see John 20:1-2).

"When He Had Risen." The section opens very abruptly, "When he had risen" *(anastas de),* literally, "and having risen." Ignoring that 16:1-8 was about Mary Magdalene and her companions (see 15:40-41, 47; 16:1), the author introduces the resurrection as if Jesus himself had just been mentioned. In the alternate ending, Jesus is not named until the last section in relation to the ascension (16:19).

In 16:9, the opening expression, "When he had risen," presumes that the resurrection had not yet been announced. The pronoun, implied in the verb, does not refer, therefore, to the young man's proclamation that Jesus of Nazareth, the crucified one, had been raised (16:6). It must then refer in general to the story of Jesus' death and his burial. It could also refer grammatically to the pronoun "him" *(auton,* 15:46), that is, Jesus, whom Joseph of Arimathea wrapped in a linen cloth and laid in a tomb. The alternate ending, however, shows no interest in the tomb of Jesus.

The style and the vocabulary of the section, as of all of 16:9-20, are very different from Mark's original ending (16:1-8), further confirmation that the author did not conceive of 16:9-20 as a continuation of the gospel beyond the visit to the tomb (16:1-8), but as an alternate ending. Mark 16:9-20 is the only account of Jesus' resurrection appearances that does not presuppose one or more visits to the tomb.

Referring to Jesus' resurrection in 16:9, the author uses the verb *anistemi* rather than *egeiro*, the verb that Mark used in the passion (14:28) and in the original ending (16:6; but see 16:14).[12] The verb *egeiro* was used in evangelization, to proclaim the resurrection of Christ, as well as in early baptismal creeds (see 1 Cor 15:3-5).

In Mark, *egeiro* was also used when Jesus took Simon's mother-in-law by the hand and raised her up (1:31), and when Jesus raised the daughter of Jairus: "Little girl, I say to you, arise!" (5:41). Very likely, both stories were part of traditional baptismal catechesis and symbolized the new life of the baptized.[13]

From the beginning, *egeiro* was part of the language of gospel proclamation and creedal response. And that is the word the young man in the tomb used proclaiming that Jesus had been raised (16:6). The alternate ending does not include a proclamation of the resurrection, making it very different from every other gospel account of the resurrection.

The verb *anistemi,* employed in 16:9, was used in Mark and elsewhere for the Jesus' prophetic announcements of the passion and resurrection of the Son of Man (8:31; 9:31; 10:34; see also 9:9).[14] The intention behind a prophetic announcement is to have people see deeply into a particular event or reality and its implications for those addressed.

In the context of apologetics, however, prophetic announcements are easily transformed into predictions. When the prediction is verified, the verb *anistemi* then becomes part of the vocabulary of

---

[12] The alternate ending does use *egeiro* in 16:14 with reference to Jesus "after he had been raised," literally, "the risen one" *(egegermenon).*

[13] In Mark, the verb *egeiro* is similarly used in 2:9, 11, 12; 3:3; 6:14, 16; 9:27; 10:49; 12:26.

[14] The subject of *anistemi* is the one who rises. The subject of *egeiro*, on the other hand, is the one who raises someone else; when the subject is the one raised, the verb is used in the passive. For example, when Jesus commanded the young daughter of Jairus to rise, the verb is *egeiro* (5:41). When, responding to Jesus' command, she rose, the verb is *anistemi* (5:42). Later, when Jesus takes a boy possessed by a mute spirit by the hand, "he raised" *(egeiren)* him, and the boy rose *(aneste,* 9:27).

apologetics. As such, it serves the apologetic purpose of the alternate ending.

"He Appeared." Referring to Jesus' appearance to Mary Magdalene, the alternate ending speaks of Jesus becoming visible or being revealed *(ephane)*. Elsewhere in the New Testament, the verb *phaino* is never used for an appearance of the risen Lord. Quite often it refers to a natural or symbolic phenomenon, whether ordinary or extraordinary, such as light (John 1:5; 1 John 5:8), a star (Matt 2:7), or lightning (Matt 23:27), or even weeds (Matt 13:26) appearing. It can also refer to an outward appearance such as one who wants to appear to be praying (Matt 6:5) or fasting (Matt 6:16, 18). Sometimes it even refers to a deceptive appearance. All in all, we have to say that the verb *phaino* is not weighty biblically and theologically.

The original ending of Mark spoke of the disciples seeing him *(opsesthe)*, a future form of the verb *horao:* "He is going before you to Galilee; there you will see [*opsesthe*] him, as he told you" (16:7). *Opsesthe,* a future form of the verb *horao,* corresponds to *ophthe,* a past form of the same verb. *Ophthe,* literally "he made himself be seen" (see 1 Cor 15:5-8), is the traditional term for an appearance of Jesus. The form *ophthe* evoked appearances of God, the angel of the Lord, and the glory of God, for example, to Abraham or to Moses, as told in the Septuagint.

"Early on the First Day of the Week." For the time of the appearance, the alternate ending refers to "early" *(proi)* on the first day of the week *(prote sabbatou),* associating the appearance to Mary Magdalene to the time she went to the tomb (John 20:1). Doing that, it replaces the visit to the tomb with the appearance. For the author, the empty tomb was not a basis for belief in the resurrection.

At the same time, the author substituted the ordinal numeral, "first" *(prote)* for traditional cardinal numeral, "one" *(mia),* traditionally used in every gospel for the day when the women went to the tomb and heard the good news that Jesus had been raised. In the early communities, it was also the day when Christians assembled as a church (1 Cor 16:2) and took part in "the breaking of the bread" (see Luke 24:13-35, 36-53; Acts 20:7-12).

In the Septuagint's literal translation of the Hebrew for Genesis 1:5, the first *(mia)* day referred to the first day of creation. In the New Testament, the first *(mia)* day of the week presented the resurrection, the experience of the resurrection, its proclamation, and its celebration as the beginning of a new creation. In favor of a more idiomatic Greek expression, the author of the alternate ending sacrificed this traditional evocation of Genesis 1:1-5. He shows little interest in literary allusions and layered evocations of the Old Testament, with the result that his references to the resurrection and Jesus' appearances have very little depth.

"First to Mary Magdalene."

"First to Mary Magdalene." Mary Magdalene is introduced as though for the first time, as one who had not been mentioned as one of the women who looked on when Jesus died, observed where he was laid, and went to the tomb early in the morning (15:40-41, 47; 16:1). The author, however, assumes that readers have heard of her. But to make sure, he identifies her as the one "out of whom he had driven seven demons."

The main reference in 16:9-11 is to the story told in John, where Jesus first *(proton)* appeared to Mary Magdalene early *(proi)* on the first day of the week. It is only later on the evening of the first day of the week that he appeared to the disciples (John 20:19). But to identify Mary Magdalene, the author refers to Luke 8:2, where Mary was introduced as one "from whom seven demons had gone out."

The reference to Luke 8:2 is quite clear, but it is not a quotation. Luke did not actually say that Jesus personally drove out the demons from her. He presented Mary as someone "from whom [*aph' hes*] seven demons had gone out [*exelelythei*]," but did not say who or what moved them to leave. In Mark 16:9, Jesus himself drove *(ekbeblekei)* the seven demons out of her *(par' hes)*. The author of Mark 16:9 recalls the event from memory, and in the process adds to the event. Making it more specific, he associated the event to Jesus' extraordinary ministry as an exorcist.

"She Went and Told His Companions."

"She Went and Told His Companions." After Jesus appeared to Mary Magdalene, she went and told "his companions," literally, "she told those who were with him" *(met' autou)*. To describe the apostles, Mark had also used the expression "being with him." When Jesus constituted *(epoiesen)* the Twelve, it was that they might be with him *(met' autou)*, that is, be closely associated with him and be in solidarity with him, in view of extending his mission (3:14). Later, while Jesus was being interrogated, one of the maids of high priest said to Peter: "You too were with [*meta*] the Nazarene, Jesus" (14:67).

When Mary Magdalene went to those who were with Jesus, she found them "mourning and weeping [*penthousi kai klaiousiv*]" at the loss of Jesus. As told in John 20:11-15, it was Mary herself who was weeping when two angels appeared to her outside the tomb. The angels said to her, "Woman, why are you weeping [*klaiousa*]?" She was still weeping when Jesus appeared to her and asked the same question. By New Testament times, the combination, "mourning and weeping" had become a stock expression for lamentation (see Luke 6:25; Jas 4:9; Rev 18:11, 15, 19).

In John, Mary was lamenting that they had taken the Lord from the tomb and she did not know where they laid him (John 20:13, 15; see 20:2). In Mark 16:10, Jesus' companions, those who were with him, lamented his death on the cross.

"When They Heard . . . , They Did Not Believe." In John, not believing is associated with Thomas, one of the Twelve, who was not present when Jesus appeared to them (see John 20:19-23). When they told him that they had seen the Lord, he answered that in order to believe he personally would have to see the mark of the nails in his hands and even put his finger into the nailmarks (John 20:24-25).

A week later, Jesus appeared to them again, and this time Thomas was with them. Jesus responded to Thomas, "Put your finger here and see my hands, and bring your hand and put it into my side, and do not be unbelieving" (John 20:27). Seeing Jesus and hearing those words, Thomas believed. Jesus then continued, "Have you come to believe because you have seen me? Blessed are those who have not seen and have believed" (John 20:29).

In the alternate ending, those who were "with him" were all like Thomas. They did not believe Mary Magdalene who reported that he was alive and that she had seen him. Like Thomas, they would not believe before they saw him with their own eyes.

In Luke, not believing is also associated with the apostles. When the women returned from the tomb and told the apostles what they saw and heard there, "their story seemed like nonsense and they did not believe [*epistoun*] them" (Luke 24:11).

In Mark 16:10, those who were with Jesus heard that he was alive *(ze)* and was seen *(etheathe)* by Mary Magdalene, but they did not believe *(epistesan)*. For the author, it was not so much that they did not believe Mary Magdalene. They would not have believed anyone else, even some of the Eleven. They simply did not believe that Jesus was alive.

The Appearance to the Two Disciples (16:12-13)

After telling how Jesus appeared to Mary Magdalene, how she reported to those who were "with him" that he was alive and was seen by her, and how they did not believe (16:9-11), the alternate ending speaks of another appearance (16:12-13). This second appearance was to "two of them," that is, two of those who were "with him," whom

Mary Magdalene had found mourning and weeping, and to whom she reported that he was alive. The second appearance was to two of those who were with him but who had not believed that Jesus was alive and had been seen by Mary Magdalene.

The appearance to the two disciples (16:12-13) is closely patterned on the appearance to Mary Magdalene (16:9-11), but is told in an even more summary form. The second appearance would not make much sense if we had not been told about the first appearance to Mary Magdalene.

As for the previous appearance, the author assumes that the readers are familiar with the story and makes no effort to retell it. This time the story is from Luke, the story of the two disciples of Emmaus (Luke 24:13-35). In Mark 16:12-13, the appearance took place while two of them were on their way to the country *(eis agron)*. The alternate ending does not even mention the village called Emmaus.

Nor does it mention that the name of one of the disciples was Cleophas. But that is understandable, since he transformed the two disciples of Emmaus, "two of them" (Luke 24:13) into two of those who were "with him," that is, two of the Eleven (see 16:14).

For the author of the alternate ending, the story itself holds no interest. Otherwise, he would surely have said that they did not recognize him when he joined them on the way but recognized him only later when they invited him to stay with them and "he took bread, said the blessing, broke it, and gave it to them" (Luke 24:30). Again the interest is narrowly apologetic.

Like the first, however, the second appearance also has a few interesting features, shedding light on the Christian setting for which 16:9-20, the alternate ending, was written. Among them, the Greek verb used for "appearing" is different from the one used for the appearance to Mary Magdalene. The author also indicates that Jesus appeared "in another form."

"After This He Appeared." For the appearance to Mary Magdalene, the verb was *phaino,* meaning becoming visible or being revealed. For the appearance to the two disciples, the verb is *phaneroo.* The same verb is used later for the appearance to the Eleven while they were at table (16:14).

Unlike *phaino, phaneroo* was used elsewhere in the New Testament with reference to an appearance of Jesus after he rose from the dead, but only in the epilogue of John's Gospel, when Jesus "revealed" *(ephanerosin)* himself again to his disciples at the Sea of Tiberias. "He revealed [*ephanerosen*] himself in this way [*houtos*]" (John 21:1). In the conclusion of the story, the verb is used again:

"This was the third time Jesus was revealed [*ephanerothe*] to his disciples after being raised [*egertheis*] from the dead" (John 21:14).

Both here in the alternate ending of Mark (9:12) and in John 21, the author associates the appearance to the way Jesus appeared. In John, it takes the whole story to describe how Jesus appeared. In the Mark 9:12, the author simply says that he appeared "in another form" *(en hetera morphe).*

The verb *phaneroo* refers to revealing or being revealed, not so much in the sense of making something visible or becoming visible, but in the sense of manifesting or being manifested. In the New Testament, the verb is associated with the whole mystery of Christ and Christian life.

The verb is associated with the incarnate life of Jesus, who in his life manifested or revealed the personal name of God. As I AM *(ego eimi),* Jesus could truly say: "I revealed [*ephanerosa*] your name" (John 17:6; see also Mark 6:50; 14:62), not just as a word made up of syllables with consonants and vowels, but as the Word made flesh.

It is also used in connection with the final coming of Christ: "When Christ your life appears [*phanerothe*], then you too will appear [*phanerothesthe*] with him in glory" (Col 3:4).

Finally, the verb is associated with the sacramental nature of Christian life in the church: "But thanks be to God, who always leads us in triumph in Christ and manifests [*phanerounti*] through us the odor of the knowledge of him in every place" (2 Cor 2:14; see also 3:3). In this same sense, Paul uses the verb to describe how the sufferings of Christ are manifested in our body. Paul was "always carrying about in the body the dying of Jesus, so that the life of Jesus may also be manifested [*phanerothe*] in our body. For we who live are constantly being given up to death for the sake of Jesus, so that the life of Jesus may be manifested [*phanerothe*] in our mortal flesh" (2 Cor 4:10-11).

"In Another Form." There are many ways in which Jesus could appear after he rose from the dead. He could appear and be manifested in many forms, just as God, the angel of the Lord, and the glory of God could appear and be manifested in many forms. In the context of the alternate ending of Mark, "another form" refers to a form different from the form in which he appeared to Mary Magdalene.

When he appeared to Mary Magdalene, at first she thought he was the gardener. It is only when he called her by name that she recognized him. For the author of the alternate ending, Jesus appeared to Mary Magdalene in the form of a gardener. When he appeared to the disciples of Emmaus, they thought he was a stranger visiting Jerusalem, one who did not know what had happened to Jesus the Nazarene, "a prophet mighty in deed and word before God and all the people" (Luke 24:18-19). For the author of the alternate ending, Jesus appeared to them in the form of one of many visitors to Jerusalem.

Using the verb *phaneroo,* the author of the alternate ending thus situates the appearance or manifestation of Jesus among other manifestations, some of them divine, some of them incarnational, eschatological, or sacramental. In the second appearance, Jesus appears in the visible form of some visitor to Jerusalem, in whom and through whom he was manifested as the risen Lord. The story in Luke tells us that Jesus appeared to the disciples on the way but they recognized him only in the breaking of the bread.

The Appearance to the Eleven (16:14-18)

First, Jesus appeared to Mary Magdalene (16:9). When she went and told the Eleven *(tois met'autou genomenois)* that Jesus was alive and had been seen by her, they did not believe, that is, they did not become believers[15] (16:10-11). They had no faith.

After this, Jesus appeared to two of the Eleven *(ex auton,* 16:12), two of those who had been with him. But when the two returned and told the others *(tois loipois),* they did not believe them (16:13). Not to believe someone is a very different statement from not being a believer.

Later, Jesus appeared to all the Eleven (16:14-18). The Eleven had not believed when Mary Magdalene told them that Jesus was alive. Nor had they believed two of their own number when they reported that Jesus appeared to them. Now, when Jesus appears to the Eleven, we expect some indication that they finally believed.

A popular saying comes to mind: "Seeing is believing!" But sometimes, popular sayings can be misleading. What should come to mind is Jesus' response to Thomas in the Gospel of John: "Blessed are those who have not seen and have believed" (John 20:29).

For the author of the alternate ending, believing, that is being a believer or having faith, is not a matter of seeing but of hearing. It comes from hearing the word of those who saw Jesus after he rose. Faith does not come from seeing Jesus after he rose from the dead. Ultimately, it comes from believing someone who saw him. In the second century, it came from believing someone who handed on the tradition (16:14).

---

[15] The verb for "they did not believe" is *apisteo.* In Mark, the verb is used only in the alternate ending (16:11, 16).

The author's immediate concern is the faith of Christians in the second century, some one hundred years after Jesus' resurrection, his historic appearances, and his ascension (16:19). His ultimate concern is the mission given originally to the Eleven and handed down by them to the Church (16:15). Pursuing and fulfilling that mission, depended on faith. At stake was the salvation of the world (16:16).

The appearance to the Eleven is the third appearance in the series of three. The first two appearances (16:9-11, 12-13) included three elements: the appearance itself, the report to the Eleven, and their disbelief. The third is very different. Like the first and second, it opens with the appearance. But unlike them, the appearance itself has no importance. It is merely the setting (16:14a) for Jesus' rebuke to the Eleven (16:14b) and his short discourse on their mission (16:15-18). In the discourse, Jesus commissions the disciples to go into the whole world and proclaim the gospel to every creature.

Like the first and second appearance, the third evokes a traditional story told in the gospels. As with appearance to Mary Magdalene and the two disciples, the author makes no attempt to retell the story. He simply refers to it, giving only enough to identify it. For all three appearances, the author assumes that his readers know about the event and are familiar with its story.

The appearance to Mary Magdalene, like the resurrection, takes place on "the first day of the week" (16:9). The author's use of the temporal indication points to a traditional story told in John 20:1-2, 11-18. The appearance to two of the Eleven took place while they were walking on the way to the country (16:12). This time, the author's use of a geographical indication points to the story of the disciples of Emmaus told in Luke 24:13-35.

The appearance to the Eleven took place while they were at table (16:14a). The author's use of a meal setting points to the story of Jesus' appearance to the Eleven when he asked them for something to eat and they gave him a piece of baked fish. The story is told in Luke 24:36-49 (see also Acts 1:3-8; 10:40-41).

As with the story of the appearance to Mary Magdalene and to the disciples of Emmaus, the author's report takes a lot of liberties with the story, transforming it into a setting for a strong rebuke to the Eleven before commissioning them to proclaim the gospel to everyone everywhere. In that, he also associates Luke's meal story with Jesus' rebuke to Thomas (John 20:24-29), who had refused to believe on the testimony of the Eleven who had seen him a week earlier on the first day of the week (John 20:19-23). He also associates both the meal story in Luke and the rebuke to Thomas with

Jesus' commission to the Eleven on the mountain in Galilee to which he had called them (Matt 28:16-20).

"As the Eleven Were at Table." Mark's Gospel never refers to the Eleven. When Jesus made or established the Twelve (3:13-19), Mark's emphasis was on the institution and the theological significance of the Twelve. In Mark, as in 1 Corinthians 15:3-5, the Twelve of Christ are comparable to the Twelve of Jacob or Israel, but their significance is radically different.

The Twelve of Israel united twelve tribes into one people. The Twelve of Christ are symbolic of the universality of the Church, and their mission is to unite all peoples into one people of God. Those who make up the list of the Twelve are also important, but the list itself is secondary to the symbolic, theological notion of the Twelve of Christ.

With that emphasis, Mark never moves away from the Twelve, even after Judas' defection. To the very end, Judas is presented as "one of the Twelve" (14:10, 20, 43).

Both Matthew and Luke place greater emphasis on those who make up the company of the Twelve. After Jesus' defection, both refer to the Eleven (Matt 28:16; Luke 24:9, 33) instead of the Twelve. Not that the institution of the Twelve was no longer important. In Acts, Luke tells how the Twelve were reconstituted and brought up to their full complement (Acts 1:15-26). Acts also refers to the Eleven in another sense, distinguishing the position and mission of Peter from the position and mission of the other apostles (Acts 2:14). At the end of Matthew's Gospel, Jesus sends the Eleven on the universal mission, suggesting that the symbolic Twelve would find its full complement through and in the mission of the Gentiles.

In its reference to the Eleven, the alternative ending has Luke 24:9, 33 and Matthew 28:16 in mind, but unlike them, does not see any need to reconstitute the Twelve. In the alternative ending, the universality of the Church and its mission is based not on the theological symbolism of the Twelve, but on the Eleven.

Jesus appeared to the Eleven while they were at table *(anakeimenois autois),* literally "while they were reclining." In New Testament times, reclining is the normal position for a formal meal. Mark described reclining at Herod's birthday banquet (6:26) and Jesus and the Twelve at the Last Supper (14:18).

Being or reclining at table, having a common meal, in itself is a sign of unity and solidarity. It also reinforces unity and solidarity among the participants. As Paul shows in 1 Corinthians 10:1-14, such unity and solidarity could be for the good, but it could also be for the bad.

In the context of Mark 16:9-14, being at table shows the Eleven united and in solidarity in their unbelief and hardness of heart. Appearing to them, rebuking them and commissioning them, Jesus transforms that unity and solidarity into one of commitment to the universal mission.

"He Appeared to Them." The verb used for the appearance of Jesus to the Eleven is the same that was used for the appearance to two of them (16:12), namely, *phaneroo* (see also John 21:1, 14). In 16:12, the verb was associated with the "other form" in which Jesus appeared. In the alternate ending, the verb *phaneroo* indicates Jesus' outward appearance and not the interior effect the appearance had on the Eleven.

A person's outward or external appearance is an objective phenomenon and can be verified by someone else. An inner or interior effect made by someone else is subjective and can be misleading. As in 16:12, therefore, the verb *phaneroo* serves the apologetic purpose of the alternate ending.

Elsewhere in the New Testament, the ordinary verb for appearing is *ophthe,* literally, "he made himself be seen" (see 1 Cor 15:5-8; Luke 24:34; Mark 16:7).[16] With *ophthe,* as with *phaneroo,* Jesus is the agent of the appearance. Unlike *phaneroo,* however, the verb *ophthe* emphasizes how Jesus' appearance had a transforming effect on those to whom he appeared. With *ophthe,* not only did Jesus manifest himself to the Eleven but he gave them the kind of sight they needed to see him.

"And Rebuked Them." When Jesus appeared to Mary Magdalene (16:9) and to two of the Eleven (16:12), he did not address them. Nor did the author indicate any purpose for the appearance. So far as the appearance goes, the focus was entirely on the fact of the appearance. What was important was that Jesus appeared.

But when Jesus appeared to the Eleven, he "rebuked them for their unbelief and hardness of heart." For the author of the alternate ending, the appearance provides a setting for Jesus' rebuke (16:14b) and his subsequent discourse (16:15-18). This time, his focus is on the purpose of the appearance, and not merely on the fact.

The Greek verb for rebuking *(oneidisen)* indicates that Jesus reproached them very severely. In rebuking them, Jesus was close to denouncing them. Elsewhere in Mark, the same verb is attributed to those who were crucified with Jesus and kept abusing *(oneidizon)* him (15:32).

---

[16] In Mark 16:7, the future form of *ophthe,* namely *opsesthe,* is used.

This is the strongest rebuke in the entire Gospel, even stronger than the one at the conclusion (8:14-21) of the Gospel's section of the mission of the Twelve (6:6b–8:21). When Jesus warned the disciples about the leaven of the Pharisees and the leaven of Herod, they had concluded it was because they had no bread. Aware of this, Jesus said to them: "Why do you conclude that it is because you have no bread? Do you not yet understand or comprehend? Are your hearts hardened [*peporomenen echete ten kardian hymon*]? Do you have eyes and not see, ears and not hear?" (8:17-18).

In the alternative ending, Jesus rebuked the Eleven for two things, first, for their unbelief *(apistia)* and hardness of heart *(sklerokardia)*, and second, for not believing those who said they had seen him after he was raised from the dead. The first, their unbelief, recalls that they remained unbelieving after Mary Magdalene reported that he was alive and had been seen by her (16:11). The second recalls their not believing two of them after Jesus appeared to them on their way (16:13).

Jesus first rebuked the Eleven for "their unbelief [*ten apistian*] and hardness of heart [*skerokardian*]."[17] In this first part of the rebuke, unbelief is taken absolutely. The noun "unbelief" *(apistia)* in 16:14 corresponds to the verb "they did not believe" *(epistesan,* from *apisteuo)* in 16:11. Mark had used the noun *apistia* (unbelief or lack of faith) when Jesus marveled at the lack of faith among those at his native place (6:6a). He used it again in the plea of the father of a boy possessed by a violent demon: "I do believe, help my unbelief!" (9:24).

The Eleven remained unbelieving. It is not simply that they refused to believe someone who witnessed to the resurrection. The first part of the rebuke addresses their continuing state of unbelief, that is, their lack of faith. In the rebuke, Jesus associates the Eleven with unbelievers.

The unbelief of the Eleven is closely associated with hardness of heart. Due to their hardness of heart, their unbelief was no ordinary lack of faith. It came from their resistance and refusal to believe.

After rebuking the Eleven for their unbelief, Jesus rebukes them for not having "believed those who saw him after he had been raised." Jesus attributed their state of unbelief, their having no faith, to an original act of unbelief. Ultimately, the reason they did not believe is that "they had not believed [*ouk episteusan*] those who saw him

---

[17] In Mark's Gospel, two Greek expressions are used for "hardness of heart," *sklerokardia,* as here in 16:14 and 10:5, and *porosis tes kardias,* as in 3:5. A related expression with the verb *poroo* (to harden) appears in 6:52 and 8:17.

after he had been raised [*egegermenon*]." The verb for believing *(pisteuo)* corresponds to the same verb when the Eleven did not believe two of their number (16:13). Not believing them, they persisted in their unbelief.

In 16:9-20, the author uses the vocabulary of belief and unbelief in two distinct ways. In relation to Mary Magdalene (16:11), he uses the verb *apisteo* in the sense of having no faith or not being a believer. In relation to two of the Eleven (16:13), he uses the verb *pisteuo* with the negative adverb *ouk* in the sense of not believing someone. The difference is then reflected in 16:14. Later, describing someone who believes and someone who does not believe, he uses the verb *apisteo* (16:16-17) in the first sense of being a believer or not being a believer.

Introducing the whole of 16:9-20, the author used the verb *anistemi* (to rise) with reference to the resurrection of Jesus (16:9). At the time, we saw that the term was associated with Jesus' prophetic announcements of the resurrection of the Son of Man. In this second reference to the resurrection, he uses *egeiro,* a term associated with Paul's proclamation of the gospel and a very early baptismal creed (1 Cor 15:3-5). The author seemingly uses the two verbs with no difference of meaning or nuance. He thereby ignores any evocative power they might have from Mark's Gospel.

The Discourse to the Eleven (16:15-18)

After telling about the rebuke (16:14b), the author presents Jesus' short discourse, which includes Jesus' missionary commission to the Eleven (16:15), the critical importance of their mission for belief and for salvation (16:16), and the signs that will accompany those who believe (16:17-18).

Jesus' extremely severe rebuke to the Eleven seems an unlikely prelude for the extraordinary commission he gives them. People who do not believe are not likely to be given an important mission, even if the rebuke was effective.

The sequence makes sense, however, if Jesus' rebuke to the Eleven is seen as a warning for Christians living many decades later. As part of the alternate ending, the rebuke is not intended for the Eleven. Its purpose is pastoral, alerting the readers about the obstacles that could impede or altogether prevent them from fulfilling their mission. The severity of the rebuke is then matched by the importance of their mission.

For the apostles, it was necessary to see Jesus personally for them to pursue their mission. That is why Jesus rebuked them. For the readers, the severity of the rebuke emphasizes the importance of believing without seeing. The Eleven should have believed without having to see Jesus. Those for whom the alternate ending was destined had to believe without seeing. Their faith depended not on seeing but on hearing the gospel of the resurrection, transmitted through those who saw him and those who believed them.

"Go into the Whole World." Jesus commissions the Eleven to "go into [*poreuthentes eis*] the whole world [*ton kosmon apanta*] and proclaim the gospel [*keryxate to euaggelion*] to every creature [*pase te ktisei*]." The commission recalls the great commission at the end of the Matthew, when Jesus appeared to the Eleven at the mountain to which he had called them: "Go [*poreuthentes*], therefore, and make disciples of all nations" (Matt 28:19). It also recalls Jesus words to the disciples assembled at the end of Luke, announcing that "repentance, for the forgiveness of sins, would be preached [*kerychthenai*] in his name to all the nations" (Luke 24:47).

The author may have had both of these in mind, but he certainly does not quote them or allude to them directly. Instead of using biblical expressions such as "all the nations" or "the ends of the earth," he refers to "the whole world" and to "every creature," terms associated with creation rather than with the history of Israel.

"Those Who Believe . . ." What follows the basic commission (16:15) is very different from the commission in Matthew and Luke. In both Matthew and Luke, Jesus continues to develop the commission. The focus is on the Eleven, those who are sent on mission. In the alternate ending, the focus shifts from those who are sent on mission to those to whom they are sent, those who should benefit from the mission.

"Whoever believes [*ho pisteusas*]," that is, whoever is a believer and has faith, "and is baptized will be saved" (16:16a); "whoever does not believe [*ho de apistesas*]," that is, who is an unbeliever and has no faith, "will be condemned" (16:16b). All the emphasis is on the absolute use of belief and unbelief, as was the case with the Eleven after Mary Magdalene told them that Jesus was alive and had been seen by her (16:9-11) and with the first part of Jesus' rebuke (16:14).

Believing is connected with baptism. In the ecclesial context of 16:9-20, believing is followed by baptism into the charismatic community of the Church (16:17-18). Mark had spoken of baptism in relation to the passion and resurrection of Jesus (10:38-39), a view very close to that of Paul in Romans 6. The alternate ending suggests an ecclesiological rather than a christological view of baptism. Since there was no question of baptism for someone who did not believe, the author did not have to add "and is not baptized" when considering the lot of "whoever does not believe."

Being a believer and being baptized is a condition for salvation. Someone who is an unbeliever will be condemned. Unbelievers are not simply people who have no faith. That could be no fault of their own. Unbelievers are like the Eleven, when they did not become believers after Mary Magdalene told them that Jesus was alive and been seen by her. Unbelievers are like the Eleven who did not believe two of their own number when they saw Jesus after he rose from the dead. In the context of the alternate ending, an unbeliever is someone to whom the gospel has been proclaimed by the Eleven, those who heard the Eleven and believed, or, later on, those who carried on the missionary tradition.

Believing and not believing is the basic theme pervading the whole of Mark's alternate ending (16:9-20). It is also a complex theme, in which believing and not believing are taken in two different senses, depending on the object of belief.

In the first sense, the object is the message itself, the gospel of Jesus' resurrection. In the second, the object is the messenger, the one who reports or proclaims the gospel of the resurrection. In reality, the two senses are very closely related. To believe the message one has to believe the messenger.

Still, the difference between the two senses is very significant. Belief in the resurrection of Jesus is at the very core of the gospel and critical for the whole of Christian faith. As Paul said to the Corinthians, "If Christ has not been raised, your faith is vain" (1 Cor 15:17). Believing the messenger, however, is but a means to that faith.

The author of the alternate ending respects the distinction, and the difference is reflected in the vocabulary.

The theme of belief and unbelief is central to each section of the alternate ending (16:9-11, 12-13, 14-18, 19-20). When Mary Magdalene told the Eleven that Jesus was alive, they did not believe *(epistesan)* the message (16:9-11). When two of them, two of the Eleven, told the others, they did not believe *(oude . . . episteusan)* the messengers (16:12-13). In the first case, they did not believe that Jesus was risen. In the second case, they did not believe the two who reported that Jesus had appeared to them.

Later, when Jesus appeared to the Eleven while they were at table, he rebuked them for their unbelief *(apistian),* that is, for not believing the gospel message of his resurrection, and that was because they had not believed *(ouk episteusan)* those who had seen him after he was raised from the dead (16:14). For the author, believing the message was paramount, but believing the message depended on believing the messengers.

This third section (16:14-18) continues with a short discourse (16:15-18), opening with the commissioning of the Eleven. They were to go into the whole world and proclaim the gospel to all creatures (16:15).

The mission of the Eleven is then described in terms of its implications for those who will believe *(ho pisteusas)* the gospel message and for those who will not believe *(apistesas)* it (16:16). For those who believe, the mission will bring salvation. For those who do not believe, the mission will bring condemnation. The third section continues to develop the theme of belief and unbelief, always in relation to the implications of the mission and the proclamation of the gospel.

"These Signs . . ." The short discourse (16:15-18) began with Jesus' commission to the Eleven (16:15) and a solemn pronouncement concerning the critical nature of their mission (16:16). It then continued by declaring that signs *(semeia)* would accompany those who will believe *(tois pisteusasin)* and by giving a list of those signs (16:17-18).[18]

"These signs [*semeia . . . tauta*, plural] will accompany [*parakolouthesei*, singular] those who believe [*tois pisteusasin*, plural]." With a singular verb *(parakolouthesei)*, the plural subject *(semeia . . . tauta)* is seen and presented collectively. What is important is that extraordinary signs will accompany those (be associated with those) who believe, even if these signs are not seen all the time and all at once.

Those who believe are also seen and presented collectively. What is important is that believers collectively will be accompanied by the signs, and not each individual believer or particular groups of believers.

The signs, therefore, are not seen as gifts or privileges offered to one who believes. Although the signs will accompany those who believe, their purpose is to reveal the power of the gospel proclaimed by the Eleven and those who succeed them. As such, the signs also show the authenticity of their mission to the whole world. The signs, therefore, are closely associated with the theme of belief and

---

[18] For the meaning and the purpose of the signs in Mark 16:17-18, see Joseph Hug, *La finale de l'evangile de Marc* (Paris: J. Gabalda et Cie, 1978) 102–28. For the use of the term "sign" in the Bible, see Karl Heinrich Rengstorf, *"semeion," Theological Dictionary of the New Testament,* edited by Gerhard Friedrich (Grand Rapids, Mich.: Wm. B. Eerdmans, 1971) VII:200–261.

unbelief, but even more closely with the theme of mission and the need to proclaim the gospel.

To appreciate the meaning of the term "signs" *(semeia)* in Mark 16:17-18, it is helpful to compare it with other usages in the New Testament. The different kinds of signs in the New Testament can be distinguished by their purpose.

Revelatory Signs. Some signs are meant to be revelatory, as the signs in John's Gospel, revealing the mystery of Jesus, his relation to God and to the history of salvation. Those same signs manifest the power and the love of God in the person of Jesus. Such signs invite contemplation and communion in the mystery they communicate.[19]

Some of the revelatory signs in the New Testament are messianic signs, revealing the abundant gifts of God in the messianic age, beginning in the mission of Jesus, as told in the gospels, and continuing in the mission of the apostles and in the Christian community, as presented in the Acts of the Apostles. In the book of Acts, the signs *(semeia)* are associated with wonders *(terata)*, recalling the acts of God in the story of Israel's liberation from bondage (2:19 [Joel 3], 22, 43; 4:30; 5:12; 6:8; 7:36; 14:3; 15:12).

Some of the revelatory signs are prophetic and apocalyptic signs, announcing and revealing the fulfillment of creation and the history of salvation. We find these in the gospels, especially in Jesus' eschatological discourse on the Mount of Olives (Mark 13:4, 22; Matt 24:3, 24, 30; Luke 21:7, 11, 25) and in the book of Revelation (12:1, 3; 13:13, 14; 15:1; 16:14; 19:20).

Authenticating Signs. Besides revelatory signs, the New Testament also refers to authenticating or accrediting signs, demanded of Jesus by unbelievers who were hostile to his mission. The intended purpose of those signs was to show that Jesus was the Messiah. The Pharisees, for example, sought from Jesus a sign from heaven to test him (Mark 8:11-13; see Matt 12:38-39; 16:1-4; Luke 11:16, 29, 30; 23:8; see also John 2:18; 6:30).

In such cases, Jesus refused to perform a sign for them. Sometimes, he announced that they would indeed receive a sign, but that sign would be the sign of Jonah (Luke 11:29-32; Matt 12:38-42). Refusing to give an authenticating or accrediting sign, Jesus announced a revelatory sign.

---

[19] For the Johannine signs, see Rudolf Schnakenburg, *The Gospel According to St. John,* Volume I (New York: Herder and Herder, 1968) Excursus IV, 515–28.

Signs in the Alternate Ending. The purpose of the signs in the alternate ending of Mark is to show that the mission of the Eleven was authentic. The intention, therefore, is to bolster the church's commitment to the universal mission entrusted to it by Jesus. The signs do that by manifesting the power of the gospel. The signs in the alternate ending, therefore, are intended as authenticating signs as well as revelatory signs: authenticating signs in relation to the messenger, revelatory signs in relation to the message.

The signs promised by Jesus are not for the benefit of those who hear the gospel. Nor are they given to particular believers for the benefit of the community. They are for the benefit of those who are entrusted with the mission.

The signs clearly serve the apologetic purpose of the alternate ending. Their apologetic purpose, however, is not to buttress the faith of those who believe, nor to persuade unbelievers to believe. The signs are associated with those who will believe, but the promise is given to Eleven. Their purpose, therefore, is to show that the mission, first given to the Eleven, is authentic and critical for the salvation of the world. The signs do that by showing the extraordinary effect of the gospel mission on those who believe.

The apologetic purpose of the signs, therefore, is to bolster the missionary effort of the Church. Those who believe, thanks to the gospel that was proclaimed to them, are accompanied with extraordinary signs. Surely, the same gospel can bring salvation to those who believe and are baptized and condemnation to those who refuse to believe.

The Five Signs. The alternate ending then gives a list[20] of five signs (16:17b-18) that will accompany those who believe:

1) in the name of Jesus, the believers will drive out demons;
2) they will speak new languages;
3) they will pick up serpents [with their hands],
4) and if they drink a deadly poison, it will not harm them;
5) they will lay hands on the sick, and sick will recover.

The list of the signs is well integrated in the context of the alternate ending. The first, driving out demons *(daimonia ekbalousin)*, recalls the description of Mary Magdalene as the one from whom Jesus had driven seven demons *(ekbeblekei hepta daimonia,*

---

[20] The alternative ending has a list of five signs. Elsewhere in the New Testament, lists include three (Matt 7:22), four (Matt 10:8), or five signs (Matt 11:5).

16:9b). Later, the very last expression in the alternate ending, describing the actual mission, refers to "accompanying signs" *(epakolouthountoun semeion),* that is, the signs that will accompany those will believe (16:20).

What Jesus did, the believers will do in his name. Indeed, all the signs will be done in the name of Jesus. The signs are therefore associated with the presence of Jesus to the Eleven, abiding through his name, working with them, confirming the word, through the signs accompanying those who believe the word and are baptized, thanks to the mission of the Eleven (see 16:20).

The context for the signs given in the alternate ending is very different from that of 1 Corinthians 12–14, where the signs are gifts *(charismata)* of the Holy Spirit, given to particular members of the community for the sake of all. The context is also different from that of Pentecost in Acts 2, where the signs are attributed to the coming of the Holy Spirit on the community of the Twelve, fulfilling the words of the prophet Joel 2:28-32 (LXX, 3:1-5).

If the author of the alternate ending had 1 Corinthians 12–14 and Acts 2 in mind, he would surely have associated the signs with the Holy Spirit. But the alternate ending does not even mention the Holy Spirit. Instead, the signs are associated with Jesus (16:17), the Lord, present with the Eleven through his name.

Four of the five signs are attested elsewhere in the New Testament. Two of them, the first and the last, are important in Mark's presentation of the mission of Jesus and the mission of the Twelve. But again, there is a difference. In Mark, it is those whom Jesus sent, the Twelve, who drove out demons or unclean spirits, not those to whom they were sent. In the alternate ending, it is those who would hear the Eleven and believe who would drive out demons. The same is true for healing the sick.

Driving Out Demons. The first sign is driving out demons in the name of Jesus. In his ministry, Jesus expelled demons or unclean spirits, demonstrating his authority (Mark 1:21-28, 34, 39; 5:1-20; 9:14-29). He also established the Twelve, "that they might be with him and he might send them forth to preach and to have authority to drive out demons" (Mark 3:14-15). Sending them on mission, he gave them authority over unclean spirits (Mark 6:7). In their mission, "they drove out many demons" (Mark 6:13). Now all those who believe will drive out demons in the name of Jesus (Mark 16:17).

The alternate ending also recalls Jesus' response when the disciples tried to stop one who did not follow them from driving out demons in the name of Jesus: "There is no one who performs a mighty deed in my name who can at the same time speak ill of me" (9:38-39; see also 9:36-37).

Speaking New Languages. The second sign, speaking new languages *(glossais lalesousin kainais),* seems to be a reference to the Pentecost event in Acts 2. But again, in the alternate ending it is not the Eleven who spoke new languages but those who believed after hearing the Eleven. Besides, Acts does not say that the apostles actually spoke new languages. What Acts says is that everyone in the huge crowd, representing "every nation under heaven" (Acts 2:5), heard the apostles in their own native language (Acts 2:6-8). In the alternate ending, it is a matter of speaking new languages. In Acts, it was a matter of hearing in different languages.

Picking up Serpents. The third sign, picking up serpents [with their hands], evokes the passage in the book of Acts where Paul inadvertently picked a serpent, while gathering a bundle of brush for the fire. The serpent fastened on his hand, but he shook it off into the fire (Acts 28:3-6). This is the only other reference in the New Testament where someone picks up a serpent.

The third sign may also recall Jesus' message to the seventy-two returning from their mission: "Behold, I have given you the power 'to tread upon serpents' and scorpions and upon the full force of the enemy and nothing will harm you" (Luke 10:19; see 11:11-12; see also Gen 3:15; Ps 91:13). But again, in the alternate ending, it is not the missionaries who pick up serpents or tread on them but those who believe and are baptized, thanks to the mission of the Eleven.

Drinking Deadly Poisons. The fourth sign, drinking deadly poisons without harm, has no parallel anywhere in the New Testament.[21] We note, however, that the author linked it with the third sign, picking up serpents, with the conjunction "and if" *(kan).* The two signs are thus presented as a double sign, both of which have to do with deadly poison. The alternate ending, however, does not mention the poison in relation to the serpent. The link may have been suggested by Psalm 58:4-6:

---

[21] Outside the New Testament, Eusebius of Caesarea quotes a fragment from Papias saying that Justus, also named Barsabbas, had drunk "a deadly poison" but, by the Lord's grace it had no ill effects on him *(Ecclesiastical History* III, 39, 9). We recall also that Ignatius of Antioch wrote of the Eucharist as an antidote (Eph 20, 2). Both Papias and Ignatius were well within the period when the alternate ending was written.

The wicked have been corrupt since birth;
    liars from the womb, they have gone astray.
Their poison is like the poison of a snake,
    like that of a serpent stopping its ears,
So as not to hear the voice of the charmer
    who casts such cunning spells.

Healing the Sick. The fifth and last sign, healing the sick by the laying on of hands, is well attested in Mark's Gospel (6:5; 8:22-26). Healing the sick is an important part of Jesus' ministry (Mark 1:29-31; 3:1-6; 5:25-34; 6:55-56; 7:31-37; 8:22-26; 10:46-52), closely associated with driving out demons (Mark 1:32-34; 3:10-11) and the forgiveness of sins (Mark 1:1-12). Someone controlled by a demon has to be cured of that demon. Someone with an unclean spirit has to be cleansed of the unclean spirit (Mark 1:21-28; 5:1-20; 7:24-30; 9:14-29). Healing the sick was also an important part of the mission of the Twelve. As in the case of Jesus, the healing mission of the Twelve is closely associated with the driving out of demons (Mark 6:13; see 9:18, 28-29).[22]

As in the alternate ending, Mark's Gospel also associates healing the sick with faith (2:5; 5:34; 6:5-6a; 10:52). But in this, as for the four previous signs, the alternate ending is very different. In Mark's Gospel, faith is a condition for being healed by Jesus or the Twelve. In the alternate ending, faith is a condition for healing others. Those who believe the gospel proclaimed by the Eleven "will lay hands on the sick, and they will recover."

All five signs, the driving out of demons, speaking new languages, picking up serpents, drinking deadly poisons without harm, and the healing of the sick, accompany those who believe and are baptized. All of them are also demonstrations of the authenticity of the mission of the Eleven, revealing the power of the gospel for salvation. In the apologetic intention of the author, the signs are not to confirm those who believe in their belief but to confirm the Eleven and their successors in their mission.

---

[22] In Luke, Jesus commissions both the Twelve and the Seventy-Two to heal the sick and associates their healing mission with the coming of the kingdom of God (9:1-2; 10:9). Then, in the book of Acts, he tells how the Twelve and the early Church fulfilled their mission (3:1-10; 4:30; 5:15-16; 8:7; 9:12, 33-34; 14:8-10; 19:12; 28:8).

The Ascension of the Lord and the Mission of the Eleven (16:19-20)

The fourth and last section of the alternate ending (16:19-20) speaks of the ascension of Jesus (16:19) and the mission of the Eleven (16:20). The section evokes the story of the ascension at the end of Luke's Gospel (24:50-53) and at the beginning of Acts (1:6-14). But like the previous three sections, this fourth section is very different from the stories in Luke and Acts.

In the alternate ending, "[the Eleven] went forth and preached everywhere" (16:20a). The ascension is followed immediately by the mission of the Eleven.

In Luke and Acts, the disciples praised God or devoted themselves to prayer. In Luke, the disciples "returned to Jerusalem with great joy, and they were continually in the temple praising God" (Luke 24:52-53). In Acts, "when they entered the city they went to the upper room where they were staying" and "devoted themselves with one accord to prayer" (Acts 1:13-14). In Luke and Acts, the ascension is followed immediately by community prayer.

In the alternate ending, the whole focus is on the Eleven, to whom Jesus appeared, first rebuking them for their unbelief, then sending them to the whole world to preach the gospel to every creature. In Luke and Acts, the story is about the whole community, including the Eleven but also those with them (see Luke 24:33) gathered in Jerusalem.

"So Then the Lord Jesus." As in Luke's Gospel, the ascension concludes Jesus' final appearance (see 24:36-49, 50-53). This is the first time in the alternate ending that Jesus is mentioned by name. The name, "Jesus," is accompanied by a title, "the Lord" *(ho kyrios),* associated with both the resurrection and the exaltation of Jesus (see Phil 2:11). The same, "the Lord Jesus," is used in connection with the ascension in Acts 1:22-23.

After speaking to the Eleven (see 16:14-18), the Lord Jesus was taken up into heaven *(analemphthe eis ton ouranon).* The verb, "to be taken up" *(analambanesthai),* is used in Luke and Acts for the ascension of Jesus (Luke 9:51; Acts 1:2, 11, 22).[23] The term is a reference to

---

[23] The same verb is used in a christological hymn included in 1 Timothy 3:16:

> Who was manifested in the flesh,
> vindicated in the spirit,
> seen *[ophthe]* by angels,

the "ascension" of Elijah as presented in 2 Kings 2:11 (see also 1 Macc 2:58), where Elijah is taken up *(analemphthe)* to heaven *(eis ton ouranon)* in a whirlwind. 2 Kings 2:11 and 1 Maccabees 2:58 say explicitly that Elijah was taken up "to heaven." The alternate ending does the same for the Lord Jesus (see Acts 1:11).[24]

The other New Testament references to Jesus' ascension (Luke 9:51; see also Luke 24:51; Acts 1:2, 11, 22) may refer to the destination, "to heaven," but only the alternate ending describes Jesus' position in heaven: "and took his seat at the right hand of God" (16:19b).

The expression, "sitting on the right side," comes from Psalm 110:1:

> The LORD says to you, my lord:
> "Take your throne at my right hand,
> while I make your enemies your footstool."

Ascended into heaven, the Lord Jesus takes his place at the right hand of God, where he will reign forever. With that the Lord Jesus has finished his personal mission on earth. Henceforth, he will continue his mission from the right hand of God in heaven.

In Mark's Gospel, the same verse was quoted by Jesus in the Temple:

> As Jesus was teaching in the temple area he said,
> "How do the scribes claim that the Messiah is the son of David?
> David himself, inspired by the holy Spirit, said:
> 'The Lord said to my lord,
> "Sit at my right hand
> until I place your enemies under your feet."'"

Describing the ascension, the alternate ending is unique in joining two biblical references, one to Elijah being taken up into heaven (1 Kgs 2:11), one to Jesus' enthronement as king (Ps 110:1).

"But They Went Forth and Preached Everywhere." After Jesus rose from the dead, he continued his mission until the ascension, appearing to Mary Magdalene, to two of the Eleven, and to the

---

    proclaimed [*ekerychthe*] to the Gentiles,
            believed in [*episteuthe*] throughout the world *(en kosmo),*
                taken up [*analemphthe*] in glory.

[24] Acts 1:11 also refers to Jesus being taken up to heaven: "Men of Galilee, why are you standing there looking at the sky? This Jesus who has been taken up [*ho analymphtheis*] from you into heaven [*eis ton ouranon*]. . ." The ascension account in Luke 24:51 uses another verb to describe the ascension: "he . . . was taken up [*anephereto*] to heaven [*eis ton ouranon*]."

Eleven. Now, with the Lord Jesus enthroned in glory (see Mark 10:37), the time has come for the Eleven to take up the mission. Jesus commissioned the Eleven for that mission when he appeared to them while they were at table: "Go into the whole world and proclaim the gospel to every creature" (16:15).

The alternate ending indicates that "they went forth and preached everywhere" (16:20). From his place in heaven enthroned in power at the right hand of God, "the Lord worked with them and confirmed the word," that is, the word of the gospel (16:15). In Mark that Gospel was the gospel of Jesus Christ [the Son of God] (1:1), the gospel of God (1:14).

Working with them, the Lord Jesus confirmed the word, the gospel they proclaimed, through the accompanying signs that would follow those who believe.

With this simple mention of the mission of the Eleven, the alternate ending comes to an end. In a new life-context, in which Christian missionaries faced new challenges, Mark 16:9-20 provides an alternate ending for "the beginning of the gospel of Jesus Christ [the Son of God]" (1:1).

Those commissioned to proclaim the gospel had to believe the gospel and those who passed it down to them. To bolster their commitment, the author spelled out its implications for those who believe and for those who do not believe. The alternate ending was written with an apologetic intention, not so much to bolster the believers, but to strengthen the missionaries in their gospel proclamation.

Index of Proper Names and Subjects

Index of Greek, Hebrew, Aramaic, and Latin Terms and Expressions

ego eimi   200, 207, 266
eis meson   264
eis telos   201
ekstasis   325
eleeson me   123
  Kyrie, eleison   123, 130
Eli eli lama sabachtani   301 n. 93,
  303
Elohim   245 n. 35
Eloi eloi lema sabachtani   130,
  297, 300, 302–03
en dolo   226
en hetera morphe   342
en parabolais   169
en to aioni to erchemeno   103–04
en to kairo touto   103–04
eparchos   274 n. 70
ephphatha   130, 300 n. 92
epitheis tas cheiras   24, 89
eremos (*topos*)   7
'erwat dabar   70–71
eschatoi   104
eucharistia   238
eulogeo, kateulogeo   88–89
euthys   5, 20, 48
exo   131, 169, 270
exousia   164 n. 2, 166–67

gat shemanim   242 n. 31
genea taute   37
  en te genea taute   37
Gittin   70
Golgotha topos   289 n. 82, 300 n. 92
gregoreite   246–47

Hades   183
hemera
  ede hemerai treis   20 n. 3
  dia trion hemeron   111, 263, 318
  he trite hemera   111
  kath' hemeran   252
  meta hemeras hex   21
  meta treis hemeras   20, 111, 183,
    263 n. 61, 318
  te hemera te trite   20, 263 n. 61,
    318

heorte   223 n. 3
hieron   154, 262
Hierosalem   19 n. 2
Hierosolyma   19 n. 2
himation, himatia   126, 147–48
hodos   7, 8–9, 11, 14, 18–19, 282, 288
  eis hodon   91
  en te hodo   17, 20, 25, 26, 29, 55,
    80, 105–06, 122, 132, 135, 179,
    282
  he hodos tou theou   177
  para ten hodon   20, 122
hora
  trite   296
  hecte   297
  enate   297
horao   95
hosanna   300 n. 92
huioi   58 n. 16
huios agapetos   173
huios tou eulogetou   265
hypage   20, 96, 131–32
  opiso mou   32, 131

idou   109
Iesous   279
inclusio   298 n. 89

kai   5, 20
kairos   158, 209, 248
kardia   72
  porosis tes kardias   72, 347 n. 17
  sklerokardia   72, 347
kat' idian   52, 197
katabaino   106 n. 42
kataklao, klao   16
katalyma   232–33
kenson   179
keros   242
khamsin   299 n. 90
klasmata   16
krateo   218, 250–51
kyrios   141, 145, 172, 209, 245

laos   226
lepton   193